M000290204

"This is no less than a trans-world colloqu[...] way on a subject of huge contemporary interest. A remarkable span of anthropologists speaking to one another, their inspiration lies at once in the provocation of Annemarie Mol's pioneering analysis of ontological multiplicity, exemplified in the medical body, and in a burgeoning field that sees its scope as multi-species studies at a moment of enhanced ecological sensitivity. The outcome is nothing less than a new dynamism in descriptive practice. Re-describing the politics wedded to a 'one world' view of life, a contemporary critical urgency, means re-describing the world. In times of crisis we constantly tell ourselves we must think again—one of the most powerful messages of these ethnographic illuminations is that this applies as much to familiar terrain for the anthropologist as to the unfamiliar. They invite us to think again about where and when and who we think we are."

–Marilyn Strathern, *Professor Emeritus, Social Anthropology,*
University of Cambridge

"If the world is more than one, the question rises how it hangs together. The contributions to this book tackle that very question. They present astutely analyzed cases of encountering, juxtaposing, intertwining, coordinating, interfering, co-existing, translating, and further kinds of going-on between different (but what is different?) versions of a wondrous world—that is less than many."

–Annemarie Mol, *Professor of Anthropology of the Body,*
University of Amsterdam

"This book can be read as an argument to the effect that 'world' should be taken as an uncountable noun. It therefore displaces the traditional debate about how many worlds there are, asking instead how much world is there in the many, otherwise uncountable multiepistemic, transpecific, extracategorial, variontological assemblages that do the real. One of the disquieting answers to be found in *The World Multiple* is that the dominant modern way of doing the real is making less and less world worth living. And yet, we cannot but remain attentive to the flourishing 'arts of living' on this damaged planet; nay, get ready to practice them ourselves."

–Eduardo Batalha Viveiros de Castro,
National Museum of the Federal University of Rio de Janeiro

"Ontological multiplicity encounters postcoloniality: this book is essential reading for all scholars interested in struggles over nature, culture, and knowledge in the asymmetrical worlds in which the profoundly different realities of modernity and indigeneity are entangled together."

–John Law, *Co-Director of ESRC Centre for Research on*
Socio-Cultural Change (CRESC) and Director of the
Social Life of Method Theme within CRESC

The World Multiple

The World Multiple, as a collection, is an ambitious ethnographic experiment in understanding how the world is experienced and generated in multiple ways through people's everyday practices. Against the dominant assumption that the world is a single universal reality that can only be known by modern expert science, this book argues that worlds are worlded—they are socially and materially crafted in multiple forms in everyday practices involving humans, landscapes, animals, plants, fungi, rocks, and other beings. These practices do not converge to a singular knowledge of the world, but generate a world multiple—a world that is more than one integrated whole, yet less than many fragmented parts.

The book brings together authors from Europe, Japan, and North America, in conversation with ethnographic material from Africa, the Americas, and Asia, in order to explore the possibilities of the world multiple to reveal new ways to intervene in the legacies of colonialism, imperialism, and capitalism that inflict damage on humans and nonhumans. The contributors show how the world is formed through interactions among techno-scientific, vernacular, local, and indigenous practices, and examine the new forms of politics that emerge out of them.

Engaged with recent anthropological discussions of ontologies, the Anthropocene, and multi-species ethnography, the book addresses the multidimensional realities of people's lives and the quotidian politics they entail.

Keiichi Omura is Professor in Anthropology at the Open University of Japan. He is the author of *Kanada inuito no minzokushi: Nichijōteki jissen no dainamikusu (Ethnography of Canadian Inuit: Dynamics of Everyday Practices)* (Osaka University Press, 2013). He is currently interested in the ethnographic study of Canadian Inuit language and knowledge, their subsistence, Inuit ways of life and social relations, and comparative studies of indigenous knowledge and modern science.

Grant Jun Otsuki is Lecturer in Cultural Anthropology at Victoria University of Wellington, New Zealand. His research focuses on technology, cybernetics, and media in Japan and North America. He is currently finishing a book manuscript entitled *Human and Machine in Formation: An Ethnographic Study of Communication and Humanness in a Wearable Technology Laboratory in Japan*.

Shiho Satsuka is Associate Professor of Anthropology at the University of Toronto, Canada. She is the author of *Nature in Translation: Japanese Tourism Encounters the Canadian Rockies* (Duke University Press, 2015). She is currently preparing a book manuscript tentatively entitled *The Charisma of Wild Mushrooms: Undoing the Twentieth Century*.

Atsuro Morita is Associate Professor of Anthropology and Science, Technology and Culture at Osaka University, Japan. In the past several years he has been exploring the global network of hydrology and water management technology, particularly the travel of technologies, ideas, and expertise among Denmark, Japan, the Netherlands, and Thailand. In this research he is particularly focusing on simulation technologies and cultural imagination about landscape transformations in the Anthropocene.

Routledge Advances in Sociology

For more information about this series, please visit: www.routledge.com/Routledge-Advances-in-Sociology/book-series/SE0511.

The World Multiple

The Quotidian Politics of Knowing and Generating Entangled Worlds

Edited by Keiichi Omura, Grant Jun Otsuki, Shiho Satsuka, and Atsuro Morita

LONDON AND NEW YORK

First published 2019
by Routledge
2 Park Square, Milton Park, Abingdon, Oxon OX14 4RN

and by Routledge
605 Third Avenue, New York, NY 10017

First issued in paperback 2021

Routledge is an imprint of the Taylor & Francis Group, an informa business

Publisher's Note
The publisher has gone to great lengths to ensure the quality of this reprint but points out that some imperfections in the original copies may be apparent.

British Library Cataloguing-in-Publication Data
A catalogue record for this book is available from the British Library

Library of Congress Cataloging-in-Publication Data
Names: Omura, Keiichi, 1966- editor.
Title: The world multiple : the quotidian politics of knowing and generating entangled worlds / edited by Keiichi Omura [and three others].
Description: Abingdon, Oxon ; New York, NY : Routledge, 2019.
Identifiers: LCCN 2018035728| ISBN 9781138314825 (hardback) | ISBN 9780429456725 (ebook)
Subjects: LCSH: Ethnology. | Ethnoscience. | Anthropology.
Classification: LCC GN320 .W746 2019 | DDC 305.8--dc23
LC record available at https://lccn.loc.gov/2018035728

ISBN 13: 978-0-367-47805-6 (pbk)
ISBN 13: 978-1-138-31482-5 (hbk)

Typeset in Goudy
by Integra Software Services Pvt. Ltd.

Contents

Figures

Tables

Contributors

Mario Blaser is the Canada Research Chair in Aboriginal Studies at Memorial University and Associate Professor in the Departments of Geography and Archaeology at Memorial University of Newfoundland, Canada. He is the author of *Storytelling Globalization from the Paraguayan Chaco and Beyond* (Duke University Press, 2010).

Cristóbal Bonelli is currently a Marie Curie Senior Researcher in Anthropology at the Institute for Water Education, IHE, Delft, the Netherlands in collaboration with the Institute of Archaeology and Anthropology, Universidad Católica del Norte, Antofagasta, Chile. He is also a researcher at the Center of Intercultural and Indigenous Research and at the Center for Integrated Disaster Risk Management. His work explores socio-natural entanglements and clashes between scientific and indigenous worlds and practices. His current research traces emerging entanglements between people and groundwater in the Atacama Desert of Northern Chile.

Marisol de la Cadena is a Peruvian anthropologist teaching at the University of California at Davis, USA. Her most recent book is *Earth Beings. Ecologies of Practice Across Andean Worlds* (Duke University Press, 2015).

Shunwa Honda (Henry Stewart) is retired Professor of Anthropology, The Open University of Japan, and author and co-editor of *Indigenous Peoples around the Globe: The Tundra World* (in Japanese; Akashi-shoten, 2005).

Taku Iida is Professor at the National Museum of Ethnology, Osaka, Japan. His most recent book is *Mi wo motte Shiru Giho: Madagasukaru no Ryoshi ni Manabu* (*Arts of Knowing through the Body: Learning among Fishers in Madagascar*, Rinsen Book Co., 2014). He is currently interested in the process of how "knowledge" and "culture" are shared in societies.

Casper Bruun Jensen is a Specially Appointed Associate Professor at Osaka University and Honorary Lecturer at Leicester University, UK. He is the author of *Ontologies for Developing Things* (Sense, 2010) and *Monitoring Movements in Development Aid* (with Brit Ross Winthereik, MIT Press, 2013) and the editor of *Deleuzian Intersections: Science, Technology, Anthropology* with Kjetil Rödje

(Berghahn, 2009) and *Infrastructures and Social Complexity* with Penny Harvey and Atsuro Morita (Routledge, 2016). His present work focuses on knowledge, infrastructure, and practical ontologies in the Mekong river basin.

Stacey Langwick, MPH, PhD, is an Associate Professor in the Department of Anthropology at Cornell University, USA. She is author of *Bodies, Politics and African Healing: The Matter of Maladies in Tanzania* (Indiana University Press, 2011) and co-editor of *Medicine, Mobility and Power in Global Africa* (with Hansjoerg Dilger and Abdoulaye Kane, Indiana University Press, 2012). Currently, she is finishing a book entitled *The Politics of Habitability: Plants, Sovereignty and Healing in a Toxic World*, which examines the emerging herbals industry in Tanzania. She is particularly interested in how herbals are (re)configuring the notions of medicine, property, chronicity, and crisis that are fundamental to global health.

Moe Nakazora is Lecturer at the Graduate School of International Cooperation and Development, Hiroshima University, Japan. She is currently finishing a book manuscript entitled *Chitekishoyu-ken no jinruigaku: Indo no seibutsusigen o meguru kagaku to zairaichi* (*Anthropology of Intellectual Property Right: Biodiversity-related Science and Indigenous Knowledge in Contemporary India*, Sekaishisosha, 2019).

Heather Anne Swanson is Associate Professor of Anthropology and Deputy Director of the Centre for Environmental Humanities at Aarhus University in Denmark. She is also a member of the Aarhus University Research on the Anthropocene (AURA) project, co-editor of *Arts of Living on a Damaged Planet* (University of Minnesota Press, 2017), and co-editor of *Domestication Gone Wild* (with Marianne Elisabeth Lien and Gro B. Ween, Duke University Press, 2018).

Anna Tsing is Professor of Anthropology at the University of California, Santa Cruz, USA and a Niels Bohr Professor at Aarhus University, Denmark, where she co-directs Aarhus University Research on the Anthropocene (AURA). Her most recent books are *The Mushroom at the End of the World: On the Possibility of Life in Capitalist Ruins* (Princeton University Press, 2015) and *Arts of Living on a Damaged Planet* (co-edited with Heather Swanson, Elaine Gan, and Nils Bubandt, University of Minnesota Press, 2017).

Antonia Walford is currently a Teaching Fellow in Digital Anthropology at University College London, a Post-Doctoral Research Associate at the Centre for Social Data Science (SODAS), University of Copenhagen, and a Research Fellow at the Centre for Interdisciplinary Methodologies, University of Warwick, UK. Her research explores the effects of the exponential growth of digital data on social and cultural imaginaries and practices, focusing particularly on large-scale digitization in the environmental sciences. She has published in several major journals and is preparing a book manuscript.

Mei Zhan is Associate Professor of Anthropology at the University of California, Irvine, USA. She is the author of *Other-Worldly: Making Chinese Medicine Through Transnational Frames* (Duke University Press, 2009).

Preface and acknowledgments

Keiichi Omura

In the winter of 2010 I attended the Nunavut Language Summit, organized by the Government of Nunavut and held in Iqaluit, Nunavut's capital. Invited were representatives of the Inuit from the Canadian Arctic and Greenland and of the Alaskan Inupiat and Yu'pik, delegates from NGOs and Canada's federal and territorial governments, and scholars studying Inuktitut (the Inuit language) and "Inuit Qaujimajatuqngit" (IQ)—Inuit knowledge—from across North America and Europe. The summit's aim was to explore possible frameworks for an official Nunavut language policy. I attended the summit as an observer, hoping to learn about the current state of Inuktitut and IQ issues. Since the creation of Nunavut as a territory of Canada in 1999, a central issue has been how Inuit forms of governance should be included in its political system. Nunavut aspires to develop self-governance in which both indigenous and Qaplunaat ("white") ways stand side by side, but the government is nonetheless structured according to modern Western models.

At a banquet during the summit, an elder, who for almost twenty years has been one of my teachers of Inuktitut and IQ, gave a speech about the future of Inuktitut and the Inuit. I was stunned when he expressed a sense of close affinity with the Japanese. He is a monolingual speaker of Inuktitut. He is highly respected as a most skillful engineer—people in his community call him a shaman because he can maintain and repair any machine in an Inuit way, without consulting manuals or Qaplunaat engineers, as though he can directly communicate with the machines. In his speech, he drew on his engineering experience to say that the Inuit should protect their language and IQ, while learning Qaplunaat technology to develop it into Inuit technology. He used the history and achievements of Japanese technology —of the likes of Nintendo, Honda, and Yamaha—to say that the Japanese have used Qaplunaat technology to develop something unique, without having their language, traditions, and identity assimilated into Qaplunaat ways of living and thinking. Rather, it was because the Japanese have maintained their language and traditions that they have been able to generate unique technologies. He declared that the Inuit should be able to do the same thing.

I have been learning Inuktitut and IQ at Kugaaruk in Nunavut since 1989, and have visited Iqaluit numerous times. I had frequently discussed with my Inuit friends how to balance Inuit and Western forms of governance in Nunavut. There are great differences in the historical and geopolitical contexts of Inuit and Japanese life, as Japan has its own colonial past and continuing neocolonial relations with other countries. But it was my teacher's speech that made me realize a common struggle we both face. Since the imperial expansion of Europe, especially during the nineteenth century, those outside European traditions have had to learn to live with knowledge, technologies, and practices that have been developed and transplanted from elsewhere. The transplants include foundational assumptions and frameworks of nation-state governance and capitalism. Under their massive normalizing power, neither of us—Inuit nor Japanese—can avoid the influence of Western ways of life. We are both "modernized" and subordinate to the Western hegemony. However, we are not entirely assimilated to it. Inuit life is full of electric appliances, snowmobiles, internet sites, wage labor, public school education, and processed foods. But it is also a life that exists in their lifeworld, *nuna*, in which hunting, fishing, trapping, and gathering maintain Inuit relationships with wildlife and each other. They live both kinds of life simultaneously. That my own life is similarly "doubled" explains the *déjà vu* I experienced when I lived in Kugaaruk: in both Nunavut and Japan, similar signifiers of the "modern West" are entangled with those of "tradition," such as when we sit directly on the floor of modern Western-style houses to share communal meals. Such "traditions" are themselves products of entanglements: the so-called "Japanese" way of life is a heterogeneous tangle of ways of life including not only those that are "Western" and "Eastern," but also Asian, Oceanian, Siberian, and so on, which have been constantly transformed through encounters, frictions, tensions, and conflicts for more than ten thousand years.

Long-standing dichotomies of modernity and tradition, or of indigenous knowledge and modern technoscience, erase everyday entanglements and multiplicity from our vision. These dichotomies are outcomes of Western colonialism and capitalism, which inevitably order the world according to a binary logic. But, if we could learn to see the entanglement of multiple ways of life and thought as common features of our everyday lives in the contemporary world, I thought the same entanglements could help us learn how to challenge and overcome ongoing colonial suppression and capitalist exploitation. So, how could we shed light on the potential of such entanglements? How could we revive the latent power of the politics in the quotidian, through which multiple ways of life and thought are continuously encountered, negotiated with, attuned to, and loosely assembled into the heterogeneous worlds in which we live?

While I was exploring such questions, I began participating in "Environmental Infrastructures," a project of my former colleague at Osaka University, Atsuro Morita, an anthropologist studying technoscience. The project aimed to explore material-semiotic processes of knowledge production and world making, including technoscience and vernacular knowledge, by analyzing the vicissitudes of infrastructure. Through this project, I developed the idea of a comparative study of indigenous knowledge and modern technoscience. The specific idea for this book germinated when I met Shiho Satsuka, an anthropologist exploring the creative potentiality of translational interactions of vernacular knowledge and technoscience, at a panel on infrastructure coorganized by Morita at the 2012 Annual Meeting of the Society for the Social Studies of Science in Copenhagen. After the panel over beer, one of the coorganizers of that panel, Casper Bruun Jensen, and a panel participant, Moe Nakazora, who have contributed chapters to this volume, also joined the conversation and helped me refine the idea.

Upon returning to Osaka, I proposed a collaborative research project with my colleagues in Japan, entitled "A Comparative Study of Indigenous Knowledge and Modern Science," to the Japan Society for the Promotion of Science. With the support of this grant (JSPS Grant-in-Aid for Scientific Research [A] 25244043), I have organized several symposia and workshops in Japan and Canada. This book is a direct outcome of one of these symposia, entitled "The World Multiple: Everyday Politics of Knowing and Generating Entangled Worlds," which was held at the National Museum of Ethnology in Osaka in December 2016. This international symposium was conceived as an experiment in entangling diverse perspectives. These included perspectives pertaining to the multiple realities of people's everyday lives under diverse historical and geopolitical settings, but also to various theoretical traditions in anthropology and in science and technology studies. Participants explored how to describe and analyze encounters and interactions between modern technoscience and *zairai-chi*, which means "knowledge" (chi) "developed as common and ordinary under local conditions" (zairai) in Japanese. Zairai-chi includes not only "indigenous knowledge," but also local, folk, traditional, and vernacular knowledges. The purpose of this experiment was to shed light on the potential of such entanglements for dismantling key dichotomies of colonialism, capitalism, imperialism, and militarism, such as tradition and modernity, nature and human, and local and global, as well as indigenous or vernacular knowledge and modern technoscience.

This book makes the results of this experiment public and calls readers' attention to the creative potential of the entanglements of multiple realities. As a result, it inhabits a crossroads of diverse theoretical approaches, including those associated with Japanese anthropology, the ontological turn, multispecies ethnography, lateral anthropology, and postcolonial anthropology. The book aims to look beyond the differences of these approaches to explore the commonalities among them, including engagement in fieldwork, which participants have conducted in diverse situations all over the world. In this sense, this book is itself a "world multiple," in which the chapters are worlds, each enacted by contributors' encounters with diverse peoples' realities, divergently generated but also attuned to each other, assembled in this book through their encounters, interactions, or frictions.

A shortcoming of this book is the absence of indigenous scholars among its contributors. The absence stems from practical matters, including scheduling, but it makes this book no more than a first step toward the further exploration of the potential of entangled realities. We hope that this book stimulates further discussion and leads to collaborations with a wider range of people, including indigenous scholars.

Because of this book's multiplicity, there are discrepancies, frictions, and tensions among its chapters. I thank the authors for their patient efforts to build mutual understanding and to engage in generous, constructive conversation across difference. Coordinating contributors with diverse analytic approaches, writing conventions, and training was a difficult task. Some expressed concern that it might be impossible to produce a coherent book with such a range of authors, including authors who are usually not in dialogue. I was told it would be easier to publish two or three different books. But I wanted to pursue this endeavor, as I owe all of the contributors for their insights. As I worked, I began to realize why people had expressed concern about the challenge. It was Grant Otsuki and Shiho Satsuka who saved this project. These anthropologists both specialize in knowledge translation and its politics between Japanese- and English-speaking worlds. I originally casually approached Shiho Satsuka just to pick her brain, and Grant Otsuki to consult regarding various expressions in English. Yet, it turned out that I had to rely almost entirely on their expertise to navigate the difficulties of publishing a book in English, which would address an unfamiliar English-speaking academic world. They put such thought into our conversations and developed the framework of the book to integrate our diverse ideas. Not only have they magically written a coherent introduction, they have taken on most of the important editorial tasks by communicating with the authors, editors, and the cover design artist to improve the book. Without their extreme generosity, patience, and capable hands, this book might not have been realized. Atsuro Morita also helped me throughout the process and contacted the publisher and endorsers using his network of connections in Europe.

I would like to thank the participants in the 2016 symposium in Osaka, who are also the authors in this volume. In addition, I thank Kazuyoshi Sugawara, who gave the concluding remarks, and the discussants—Kazunori Kondo, Sachiko Kubota, Gergely Mohácsi, Atsuro Morita, Grant Otsuki, and Goro Yamazaki. Yen-ling Tsai and Joelle Chevrier together with Anna Tsing presented a live performance of their *Golden Snail Opera* accompanied by a video filmed by Isabelle Carbonelle. I am grateful to Taku Iida who made it possible to have the symposium at the National Museum of Ethnology, and to Atsuro Morita and Moe Nakazora, who helped me host the international participants. I also gratefully acknowledge the logistical assistance of Fukachi Furukawa, Yulong Jia, and Asli Kemiksiz at the 2016 symposium. Junko Omura provided immense support. Moe Nakazora made special contributions as the chief editorial assistant. I also owe thanks to Asli Kemiksiz and Liv Nyland Krause for their editorial assistance; to Molly Mullin, Caroline Jennings, and Jessica Ruthven, who conceptually edited the chapters; and to Elaine Gan, who designed this book's beautiful cover.

I acknowledge the assistance of Osaka University and the National Museum of Ethnology, especially the staff of the accounting office and the Nakanoshima Center of Osaka University. I thank especially Aki Hyoudou, Keiko Akamatsu, Yuka Ikuo, and Emiko Nio for assistance with the 2016 symposium, this book, and the other associated workshops and symposia I have organized. I gratefully acknowledge the logistical assistance of Akina Tagawa, Wakana Suzuki, and Marina Samukawa at those other events. In Canada, I am grateful to Joshua Barker, Bonnie McElhinny, Andrea Muehlebach, and Michelle Murphy for sharing ideas at the sister workshop in Toronto in May 2017, as well as Sabrien Amrov, Jessica Caporusso, Columba Gonzalez, Veronica Grigio, Jacob Nerenberg, Emily Simmonds, and Lindsay Small for their stimulating comments. I thank Brenton Buchannan, Bronwyn Frey, and Johanna Pokorny for organizing the workshop at the University of Toronto, and I thank the staff of the Anthropology Department there for their assistance.

I give special thanks to Milton M. R. Freeman, who suggested the framework of the research project, "A Comparative Study of Indigenous Knowledge and Modern Science." Conversations with Paul Nadasdy also provided inspiration. Thanks to participants in various other meetings related to this project, who contributed to the explorations of this book but were unable for various reasons to contribute to it: Anders Blok, Shuhei Kimura, Gergely Mohácsi, and Tak Uesugi. I thank the guest speakers and commentators for the workshops of the research project, who provided much inspiration—Hiroyuki Aoki, Yukio Gunji, Yuka Mizutani, Sho Morishita, Osamu Nakagawa, Kazuto Nakatani, Motomitsu Uchibori, and Tadashi Yanai—and to the anonymous referee who made many useful suggestions for improving the book's frameworks.

I gratefully acknowledge the financial support we have received from the Japan Society for Promotion of Science and Osaka University. Their support made the workshops and symposia possible.

Finally, this book owes much to the indigenous peoples and other interlocutors that I and the contributors have encountered all over the world. I especially thank my teachers and friends: Martha Tunnuq, Simon Inuksak, Jose Angutingnungniq, Levi Illuittuq, Emily Illuittuq, Christian Nalungiaq, Guy Kakkiarniun, Attima Hadlari, Shuvinai Mike, Peter Itinnuaq, and Peter Irniq. They are central to our explorations of the world multiple.

Chapter 1

Introduction

Grant Jun Otsuki, Shiho Satsuka, Keiichi Omura, and Atsuro Morita

At 5:00 a.m. in Nunavut, in the Canadian North, an Inuit elder leaves his comfortably heated home to look out at the sea and check on weather and ice conditions. His extended family lies fast asleep. Satisfied with his grasp of the morning, he goes back inside and switches on his living-room radio. As the aroma of his morning tea fills the room, he plays a hand of solitaire while listening to a weather report in the Inuktitut language and waits for his family to wake. Around 7:00 a.m., one of his sons enters the living room and asks the elder whether today will be for hunting. The elder gestures for his son to check the forecast on the computer. They then sit to discuss the weather on the basis of information from the radio and the internet, the elder's own early morning observations, and his *Inuit Qaujimajatuqangit*—Inuit knowledge, IQ. As the elder's other sons join them from their own homes, the day's plan is fixed. Some prepare to hunt, donning thermal clothing, fueling snowmobiles or outboard motors, and bringing out rifles, harpoons, and nets. Just before 8:00 a.m., a group leaves to hunt for *niqinmarik*—the *real* food of fish and meat. The niqinmarik will be shared among the hunters' families. This fulfills a moral responsibility: the animals will offer their bodies to the hunters only if, in return, the hunters share the food with kin. Sharing the meat in this way makes it possible for the animals' spirits to be reincarnated. While some members of a family are hunting or fishing, others will go to work at the co-op or the hamlet office to earn the money needed for equipment and fuel. All of this needs to be done to generate their world, *nuna*.

Inuit hunters live complex realities where the world of technoscience and that of their indigenous knowledge, IQ, are entangled. Nuna is an intricately con-nected world of humans and non-humans which the Inuit know, generate, and maintain through a long tradition of hunting activities. At the same time, nuna is a world filled with modern technologies, such as the internet and snowmobiles, and market relationships and wage labor as people in the community work as government officials, co-op managers, and artists. When preparing their equip-ment for an expedition, they link labor at government offices with the moral obligation to participate in the reincarnation of wildlife. On the ice, they use snowmobiles and rifles to fulfill their responsibility to share niqinmarik among kin. Hunting is an important act of negotiating with animal worlds while connecting with spirits, ancestors, and people in the community. Their use of internet weather reports and snowmobiles to hunt seal or polar bear maintains nuna, but also entangles their lives with a national weather-monitoring network, the conservation policies of the Canadian nation-state, and a planetary satellite system. These practices create channels to worlds outside their immediate communities, making everyday Inuit life irreducibly multidimensional (see Omura, Chapter 5 in this volume). These practices sustain nuna, although they are never free from friction, tension, or transformation. Nuna is a world multiple, an assemblage of partially incommensurable knowledges and partially connected practices.

Nuna is not another interpretation of a single material world. Such a conceptualization is a product of what John Law (2015) calls the "one-world world" doctrine. This doctrine assumes the existence of only one natural world, and takes different cultures to be no more than interpretations of that world. This doctrine makes it possible to believe that the truth of these cultures can be measured by the standard of the natural world, privileging modern science as the authoritative means of knowing it.

The world multiple is an inspiration and a guide for thinking beyond the one-world world. The world multiple is both a world and worlds. It is fractal (cf. Law 2015); it may be constituted by more worlds inside, and may be itself part of another world, none necessarily simpler or more complex than others. To paraphrase Donna Haraway, one world is too few, but two are too many (Haraway 1991, 177; cf. Strathern 2005, 36). In our use, the singular form will always imply the plural, and vice versa. But the question of how many worlds there actually are is of little importance. What matters more is to make sense of the complex and multidimensional realities that people like the Inuit hunters are living. To do this, we need to consider the relationships between modern technoscience and other forms of knowledge and practices—often described as indigenous, traditional, folk, or vernacular—in people's engagements with the world. How should we attend to the simultaneous existence of the different material consequences generated by the entanglement of modern technoscience and other knowledges and practices? This book represents a collective experiment in exploring these questions with the figure of the world multiple.

From body into world

The idea of "the world multiple" emerged in initial conversations between Keiichi Omura and Shiho Satsuka about the key theme for the workshop that led to this book, which was held in Osaka, Japan in 2016. The workshop was a part of Omura's collaborative research project, funded by the Japan Society for Promotion of Science. While the title of his funded project was "A Comparative Study of 'Indigenous Knowledge' and 'Modern Science,'" Omura had been searching for an analytic framework that would avoid the binary opposition of "indigenous knowledge" and "modern science."[1] From the nearly three decades that Omura has been working with the Inuit, he has become deeply committed to their IQ advocacy project. He feels uncomfortable with the framing of the Inuit and other indigenous peoples as passive recipients of global forces such as modern science, which makes the creative and multidimensional reality of their everyday practices invisible.

In Omura's observations of heterogeneous practices among the Inuit and in his attention to the material aspects of reality and ontological multiplicity, Satsuka detected resonances with Annemarie Mol's *The Body Multiple* (2002). In her ethnographic analysis of atherosclerosis treatments in a Dutch hospital, Mol illustrates the ontological multiplicity in a diseased body—a disease is not a single objective reality waiting to be discovered and diagnosed, but a phenomenon made real through the coordination of different medical practices. She demonstrates that these practices do not all fit together easily to generate a single reality; inasmuch as different specialists in various disciplines act on the body using different forms of practice, and as patients experience the disease, the body manifests materially in different ways. Yet these different practices are coordinated to make a diagnosis. The body with atherosclerosis is the ontological achievement of these coordinations. Mol's analytic approach seemed relevant to Omura's, but the conjuncture also brought Satsuka new realizations about the contradictory and complementary practices of mushroom scientists and their material effects that she has been observing over the past ten years. She had been wondering how to make sense of the tension in her scientific interlocutors' project on artificially cultivating matsutake mushrooms, a project that can potentially belong to both the world of capitalist resource extraction and that of interspecies care and affection (see Chapter 14 in this volume). Satsuka thus presented Omura with the challenge to extend Mol's insights from the body to the world multiple.

During the 2016 symposium that first brought the contributors to this book together in one place, the possibilities of the world multiple came alive as ethnographic insights drawn from around the world crossed with diverse conceptual tools. But moving away from a hospital in the Netherlands to diverse settings in the world required us to deal with a broader array of unanticipated connections, unruly companions, and unfinished historical business. Mol's work provided us with a powerful provocation, but the "intricately coordinated crowd" (Mol 2002, 9) of the body multiple is a rather cordial one. In Mol's hospital, different bodies are enacted in the practices of experts in different departments, providing a map with which to trace the multiple embodiments of atherosclerosis. In the world beyond the hospital, crowds are rarely so easily managed. Everyday life is full of people engaging with practices from competing or incommensurable ontological genealogies. Our fields are often messy; practices do not neatly correspond to the social order that defines different communities of experts. Furthermore, in other worlds it is impossible to turn a blind eye to the legacies and ongoing practices of colonialism, imperialism, militarism, and capitalist exploitation. These require us to consider how we encounter and think about multiplicity in the world, which we may find mangled by politics or disfigured by violence imposed on human and other-than-human beings. Attention to worlds brings into stark relief the political, historical, and social chains that encumber what kinds of worlds are possible.

Entangled realities for livable world

At the symposium, our interest in challenging the one-world world took on a new sense of urgency. We were asking questions about how others strive to make worlds worth living in and for, and how anthropologists might best become part of these worlds. The past few decades have witnessed a heightened concern over environmental issues framed on a planetary scale: climate change, rising sea levels, contamination of the biosphere, and species extinctions. The term "Anthropocene" (Crutzen and Stoermer 2000) was coined to signify the intensity of human impact on the Earth, indicating that human activities have become a major geological force working on a planetary scale. It has caught the popular imagination for how it epitomizes an awareness of the past centuries of industrialization and devastating resource extraction inscribed on the Earth. It also captures anxieties about the livability of our planet in the future. The sciences and technologies of global environmental change—modeling, simulation, and remote sensing—have guided our optics toward a planetary view of the environment. This planetary consciousness has generated momentum among social scientists who have been critically reflecting on the centuries of colonialism, imperialism, and militarism that have caused the violent exploitation of humans, and enabled the destruction of many other-than-human beings on the Earth. This moment requires both contending with the technoscientific consensus that human activity is impacting life at a planetary scale, while maintaining a suspicion of universals and the politics and interests they might obscure (Chakrabarty 2009, 221). How might we join critical reflections on the violence imposed upon humans and non-humans on this planet? How can we do so while remaining critically wary of the holisms conjured forth by this new planetary consciousness?

Parallel with this development, indigenous and traditional environmental knowledge has drawn interest as a way of navigating the twilight of late modernity. Modern science is often critiqued as abstract, mechanistic, and reductionist, perceiving the natural world based on a dualistic ontology that separates nature from human society. In opposition, indigenous knowledges are characterized as embodied, organic, holistic, and composed from entangled relationships between humans and the other-than-human. This binary has long cast IQ explanations of hunting interactions as little more than irrational myths, because they "inappropriately" mix the human and the animal, with neither clearly belonging to the domain of the "natural" or the "social."[2] But now, the very entanglement of the natural and the social in indigenous knowledges such as IQ is being considered the key to overcoming the limitations of the abstract technoscientific approach. Since the 1980s, social scientists have advocated for the effectiveness of indigenous and other traditional knowledges in conserving biodiversity (e.g., Collings 1997; Freeman 1985, 1993). As a result, these knowledges have gradually been incorporated into decision-making processes, and consulting with their practitioners has become a policy requirement in some governments in North and South America (e.g., Blaser 2009; Nadasdy 2003; Omura 2005, 2013; Usher 2000; Wenzel 2004). Yet, as many critics have pointed out, indigenous and traditional knowledges have been assumed to be static cognitive frameworks: the holders of these knowledges are treated as though they are in the grip of epistemological paradigms that have remained unchanged from ancient times (Agrawal 1995; Krupnik and Vakhtin 1997; Omura 2007). While there is an inclusive drive to make up for past epistemic discrimination and violence, the "incorporation" (Nadasdy 1999) of indigenous and traditional knowledges into existing frameworks prolongs the hegemony of modern technoscientific expertise, and its basic assumption of a one-world world. How might we think beyond "incorporation," and give heed to the interactions between modern, indigenous, and traditional forms of life?

The world multiple also reverberates with the fundamental rethinking of space and time that we have learned about from interlocutors in the sciences. Karen Barad's writing on quantum physics (2007, 2017) shows how science itself is not all about a one-world world, but can offer up provocative ways to think about how worlds come into material being through entangled relationships. Using quantum physics pioneer Niels Bohr's writings on the behavior of light, Barad (2007) explains that the way matter exists in the world cannot be determined prior to its "intra-actions" with its surroundings. The quantum puzzle of whether light is *really* a wave or a particle misses the point that light *becomes* wave or particle depending on the constitution of the socio-material assemblages—that is, the experimental apparatuses—with which it is entangled. Moreover, this does not simply change how we think about "what" light is, but also "when" and "where." Light is not a thing that flies freely against the background of a flat, Newtonian space-time. It demands different times and spaces depending on whether it becomes a point-like particle or an arrow-like wave. Light exists as a heterotemporal, heterospatial matrix which shifts the nature of its being, time, and space contingent upon the specific relations in which it is placed. Anthropologists may usually have little to do with the ontological multiplicity of photons, but we have yet to fully come to terms with the fact that flat Newtonian space-time is no more than a partial way of imagining the world. As beneficiaries of modernity, we easily fall back into thinking about worlds as flat spaces and times occupied by our human interlocutors. But we can take insights like Barad's as a warrant to explore the dynamics of multiple, entangled realities that people are already engaging with. How, then, might we learn to sense and speak of these multiplicities?

Quotidian politics of worlding

The chapters assembled here are diverse in their aims, interests, and styles of argumentation. Yet they converge in how they explore the quotidian politics of worlds inspired by postcolonial perspectives. In doing so, these chapters show us that we need to focus on how worlds are socially and materially generated in practice within specific power relations. In other words, they show us that we need to attend to *worldings* and their politics (Tsing 2010, Chapter 15 in this volume; Welland 2018; Zhan 2009, 2012). Worldings are "different stagings of the world" that engender a sense of what is "natural" (Welland 2018, 29). They are situated "figurings of relevant worlds," articulations of who and what matters in a particular form of life (cf. Tsing 2010, 48). These practices are not acts that can be performed by a lone individual, but material-semiotic "enactments" (Law 2015, Mol 2002) or "intra-actions" (Barad 2007) that always involve associating with human and non-human others (Latour 2005). Worldings may conjure an aura of totality, but they are practices that are always partial and incomplete on their own. Conversely, worldings may be polyvalent, generating the conditions of possibility for more than one world at the same time. They are unstable in their form and effects, and open to critique, resignification, and transformation (Welland 2018, 40).

Worlding has appeared in anthropology with multiple genealogies, primarily in literary studies and postcolonial studies (Spivak 1985; Tsing 2010; Welland 2018), but in the Western canon most trails pass through the work of Martin Heidegger (1993).[3] For Heidegger, a world is a space in which humans emerge as human beings through their relations with other things— human, animal, plant, and otherwise. It is the what and the where that make up the conditions of possibility of being human, encompassing both the actual realm of the humanly perceivable and the virtual realm of the humanly possible (Heidegger 1993, 170). Conversely, the human being is a condition of possibility for a particular world. This feedback relation is what it means for a world (n.) to world (v.). For Heidegger, the world emerges out of what he calls "earth," which is the stable, enduring, and nourishing ground which must constantly recede for worlds to come "into full radiance" (141–142) as figures. Heidegger's first articulation of worlding appeared in thinking about art as a form of being; it has since been used by postcolonial theorists to think about art and literature as materially generative of worlds, not as mere representations of the world. But where Heidegger takes "world" and "being" (*Dasein*) as singular in relation to each other (see Derrida 1982; Spivak in Derrida 1997, xvii), postcolonial scholars have emphasized the possible and actual other worlds that are generated at the margins of hegemonic ones—hence Gayatri Spivak's attention to "the Third World" (1985), Sasha Su-Ling Welland's decolonizing "art worlds" in China (2018), or Mei Zhan's *re*-worlding of Daoist oneness (2012). It is this postcolonial focus on worlding as a generative and critical practice that inspires this book.

The chapters in this volume take on the analytic challenge of considering the specificities of each ethnographic scene and how a multitude of practices among different actors generate the worlds in which they dwell. The attention to worlding changes where we must look for diversity. Anthropologists have classically used the concept of culture to explain why human ways of life can differ so much across space and time. Though culture has been defined in countless ways, it is usually opposed to the natural world, the material realm that exists independently of what humans might think of it. Anthropologists, like those in many other modern disciplines, have seen cultures as human interpretations of this naturalized "one-world world." But if our practices *make* reality, then human diversity is not about differing cultures, but about differing worlds.

This also means that we do not take humans to be the only beings that act in the world. As the Inuit example implies, humans can play an important role in generating nuna, but their world cannot wholly encompass the worlds of animals. Moreover, the chapters show worlding as a multilayered practice, in which one actor can simultaneously participate in incommensurable worlds (see e.g., Omura, Chapter 5 in this volume; Langwick, Chapter 10; Satsuka, Chapter 14), or one group of people can become a site of contestation among different worlding practices (see Iida, Chapter 12). Multiple worlding practices come into contact and "fold" into tentative and tense stability (see e.g., Swanson, Chapter 7; Bonelli, Chapter 8) or, as de la Cadena discusses in Chapter 2, produce "not only" their intended effects but also significant "excesses." Worldings are practices that involve heterogeneous actors and heterogeneity within actors. In this way, as Tsing explicates in Chapter 15, many of the chapters in this book are informed by, and build on, recent anthropological discussions of ontologies (e.g., Gad, Jensen and Winthereik 2015; Henare, Holdbraad and Wastell 2007; Holbraad and Pedersen 2017; Viveiros de Castro 2004) and ethnographies that take non-human species seriously (e.g., van Dooren, Kirksey and Münster 2016; Kirksey and Helmreich 2010; Kohn 2013; Ogden, Hall and Tanita, 2013; Schrader 2010).

Our focus on practices of worlding points towards subtle forms of politics embodied by worlds multiple. Worlding always entails building some relation-ships and ignoring possibilities for others; or being affected by some actors and indifferent to others. In this sense, there is a politics embodied in the socio-material constitution of worlds. This pushes us to rethink what counts as political. The political is often glossed in terms of questions of representation. As Gayatri Spivak points out, in this politics, it is assumed that an oppressed people "can [if given the chance,] speak and know their own conditions" (Spivak 1999, 269). The project of this politics is to create space for the self-representation and self-determination of the oppressed and provide that chance. This book indicates the limitations of this way of thinking. The subtle politics of multiplicity in practice are prior to representational politics in that they are enacted and can make their effects felt whether or not the actors involved are recognized by anyone as political subjects as such.

Representational politics is a product of the Enlightenment and modern liberalism, which assumes humans are rational individuals with universal and intrinsic rights who possess the agency to resist external forces. But our everyday worlds are filled with politics that fit uneasily within this representational regime. They are populated by peoples whose subjectivities can be represented only if they are painfully and violently distorted. Our critique of the "one-world world" questions the subjectivity assumed by this conventional politics, pushing us to focus on the *quotidian*.

The quotidian conventionally refers to the ordinary, the everyday, and the mundane.[4] In this sense, our exploration of quotidian politics is influenced by Michel Foucault and his discussions of micropolitics in the basic conduct of life (Foucault 1988). Foucault forcefully illustrates the process in which modern liberal governmentality has been formed through the production of modern subjects who deeply internalize the norms of liberalism through their everyday conduct, disciplining themselves into productive workers and law-abiding and rational citizens (Foucault 1991). His work does not take the modern subject as a given, but as formed through quotidian practices. Thus, Foucault took an important step toward examining the foundational processes that made the one-world world. Beyond this, many of the chapters in this book suggest that possibilities for an "otherwise" can be found in quotidian practices, if we remain ambivalent about the notion of a single totalizing world that enframes them. The quotidian is a notion capacious enough to hold other forms of worlding.

Ethnography provides a way of engaging with the world multiple. Indeed, ethnography may itself be thought of as a worlding practice entangled with concrete moments from the lives of our interlocutors (see Jensen, Chapter 3 in this volume and Walford, Chapter 13). One may thus think of the quotidian as the experiential world that the anthropologist might come to share—or perhaps only glimpse—as she or he makes relations with his or her interlocutors using the practices of fieldwork. Accordingly, many of the chapters in this book work with an ethnographic "jeweler's eye" (Fischer 2007) to bring into relief the concrete and specific character of the relationships that generate specific worlds. As postcolonial scholars have shown (e.g., Asad 1991), the ways that anthropologists represent other worlds can never be free of the modern, colonial world for which our discipline was established. But we hope that insofar as it is a worlding, our writing can be multiple, polyvalent, and gesture to an otherwise.

The diversity of styles of argumentation, representation, and analysis embodied by this book's chapters show how anthropology itself is more than a singular mode of engagement with the world. Readers of this book will notice stark and even jarring shifts of tone between chapters. These are the traces of the authors' diverse backgrounds—their languages, the places where they grew up and developed their thoughts, their disciplinary training, and the times and locations they received that training. They also reflect differences in the worlds that each author attempted to approach, which called for their own ways of being theorized and narrated. Anthropologists enact worlds multiple, entangling them with our various disciplinary and political dispositions to generate different relationships, possibilities, and written representations. With their attention to quotidian politics, the chapters push our ability to see, listen to, and touch other worlds in subtle but profound ways, so that we might perhaps recognize new affinities, obligations, and responsibilities. And, like all good experiments, they provoke unexpected questions and reveal new directions to explore, even as they give us empirical confidence in the important lessons we have learned together.

Chapter organization: Entangled worldings, space-time multiplicities, exploring quotidian politics

Befitting the theme of this volume, readers will sense multiple ways of connecting its chapters. Some chapters share an emphasis on multiplicity in a particular region of the world: South America (de la Cadena, Bonelli, and Walford: Chapters 2, 8, 13); Asia (Swanson, Nakazora, Zhan, and Satsuka: 7, 9, 11, 14); the Arctic and circumpolar regions of Canada (Blaser, Omura, and Honda: 4–6); and Africa (Langwick, Iida: 10, 12). Lateral linkages also exist in terms of our contributors' perspectives on plants or fungi (Nakazora, Langwick, Satsuka, and Tsing: 9, 10, 14, 15); science and technology (Swanson, Iida, and Satsuka: 7, 12, 14); fraught conceptions of "indigeneity" (de la Cadena, Jensen, Nakazora, and Walford: 2, 3, 9, 13); or anthropological knowledge production (Jensen and Walford: 3, 13). While all of our contributors explore the potential of the world multiple, analytic and empirical trajectories differ. We have grouped them roughly according to how they navigate the contemporary problem space of the world multiple. These groupings are not mutually exclusive, but we offer them as three reference points for reading through this book.

The authors in Part I—*Entangled worldings*—explore how forms of being enacted in worlding practices embody and enable forms of multiplicity both within and beyond the worlds of ongoing colonialist and imperialist projects. Marisol de la Cadena's chapter (2) is exemplary here for her sensitive account of her own incapacity to fully occupy the worlds which her Andean interlocutors inhabit with ordinary ease. She describes how earth-beings (*tirakuna*) and Andean persons (*runakuna*) exist with and beyond mountains and human beings, exposing in the process the violence in the translation and imposition of the notion of religion. Her refrain of "not only…"—"religious, but not only…," "a mountain, but not only…"—marks the limits of translation and gestures towards the simultaneous existence of other worlds.

Casper Bruun Jensen's chapter (3) carries de la Cadena's argument forward to consider both classical debates in anthropology about emic versus etic standpoints, and contemporary debates stemming from the ontological turn. Jensen explores the consequences of de la Cadena's work in the Andes, as well as ethnographic reflections on infrastructures in the Thai Chao Phraya Delta, to argue for an emetic approach to anthropology, which faces the nausea induced by ontological instabilities to think about multiplicities of being.

In working through what Jensen calls an emetic approach, de la Cadena invokes Isabelle Stengers' notion of divergence to refer to "an ecology of practices [that are not] contradictory or incommensurable [but] heterogeneous" (2015, 112), producing multiple worlds and beings that "[continue] to be distinct" (de la Cadena, Chapter 2). Mario Blaser's chapter (4) looks at such an ecology in Labrador, Canada, in which the biological species of "caribou" diverges from but also remains tied to the being known by Innu hunters as *atîku*. Blaser's ethnography follows this ontological divergence to highlight the political stakes it has for environmental conservation, resource-hungry states, and the continuation of Innu forms of life.

Keiichi Omura's chapter (5) also focuses on divergence among indigenous hunters in Canada, but his concern is with understanding maps of the land as material-semiotic objects that translate between different worlds. Omura thinks of the topographical map as a "boundary translational matrix," and he explores the "strategic" and "tactical" practices (a distinction made by Michel de Certeau) that Inuit hunters use to mediate between their world and the world of the Canadian Government.

Shunwa Honda's chapter (6) is the third in the trilogy of chapters about the North. Like Omura, Honda is concerned with the lives of the Inuit, but his chapter examines multiplicities within the category "Inuit" itself. Climate change has impacted and is received in radically different ways by Inuit in west Greenland versus north Greenland and Nunavut, Canada, which are structured by differing experiences of colonization, governance, economic development, and physical environment. Honda's chapter provides comprehensive empirical insights into Inuit life, and in this sense it complements Omura's chapter. But his main contribution is to present the diverse perceptions and responses that Inuit communities have had to climate change, demonstrating the multiplicity of ways to be Inuit.

Part II—*Space-time multiplicities*—is a cluster of essays concerned with how worlds multiple imply overlapping and diverging spatialities and temporalities. The relationships among materiality, spatiality, and temporality form the center of Heather Swanson's chapter (7) dealing with the making of salmon bodies and landscapes in the most northern of Japan's main islands, Hokkaido. The worldings wrought in the practice of comparison provide the path Swanson follows for examining how salmon and landscape have been entangled since the onset of Japan's modernization and colonization endeavors in the nineteenth century. Comparisons between Hokkaido's salmon and those of the Columbia River, and between its landscapes and the frontiers of the American West, transformed species and landscape and also spurred the development of technologies, commodities, and a new place for Japan in the modernizing world. This assemblage of humans and non-humans is a materialized multiplicity of comparisons that have coordinated a way to "hang together" in time.

Cristóbal Bonelli's chapter (8) argues that the domination of the "one-world world" is also an imposition of a "one-time-temporality." To draw out the divergent temporalities that dwell in the world, Bonelli offers an ethnographic and philosophical meditation on the "politics of when"—a form of politics in addition to the representational "politics of who" and the ontological "politics of what." He draws together singular inscriptions of names—those of Chilean dictator Augusto Pinochet on a sacred stone and of Miguel Cuevas Pincheira, one of his victims, on the bridge where he disappeared—with the Spinozan notions of *conatus* and "striving" to think about the entangled politics of duration, ontological persistence, and the material act of inscription.

If Swanson and Bonelli look at the multiple pasts that inhere in the present, then Moe Nakazora's contribution examines worldings in which what count as past, present, and future is at stake. An outgrowth of her extensive work on Ayurvedic medicine in India, this chapter (9) examines how Ayurvedic knowledge is translated with modern biomedical knowledge in the construction of biodiversity databases. Against the background of global and national agreements for protecting biodiversity, Nakazora shows how database projects for collecting Ayurvedic knowledge about plants in Uttarakhand become contentious "contact zones" (cf. Pratt 1992), where multiple knowledges and practices encounter each other to generate new temporalities in which plants and various practitioners live.

Part II concludes with Stacey Langwick's ethnographic evocation of the lushness engendered by plants in Tanzania (Chapter 10). "Lushness" is a particularly apt word with which to imagine the verdant and vibrant multispecies relations that *mlonge*—a tree used to produce herbal therapies—calls forth around it. Langwick shows us how Tanzania is a place where the often overbroad notion of the "Anthropocene" (see Morita, Afterword) is manifested in the quotidian as pervasive toxicity. Mlonge and the way it strives for life with others then become Langwick's more-than-human guides for thinking about what worlds are possible in toxic times.

Anthropological analysis has always been in some sense about finding ways to talk about worlds: analysis is a worlding practice, albeit one that necessarily leans heavily on translating the quotidian into text, usually in a Western, academic idiom. The chapters in Part III—*Exploring quotidian politics*—acknowledge this ecology of practices. But they refuse to sever abstractions from the quotidian worlds that they make available in text so that they can offer analytics that stay entangled with worlds multiple. Such entanglements lie at the center of Mei Zhan's chapter (11) on entrepreneurial experiments with traditional Chinese medicine. These experiments are both classical and contemporary in orientation, but this is not a contradiction: Zhan argues that Daoism, Max Weber's problematic studies of Chinese religion, and Maoist materialism, among others, are not successive systems of thought, but tangles of worldly relations that Chinese medical entrepreneurs grasp at or sweep aside as they work to re-animate the "primal spirit" of traditional Chinese medicine.

By doing so, her essay challenges our reverence for critical analysis as an epistemological act that is done to the world; instead, Zhan shows how critical analytics are *in* the quotidian doings of worlds.

A similar irreverence is evident among Vezo fishers in Taku Iida's chapter (12), a careful study of the development, sharing, and transformation of various kinds of knowledge in southern Madagascar. Iida shows how relations among villagers and between fishers and foreign NGOs can help reveal how knowledges transform, multiply, and adapt over time. Iida distinguishes between knowledge and "information" in Gregory Bateson's sense, to develop a model that sees knowledge as a practice and information as relations, and uses this to ponder, among other things, what this reveals about commonly held distinctions between "technoscientific" and "local" knowledges.

Antonia Walford's chapter (13) takes us from analyses of knowledge to reflections on self-knowledge. São Gabriel da Cachoeira is a city located at the confluence of the Rio Negro and the Rio Uaupés in Brazil. Walford attends to how the people she encounters there, both "indigenous" and "outsider," speak about the "world of the Indians" and the "world of the whites." Comparison appears here as the practice of interest, but in contrast to Swanson's approach, Walford is interested in how people iterate comparisons between "Indians" and "whites" in ways that provide both unexpected sources of stability for some indigenous interlocutors and anxiety-inducing, perhaps "emetic" experiences for others. Walford uses these to think about the concept of "equivocation" (Viveiros de Castro 2004; see Chapters 2–4 and 15 in this volume by de la Cadena, Jensen, Blaser, and Tsing), and how to more carefully theorize encounters between multiple worlds.

Shiho Satsuka's chapter (14) takes us into a forest of multispecies relations and introduces us to the work of matsutake mycologists and "meisters," scientists and farmers brought together by the charisma of the matsutake mushroom in Japan. Satsuka's questions concern the multiple, overlapping, and divergent worlds that mushrooms, scientists, and meisters enact through their relations with each other. Not unlike Langwick's interest in the lushness surrounding the mlonge tree, Satsuka attends to the multidimensional engagements that these actors have with each other, which both connect worlds and hold them apart, emphasizing the omnipresent but thoroughly situated potentials for the *otherwise* that inhabit worlds multiple, which epitomizes this volume's focus on subtle politics.

Anna Tsing concludes Part III with a chapter (15) that is wary of holism but hungry for connection. Her essay stages an encounter between two ways of thinking about humans and non-humans in anthropology today—ontological anthropology and multispecies ethnography—to ponder their differences and feel out their resonances. Tsing traces a path from there through Annemarie Mol's work, Satsuka's analytic focus on "translation" (2015), and Morita's intervention in "infrastructure" (2016) to discuss the importance of "encounter" and "coordination" in thinking about worlds multiple. She moves on to her own recent ethnographic experiments for evoking worlds multiple, such as the Matsutake Worlds Research Group (Matsutake Worlds Research Group 2009a, 2009b), and especially her collaboration with the visual artist/scholar Elaine Gan, and the "Golden Snail Opera" (Tsai et al. 2016), to suggest ways of intervening generatively in contemporary anthropological debates.

Atsuro Morita provides the Afterword. Drawing our attention to the horizons of anthropology, Morita connects the contributors' experiments back to Marilyn Strathern's (1995) reflections on the local and global. The "global" for Strathern was an imagined, encompassing scale or an "ever-expanding horizon" against which the "local" becomes a meaningful relational object, though in shifting ways. Morita argues that, in contrast, the "world" of the world multiple is not a self-evident background for local relations, but is itself a relational object. This is due to, among other things, the realization that human life does not just imagine the globe, but constructs it in the age of the Anthropocene. Morita shows how this leads the contributors in this volume not simply to replace "globe" with "world," but to sound out the elusive depths of the worlds generated in complex, ceaseless, recursive movements between objects and their backgrounds.

The practices found and documented in these chapters point towards ways that the world multiple might help us cultivate "arts of living on a damaged planet" (Tsing et al. 2017). The world multiple is a modest experiment with "speculative fabulation" (Haraway 2015) to explore possibilities of life in a world respectful of multiplicity.

Acknowledgments

Our thanks to the participants in the 2016 "The World Multiple" symposium for inspiring this discussion. We are particularly grateful to Mei Zhan, who offered close readings and helpful feedback that have improved the final text. Otsuki also thanks Jeff Sissons, Eli Elinoff, and Callan Sait for their feedback on earlier versions. Satsuka thanks the participants of her graduate seminars "Postcolonial Science Studies" and "Politics of Cohabitation" at the University of Toronto for discussing the issues addressed in this introduction and helping her develop the ideas.

Notes

1 Omura was also not satisfied with the sensationalization of the Inuit "adoption" of modern technologies, such as the internet and snowmobiles. The spirit of this book is also to explore analytic frameworks alternative to the conventional assimilation or acculturation model exemplified by the sensationalization of indigenous creativity, which also reinforces the hegemony of modern "Western" technology.

2 As Roy Wagner (1981) argues, in the modern Western ontology, social relations belong to the domain of culture as a product of creative human agency, while things must stay in the domain of nature as inert and given. From this perspective, applying social categories to the domain of nature inevitably looks like subjectivism, an unjustifiable extension of the logic of the cultural to the natural (cf. Ingold 2000).

Indigenous knowledges, as typified by IQ, are characterized as not being constrained by modernist boundaries between animals and humans; seeing homologies between ecological interspecies relations and social interpersonal relations; and explicitly relating ecology and biology with religion, kinship, political organization, and myth.

3 Zhan (2012) argues that Heidegger's "unworlded" Daoism, by failing to acknowledge its influence on his thought, makes Daoist ideas "invisible and unimaginable as analytical frameworks" (113). Heidegger was also influenced by Jakob von Uexküll's notion of "*umwelt*" ("around space") (Mazis 2008, 32–33).

4 In this sense, the quotidian may resemble the traditional "local" field site of anthropology experienced in real-time. Our use of the quotidian is compatible with this meaning, but the contributors to this book show how worldings often do not respect the boundaries of things like the "local." Worlding practices bring into range many things that affect us, or are affected by us. The quotidian is this space-time that both is made in practice, and is where those practices take place.

References

Agrawal, Arjun. 1995. "Dismantling the Divide Between Indigenous and Scientific Knowledge." *Development and Change* 26 (3): 413–439.

Asad, Talal. 1991. "Afterword: From the History of Colonial Anthropology to the Anthropology of Western Hegemony." In *Colonial Situations: Essays on the Contextualization of Ethnographic Knowledge*, edited by George W. Stocking Jr. Madison, WI: University of Wisconsin Press.

Barad, Karen. 2007. *Meeting the Universe Halfway: Quantum Physics and the Entanglement of Matter and Meaning*. Durham, NC: Duke University Press.

—. 2017. "No Small Matter: Mushroom Clouds, Ecologies of Nothingness, and Strange Topologies of Spacetimemattering." In *Arts of Living on a Damaged Planet*, edited by Anna Tsing, Heather Swanson, Elaine Gan, and Nils Bubandt, 103–120. Minneapolis, MN: University of Minnesota Press.

Blaser, Mario. 2009 "The Threat of the Yrmo: The Political Ontology of a Sustainable Hunting Program." *American Anthropologist* 111 (1): 10–20.

Chakrabarty, Dipesh. 2009. "The Climate of History: Four Theses." *Critical Inquiry* 35 (2): 197–222.

Collings, Peter. 1997. "Subsistence Hunting and Wildlife Management in the Central Canadian Arctic." *Arctic Anthropology* 34 (1): 41–56.

Crutzen, P. J. and E. F. Stoermer. 2000. "The Anthropocene." *IGBO Global Change Newsletter* 41: 17–18.

Derrida, Jacques. 1982. "The Ends of Man." In *Margins of Philosophy*, translated by Alan Bass. Brighton, UK: Harvester Press.

—. 1997. *Of Grammatology*. Translated by Gayatri Chakravorty Spivak. Baltimore. MD: Johns Hopkins University Press.

van Dooren, Thom, Eben Kirksey, and Ursula Münster. 2016. "Multispecies Studies: Cultivating Arts of Attentiveness." *Environmental Humanities* 8 (1): 1–23.

Fischer, Michael M. J. 2007. "Culture and Cultural Analysis as Experimental Systems." *Cultural Anthropology* 22 (1): 1–65.

Foucault, Michel. 1988. "Technologies of the Self." In *Technologies of the Self: A Seminar with Michel Foucault*, edited by Luther H. Martin, Hugh Gutman, and Patrick H. Hutton, 16–49. Amherst, MA: University of Massachusetts Press.

—. 1991. "Governmentality." In *The Foucault Effect: Studies in Governmentality*, edited by Graham Burchell, Colin Gordon, and Peter Miller. Chicago, IL: University of Chicago Press.

Freeman, Milton M. R. 1985. "Appeal to Tradition: Different Perspectives on Arctic Wildlife Management." In *Native Power: The Quest for Autonomy and Nationhood of Indigenous Peoples*, edited by Jens Brøsted, Jens Dahl, Andrew Gray, Hans Christian Gulløv, Georg Henriksen, Jørgen Brøchner, and Inge Kleivan, 265–281. Bergen, Oslo, Stavanger, Tromso: Universitetsforlaget.

—. 1993. "Traditional Land Users as a Legitimate Source of Environmental Expertise." In *Traditional Ecological Knowledge: Wisdom for Sustainable Development*, edited by Nancy Williams and Graham Baines, 153–161. Canberra: Center for Resource and Environmental Studies, Australian National University.

Gad, C., C. B. Jensen, and B. R. Wintghereik. 2015. "Practical Ontology: Worlds in STS and Anthropology. *NatureCultures* 3: 67–86.

Haraway, Donna J. 1991. "A Cyborg Manifesto: Science, Technology, and Socialist-Feminism in the Late Twentieth Century." In *Simians, Cyborgs, and Women: The Reinvention of Nature*, edited by Donna J. Haraway, 149–181. New York: Routledge.

—. 2015. *Staying with the Trouble: Making Kin in the Chthulucene*. Durham, NC: Duke University Press.

Heidegger, Martin. 1993. "The Origin of the Work of Art." In *Basic Writings*, edited by David Farrell Krell, 139–212. New York: HarperCollins.

Henare, Amiria, Martin Holdbraad, and Sari Wastell, eds. 2007. *Thinking Through Things: Theorising Artefacts Ethnographically*. London and New York: Routledge.

Holbraad, Martin and Morten Axel Pedersen. 2017. *The Ontological Turn: An Anthropological Exposition*. Cambridge: Cambridge University Press.

Ingold, Tim. 2000. *The Perception of the Environment: Essays on Livelihood, Dwelling and Skill*. London and New York: Routledge.

Kirksey, S. Eben and Stefan Helmreich. 2010. "The Emergence of Multispecies Ethnography." *Cultural Anthropology* 25 (4): 545–576.

Kohn, Eduardo. 2013. *How Forests Think: Toward an Anthropology Beyond the Human*. Berkeley, CA: University of California Press.

Krupnik, Igor and Nikolay Vakhtin. 1997. "Indigenous Knowledge in Modern Culture: Siberian Yupik Ecological Legacy in Transition." *Arctic Anthropology* 34 (1): 236–252.

Latour, Bruno. 2005. *Reassembling the Social: An Introduction to Actor-Network-Theory*. Oxford; New York: Oxford University Press.

Law, John. 2015. "What's Wrong with a One-World World?" *Distinktion: Scandinavian Journal of Social Theory* 16 (1): 126–139.

Matsutake Worlds Research Group (Timothy K. Choy, Lieba Faier, Michael J. Hathaway, Miyako Inoue, Shiho Satsuka, Anna Tsing). 2009a. "A New Form of Collaboration in Cultural Anthropology: Matsutake Worlds." *American Ethnologist* 36(2): 380–403.

—. 2009b. "Strong Collaboration as a Method for Multi-sited Ethnography: on Mycorrhizal Relations," In *Multi-Sited Ethnography*, edited by Mark-Anthony Falzon, 197–214. Farnham, UK: Ashgate Publishing.

Mazis, Glen A. 2008. *Humans, Animals, Machines: Blurring Boundaries*. Albany, NY: SUNY Press.

Mol, Annemarie. 2002. *The Body Multiple: Ontology in Medical Practice*. Durham, NC: Duke University Press.

Morita, Atsuro. 2016. "Infrastructuring Amphibious Space: The Interplay of Aquatic and Terrestrial Infrastructures in the Chao Phraya Delta in Thailand," *Science as Culture* 25 (1): 117–140.

Nadasdy, Paul. 1999. "The Politics of TEK: Power and the 'Integration' of Knowledge." *Arctic Anthropology* 36 (1/2): 1–18.

—. 2003. *Hunters and Bureaucrats: Power, Knowledge, and Aboriginal–State Relations in the Southwest Yukon.* Vancouver and Toronto: UBC Press.

Ogden, Laura A., Billy Hall, and Kimiko Tanita. 2013. "Animals, Plants, People, and Things: A Review of Multispecies Ethnography." *Environment and Society* 4 (1): 5–24.

Omura, Keiichi. 2005. "Science against Modern Science: The Socio-political Construction of Otherness in Inuit TEK (Traditional Ecological Knowledge)." In *Indigenous Use and Management of Marine Resources,* edited by N. Kishigami and J. Savelle, 323–344. Osaka: National Museum of Ethnology.

—. 2007 "From Knowledge to Poetics: The Sophia of Anti-essentialistic Essentialism in Inuit Traditional Environmental Knowledge." *Japanese Review of Cultural Anthropology* 7: 27–50.

—. 2013. *Kanada inuito no minzokushi: Nichijōteki jissen no dainamikusu (Ethnography of Canadian Inuit: Dynamics of Everyday Practices).* Osaka: Osaka University Press.

Pratt, Mary Louise. 1992. *Imperial Eyes: Travel Writing and Transculturation.* New York: Routledge.

Satsuka, Shiho. 2015. *Nature in Translation: Japanese Tourism Encounters the Canadian Rockies.* Durham, NC: Duke University Press.

Schrader, Astrid. 2010. "Responding to *Pfiesteria piscicida* (the Fish Killer): Phantomatic Ontologies, Indeterminacy, and Responsibility in Toxic Microbiology." *Social Studies of Science* 40 (2): 275–306.

Spivak, Gayatri Chakravorty. 1985. "Three Women's Texts and a Critique of Imperialism." *Critical Inquiry* 12 (1): 243–261.

—. 1999. *A Critique of Postcolonial Reason: Toward a History of the Vanishing Present.* Cambridge, MA: Harvard University Press.

Stengers, Isabelle. 2015. *In Catastrophic Times: Resisting the Coming Barbarism.* Translated by Andrew Goffey. Lüneburg, Germany: Open Humanities Press.

Strathern, Marilyn, ed. 1995. *Shifting Contexts: Transformations in Anthropological Knowledge.* London and New York: Routledge.

—. 2005. *Partial Connections.* Updated edition. Walnut Creek, CA: Altamira Press.

Tsai, Yen-Ling, Isabelle Carbonell, Joelle Chevrier, and Anna Lowenhaupt Tsing. 2016. "Golden Snail Opera: The More-than-Human Performance of Friendly Farming on Taiwan's Lanyang Plain." *Cultural Anthropology* 31 (4): 520–544.

Tsing, Anna. 2010. "Worlding the matsutake diaspora: Or, Can Actor-Network Theory Experiment with Holism?" In *Experiments in Holism: Theory and Practice in Contemporary Anthropology,* edited by Ton Otto and Nils Bubandt, 47–66. Malden, MA: Wiley-Blackwell.

Tsing, Anna, Heather Swanson, Elaine Gan, and Nils Bubandt, eds. 2017. *Arts of Living on a Damaged Planet.* Minneapolis, MN: University of Minnesota Press.

Usher, Peter J. 2000. "Traditional Ecological Knowledge in Environmental Assessment and Management." *Arctic* 53 (2): 183–193.

Viveiros de Castro, Eduardo. 2004. "Perspectival Anthropology and the Method of Controlled Equivocation." *Tipití: Journal of the Society for the Anthropology of Lowland South America* 2 (1): 3–22.

Wagner, Roy. 1981. *The Invention of Culture*, 2nd revised edition. Chicago, IL: University of Chicago Press.

Welland, Sasha Su-Ling. 2018. *Experimental Beijing: Gender and Globalization in Chinese Art*. Durham, NC: Duke University Press.

Wenzel, George. 2004. "From TEK to IQ: Inuit *Qaujimajatuqangit* and Inuit Cultural Ecology." *Arctic Anthropology* 41 (2): 238–250.

Zhan, Mei. 2009. *Other-Worldly: Making Chinese Medicine Through Transnational Frames*. Durham, NC: Duke University Press.

—. 2012. "Worlding Oneness: Daoism, Heidegger, and Possibilities for Treating the Human." *Social Text* 29 (4 109): 107–128.

Part I

Entangled worldings

Chapter 2

Earth-beings: Andean indigenous religion, but *not only*

Marisol de la Cadena

It is impossible to take from them this superstition because the destruction of these *guacas* would require more force than that of all the people of Peru in order to move these *stones and hills*.

(Cristóbal de Albornoz, 1584; emphasis added)

[We have to] defeat those absurd pantheistic ideologies that believe that walls are gods and the wind is god. [To believe that] means to return to those primitive forms of religiosity that say do not touch that *mountain* because it is an *Apu* [a powerful earth-being] full of *millenarian spirit* or whatever. Ok, if we get there, we'd rather not do anything, not even mining. [...] We return to primitive animism.

(Alan García Perez, former president of Peru, 2011;[1] emphasis added)

Cristóbal de Albornoz, the sixteenth-century author of the first quotation, was a relatively well-known "extirpator of idolatries." He identified *guacas* as the source of the superstitious practices of Andean Indians, whom he deemed the Devil's easy prey. Acknowledging the risk of anachronism, I am going to say that guaca is the colonial term for what I have called "earth-beings," translating from the Andean word *tirakuna* (see also Allen 2002). This is the Quechua plural of *tierra*, or earth: *tierras*. Accordingly, "earths" would be the literal translation. In contemporary Cuzco, tirakuna with *runakuna* (Quechua plural for *runa*, or person) form *ayllu*—a concept to which I will return. Intriguingly, de Albornoz translated guacas as "stones" and "hills" and consequently he was able to attribute blame for the difficulty he experienced attempting to eradicate idolatries: removing them appeared impossible for guacas were "earths!" Five hundred years later, "earths" present the same challenge to new eradicators: mining corporations translate them as mountains and a source of minerals, and therefore wealth. They find allies in chiefs of state like Alan García, former president of Peru and author of the second epigraph, a statement he made on television in June 2011. While the ex-president seems to rely on modern idioms of separation between the sacred and the secular, his words have uncanny resonance with the sixteenth-century extirpation of idolatries that de Albornoz practiced. Yet, the plight of modern extirpators is lessened by the might of corporations that, unlike their colonial counterparts, have the power to remove mountains, redirect rivers, or replace lakes with efficient reservoirs for water. Also different is that modern extirpators have non-indigenous opponents: Alan García's infamous remarks prompted disagreement from leading leftist politicians, who accused the then president of racism and religious intolerance and defended the right of indigenous peoples to their spiritual beliefs (Adrianzén 2011). Yet, when these politicians joined the defense of what they called "indigenous sacred mountains," people who live in the surroundings of Ausangate, one of the endangered tirakuna, regardless of whether they were for or against mining, vacillated over whether to consider practices with earth-beings "religious." The dispute, then, housed an important paradox: while for Peruvian politicians (left and right), "indigenous practices" with earth-beings were evidently religion, for practitioners, their relations with earth-beings were not self-evident as religion, and yet it was far from certain that those practices were not religion.

This paradox is not insignificant. The vacillation makes uncomfortable those modes of analysis that seek straightforward answers, and it provokes thought about the practice of categories, which in this case are categories that name practices. Local dwellers of communities affected by mining prospects negotiated their being with tirakuna in ways that opened up to discussion the qualification of their practices as religion—apparently they were *not only* such. This provoked my question: could it be that runakuna practices with Ausangate enacted divergent entities (and were therefore not the same practice) even as the event happened at the same time and place?

To start unraveling the paradox that motivates this chapter, I propose something that will sound obvious: relations with earth-beings as religious practices emerged in translation through practices that transpired along with colonial processes of conversion, first to Christianity (executed through faith by the Church and its representatives) and later to secular modernity (executed by the state and its representatives). In the transition from the former to the latter, the Devil—the entity extirpators declared to be the instigator behind the "worship of hills"—became "beliefs in animated nature." As illustrated by the tension between García and his opponents, such practices continued to be considered superstitions or were redescribed as indigenous religion.

To what they called America, the sixteenth-century newcomers brought a world where God was the supreme power, the Creator of human and nature, entities with and without soul, respectively. In the Andes, the newcomers encountered what local people called guacas. Their difference from people was considerable, and it could include power. Yet, the distinction Andeans made between people and what de Albornoz called "hills and stones" did not preclude continuity. Instead, the opposite was the case: guacas were *with* people, makers and watchers of the places they also were. Also with (and like) people, some were more powerful than others, and the relation across and within these connections was one of respect, care, and gifts (Dean 2010).[2] The likes of de Albornoz also learned that people could also be wank'a or become one, in a process extirpators called "petrification"—this surprised them, even scared them. I want us to take their surprise into consideration, for the possibility of becoming wank'a (translated as "becoming rock") speaks of the divergence between "Spanish humans" and "Andean people" (or runakuna) in spite of their also apparent similarity. I want to take this divergence as an opportunity to suggest that the conception of a discontinuous overlap between, on one hand, practices between people and mountains and, on the other, practices through which runakuna become (inherently) with earth-beings, may allow us to conceive an assemblage that emerges as religion but is *not only* such. The assemblage would house *excesses* between mountains and earth-beings, as I have mentioned in previous works, (de la Cadena 2010, 2015), and it would also be composed by the divergence between, on one hand, runakuna with earth-beings and, on the other, the human separated from nature that enacts and is enacted through religious practices in the Andes. I will resume this point later in the chapter; for now, a brief word about divergence. I borrow the notion from Isabelle Stengers (2005) and use it as a tool to look at practices that are not the same and do not make up the same entity, yet occupy the same time-place and become with each other while continuing to be distinct. In the Andes, from early colonial faith to current sacred mountains, or mountain spirits, the language of religion has acted as a tool for a capacious translation housing divergence among worlds that enact ontological discontinuities between humans and non-humans and worlds that do *not only* enact such discontinuities. "Indigenous religiosity" in the Andes is a complex field, the result of a series of historical translations and ecologies of practices across geographies, fields of power, and epistemic and ontological scapes. And within this field the practices that might be named "religious" may also be *not only* such.

My intention is not to declare the notion of "indigenous religion" spurious. Instead, and using the words of religious studies scholar Tomoko Masuzawa, I want to avoid the

> rather monumental assumption that is as pervasive as it is unexamined, namely that religion is a [...] ubiquitous phenomenon to be found any-where in the world at any time in history, albeit in a wide variety of forms and with different degrees of prevalence and importance.
>
> (Masuzawa 2005, 1)

The assumption is persistent in contemporary descriptions of early colonial encounters between the Spanish and the people they found in the Andes. Take, for example, the following sentence: "Catholic missionaries encountered religions that had no previous contact with Europe" (Stevens-Arroyo 2003, 62).[3] Consider also a recent title: *The Archaeology of Wak'as: Explorations of the Sacred in the Pre-Columbian Andes* (Bray 2015), an excellent edited volume on the idols that de Albornoz considered devilish. A question in response to Stevens-Arroyo's statement: Was it "religion" that the missionaries encountered? And a question in response to the title of Bray's book: What genealogy is current scholarship implicitly inheriting when it qualifies sixteenth-century guacas as sacred? What would happen both to guacas and the sacred if the genealogy were to be made explicit?

Translation as conversion: Fields of equivocation

That friars might have translated the practices they encountered using questions and vocabularies from the field with which they were familiar is not a new idea. Apparently it was a frequent practice, and also not without doubts. For example, according to Owen Chadwick, a scholar of Christianity: "The Jesuits in China contended that the reverence for ancestors *was a social, not a religious act, or that if religious*, it was hardly different from Catholic prayers for the dead" (emphasis added). Also: "in 1631, a Franciscan and a Dominican from the Spanish Zone of Manila travelled [...] to Peking and found that to translate the word 'mass,' the Jesuit catechism used the character *tsi*, which was the Chinese description of the ceremonies of ancestor-worship" (Chadwick 1964, 338; quoted in Asad 1993). Vicente Rafael (1993) observes a similar situation in the Philippines. He reports that translating the entity that the Tagalog called *nono* with the notions they had at hand, Spanish friars made an equivalence between this entity and the tutelary spirits of ancient Romans; also, continuing the equivalence, because nono referred to ancestors, the friars assumed they were similar to the ancestors the Chinese worshiped. As in the Andean case, the friars identified the offerings as "superstition." Complicating the friars' translation, Rafael's inspection of the word nono reveals that, more than spirits, these entities evoked "indeterminate auras emanating from certain objects [...] trees, rocks, rivers, even crocodiles." And explaining how the translation worked, he states: "to identify those offerings with idolatries was to conflate the nature of the natives' offerings with those of Christians" (Rafael 1993, 112–113).[4]

But translation was a complex practice: as faith made itself local to convert things indigenous, the very things that were converted exceeded conversion, either because faith feared them (and decided to leave them alone) or simply because practices were recalcitrant to capture by faith. For example, scholars of the colonial Andes have famously suspected that during the initial centuries of Spanish rule, the "procession of Saints," part of the celebration of Corpus Christi in Cuzco, was also a commemoration of the deceased rulers whose "mummies" were supposedly hidden under the image of the Christian Saint. Less famous examples abound: alleged "offerings to the saints" could have hidden (from view and conception) the relation of runakuna being with guacas or other earth-beings of lesser import (Gose 2008). In any event, through effective conversion, practices indigenous to the Andes were moved into a field —that of Christian faith—that *also* could not recognize them. The friars would have been disappointed to learn that, even when effective, conversion remained a partial practice: it did not work with "wholes," for, rather than discrete units, practices are knots of connections with the capacity for endless fragmentation. Conversion worked through these knots, with practices both emerging in translation through conversion and escaping it, thus also remaining part of the practice that through conversion appeared included in faith (and later on in religious practice)—and also escaped, and endlessly like this. Practices recalcitrant to conversion (that were also with it) could be ignored, denied existence, or made irrelevant to the world of the Christian God. But regardless of which of the three options they fell into, practices that I am calling indigenous to the Andes and recalcitrant did not cease to enact something that was also in excess of Christianity. Rafael makes a similar point about the Philippines:

> It was as if the Tagalogs, in confronting the discourse of clerical-colonial authority, always had something else in mind which the procedures of missionary translation and conversion were unable to circumscribe. So things in Tagalog culture could not be unequivocally restated in Spanish-Christian terms, just as some aspects of the vernacular exceeded the limits that the missionaries sought to set for it.
>
> (Rafael 1993, 110)

I'd like to make two proposals: The first is that we consider that what the Christians who arrived in the Andes encountered might not have been "religion." The heterogeneous notions of religion that we now use date from complicated geopolitical processes spanning at least the eighteenth and nineteenth European world-making centuries.[5] Also, important entities like the Devil and God, and the discontinuities between humans and nature, soul and body, which practitioners of Christian faith utilized to translate the practices they encountered into "idolatry" and "superstition," came to be in the Andes through the process of colonial translation (of words and practices) that created the conceptual field (and the vocabulary) that served as a genealogical foundation for the emergence of "indigenous religion." In producing current critical notions of religion, we tend to obviate the conversion/translation through which "religion" became (by which I mean was made real); this is a habit that draws from the political thought that composed a region where Christianity played an important geopolitical, ontological, and epistemic role.

Second, keeping an eye on "conversion," I propose that translations between the world of guacas and the world of the Christian God created what, drawing from (and tweaking) Eduardo Viveiros de Castro (2004), I want to call *fields of equivocation*, or onto-epistemic spaces of action that can both host practices that enact more than one world *and* not infrequently translate forcefully (even disregarding their own hesitation, like the colonial friars) into the practices of the world made hegemonic through the same translation practices.[6] Fields of equivocation are thus fields where onto-epistemic politics—negotiations of what is, or the conflict among practices to be—take place along with and through practices of translation (that make one out of what is entangled in the multiple) that often go unacknowledged.

Is it enough to replace the universality of religion with religious plurality?

Religion has been historicized. Critique of its universality has also localized its specificity to geopolitical and epistemic formations. A landmark in this respect is Talal Asad's discussion of Clifford Geertz's analysis of religion as a system of beliefs. Using a Foucault-inspired genealogical argument, Asad explained, counter Geertz, that concepts of "religion qua belief in the sacred" were contingent to the power formation of Christianity that articulated Europe and its expansions in the Post-Reformation seventeenth century (Asad 1993). During that period,

> the idea gradually crystallized among European thinkers that in *every society* people *believed in supernatural beings* and told *stories about the origin of the world* and about what happens to the individual *after death;* that in every society people instituted *rituals of worship* and deferred to *experts* in these matters; and that therefore religion was not something only Christians had.
>
> (Asad 2012, 37; my emphasis)

Inherited from this political formation is the nineteenth-century notion of "world religions." Edward Burnett Tylor's definition of religion as "belief in spiritual beings," and the early concept of "animism" as (primitive) belief in the animate nature of the natural—such as rocks or mountains—represents such a notion. Yet, the inheritance was not unchanged. A contemporary of the then also budding notions of "race" and "culture," thus sharing with them the evolutionary imagination of the time, "world religions" transformed the previously prevalent view of the world as composed of Christians, Jews, Muslims, and "the rest" into a new hierarchical division that, ranked from civilized to primitive, offered the possibility of religion to all peoples in the world (Masuzawa 2005, xi). Curiously, "religion" achieved geopolitical universality as intellectuals endowed it with provincial capacity, that is, as they granted it the ability to include local practices that while deemed "strange (cultural) beliefs" had similarities with either Catholic faith or Post-Reformation notions of belief—and at times with both (Keane 2008). That the relationship among local and European versions was hierarchical certainly helped congeal the imagination of "world religions" even as "the concept of religion itself remained virtually unexamined" (Masuzawa 2012, 37).

Critical commentary about the relation between religion and secular formations has been another important thread in the historicization of religion. Especially influential (but not the only important influence) has been Asad's argument about the imbrication between notions of the secular and the religious as historically specific to the modern Euro-American state and politics. Accordingly, when emerging from another genealogy (Islam, for example), the public sphere of politics is not secular; that it is required to be so responds to the world-making power of the West and the continuing work of Christianity through what is purportedly a secular sphere (Asad 2003).

The work of historicization has undone the universality of the category. Resulting from it, "religion" surfaces as plural in its grammars, temporalities, institutions, and practices, and so does the "secular" and, of course, politics. The idea that religion becomes—or acquires its truth—through different kinds of practices, material and immaterial, is well established. Moving toward this idea is Asad's recommendation that "the anthropological student of particular religions should therefore begin [. . .] in a sense unpacking the comprehensive concept that she or he translates as 'religion' into heterogeneous elements according to its historical character" (Asad 1993, 54.) This resonates with that other recommendation whereby, following Walter Benjamin, Asad called for the language of the translator to be inflected by the one from where she was translating, that is (in this case), religion inflected by that which makes it (in translation) what is also not religion. It seems to me that the recommendation has been indecisively followed, for while the postcolonial critique has undone the universality of religion and has produced definitions that attend to local conditions, the question of why "religion" would be a worldwide practice has yet to be fully posed. If we consider that scholars have also remarked that the word "religion" became part of the lexicon of many collectives only after colonial encounters, the hesitancy toward the question becomes striking. A relatively recent volume by religious studies scholars does address it: in their introduction the editors emphasize that

> it is perfectly possible to organize societies without the concept "religion" or religious–secular interventions. Japan, China, and India are perfectly good examples of such cultures. There is increasing empirical evidence that what we today call Hinduism, Sikhism, and Buddhism only became part of the "world religions" group as late as the nineteenth and early twentieth centuries. *It is therefore worth asking why "we" continue to speak of Indian, Japanese, or Chinese religions.*
>
> (Dressler and Mandair 2011, 17; my emphasis)

I agree—the question needs to be asked. Unlike both colonial friars and ex-president Alan García, current Andeanist scholarship does not translate indigenous relations with earth-beings as idolatries, or earth-beings as idols or fake gods; also unlike García, leftist politicians (like the one who confronted the president) as well as scholars reject the evolutionary premises that led to "indigenous religion" being considered "a primitive cult of nature." Yet, it is not unusual for Andeanist scholarship and politicians of the left to translate local practices with earth-beings as religion *without acknowledging the translation*. Thus, discrepancies notwithstanding, they all share a common ground (sustained by the field of equivocation) where hegemonic understanding ignores what escapes it. Acknowledging the translation may be a first analytic step to unsettling the hegemony—to uncommon the ground, so to speak—and perhaps work toward the inheritance of "indigenous religion" as a decolonized event.[7]

Not only, or a formula to acknowledge the translation and signal its limits

Not only is a phrase frequently used in analyses when referring to a plurality of things (two or more) occurring simultaneously or in a sequence. I learned to give this phrase a post-plural conceptual valence from conversations with Mariano Turpo, a friend with whom I co-labored the ideas that came into the book I published not long ago (de la Cadena 2015). A Quechua speaker and a commuter across some of the worlds that make what Mariano and I call "our country" (Peru), Mariano would insist that what to me *was* (for example, a mountain) was *not only* that. And it was possible that I could eventually *not know* what *it* not only was! To accept that eventuality, I patiently labored my own scholarly habits to let go of two scholarly convictions: first, that I *knew what we were talking about* (a mountain of course!), and, second, that my questions to Mariano would elicit responses after which I *would know* what I did not know before the conversation (i.e., if I did not know what else a mountain was before I elicited Mariano's explanations, once he explained, I would know what he was talking about). This required me to work on my own habits of thought—fieldwork became also about me. Coming to terms with what was *not only* that which emerged through my habitual practice of thought, in addition to taking time, required working at a permanent interface where Mariano's worlding practices and mine were seemingly alike, and at the same time different (de la Cadena 2014, 2015). And what emerged at the interface, rather than "the" entity or practice in question, was an awareness of our concepts and practices (Mariano's and mine) frequently exceeding each other as they also overlapped. *Not only* signaled translation as a practice that allowed for conversation while also insinuating its limits, thus evoking a possibility for that which the same translation that allowed for communication could not contain.

Signaling the limits of translation, *not only* also suggested itself as an ethnographic tool to displace analytics (categories, arguments, grammars) that appeared unable to allow the conditions that I intuited (or was told) were *not only* what to me were (for example, a mountain). And as *not only* suggested its work of displacement, it created possibilities to redescribe those conditions that then appeared different from, but still connected to, what (who or how) they had initially been to me (for example, that mountain!). I borrow displacement and redescription as ethnographic practices from Marilyn Strathern.[8] I also tweak her concepts a bit to make them useful for what I call the "ontological openings" that may result from a disposition to co-labor with the situation at hand. Displacement results from controlling—without canceling— (the practice of) categories, concepts, or analytics that may overpower, perhaps even kidnap, the situation that is up for description. Strathern calls what results from this ethnographic practice "a better description"—one that also indicates the limits and therefore excesses to the displaced categories/practices that, while present yet controlled, cannot further explain away the situation in question. The situation remains open to a "better description"—and this, without closure for that "better description," may be *not only* what it also is. Thus, "*not only*" allows for representation and also suggests its displacement.

Persisting with *not only*, I found ayllu a relational form to redescribe "indigenous religion," which is usually described as a field where people worship/believe in/enact mountains as sacred, or as spirits or deities of some sort. Regardless of the verb or noun, the description hosts a form of relation that connects people and mountain so that if without ayllu they are also without each other. As an ethnographic analytic, ayllu has the capacity to displace relations between entities that *are* without each other (and the subject and object grammar that expresses them) and propose a different one: runakuna and tirakuna in-ayllu *are* inherently related (i.e., never without each other) and as such *take place*—a phrase where time (when it happens) and space (where it happens) are inherent to each other as well. In-ayllu, tirakuna are not an external object of human worship but inseparable from runakuna: they take place and are inherently related to one another in a worlding practice that makes time-space simultaneous.

Being in-ayllu is enacted through a variety of practices—among them, *despacho* may be the most charismatic and also complex. To begin with, a "despacho" is an object: a bundle of assorted dry foodstuffs, a llama fetus, and flowers, all wrapped in white paper that can be bought in marketplaces. "Despacho" is also a Spanish noun, rooted in the verb *despachar*, which means to send something from one place to another. It has a Quechua equivalent in the word *haywayku*, which translates as *alcanzar* in Spanish: to stretch one's hand to reach or offer something. Some features of despachos are similar to Catholic practices; for example, offering the coca leaves during a despacho (either to other runakuna or to earth-beings) follows a pattern similar to the movement of a priest presenting the host, the consecrated body of Christ. Also, the address to the earth-being by the despachante (the person performing a despacho) may have the intonation of Catholic prayers. My friend Antonio, a Jesuit priest, used to perform despachos with Mariano and Nazario—he may still do so with Rufino or Víctor Hugo, Nazario's son and son-in-law, respectively. Also with runakuna, Antonio practices the *k'intu* and the *tinka*. The first consists of blowing one's breath on an arranged set of coca leaves and directing it to the surrounding earth-beings; the second requires pouring drops of one's drink on the ground to share with earth-beings. For more than fifty years, liberation theology has translated all three (despachos, k'intu, and tinka) into their catechisms and pastoral work as indigenous religious practices; similarly, the Andean ethnographic record describes them as offerings to supernatural beings, mountain spirits, or *Pachamama* (Mother Earth). Antonio does not think earth-beings are deities, but he explains that by making despachos, k'intu, and tinka he communes with the Christian God, who is in every entity He created, including runakuna and tirakuna of course. From a theological viewpoint, and coinciding with liberation theology, he thinks of these practices as "natural religion," and with that caveat he would agree with Andean ethnography: despachos, kint'u, and tinka are integral to indigenous religion. I would not contradict that statement, let alone in relation to Antonio's practices—yet I would say that they are *not only* religion. Those relations are also ayllu—runakuna with tirakuna inherently together taking place. Andean indigenous religion, a practice that if Catholic would also include my friend Padre Antonio, the Jesuit priest, and would thus be hybrid —not after the mixture of two religious traditions but through its becoming through both, Catholicism *and* ayllu, the condition through which runakuna and tirakuna cannot be pulled apart.

Now I will risk anachronism again for the sake of a thought exercise: in addition to replacing allegedly spurious beliefs with legitimate ones, the sixteenth-century practice of extirpating idolatries might have required replacing the condition that made runakuna *with* guacas with a conceptual grammar that conceived of humans as distinct from nature. Seemingly, then, the immensity of guacas was not the only obstacle to the extirpators' task, and neither was conversion limited to changing native beliefs. The friars' mission might have included making the human that conversion required—and this human was not what runakuna were, for they could become with tirakuna (even become one!). What the friars needed to extirpate was this condition—the relational being runakuna-with-guacas—and convert it into a relation in accord with God's creation: humans and nature. This alters the usual imaginary of colonization: accordingly, rather than the denial of humanity, colonization might have required in the first place the imposition of humanity to the colonized—and this entailed the extirpation of specific forms of being person. Fighting against earth-beings and runakuna becoming together, colonial and later modern Christian conversion/translation would have created the entities that first faith and then religion required: mountains and humans to worship them.

It may be difficult to fathom that both relations (the one that separates humans and earth-beings via belief or practices and the one through which runakuna and tirakuna emerge together in ayllu) may occur simultaneously. And it may ease the difficulty if we remember that indigenous religion in the Andes is *not only* such. If we slow down its utterance, we may sense that such condition is already in the terms "indigenous" and "religion," each word already indicating its historical emergence in excess of the other—and together. Made with practices that exceed it, indigenous religion is a complex phenomenon, the coherence of which is partial, for it also emerges through ayllu. Vice versa might also be the case. Neither is reducible to a single dimension, nor do they do not exist as a plural coherence of two separate and independent practices.[9] Conversion was effective, and resistance to it was perseverant. Thinking both processes simultaneously yields complex conditions: entities and practices that are *not only* what they also are. Despacho is the example I have used; pilgrimages to shrines can be another one. They all suggest composites where religion, humans, or mountains are *not only* such. They are also runakuna with tirakuna in-ayllu, without this canceling their being religion, humans, and mountains.[10]

Not only: A tool for ontological openings

Not only was inspired at the crossroads—remote from usual imagination—where the life and words of Mariano Turpo met my readings of Isabelle Stengers's cosmopolitics. Enabling the practice of ethnography at the interfaces of what is both the same and not—for example my world and Mariano's, a condition of world multiple, simultaneously distinct and historically coordinated into singularity—*not only* may be a formula to perform what I am proposing as "ontological openings": a proposal to think that, as they become through enactments, anything—events, relations, practices, entities—might be other than what it also is. A tool for partial connections (Strathern 2004), *not only* is not a formula to "add" known possibilities (for example, as in "*not only* happy, also unhappy"), to denote two conditions combined into a third one ("*not only* black, also white and thus mulatto"), or to make a list of things that might eventually be completed. Instead, like Mariano's challenge to me and as in Stengers's proposal, my intent with *not only* is to slow down our practice of knowing (events, relations, practices, entities). Slowing down our knowing habits *not only* indicates a potential emergence that could challenge what we know and the ways we know it, and even suggest the impossibility of our knowing, without such impossibility canceling the emergence. *Not only* works with the empirical also to open it up beyond its limits, toward what may be in a different mode and without its binary opposite, "theory." Thus, *not only* indicates that the empirical and its counterpart, abstract theory, are not the only conditions of emergence of entities, relations, or practices. In so doing, *not only* arrests the analytic urge to cancel the eventfulness of relations, practices, or entities that do not meet the empirical conditions that modern epistemology currently requires to abstract knowledge from its objects. Practicing *not only*, we may *attend* to that which *is* (or may emerge) beyond the limit of epistemic knowledge and thus exceeds the way "we" know. Different from knowing, attending in the previous sentence means acquiescing, without requirements, to a presence whose manner of being we may not fathom.

Not long ago, Francisco Pazzarelli, an Argentinian anthropologist, called my attention to a phrase that Claude Lévi-Strauss used throughout the volumes of *Mythologiques* (1968, 1970, 1971, 1973.) The phrase is *"ce n'est pas tout"*, or "that is not all," and with it, Lévi-Strauss practices the relentless work of structural analysis in which what objects are is never settled, for they emerge within a system of transformations whose limits are always relational and thus unclosed (Viveiros de Castro n.d.). The work of *not only* as suggested by Mariano appears uncannily similar to *ce n'est pas tout* and also different. Both phrases operate like keys: they open and close possibilities. However, the will behind those keys is different, and so is what they open and close. *Ce n'est pas tout* is a tool that constantly opens possibilities of transformations in the analysis of a large body of myths in order to close them into a system of connections and thus know them. As Viveiros de Castro explains it:

> In *Mythologiques*, Lévi-Strauss repeatedly insists on the "closureness," [*cloture*] of the system he analyzes, on the roundness of mythology's Earth, the completeness of the circle that takes him from the savannahs of Central Brazil, to the foggy coasts of Washington state and British Columbia, as well as on the several clotures of the sub-mythical groups within that circuit."
>
> (Viveiros de Castro n.d.)

Like *ce n'est past tout, not only* also closes; but what it closes is the conception (even the hope) that there is an *all*, a *"tout"* that can be captured by ethnographic knowledge. Allowing for divergence from modern epistemic knowledge, while also being with it, *not only*—like the Lévi-Straussian con- cept—indicates that nothing is everything. Yet, it also calls attention to what calls itself everything—the forces and practices that translate world multiple into a singular one—by indicating the excesses of such translation, even if these excesses have not been confirmed through empirical experience. If one of the characteristics of world multiple is that singularity is also its condition, one of the tasks of *not only* is to make singularity an ambiguous condition—one that can be other than what it also is—and therefore unsettle the imposition of singularity over multiplicity while maintaining its possibility. *Not only* may thus perform as a conceptual tool for a decolonial analysis of the dynamic of the world being more than one and less than many. Interrupting the imposition, and working to open possibility beyond its limits, *not only* is an analytic formula to attend to marginalized (even deemed impossible) intra-relationalities.

In closing, I want to make two points that might appease scholarly criticism about the current use of ontology as analytics. The first is that rather than a tool for a turn away from culture, the ontological openings that *not only* may perform are mindful of Roy Wagner's idea that anthropology's invention of culture has created the conditions whereby "*we* incorporate *them* within *our* reality, and so incorporate *their* ways of life within *our own self-invention.*"[11] The italics are not in the original. I have added them to emphasize that Wagner's idea suggests both that neither way of life—*theirs* or *ours*—is without the other, that the form of the difference the pronouns indicate is invented (and always re-invented) therefore not without its vehicle (anthropology, thus made complex), and that ethnographic practice may allow this awareness. Alertness to such complex and always unsettled junctures (those of constant re-invention of a relational us-making-other-making-us) may help slow down our analytic eagerness and invite us to take the risk of entertaining entities whose presence emerges in divergence from what is to "us" (nature or religion, for example)—while also being with it.[12]

With the second and final point I want to appease all those concerned with the risks of depoliticization that may result from using ontology as an analytical tool. Thus, let me go to the paradox that initially suggested my questions: a vacillation emerged between runakuna practices with tirakuna and "religion" as politicians named those practices. The background of the controversy was extractivism: it is the most ubiquitous human geological force through which what is currently known as the Anthropocene makes itself present in Latin America, mightily destroying entities and the relations from where they emerge. Against this destruction, environmentalists have joined indigenous claims to their rights to well-being, culture, territories, and sacred lands. While with obvious difficulty, these claims achieve some of their goals in defense and, in so doing, they may also coordinate the world multiple into a singularity. Transpiring through the material-semiotic field of culture (indigenous religion, for example), this defense may perform an unsurprising (because hegemonic) disregard of the circumstances when nature is *not only* such. It thus asserts the onto-epistemic practice that makes beliefs out of worlding practices (for example, those through which runakuna with runakuna take-place in ayllu—take-place is hyphenated to indicate the in-ayllu simultaneity of time and space) and thus meets the coloniality of their adversaries, the proponents of extractivism in any of its versions. *Not only* opens room for the initial vacillation to become public, a matter of political discussion disrupting the human-only modern sphere of politics that offers no other guarantee than the way it disrupts the hegemonic one-world world, allowing instead a dynamic between the world multiple and its coordination into singular that may be decolonial. As a tool for the analytic practice of world multiple, *not only* allows a glimpse of the unending work of political negotiations that, while divergent and therefore in constant excess, overlap in the disputation of what can and cannot be.

Notes

1 "Alan Garcia Perez (President of Peru 1985–1990; 2006–2011) against pantheistic absurd ideologies." http://www.youtube.com/watch?v=2Vf4WfS5t08 accessed March 27, 2013. Also quoted in *La República*, June 25, 2011.
2 Dean, an art historian, mentions that what we practice as rock Andeans enacted as place-person. The most important ones were considered pernicious and portrayed as idols. She defines wank'a as a "presentational stone" or "a rock that is that which it embodies" (Dean 2010, 41; see also Mannheim and Salas C. 2015.)
3 These expressions participate in a long Andean genealogy that includes prominent scholars. For example, historian Sabine MacCormack wrote: "Inca religion in the narrow sense consists of the beliefs and rituals that the Incas practiced in their homeland, in and around Cuzco" (1991, 3).
4 The discussion of translation and religion has been frequent in anthropology. For example, in 1965 the British anthropologist Evans-Pritchard wrote that: "One may, indeed, find some word or phrase in one's own language by which to translate a native concept. We may translate some word of theirs by 'god' or 'spirit' or 'soul' or 'ghost', but then we have to ask *not only* what the word we so translate means to the natives but also what the word by which it is translated means to the translator and his readers. We have to determine *a double meaning*; and at best *it can be no more than a partial overlap of meaning between the two words*" (Evans-Pritchard 1965, my emphasis). I agree, and would add that I am interested in what exceeds the overlap and indicates their divergence.
5 About the origins of the word "religion," see the fascinating article by Hoyt (1912).
6 The reader may recognize in the second of the two clauses an argument that Talal Asad (1986) made classic thirty years ago: more powerful languages/practices obtain the translation.
7 There is effort being displayed in that direction and having to do precisely with opening up "indigenous religion" to inspection rather than flatly stating the category. Important work in that respect is by Tafjord (see especially his "Toward a Typology of Academic Uses of 'Indigenous Religion(s),' or, Eight or Nine Language Games that Scholars Play with this Phrase" (unpublished manuscript).
8 See also Jiménez (2015); Lebner (2017).
9 Here I am paraphrasing Law (2004).
10 People in the Andes may be labeled animists—as noted in recent scholarship, this is an intriguing thought. For example, Harvey (2005, 83) writes "Animists are people who encounter other persons, only some of whom are human, as cultural beings." Intriguing as this specific concept of animists is, it introduces an important doubt: would earth-beings be "animists" or "animated"?
11 Wagner, 1981, 142.
12 Divergence, it must be remembered, avoids the practice of sameness that the use of difference as analytics may carry with it. For example, Catholic saints are *different* from sacred mountains as they are within the same semantic-ontological field: that of religion. Both diverge from earth-beings as the latter *exceed* the religious practices through which they may also become—in divergence.

References

Adrianzén, A. 2011. "La Religión del Presidente." *Diario La República* June 25.
Allen, Catherine J. 2002. *The Hold Life Has: Coca and Cultural Identity in an Andean Community*. Washington, DC: Smithsonian Institution Press.

Asad, Talal. 1986. "The Concept of Cultural Translation in British Social Anthropology." In *Writing Culture: The Poetics and Politics of Ethnography*, edited by James Clifford and George E. Marcus, 141–164. Berkeley, CA: University of California Press.

—. 1993. "The Construction of Religion as an Anthropological Category." In *Genealogies of Religion: Discipline and Reasons of Power in Christianity and Islam*, 27–54. Baltimore, MD: Johns Hopkins University Press.

—. 2003. *Formations of the Secular: Christianity, Islam, Modernity*. Stanford, CA: Stanford University Press.

—. 2012. "Thinking about Religion, Belief, and Politics." In *The Cambridge Companion to Religious Studies*, edited by R. A. Orsi. Cambridge and New York: Cambridge University Press.

Bray, Tamara L., ed. 2015. *The Archaeology of Wak'as: Explorations of the Sacred in the Pre-Columbian Andes*. Boulder, CO: University Press of Colorado.

de Albornoz, Cristóbal. 1988. "Instrucción para Descubrir Todas las Guacas del Pirú y sus Camayos y Haziendas (1584)." In *Fábulas y Mitos de los Incas*, edited by Henrique Urbano and Pierre Duviols, 161—198. Madrid: Historia 16.

de la Cadena, M. 2010. Indigenous Cosmopolitics in the Andes. Conceptual reflections beyond "politics' in *Cultural Anthropology* 25(2): 334-370

—2014 Runa: Human but *Not Only*. HAU: *Journal of Ethnographic Theory* 4 (2): 253–259.

—2015. *Earth Beings: Ecologies of Practice Across Andean Worlds*. Durham, NC: Duke University Press.

Chadwick, Owen. 1964. *The Reformation*. London: Penguin.

Dean, Carolyn J. 2010. *A Culture of Stone: Inka Perspectives on Rock*. Durham, NC: Duke University Press.

Dressler, Markus and Arvind-Pal S. Mandair, eds. 2011. *Secularism and Religion-Making*. Oxford: Oxford University Press.

Evans-Pritchard, E. E. 1965. *Theories of Primitive Religion*. Oxford: Oxford University Press.

Gose, Peter. 2008. *Invaders as Ancestors: On the Intercultural Making and Unmaking of Spanish Colonialism in the Andes*. Toronto: University of Toronto Press.

Harvey, Graham. 2005. "Animism: A Contemporary Perspective." In *The Encyclopedia of Religion and Nature*, edited by Bron Taylor, 81–84. London: Bloomsbury.

Hoyt, Sarah F. 1912. "The Etymology of Religion." *Journal of the American Oriental Society* 32 (2): 126–129.

Jiménez, Alberto Corsín. 2015. "The Capacity for Re-Description." In *Detachment Essays on the Limits of Relational Thinking*, edited by Thomas Yarrow, Matei Candea, Catherine Trundle, and Jo Cook, 179–196. Manchester: Manchester University Press.

Keane, Webb. 2008. "The Evidence of the Senses and the Materiality of Religion." *Journal of the Royal Anthropological Institute* 14: 110–127.

Law, John. 2004. After Method: Mess in Social Science Research. New York: Routledge.

Lebner, Ashley, ed. 2017. *Redescribing Relations: Strathernian Conversations on Ethnography, Knowledge and Politics*. Oxford: Berghahn Books.

Levi-Strauss, Claude. 1968. *Mythologiques I L'Origine des manieres de table*. Paris: Plon.

— 1970. *Mythologiques II The Raw and The Cooked*. New York: Harper & Row.

— 1971 *Mythologiques III L'Homme nu*. Paris: Plon.

— 1973. *Mythologiques IV From Honey to Ashes*. New York: Harper & Row.

MacCormack, Sabine. 1991. *Religion in the Andes: Vision and Imagination in Early Colonial Peru*. Princeton, NJ: Princeton University Press.

Mannheim, Bruce and Guillermo Salas Carreño. 2015. "Wak'as: Entifications of the Andean Sacred." In Tamara L. Bray, ed., *The Archaeology of Wak'as*. Boulder, CO: University Press of Colorado, 47–72.

Masuzawa, Tomoko. 2005. *The Invention of World Religions, or, How European Universalism was Preserved in the Language of Pluralism*. Chicago, IL: University of Chicago Press.

Rafael, Vicente. 1993. *Contracting Colonialism: Translation and Christian Conversion in Tagalog Society under Early Spanish Rule*. Durham, NC: Duke University Press.

Stengers, Isabelle. 2005. "Introductory Notes on an Ecology of Practices." *Cultural Studies Review* 11 (1): 183–196.

— 2015. *In Catastrophic Times*. Lüneburg, Germany: Leuphana and Open Humanities Press.

Stevens-Arroyo, A. 2003. "Earth Religions and Book Religions: Baroque Catholicism as Openness to Earth Religions." *Comparative Civilizations Review* 49 (49): 54–75.

Strathern, Marilyn. 2004. *Partial Connections*. New York: Altamira.

Viveiros de Castro, Eduardo. 2004. "Perspectival Anthropology and the Method of Controlled Equivocation." *Tipití: Journal of the Society for the Anthropology of Lowland South America* 2 (1), 3–22.

— n.d. "Claude Lévi-Strauss, fundador del posestructuralismo."

Wagner, Roy. 1981. *The Invention of Culture*, 2nd revised edition. Chicago, IL: University of Chicago Press.

Chapter 3

Vertiginous worlds and emetic anthropologies

Casper Bruun Jensen

The world multiple depicts a scene of radical heterogeneity. The study of practical ontologies (Gad, Jensen, and Winthereik 2015) takes an interest in how, and by whom, this multiple world is composed and what it adds up to (or not). This, of course, is easier to say than to do. For one thing, it raises the thorny question—central to debates about the "ontological turn"—of whether practical ontologies are empirical objects, found, for example, in the mundane experiences of lived reality, or whether they are anthropological inventions generated through a labor of conceptualization, or whether they are something else altogether, which does not map on to the distinction between the empirical and the conceptual. What is clear is that any attempt to give meaning to the world multiple must also deal with the question of where in the world the anthropologist sits, and what he or she does, or should be doing. Here, I carry out such an examination of the relation between the anthropologist and the world multiple. It leads to a characterization of what I call emetic anthropologies.

The emic and the etic

The "moderns" are often seen as distinguished by their ability to objectify the world through science. Isabelle Stengers (2000, 164) describes the situation as follows:

> To be sure, all peoples believe themselves to be very different from others, but our belief in ourselves permits us to define others both as interesting— it was we who invented ethnology—and as condemned in advance, in the name of the terrible differentiation, of which we are the vectors, between what is of the order of science and what is of the order of culture, between objectivity and subjective fictions.

In other words, while everybody views themselves as different from others, only modern Westerners have systematized that difference *as* science, including, crucially, the sciences *of culture*. It is thus more than coincidental that Stengers's "terrible differentiation" hinges on the invention of ethnology. From the perspective of the sciences of culture, while "they" may have views of "us," only "we" are able to truly know "them."

To use a somewhat older vocabulary, science has generally been thought of as an *etic* endeavor. Originally, the linguist Kenneth Pike (1967) developed this term and its contrast, *emic*, as a way of describing different approaches to the study of language. While the etic approach entailed a study of the "mechanisms and acoustics of speech production" (Jardine 2004, 263) the emic approach centered on understanding "the categories of sounds through whose recognition native speakers identify and discriminate meaningful utterances" (ibid.) More generally, etic approaches study "behavior as from outside of a particular system," while emic approaches begin "from the inside of a system" (ibid. 264, citing Pike 1967, 37).

Marvin Harris (1979, 32) argued that the difference between objectivity and subjectivity does not map neatly onto the distinction between etic and emic. Rather neatly exemplifying Stengers's "terrible differentiation," however, Harris defined objectivity as a trademark of those capable of adopting "epistemological criteria" with which to distinguish science "from other ways of knowing" (Harris 1979, 34–35). Yet, even as Harris insisted that only a properly etic approach—specifically cultural materialism—could aspire to the status of a real science of culture, critics ironically renamed his solution an emics of the observer (Fisher and Werner 1978). Thus, Harris's attempt to create the grounds for objective anthropological explanation was redescribed as nothing but an elevation of his own subjective viewpoint.

In contrast with what Harris had in mind, the premise of contemporary sociocultural anthropology is overwhelmingly emic, in the sense of being oriented to what is "significant, meaningful, real, accurate or in some other fashion regarded as appropriate by the actors themselves" (Jardine 2004, 264, citing Harris 1968, 571).[1] This orientation aligns with the method of participant observation and the notion of "working with" people rather than studying them from a detached position. As for the people with whom one "works," they are often treated as having exclusively emic perspectives.

Entanglements

Sociocultural anthropology, then, has largely shed its previous etic inclinations, donning instead an emic mantle. Yet, before celebrating this state of affairs, we might want to pause. Is the distinction between outside and inside, objective and empathetic, really so clear-cut? On closer inspection, the hierarchy between these terms, gradually turned upside down over the past several decades, appears instead as a set of unstable and shifting entanglements.

Even the accumulation of facts *meant to be etic* has always been bound up with linguistic and interpretive problems. Nigel Barley (1983, 44) offered an ironic description of this situation:

Someone may have studied French at school for six years and with the help of language-learning devices, visits to France and exposure to the literature and yet find himself hardly able to stammer out a few words [...] Once in the field, he transforms himself into a linguistic wonder-worker. He becomes fluent in a language much more difficult [...] without qualified teachers, without bilingual texts, and often without grammars and dictionaries. At least, this is the impression he manages to convey.

But if linguistic competence is limited, as it often is, the status of any collected "fact" will be correspondingly uncertain. Moreover, as Paul Stoller noted at his own expense, relative fluency doesn't guarantee successful fact collection either. After having conducted 180 interviews with the Songhay of Niger, he found that every single informant had lied (Stoller and Olkes 1987, 9). As Stoller and Olkes write, the reasons why people can't be bothered to tell the truth are many: they don't care, they don't know you, or they don't trust you. In effect, therefore, the firm line between emic and etic blurs even from *within the etic*.

Conversely, the etic also appears within the emic. Consider, for example, mundane experiences and lived worlds. In one sense, the study of such worlds and experiences depends on taking an empathetic insider's perspective, thereby exemplifying and embodying the very meaning of the emic. Yet, how does the anthropologist know about the importance of lived worlds and experiences? After all, these are not categories used by the people whose lives are studied. Instead, their importance has been inculcated as a central part of what it means to do good (emic) anthropology. That is, rather than being based on what is significant and meaningful for actors in the world, the conceptual categories undergirding these forms of analysis have been prefigured on the basis of "distinctions judged appropriate by the community of scientific observers" (Jardine 2004, 264). This, however, is a definition of how etic analysis proceeds. Moreover, conceptual categories like mundane experience and lived worlds are usually not seen as falsifiable by actors' notions of "what is significant, real, meaningful or appropriate" (ibid.). In this sense, too, the mode of analysis is effectively etic.

So far, I have addressed some complications that occur within single-site ethnographies. At the present time, however, many ethnographies are multisited. Ethnographers recognize that people move in and out of places. Foreign (outside) ideas and technologies enter "indigenous" (inside) settings and mingle with them. Outsiders, including scientists, also come and go. And some anthropologists study those scientists. A new set of complications thus arises, which is at once internal to each "world" and elicited in movements between them.

As noted, "local people" are conventionally seen as taking an inherently emic—insider's—perspective on their worlds. Per definition, this is a consequence of their lack of attempt to objectify those worlds in a way that conforms to the protocols of Western science. At the same time, however, people are, of course, involved with many "others," whose activities and motives they do make sense of using their own (emic) categories. The development professionals I am studying, for example, routinely offer observations and interpretations of the rural Cambodians whose lives they take it as their job to try to improve.[2] Conversely, rural people deploy their varied understandings to make sense of international development initiatives. If these understandings are obviously not objective, in both cases they nevertheless come from the outside. In other words, while there are certainly always many emic viewpoints, they become at least quasi-etic as soon as one switches focus to another group. Each ethnographic situation, therefore, is invariably characterized by the co-existence and entanglement of perspectives that are variably emic and etic (see Jensen 2017).

However, this issue is often elided by the fact that anthropologists are typically not *equally interested* in all these perspectives. In fact, perspectival asymmetries are built into all ethnographies. This is particularly manifest whenever anthropologists deal with what they consider unequal power relations—for example, between doctors and patients, or state officials and local people, or scientists and indigenous populations. In the latter case, for example, studies are typically undertaken from an ethnographic location among indigenous people rather than among scientists, and with a primary view to understanding the perspectives of the former. The consequence is that the knowledges and practices of the latter are often taken as self-evidently decontextualizing, reductive, or objectifying.

Fractals

In some ways, the negative depiction of science as reductive and objectifying is at odds with popular images, textbook descriptions, and philosophical characterizations that tend to present science in a positive light. In another sense, however, the two are simply mirror images. Sharing the assumption that objectivity really captures the distinctiveness of science, they differ only in their appraisal of the trait. For those out to protect indigenous people against the onslaught of modernization, objectivity sounds bad. For those who aim to uphold the virtues of science against the supposed dangers of postmodern theory and the real ones of post-factual politics, it sounds good. The question of whether the distinction itself makes any sense is rarely raised.

At the same time, objectivity and its correlates, including neutrality and factuality, are also words often used to distinguish natural science from critical and interpretive scholarship in the humanities and social sciences. Among those who study science and technology historically, sociologically, or anthropologically, however, these terms are widely recognized as chimerical. Rather than being homogeneous, science exhibits a disunity of styles, practices, methods, types of knowledge, and forms of theory, which fail to map on to the standard dichotomies (e.g., Galison and Stump 1996; Knorr Cetina 1999).

Just as emic and etic cannot be used to distinguish forms of anthropology—since they are entangled—the distinction between objective facts and subjective interpretations is of very limited use for understanding the actual practices of either the sciences or the humanities. Here, too, they mix. Even though some scientists and philosophers argue for the objectivity of natural science, for example, it has been amply demonstrated that all kinds of scientific research have an integral interpretive dimension (e.g., Jasanoff et al. 1995). Complicating the issue further, a broad range of phenomena, including such anthropologically pertinent ones as *language* and *culture*, are studied *both* emically and etically by different scientific subfields and practitioners (Smith 2005, 110). Some fields, like Japanese primatology, actively cultivate emic approaches (e.g., Strum and Fedigan 2000; de Waal 2003). And, to gesture at an example to which I return later, the philosopher Vinciane Despret (2010, 1) notes that certain ethologists are becoming aware that birds "tell very different stories according to the one who observes them."

As noted, Marvin Harris strenuously held on to the etic–emic distinction, locating his cultural materialism squarely within the former, and asserting that its destabilization would be "epistemologically intolerable" (Harris 1976, 338). Ward Goodenough (1970, 112) countered that the etic and emic are really complementary, but like Harris he left the underlying logic of insides and outsides intact. As I have suggested, however, we find ourselves within a fractal ecology of practices no matter where we go (Jensen 2014; see Strathern 1991 for anthropology; Abbott 2001 for social science). Unfortunately—for Harris at least—one of the defining features of this ecology is precisely an "intolerable" lack of stability.

Emetic anthropologies

So there we are. Sociocultural anthropology is often seen as an emic endeavor but it contains etic components. The emic infuses the etic and vice versa. Indigenous knowledge is presumed emic, but since there is always more than one kind of knowledge, the emic must be constantly calibrated with respect to what, and whom, it is emic *for*. Meanwhile, scientific knowledge does not offer a single, or simple, *etic* alternative, or opposition, to either anthropological or indigenous knowledges. Consisting of variable constellations of actors, forms of knowledge, and practice, each domain exhibits fractal properties. Where does this leave us in terms of the world multiple?

One answer is given by lateral anthropology, which draws analytical power from the study of mobile constellations of knowledge and practice that *move between* anthropological and other forms of Western knowledge, and between different ethnographic fields (see e.g., Helmreich 2011; Maurer 2005; Strathern 1988, 1991). Another is given by the ontological turn, which (also) draws inspiration from Marilyn Strathern, as well as from Roy Wagner (1975) and Eduardo Viveiros de Castro (1998). As one controversial statement has it, the ontological names an effort to mine indigenous thought for resources that allow the ethnographer to set conventional anthropological truths in motion (Holbraad 2012).

Usually, lateral and ontological approaches are seen as quite different, and their proponents are not always mutually supportive.[3] In my view, however, they share some close affinities. Importantly for the present context, both entail experimentation with the emic–etic relation. To capture what they share, it is thus tempting to collapse the dichotomy. The approaches are similar in being *emetic*.

In medicine, the term emetic describes substances that induce nausea and vomiting. Surprisingly, more than half a century ago the term also made a brief appearance in anthropology. At that time, Gerald Berreman (1966, 350) drew a contrast between a purely etic approach, which would remain anemic (bloodless) in its "humorless scientism," and a strictly emic approach, which would be emetic (nauseous) in its display of "empty ingenuity." He argued that the relevant question was not whether to be scientific (etic) or humanistic (emic) but rather "how to be *both*" (347, emphasis in original). Similar to Harris and Goodenough, however, the problem with this "best of both worlds" solution is the assumption of a static relation between the two approaches.

In what follows, I tweak the emetic to describe approaches that suspend the assumption of such a static relation. At this point, the medical connotations once again come in handy, because emetic anthropological approaches, including lateral and ontological ones, are in fact often seen as "epistemologically intolerable" to critics (e.g., Bessire and Bond 2013; Graeber 2015). Indeed, emetic approaches appear to make quite a few readers and commenters sick to their stomachs.[4]

In spite of its unpleasantness, however, nausea is not always evaluated negatively. In *Thus Spoke Zarathustra*, Friedrich Nietzsche (1966) depicted the great nausea as one step toward overcoming resentment. Along this trajectory, emetics can be affiliated with what Foucault described as an "ethic of discomfort" (2000, 443–9) that paves the way to different kinds of insight. In quite a different register, shamans and others imbibe substances that *first* make them vomit, and then make them *see* (Kopenawa 2013). Emetics can thus also be used to describe the vertigo experienced as one is drawn toward what Marisol de la Cadena (Chapter 2 in this volume) calls ontological openings.

Co-existence

To articulate some relations between the emetic and the vertigo of ontological openings, I turn to *Earth Beings: Ecologies of Practice Across Andean Worlds*, de la Cadena's (2015) fascinating ethnography of the historically changing relationship between the *runakuna* living in the Andes, and Peruvian enterprise and state-making. For decades, the runakuna were forced to work on *haciendas* under brutal conditions. After a lengthy battle to get the land returned to indigenous hands, the haciendas were eventually closed by governmental decree and local cooperatives took over. However, corrupt politicians and administrators quickly took advantage of the situation, which did not significantly improve conditions for the Indians themselves. Continuing to live in poverty, some have found new positions within a neoliberal order, in which, among other things, their "indigenous" knowledges have been translated into various foreign idioms including environmental tourism and new age shamanism.

The story has a number of familiar aspects. For example, it can easily be interpreted in terms of co-optation and repression. In a conventional left-wing narrative, Indians figure as workers struggling to avoid exploitation and bonded labor. Further, from the point of view of indigeneity, it can be said that the runakuna knowledges that sustain local communities have been pushed to the margins of history. What makes *Earthbeings* emetic, however, is de la Cadena's insistence that while *it is not wrong* to depict the situation in either of these ways, it is also not *quite right*.

While the runakuna collaborated with critical social scientists, communists, activists, and lawyers in Lima—all of whom viewed the hacienda system as exploitative in a Marxist sense—the runakuna continued to live in *ayllu*.

Schematically, ayllu can be described as living with a group of people related by kinship, while also cohabiting with various nonhuman others (de la Cadena 2015, 43). These others include what we could call animals, plants, and mountains, or as the runakuna call them, *tirakuna*. Translating tirakuna as "earth-beings," de la Cadena describes them as *enacted presences* (26). They are enacted, for example, by *k'intu*, the presentation of coca leaves, or by the sending off of *despachos*, packets of "food, seeds, flowers and kind words" (228).

Note that, unlike a term such as labor exploitation, tirakuna, k'intu, and despacho are emic terms. Thus, we are on the path of recognizing indigenous knowledges and practices, which continue to exist even if they remain hidden and irrelevant from the point of view of modern knowledges. This recognition is certainly also *not wrong*, and de la Cadena spends much energy insisting on the point. However, this does not lead her to prioritize a properly emic approach, for approaching the problem in terms of a choice between incommensurable knowledge forms is *also not quite right*.

For one thing, the indigenous knowledges and practices of the runakuna are partially related to, and have to some extent been transformed by, outsiders. Certainly, one important dimension of such transformation is the long history of colonial violence. Yet, this is not the only vector of change, for as noted some runakuna have also seized the opportunity of making better lives *through* new relationships. For example, as a consequence of his work with the curators of the Quechuan exhibition at the National Museum of the American Indian in Washington, DC, de la Cadena's friend and informant Nazario Turpo gained a certain kind of indigenous "authority," which he could subsequently leverage to become an Andean "shaman" and tour guide.

In telling this story, de la Cadena does not aim to sort out these mixed categories in order to get to what is really indigenous. Instead, she explains why this is an impossible task. In part, as she insists, this is due to the fact that her ethnography is necessarily more than a transcription of runakuna realities, since it was generated through complex entanglements with these realities. Since ethnography is itself an outcome, or effect, of ambiguous, equivocal, and partial relations, even seemingly emic concepts such as ayllu or tirakuna invariably gain new form in the act of redescription. That form is not quite emic without being etic.

What, for example, is an earth-being? We simply cannot describe what it is for the runakuna. We can say, as de la Cadena (2015, 25) does, that tirakuna is neither a material nor a spiritual category, but rather an entity continuously made present. That, of course, is not *really* how the runakuna experience the matter, and certainly not how they speak of it. Conversely, no matter the degree of earnest ethnographic immersion or intellectual effort, what runakuna experience effortlessly as tirakuna, the anthropologist will continue to perceive and experience as a mountain.

The alluring choice between emic and etic strategies emerges at this juncture. Staying firmly on the etic side, one may argue, á la Harris, that irrespective of what the runakuna *believe* about entities like the Ausangate, at the end of the day it is *really* a mountain. At the risk of repetition, this solution precisely instantiates Stengers's "terrible differentiation," which defines objectivity as Western knowledge and relegates the indigenous to the status of fictions and beliefs. Contemporary sociocultural anthropologists, of course, will usually take an emic route. Indeed, some may claim that proper ethnographic immersion facilitates something like a conversion that would make it possible to experience as indigenous people do.

The emetic quality of de la Cadena's ethnography lies in its simultaneous rejection of both these options and the "terrible differentiation" on which they are premised. Unable to experience the tirakuna as such, and unable, too, to prevent the tirakuna from being transformed in the very act of ethnographic description, de la Cadena (2015, 25) proposes that tirakuna and mountains can nevertheless be enacted in a manner that enables them to co-exist without one necessarily detracting from the other.

The emetic image of partly incommensurable yet co-existing worlds that do not detract from one another allows de la Cadena to characterize the Cuzco area as a "complexly integrated hybrid circuit" (2015, 20) where the "indigenous and nonindigenous infiltrate and emerge in each other" (2015, 5). While the area is composed of emic "wholes"—languages, understandings, and practices—these wholes intrude on and permeate one another. Emetically, they become "inseparable fragments of each other," *without merging into unity*.

With a certain liberty, I might use Despret's (2010, 4) description of a scene "full of beings [...] with intention, will, perspectives, [and] meanings and who respond to each other" to characterize de la Cadena's wager. It is a wager, rather than a description, because everything suggests that not all "beings" in fact respond to each other in this capacious manner. The central point is that through writing, de la Cadena is creating a lure for feeling that makes it possible to conceive of, and perhaps to some extent feel or experience, Cuzco worlds as amenable to co-existence without detraction. More than a "mere" description, it is an invitation to search for, and perhaps enter, ontological openings.

When Despret wrote of mutually responsive beings with will, perspectives, and meanings, she was not dealing with an anthropological context. Quite differently, she was re-enacting a different set of ontological openings within the field of ethology. In stark contrast with the conventional assumption that proper science is inherently etic, Despret explained that some ethologists

> do not study what an animal is, [but] rather what an animal becomes in responding to the way he/she is questioned, in responding to what is expected from him/her. The situation is a co-inventive situation of knowledge, which creates opportunities for new behaviors. The animal's perspective upon the situation is, for these few scientists, at the center of the whole matter.
>
> (Despret 2010, 4)

Far from embodying the cliché of distanced objectivism, then, these scientists *begin with* the emic question of the animal's perspective. Indeed, Despret (2010, 3) describes some ethologists in the tradition of Jakob von Uexküll as practicing "a kind of 'alter-subjectivity'" with the animals they study. Based on the recognition that "animals do not feel and think like us [...] do not share our point of view," they are engaged and understood via "a system of contrasts and differences."

But if these ethologists begin with an emic interest in the animal's world, they do not end with it. By experimenting with set-ups that enable mutual learning between scientists and animals, producing "alter-subjectivities" in the process, they attempt to provide birds, sheep, or cats with the chance to differ not only from the ethologists' own starting assumptions, but also from themselves, since, in response to novel situations, they begin to learn new things and act differently.

There are, of course, innumerable differences between this situation and that of the ethnographer, not least the inability of the latter to control and manipulate the settings in which s/he studies. Yet, there is also a significant resonance between Despret's alter-subjective ethologists and de la Cadena's exploration of a hybrid Cuzco. Both experiment with the question of what it takes to allow one's interlocutors—who or whatever they are—to be, and to become, different. In both cases the search for—and construction of—ontological openings required abandoning the etic–emic dichotomy.

Materializations

Practical ontologies are certainly made of cosmologies, perspectives, and view-points. But they are also made of (other) *things*. As we begin to examine the material dimension of the emetic, we are, as Bill Maurer (2015, 28) writes, "confronted with [. . .] infrastructures." I offer two brief examples of what such a confrontation entails (see also Harvey, Jensen, and Morita 2016). The first is taken from Maurer's work on the social implications of new forms of techno-logically mediated payment in Kenya. The second concerns the hundred-year-long transformation of Thailand's Chao Phraya delta landscape, as studied by Atsuro Morita. Despite very different temporalities and settings, both examples provide insight into the emetics of materialization.

In 2007, the mobile phone payment system M-Pesa was introduced in Kenya, where over a mere decade it attracted 17 million customers and revolutionized money transactions. Changing more than flows of money, text messages and mobile payments also began changing the capacities of young Kenyans for making social relations, providing "a route to financial stability and inclusion for people without access to or, more important, the means to afford a bank account" (Maurer 2015, 11). Thus, it encoded alternatives for how to live differently, and for how to think differently about how one might live.

Of course, the new payment infrastructure relied on principles and ideas initially foreign to its users. Quickly, however, Kenyans started experimenting with its possibilities, tweaking M-Pesa in creative ways to accomplish what they wanted. Thus, for example, people invented ways of acquiring goods from distant places using a mixture of texting and mobile money transfers between friends and extended kin. M-Pesa and its users were mutually modified, both gaining new qualities through the interaction.

As Maurer argues, these reconfigurations provide materials for rethinking the ontological status of money. Rather than an abstract, rationalizing force, money consists of materialized relations that extend across time and space "linking us to our ancestors, descendants, and fellow humans" while also contributing to the remaking of those links (2015, 136). Rather than an abstract flow, Maurer surmises, on closer inspection, monetary relations begin to resemble a delta with many "rivulets, side currents, eddies, and pools." Conversely, as I now indicate, deltas, while certainly composed of flowing materials, are also made from ideas and abstractions. As much as money, they are emetic.

Historically, the Thai Chao Phraya delta has been modified, primarily by local farmers. However, in 1902 the Dutch engineer Homan van der Heide came up with a plan of unprecedented scope and ambition. His aim was to radically extend and transform the canal system, making it more suitable for agriculture (Brummel-huis 2007; Morita 2016). Though his plan was long dismissed by the Thai elite, the idea to modify the delta on a massive scale remained in circulation.

Taking the basic stance that water is an element situated inconveniently on top of land, the Dutch engineer wanted more than anything to drain excess water to create space for dry crops, as had been done previously in the Netherlands. Yet, to the Thai, who were used to river transportation and seasonal flooding, it was far from obvious that water was an element to be removed. Indeed, they might have seen land as what, only sometimes, emerged out of water.

These differences between inside and outside perspectives extended into other domains, such as politics, where the "rational" arguments pursued by the blunt Dutchman were deflected by Thai political aesthetics, and where assumptions of European *realpolitik* encountered the galactic polities discussed by Stanley Tambiah (1977; see also Morita 2017; Morita and Jensen 2017). Homan van der Heide himself clearly found the experience emetic—vertiginous, confusing, and infuriating. So did many of his Thai partners and interlocutors, though, of course, for different reasons.

Since the mid-twentieth century, when van der Heide's plan finally started to materialize, radical changes in the delta infrastructure began spilling over into Thai lives and ways of thinking. Presently, most people do not sail but drive, and it is likely that the liquid perceptions (Thaitakoo and McGrath 2010) of previous generations have begun shifting. Perhaps it is indeed the case that many Thai people now *do* think that water is an element sitting on top of land.

Akin to previous discussions, then, the inside and the outside refuse to stay put. Dutch ideas slowly began influencing Thai practices, leading to modifications of the delta infrastructure, which in turn influenced Thai capacities for thinking of the delta itself. At the same time, infrastructural transformations generated something like a materialized figure-ground reversal at the level of the delta's practical ontology: while land used to sit on top of water, water now flows on top of land.

Paradoxically, this transformation is now recognized to have reduced the flood resilience of the delta landscape, and particularly of Bangkok. After seventy-five years of Western modernization, experts are now looking to Thai solutions similar to those squeezed out by foreign infrastructures in the first place. Presently, rediscovered or newly invented "indigenous" forms—from houses on stilts to floating car parks—are beginning to reshape delta imaginaries and forms of materializations.

As discussed in previous sections, the emetic is, in one sense, an effect of a movement between internal and external perspectives. But in another sense, as I have added in this section, it describes the vertigo set in motion by novel processes of materialization. As infrastructures materialize new worlds, they also modify peoples' sense of who they are and what they can do. Rather than subtracting from indigenous knowledges and lived experiences, therefore, material transformations add to and mutate such knowledges and practices (see also Gow 2001; Jensen 2015). In turn, people tweak and twist infrastructures in unpredictable ways.

While Maurer noted that abstractions start to look like deltas when considered from the point of view of their material forms, deltas are thus also materially shaped and reshaped by imaginaries. Money is like deltas, but deltas are made in part by ideas, which flow like deltas... We are, indeed, in vertiginous worlds.

Vertiginous worlds

Ignoring the constraints of ethnographic reality, lateral and ontological anthropologists feel authorized to create concepts and theories that have no proper ground. Even worse, these approaches and concepts provide hardly any ammunition in the battle against Western colonialism and hegemony. Or so their anthropological critics would have it.

Two dimensions of these critiques are noteworthy. First, they rely on the very same opposition between truth and fiction characterized by Stengers as the unique trait of the moderns. Second, this critical position is defined with "reference to a past [the critic] would like to regret" (Stengers 2000, 149).

Offering an alternative to the vision of critique as atonement, Nietzsche advocated a process of "active forgetting." While perpetual remembrance of past wrongs holds people hostage to their violent and unjust history, he argued, active forgetting can operate as a "plastic, regenerative and curative force" (cited in Deleuze 1983, 113), and thus as a selective principle for making new thought and action possible. I would suggest that emetic approaches wager on this plastic force. In search of ontological openings, they experiment with possible antidotes to Stengers's terrible differentiation between the moderns and everyone else.

In consequence, "scientific" and "indigenous" forms of knowledge and practice come into view as relational effects. This is not an argument for a spurious identity or equality between forms of knowledge and practice. Rather, attending to fractal patterns of similarity and difference, emetic approaches replace the vast chasm assumed to separate the indigenous from the modern, or the subjective from the objective, or the inside from the outside, with a multiplicity of smaller and larger gaps and bridges crisscrossing the terrain in many directions. The image is one of permeable domains emerging and transforming over time (e.g., Jensen 2017). In the aggregate, these practical ontologies could be named the world multiple.

Within the world multiple, it is not only the "others" who are different from "us." As Stengers emphasizes, moderns, too, are "already very different from what we believe ourselves to be" (2000, 165). Rather than inhabiting a dual landscape in which objectivist reductions of scientific knowledge are pitted against empathetic engagements with the lived world experiences of indigenous people, the anthropologist finds him/herself moving dizzily through a fractal ecology. Rather than working as a curator, interpreter, or activist on behalf of the worlds of others, he or she assumes, not as a matter of choice but as a condition, the position of an ontological co-inventor of such entanglements (Jensen 2012). If one grapples with the continuous emergence and transformation of the relations that make up the world multiple, vertigo may, after all, turn out to be generative.

Notes

1 For Harris (1979, 45), the claim that all knowledge is insider's knowledge amounted to nothing less than a "surrender of our intellects to the supreme mystifications of total relativism."

2 Since 2013, I have studied development and urban infrastructure in Cambodia. My current research focuses on how experts and organizations model the Mekong river basin and delta, and how they try to use such models to induce changes in environmental and infrastructure policies.

3 Whereas lateral experiments are often viewed, whether positively or negatively, as the reflexivist inheritors of *writing culture*, ontological approaches are derided simultaneously for returning anthropology to essentialism and for engaging in "philosophy" to the detriment of ethnographic reality and political responsibility (see Gad, Jensen, and Winthereik 2015).

4 This was most vividly exhibited by the now discontinued anonymous "procto-ontologist" blog and Twitter account. Trading in personal attacks on proponents of the ontological turn using graphic scatological and sexual language, these descriptions were widely circulated and evidently seen as a matter of "getting what one deserves" by many readers. On the *Savage Minds* blog we find the observation that the: "Procto-ontologist is very much needed to burst the bubble of high-falutin silliness that is 'ontology' in anthropology." Referring to the procto-ontologist as "hysterically funny," and comparing his writing to the satire of Jonathan Swift, another commentator added: "But where ontologicality and the proctological meet is not at the sphincter—that would mean depth, darkness, stench—but at the level of buttocks—sameness separated by difference of the line, of the butt-crack." [From https://savageminds.org/2014/01/25/on-taking-onto logical-turns/ accessed March 8, 2018]

References

Abbott, Andrew. 2001. *Chaos of Disciplines*. Chicago, IL: University of Chicago Press.

Barley, Nigel. 1983. *The Innocent Anthropologist: Notes from a Mud Hut*. Long Grove, IL: Waveland Press.

Berreman, Gerald D. 1966. "Anemic and Emetic Analyses in Social Anthropology." *American Anthropologist* 68 (2): 346–354.

Bessire, Lucas and David Bond. 2013. "Ontological Anthropology and the Deferral of Critique." *American Ethnologist* 41 (3): 440–456.

Brummelhuis, Han ten. 2007. *King of the Waters: Homan van der Heide and the Origin of Modern Irrigation in Siam*. Chiang Mai: Silkworm Books.

de la Cadena, Marisol. 2015. *Earth Beings: Ecologies of Practice Across Andean Worlds*. Durham, NC: Duke University Press.

Deleuze, Gilles. 1983. *Nietzsche and Philosophy*. London: Athlone.

Despret, Vinciane. 2010. "Ethology Between Empathy, Standpoint and Perspectivism: The Case of the Arabian Babblers." http://www.vincianedespret.be/2010/04/ethology-between-empathy-standpoint-and-perspectivism-the-case-of-the-arabian-babblers/ accessed April 3, 2016).

Fisher, L. E and O. Werner. 1978. "Explaining Explanation: Tension in American Anthropology." *Journal of Anthropological Research* xxxiv: 194–218.

Foucault, Michel. 2000. "For an Ethic of Discomfort." In *Power: Essential Works of Foucault 1954–1984*, edited by James Faubion, 443–449. New York: New Press.

Gad, Christopher, Casper Bruun Jensen, and Brit Ross Winthereik. 2015. "Practical Ontology: Worlds in STS and Anthropology." *NatureCulture* 3: 67–86.

Galison, Peter and David J. Stump, eds. 1996. *The Disunity of Science: Boundaries, Contexts, and Power.* Stanford, CA: Stanford University Press.

Goodenough, Ward H. 1970. *Description and Comparison in Cultural Anthropology.* Chicago, IL: Aldine.

Gow, Peter. 2001. *An Amazonian Myth and its History.* Oxford: Oxford University Press.

Graeber, David. 2015. "Radical Alterity is Just Another Way of Saying 'Reality'": A Reply to Eduardo Viveiros de Castro." *HAU: Journal of Ethnographic Theory* 5 (2): 1–41.

Harris, Marvin. 1968. *The Rise of Anthropological Theory: A History of Theories of Culture.* New York: Crowell.

—. 1976. "History and Significance of the Emic/Etic Distinction." *Annual Review of Anthropology* 5: 329–350.

—. 1979. *Cultural Materialism: The Struggle for a Science of Culture.* New York: Random House.

Harvey, Penny, Casper Bruun Jensen, and Atsuro Morita, eds. 2016. *Infrastructures and Social Complexity: A Companion.* London and New York: Routledge.

Helmreich, Stefan. 2011. "Nature/Culture/Seawater." *American Anthropologist* 113 (1): 132–144.

Holbraad, Martin. 2012. *Truth in Motion: The Recursive Anthropology of Cuban Divination.* Chicago, IL: University of Chicago Press.

Jardine, Nicholas. 2004. "Etics and Emics (not to mention Anemics and Emetics) in the History of the Sciences." *History of Science* xlii: 261–278.

Jasanoff, Sheila, Gerald E. Markle, James C. Petersen, and Trevor Pinch, eds. 1995. *Handbook of Science and Technology Studies.* Thousand Oaks, CA: Sage.

Jensen, Casper Bruun. 2012. "Proposing the Motion: The Task of Anthropology is to Invent Relations." *Critique of Anthropology* 32 (1): 47–53.

—. 2014. "Continuous Variations: The Conceptual and the Empirical in STS." *Science, Technology and Human Values* 39 (2): 192–213.

—. 2015. "Experimenting with Political Materials: Environmental Infrastructures and Ontological Transformations." *Distinktion: Journal of Social Theory* 16 (1): 17–30.

—. 2017. "Mekong Scales: Domains, Test-Sites and the Micro-Uncommons." *Anthropologica* 59 (2): 204–215.

Knorr Cetina, Karin. 1999. *Epistemic Cultures: How the Sciences Make Knowledge.* Cambridge, MA: Harvard University Press.

Kopenawa, Davi. 2013. *The Falling Sky: Words of a Yanomami Shaman.* Cambridge, MA: Harvard University Press.

Maurer, Bill. 2005. *Mutual Life, Limited: Islamic Banking, Alternative Currencies, Lateral Reason.* Princeton, NJ: Princeton University Press.

—. 2015. *How Would You Like to Pay? How Technology is Changing the Future of Money.* Durham, NC: Duke University Press.

Morita, Atsuro. 2016. "Infrastructuring Amphibious Space: The Interplay of Aquatic and Terrestrial Infrastructures in the Chao Phraya Delta in Thailand." *Science as Culture* 25 (1): 117–140.

—. 2017. "In Between the Cosmos and 'Thousand-Cubed Great Thousands Worlds': Composition of Uncommon Worlds by Alexander von Humboldt and King Mongkut." *Anthropologica* 59 (2): 228–238.

Morita, Atsuro and Casper Bruun Jensen. 2017. "Delta Ontologies: Infrastructural Trans-formations in Southeast Asia." *Social Analysis* 61 (2): 118–133.

Nietzsche, Friedrich. 1966. *Thus Spoke Zarathustra: A Book for None and All.* New York: Penguin Books.

Pike, Kenneth L. 1967 [1954]. *Language in Relation to a Unified Theory of the Structure of Human Behaviour.* 2nd edition. The Hague: Mouton & Co.

Smith, Barbara Herrnstein. 2005. *Scandalous Knowledge: Science, Truth and the Human.* Edinburgh: Edinburgh University Press.

Stengers, Isabelle. 2000. *The Invention of Modern Science.* Minneapolis, MN: University of Minnesota Press.

Stoller, Paul and Cheryl Olkes. 1987. *In Sorcery's Shadow: A Memoir of Apprenticeship among the Songhay of Niger.* Chicago, IL: University of Chicago Press.

Strathern, Marilyn. 1988. *The Gender of the Gift: Problems with Women and Problems with Society in Melanesia.* Berkeley, CA: University of California Press.

—. 1991. *Partial Connections.* Lanham, MD: Rowman & Littlefield.

Strum, Shirley C. and Linda M. Fedigan, eds. 2000. *Primate Encounters: Models of Science, Gender, and Society.* Chicago, IL: University of Chicago Press.

Tambiah, Stanley J. 1977. "The Galactic Polity: The Structure of Traditional Kingdoms in Southeast Asia." *Annals of the New York Academy of Sciences* 293: 69–97.

Thaitakoo, Danai and Brian McGrath. 2010. "Bangkok Liquid Perception: Waterscape Urbanism in the Chao Phraya River Delta and Implications to Climate Change Adaptation." In *Water Communities*, edited by Rajib Shaw and Danai Thaitakoo, 35–50. Bingley, UK: Emerald Group Publishing.

Viveiros de Castro, Eduardo. 1998. "Cosmological Deixis and Amerindian Perspectivism." *Journal of the Royal Anthropological Institute* 4 (3): 469–488.

de Waal, B. M. 2003. "Silent Invasion: Imanishi's Primatology and Cultural Bias in Science." *Animal Cognition* 6: 293–299.

Wagner, Roy. 1975. *The Invention of Culture.* Englewood Cliffs, NJ: Prentice Hall.

Chapter 4

Doing and undoing caribou/atîku

Diffractive and divergent multiplicities and their cosmopolitical orientations

Mario Blaser

"More than one and less than many" has become a refrain to depict the notion of multiplicity. Annemarie Mol (2002) used it to succinctly capture the result of operations that make a variety of practices hold together as a singular thing. In this chapter, I explore some consequences of the proposition that multiplicity can be figured in at least two different ways: as diffraction, where the operations of singularization explored by Mol are more easily carried out; and as divergence, where singularization is not necessarily an option. The exploration is part of a larger project to rework the notion of cosmopolitics proposed by Isabelle Stengers (2005) and Bruno Latour (2004, 2007). Elsewhere (Blaser 2016), I have argued that their conception of cosmopolitics as a project oriented towards the composition of a common world is informed predominantly by the figuration of multiplicity as diffraction, and thus it very much resembles a process of singularization writ large. In this context, foregrounding multiplicity as divergence opens a path to probe the limits of this conception of cosmopolitics, inquire into the different ways in which multiplicity holds together, and envision alternative forms of cosmopolitics.

I organize my exploration around two entities, caribou and *atîku*, that, so to speak, occupy the same space at the same time in terms of bodily presence, albeit dominant common sense would have it that atîku and caribou are two words for the same entity. I begin by looking at caribou in a similar way as Mol did with atherosclerosis in her book *The Body Multiple*. Using Mol's work as a template and counterpoint, I highlight similarities and differences between the caribou and atherosclerosis cases. In the second section I show how what Innu people of Labrador call atîku is different from caribou, a difference that makes evident multiplicity as divergence. Yet, a question remains, how can multiplicity as divergence nevertheless "hold together" in such a way that gives credence to the idea that atîku and caribou are just two words for the same "thing"? I tackle this question in the third section, discussing the important role that equivocations play in "holding on together in divergence." In the conclusions I draw together the points raised by this exploration and reconnect them to the larger project of rethinking cosmopolitics.

The caribou multiple

"What is Caribou?" Thus opens *Caribou and the North: A Shared Future* (Hummel and Ray 2008), a publication bringing into the public eye the need for urgent actions to save caribou from Alaska to Labrador. The question is not an ontological one, the authors know what caribou is: "a large-bodied ungulate [that] belongs to the group *Artiodactyla*" and that "despite the fact that [they] actually encompass a remarkable variety of different forms of the same animal" it is one single species, *Rangifer tarandus* (ibid. 29–30). The challenge that the question foregrounds is the proper classification of the species into "types" on the basis of morphological differences (shape, size, antler form), behavioral differences (migratory and sedentary); and into ecotypes on the basis of where the caribou lives (tundra, boreal forest, mountain). Why is this classification important?

> "[A] good classification system [...] captures the full diversity of the wildlife species being classified, at a scale that is meaningful for both conservation and management purposes. For any given caribou herd or population, we need to know what behaviors, movements, foods, pressures and habitats might be unique. Only then can we [...] make sure caribou are maintained in healthy populations across the different landscapes where they are found."
>
> ibid. 41

After an overview of what characterizes each caribou type, the book moves on to discuss the natural and anthropic pressures affecting the herds' health, a discussion that leads to a logical conclusion—specific steps to protect the herds —upon which the various perspectives of stakeholders would have to converge.

The challenges of making different perspectives on a given "natural resource" converge for "co-management" has generated very intense debates, particularly when indigenous "perspectives' are involved. I will not dwell on these debates (for an overview see Spaeder and Feit 2005) apart from pointing out that the old relativist/universalist debate is not far from the surface in them and, as such, at bottom they share a common assumption, that the problem is epistemological: it is about perspectives on "the world" (singular) and the possible relations they may hold, or not.[1] As readers of this book will be aware, material-semiotics versions of Science and Technology Studies (STS) would engage the differences being alluded to by the word "perspectives" as involving the performance of different reals. Works in this "tradition" call for a sort of displacement of the gaze from the "thing" at stake—which, according to the standard realistic assumption, supposedly pre-exists the perspective that some might have upon it—to the practices that perform the "thing." Annemarie Mol's book *The Body Multiple* (2002) is now a classic example of this approach.

In that book, Mol shows how the practices of radiologists, clinicians, and pathologists in a Dutch hospital perform different versions of atherosclerosis and, then, how this multiplicity is rendered singular, even if temporarily for the purpose of intervention. This, she argues, is accomplished through coordination and distribution: operations by which different performances either are made to hold together as a single entity or are kept apart to avoid mutual interference. Succinctly, co-ordination works by adding performances as if they were multiple perspectives on a single object and by discarding dissonant ones. Distribution, in turn, works by keeping different performances apart so that inconsistencies between them do not turn into clashes where some sort of adjudication of "truth" has to occur to preserve the unity of a given object.

In our case, to follow a similar approach would imply looking at the different practices that in the book *Caribou and the North* are presented as being the "perspectives" of stakeholders. Without constituting an exhaustive list, the participants gathered at the North American Caribou Workshop that has been meeting for the past fifteen years provide an entry point to briefly explore what these different practices might entail. These meetings are attended by caribou biologists, wildlife managers, and representatives from environmental NGOs (e.g., World Wide Fund for Nature, Wildlife Conservation Society of Canada), outfitters' associations, resource extractive industries, and Indigenous groups.

Each of these "stakeholders" is involved in practices that render slightly different versions of caribou. For instance, biologists "do" caribou as a techno-scientific artifact, the animal species *Rangifer tarandus*. This artifact is done through the mobilization of a variety of practices nested into each other in the forms of established theories (e.g., from genetics and etiology); techniques (e.g., statistical sampling, aerial tracking of movements, surveys); instruments (e.g., satellite collars), and institutions (e.g., universities and government agencies), to mention a few. Wildlife managers in turn enfold this techno-scientific artifact as part of a complex "equation" that must estimate how human activities impact on the herds and strike a (hypothetical) balance. The unstated points of reference for the balance are (supposedly) the minimum required for the sustainability of a herd and the maximum profit that any activity that affects them can obtain. As the authors of *Caribou and the North* point out, "[r]esearch is needed to better understand thresholds of human harvest, as well as *our industrial footprint with its corresponding deterioration in habitat quality. How much of this can be tolerated by caribou, and what are their minimum protection needs*" (189, emphasis added). The quote also indicates why corporations involved in forestry, mining, and oil and gas extraction are prominent sponsors of the annual North American Caribou Workshop, and how they do caribou. Articulated with environmental legislation, and nested within the wildlife managers' equations, this techno-scientific artifact commonly called "caribou" is another element in their own equations to plan operations and perform their calculus of profitability; for instance, mitigating the impact of their activities on caribou, or the public relations costs of disregarding such impacts, might be too onerous. Outfitters do caribou in a similar but slightly different fashion, the resource being the herds themselves: their calculus is more directly aligned with having continued access to it. Environmental NGOs, in turn, might do caribou as part of larger entities such a "species at risk," biodiversity, symbol of the North, and so on. I will leave Indigenous practices aside as I focus on them in the next section. For now, and using Mol's analysis of atherosclerosis as a template and counterpoint, I want to explore briefly how the different versions of caribou that I have characterized schematically here hold together.

To use Mol's terminology, the predominant operation that holds together the various versions of caribou is co-ordination through adding up. More often than not, caribou as techno-scientific artifact is the invariant term upon which the addition is performed. This is reflected in *Caribou and the North*, where the discussion about "what is caribou" is solely based on the disciplinary practices of biology. This does not mean there are no controversies and dissonances between different versions of caribou, but these tend to refer back to controversies between performances of caribou as a techno-scientific artifact. For example, to refuse a course of actions that contradict their own versions, wildlife managers, environmental NGOs, corporate representatives, outfitters, and Indigenous groups might back their own position on how to manage herds by reference to contending methodologies used to establish "significant units" for management; or might find fault with specific techniques used to generate data; or might refer to the uncertainty and perfectibility inherent to scientific knowledge. What rarely happens is that caribou as a techno-scientific artifact is simply discarded or kept apart, as may happen with other versions. For instance, caribou as a source of income for outfitters might have to be discarded if it runs against what biologists say. While extractive industries' version of caribou might be harder to simply discard, they can only persevere as long as they can claim grounding on the techno-scientific version. By distinguishing in their practices aspects that can be attributed to culture (e.g., the "belief" in spirit owners of the animals) and those that can be attributed to "empirical observation" (e.g., of migration routes), Indigenous versions can be kept apart, in the first case, or added up, in the second. In a similar way, environmentalists' positions grounded on "objective" scientific observations will be engaged, while positions perceived as "emotional" would be kept apart.

The predominance of one version of caribou reflects some illuminating differences between Mol's and our case. First, in the Dutch hospital, the various versions of atherosclerosis are in principle relatively symmetrical to each other; there is no established hierarchy between them. Second, the practices of the radiologist, the pathologist, and the clinician are about diagnosing a condition, and hence any one of them being asked "show me atherosclerosis" will show something different that relates to their practice (a graph, a calcified artery, claims of pain by a patient). Then, and given the first point raised before, how this multiplicity is ordered and sorted in such a way that holds together constitutes a question that can only be answered case by case, for there are no established hierarchies between practices. In our case, asking anyone "show me caribou" would result in a finger pointing to a four-legged being with antlers. Here it *seems self-evident* that caribou exists out-there, holds together, and pre-exists the various practices of knowing.[2] This reinforces a series of assumptions about the basic stability, orderliness, and "givenness' of the world/reality that is independent and prior to knowledge practices. As John Law (2004) has argued, these assumptions are commonsensical for moderns, and call for a specific way of knowing which is epitomized in the "the scientific method." Thus, for a variety of reasons—including, but not limited to, the perfect fit between a commonsensical notion of what the scientific method can achieve and dominant assumptions about the nature of reality—the techno-scientific version of caribou has become dominant when it comes to specifying what this "thing" is and, thus, how humans have to manage it.

The role that commonsensical assumptions about reality play in establishing a hierarchy of versions of caribou raises a larger question about their role in enabling the kind of relatively "civil" process through which the various versions of atherosclerosis are made to hold together in Mol's case. The point becomes sharper if we attend to practices that, operating on different assumptions (surprisingly close to those of these material-semiotics versions of STS), are not as easily enrolled in processes of singularization. To this we turn next.

Atîku: disturbing multiplicity

What is atîku?

> Once an old man and his son were very expert in hunting. And it happened that the son dreamed that he cohabited with the caribou. [...] he said to his father "I will depart. And I will kill caribou enough for the whole winter. So do not wait for me [...] I am going to go with the caribou." Then he sang: "The caribou walked along well like me. Then I walked as he was walking. Then I took his path. And then I walked like the caribou, my trail looking like a caribou trail where I saw my tracks. And so indeed I will take care of the caribou. I indeed will divide the caribou. I will give them to the people [...] He who obeys the requirements is given caribou, and he who disobeys is not given caribou [...] For so now it is as I have said. I, indeed, am Caribou Man (Ati'k'wape'o) [a.k.a. Kanipinikassikueu]."
>
> Speck 1977, 81

This is one of the many versions of an *atanukan* (narratives about the origin of the current status of "things") accounting for the special relation the Innu sustain with *atîku*, what Speck translates as "caribou." The underlying assumption in these stories of how things came to be as they are now is that nothing begins *ex nihilo*; thus, reality is conceived as in a permanent state of becoming, the emergent effect of relations, and therefore "relatedness" or "relationality" is primordial (see Cajete 2000; Deloria, Deloria, and Foehner 1999). The pre-eminence of relatedness or relationality grounds a specific epistemology: knowledge is mainly about attunement with the ongoing unfolding of life-giving relations (see Burkhart 2001). This way of knowing is not about generating (mental) representations of an already existing world to then inform action, but about participating through appropriate actions in the worlding of a world of which the knower is part.

In this framework, hunting is a way of participating in a particular kind of worlding. Atîku (as other non-humans) have full personhood and will of their own, therefore hunting is not mainly about outsmarting "animals" but rather about enticing these fully volitional beings and their leader, Kanipinikassikueu, to be generous with their bodies (Castro 2015; Henriksen 2009). This is achieved through practices that show respect and recognition of these generous acts, such as protocols to dispose of the bones of hunted atîku, the injunction to not waste any part of their bodies, and the requirement that meat has to be generously shared among people. Other prescriptions, like keeping atîku in one's thoughts through storytelling, singing and drumming, and celebrating a ceremonial meal (*mokoshan*), are geared to receive the blessings that this relationship generates for the general wellbeing of *nitassinan*, the land (see Andrew and Castro 2016; Armitage 1992; Henriksen 1973).

For many Innu, a decrease in the frequency of atîku giving themselves to hunters is a symptom that Kanipinikassikueu is angry. This is the key in which most of Innu elders and hunters understand the ongoing decline of atîku.[3] Since the 1990s, when it numbered about 800,000 individuals, the George River Herd has been decreasing exponentially, down to 9,000 in 2016.[4] In conversations about the crisis, elders and hunters said that the disrespect of younger generations for atîku was rampant. They spoke of atîku remains being carried away by dogs, of people selling meat, and of a general lack of interest about life on the land. For most of these Innu, the consequences of all this are obvious in the decline of the herds as well as in the epidemic of addiction, suicide, and diabetes that has plagued younger generations of Innu for the past twenty years (see Samson 2003).

In 2010, the Newfoundland and Labrador provincial government commissioned a study to evaluate the status of the George River Herd in order to generate a management plan. The measures proposed hinged mostly on the study's conclusion that hunting was "now significant and cumulative to natural mortality," in other words, caring for the caribou population would require hunting to be restricted (Newfoundland and Labrador Wildlife 2010). The government made clear that its position was that conservation took precedence over Aboriginal rights to hunt. Since then, non-Aboriginals began to mount strong pressure on the government to put a ban on all hunting of the species.[5]

Finally, on January 28, 2013, the government, citing scientific evidence and recommendations, announced a five-year hunting ban on caribou.[6] The next day, Prote Poker, the Innu Nation Grand Chief, said that the Innu elders did not agree with the ban and the communities would continue hunting.[7] Thus, the hunting ban has been a matter of constant friction between the Innu and the provincial government as the former consistently refuse to follow it. Although several instances of consultations and discussion have been put into place, and the two Inuit groups of Labrador have accepted the argument that the ban is necessary to respond to the decline, the Innu "perspective" cannot be brought into compliance. This foregrounds that, rather than one of the practices/versions that constitute the caribou multiple, atîku is an altogether different "thing" and, therefore, recalcitrant to the usual operations of singularization.

Elsewhere (Blaser 2016) I have argued that the multiplicity at stake in this case is different from the multiplicity on which Mol and other STS scholars have focused. For the latter, the refrain that multiplicity is "more than one but less than many" can be captured by the image in Figure 4.1.

As with Mol's praxiography of atherosclerosis, multiplicity can be seen in the image as the various traces of the contour of the caribou, which do not quite coalesce in a single line. When seen through practices (or the lines) the "oneness" of atherosclerosis (or the caribou) appears diffracted, multiplied. Yet as happens with the image of *a caribou*, the assumption that there is a single

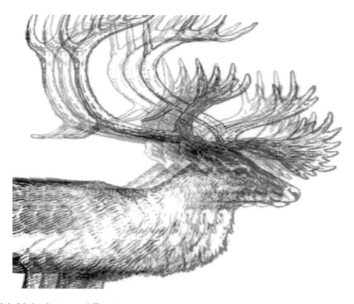

Figure 4.1 Multiplicity as diffraction

thing called atherosclerosis also contributes to hold this multiplicity together. The multiplicity of caribou can be also thought along these lines. The techno-scientific, wildlife management, environmentalist, corporations', and outfitters' versions of caribou do not always quite align with each other, but they are all oriented by a similar assumption, that there is a "thing" out there, the animal caribou. Such an assumption, and the tacit acceptance that the most accurate perspective on the "thing" is the scientific, enables the operations that allow the different practices to hold together. And I would add that such an assumption also plays a role in enabling the relatively "civil" procedures radiologists, clinicians, and pathologists use to stabilize and singularize the multiplicity of atherosclerosis when their practices are rendered as perspectives.

Taken on their own, the concrete practices that constitute atîku perhaps could be described in a similar way, that is, practices such as pursuing atîku, singing to it, dreaming with it, sharing meat, or performing rituals might not align all perfectly with each other. But there is an important caveat: in contrast to caribou, there is here an awareness that each of those practices are intrinsic to the being of atîku, hence the constant concern that the practices be carried out in the proper ways, and that carelessness is very dangerous as it will not render the "state of affairs" being sought.

Now, given that the practices associated with caribou and atîku encounter each other in the flesh of a being (so to speak), as I pointed out before, the multiplicity at stake is different. Better captured perhaps by a popular trick image as in Figure 4.2.

Here we have a bird looking to the left and a rabbit looking to the right, more than one but less than two. There is a bird and a rabbit, and yet they are not two units; and while the traces overlap, there is not just one drawing. If we imagine that the bodies of the bird and the rabbit do not overlap as neatly as

Figure 4.2 Multiplicity as divergence (duck–rabbit illusion)

their heads, we can grasp the idea that there might be partial co-occurrence of the entities, but the difference is not cancelled. In a similar fashion, the material-semiotic assemblages and practices from which the more than one, less than many atîku/caribou emerges *partially* co-occur (most evidently in bodily presence) but they remain distinct.[8] In this case, multiplicity refers to mutually entangled but divergent worldings.

Although the specific multiplicity of atîku/caribou has often been a factor in the conflicts between the Innu and various agents of the nation-state and corporations, it had not before irrupted in such a way as it has now with the hunting ban, a situation that makes it more visible that different worldings are at stake here. In other words, before the conflict over the hunting ban, atîku/caribou held together well enough to give credence to the idea that each word represented cultural perspectives on the same "thing." In the next section we will take a closer look into how this multiplicity was made to hold together and why it cannot be made to do so any longer.

Holding on together in divergence

As pointed out above, caribou population studies are central to governmental decision-making regarding management of the species. These studies are the aggregate result of theories and models about population cycles and ethology; aerial surveys; tracking of movement using radio collars; analysis of individual specimens' physical status (body fat, weight, parasites, etc.); and reports from hunters (including harvest data, location of herds, observation of body condition of specimens hunted, and so on). Here, we have a first "crossing" of practices that we can follow in pursuit of understanding how the multiplicity of caribou/atîku has held together.

While hunting practices contribute "data" for population studies, some research practices contribute to the performance of hunting practices. In effect, until recently, the location of the George River Herd transmitted by radio collars was posted with very little delay on a website of the Quebec Ministry of the Environment. Innu hunters in Labrador used this information to travel to those areas where the hunt was more likely to be successful. Neither the data provided by the hunters nor the location the radio collars provided is determinant to either set of practices (hunting atîku and researching caribou), but they reinforce each other, even if unwittingly. Notice that in this case atîku and caribou (or some of the practices that constitute them) relate to each other in "productive" ways without a requirement that both entities be mutually equivalent. Somehow, the difference between entities remains invisible or irrelevant; they both "flow" without interrupting each other. But this is not always the case.

In a recent ethnography, Damian Castro, one of my collaborators, reports an incident that shows how the contrasting assumptions about atîku and caribou might engender conflicts involving the collars.

One day, while I was in the Innu Nation office, a very experienced hunter who had been recently charged with illegal hunting came to the office where I was working and told me "they found a Red Wine [protected herd] collar close to lake Kamistastin; see, atiku *wants* to go there". Lake Kamistastin is located about 400 kilometers north of Sheshatshiu, very far from the Red Wine herd range, and right in the migration area of George River herd. This information, as he and other Innu argue, shows that the Red Wine woodland herd and the George River migratory herd intermingle, therefore, there is no point in declaring the hunt illegal on the basis of the assumption upheld by government scientists that the herds are different: for the Innu there is only atîku. Furthermore, the words of this hunter obliquely indicate differences in how the collar information is used. The government uses it to obtain the information the scientists need to learn about caribou behavior, such as their whereabouts, while the Innu use this information to know *what atiku wants*. In other words, while the government administer the collars to satisfy their will to learn, the Innu use it to learn the will of atiku. Like human beings, atiku has will.

(Castro 2015, 54–5)

The collars are a key component of caribou population studies and the calculations that inform regulations impacting the practices of hunters. But regulating hunting is only the tip of the iceberg of a larger wildlife management dispositive. Let's take a look at how atîku and caribou encounter each other in this larger dispositive of management.

In 1996, the Voisey's Bay Nickel Company Ltd. filed an application to proceed with a mine and mill project in northern Labrador. Subsequently, and following standing legislation, the company had to present an environmental impact assessment (EIA) study that would then become part of a larger process of EIA by an independent review panel. The Innu refused to participate in the EIA study as they staunchly rejected the project due to the effects it could have on atîku and other non-humans (Innes 2001). Nevertheless, the EIA went ahead, including an estimation of the impact the project would have on the George River Herd that hinged upon studies made on that population. Based on these estimates, the review panel made recommendations to mitigate the impacts and that would allow the project to proceed. Thus, nested within them, the techno-scientific artifact "caribou" (at the center of caribou population studies) became a building block of the EIA, the recommendations of the panel, and the planning of operations of the mine.

Although the Innu struggled and opposed the mining project, they were aware that the deck was stacked against them:

What choice do we have to protest or negotiate? We are trying to protect the land and the animals and on the other hand [are] the big companies. No matter where we stand, it's like giving away our land.

And if we try to stop it, we won't go nowhere. Mining developments will go ahead anyway.

> (George Gregoire, the Innu Nation Officer, cited in Innes 2001)

Eventually, the Innu signed an Impacts and Benefits Agreement with the mine. The mine's website provides a concise and clear explanation of what an Impacts and Benefits Agreement is:

> Impacts and Benefits Agreements (IBA) are typical where a significant project is proposed for development on a First Nation's "traditional lands". Traditional lands are the First Nation's ancestral lands over which they have Aboriginal rights. Mining projects, as an example, have the potential to have social, cultural and environmental impacts on traditional lands and on local communities [...] IBAs are formal, written agreements between companies and First Nations that help to manage the predicted impacts associated with an industrial development and to secure economic benefits for neighboring communities affected by that development.
>
> (Vale n.d.)

Although the terms of the IBA that the Innu reached with the mining company are confidential, some of the economic benefits derived from it have been used to sustain an outpost program where Innu families are supported in going by aircraft to live in camps in the bush for as long as three months (Castro 2015). These kinds of programs have become very important for those Innu who have been progressively driven to live in permanent settlements and depend largely on wage labor, yet want to sustain their connection with nitassinan and Kanipinikassikueu. Hence, here we have another (more mediated) "crossing" of practices that at the same time disrupt and reinforce each other. In effect, the caribou population studies "nested" within the EIA and the review panel's recommendations paved the way for calculations that would make feasible a project that disrupts hunting practices in a certain place. The defense of these hunting practices (and more generally nitassinan) led the Innu to initially reject the project, which in turn led the mine to the negotiation of an Impacts and Benefits Agreement that now contributes to sustain Innu hunting practices in the present circumstances.

Thus, while in a particular place/moment (the EIA) the nested practices of caribou population studies, on the one hand, and hunting, on the other, interrupt each other, in another place/moment (the Impacts and Benefits Agreement) the interruption is worked around (although not eliminated), enabling the continuation of both (including, of course, the entities which they contribute to enact, i.e., atîku and caribou). We do not have here a process that produces "common ground," but rather a process that through displacement enables the sustenance of divergent yet entangled entities; but only up to a point. In effect, the divergence is grounded on an asymmetrical equivocation, and thus the "holding on together" is not very robust. An equivocation refers to a situation in which interlocutors appear to be speaking of the same thing when they are actually referring to different ones (Viveiros de Castro 2004); in our case, assuming that caribou and atîku refer to the same thing would be an equivocation. However, this equivocation is not symmetrical. For those mobilizing caribou, atîku is seldom anything more than a "word" in another language to reference the same "thing." The signing of the Impact and Benefits Agreement enabled this presumption of synonymity to hold after a period of turbulence (while the Innu opposed the project), after all the agreement was based on the EIA study within which was nested caribou as a techno-scientific artifact. For the Innu, in contrast, that caribou is not exactly atîku is made evident by the constant interruptions of the practices that bring the latter into being. Just remember the reference in Castro's quote above to the hunter charged with illegally hunting caribou from what biologists have established is a protected and distinct herd different from another one that was not then protected. In this sense, "displacement" is different from Mol's "keeping apart" practices—so that they do not force an adjudication—in that the adjudication is only deferred. In effect, while for those doing caribou the agreement may push the equivocation to the background, for the Innu it is evident that the equivocation can hold only so long; as Edward Piwas, an Innu elder, presciently stated:

> The smog from the milling plant will kill the plants and animals. And it will float into our community. We will not see the smog—it will slowly kill the animals and us [...]. The wildlife officer will know when he can't find any animals. He will blame us for the lack of them but he will not think about the drilling.
>
> (cited in Innes 2001)

In relation to my argument, I take the statement to indicate that the practices that constitute caribou (and through it, the EIA study and its suggested mitigation measures) would not sustain atîku and this would become evident in time, and when this happens those doing caribou will not question their own practices, such as industrial activities enabled by the caribou artifact, but those that do atîku, such as hunting. The passing of the ban in 2013 brought this scenario to fruition. But, in contrast to what happened with Voisey's Bay, now the interruption of atîku cannot be displaced as it hits in one of the most crucial practices that constitute it, hunting (as the giving and receiving of gifts from Kanipinikassikueu). Hence, the Innu refusal to accept the ban. The asymmetry in the equivocation of assuming that caribou and atîku are the same is foregrounded by an ironic call by Simeon Tshakapesh, chief of Natuashish, to make caribou and atîku symmetrical in practice:

> If they're so sincere about the George River herd [...] I think they should stop the [...] mining and exploration. I wouldn't hunt if they say, "Okay,

we want to save the caribou herd, we're going to shut all the exploration, mining companies, and other projects—we're going to shut it down for the next five years."[9]

In other words, by making what he knows is an impossible demand on the colonial state Tshakapesh tries to foreground the extent to which the ban is an impossible demand for the Innu as well. Symmetry by the negative.

Conclusions

As I pointed out in the introduction, and have developed elsewhere (Blaser 2016), the conception of cosmopolitics as a project oriented towards the composition of a common world is predominantly informed by the figuration of multiplicity as diffraction, and is thus conceived as process of singularization writ large. Bringing forward an example of another kind of multiplicity enables us to probe the limits of this conception of cosmopolitics. In my previous work (ibid.), I pointed out that such conceptions of cosmopolitics have little space for the multiplicity as divergence revealed by the atîku/caribou case. Quoting Latour, I pointed out that the divergent multiplicity of atîku would be rendered an externality about which "an explicit collective decision has been made not to take them into account; they are to be viewed as insignificant" (ibid. 663–4), and concluded that this conception of cosmopolitics can at best offer a slowing down of this externalization and a recognition of the victims thereby generated. Taking as leads some events that had happened before and after the passing of the hunting ban, I argued that another cosmopolitics might be possible if we took divergent rather than diffractive multiplicity as the starting point. If the original conception of cosmopolitics as the constitution of the common world was built on the observation of situations (usually in laboratories) in which matters of concern are progressively transformed into matters of fact, the possibility of another cosmopolitics would hinge upon an (ethnographically rich) exploration of how divergent multiplicity operates in such a way that it holds together. This is what I have started to do in this chapter.

From our brief overview of "crossings" in the caribou/atîku case it is evident that, rather than singularization, what "hold together" divergent multiplicity are different versions of equivocation, that is, situations that by chance or design allow for divergence to be sustained through the connection or the crossing. This may occur through equivocations that allow different practices to connect either without interference with each other, or even enabling each other. In a similar fashion, the situation that led me to further explore multiplicity as divergence involved a consciously staged equivocation that would enable atîku and caribou to hold together symmetrically in the context of the hunting ban (Blaser 2016, 564–5). Succinctly, my Innu collaborators proposed to wildlife managers that a limited hunt of atîku be allowed to the Innu communities under their strict "traditional" protocols. The pitch they made was that the amount of work required to follow the protocols and their enforcement by the communities themselves would have better results in terms of addressing the biologists' concerns than a ban that no Innu would abide by. The idea was taken up by the wildlife officers but soon after, under public pressure, the Environment Minister passed the ban. Nevertheless, we have here a number of examples showing how equivocations (might) help multiplicity as divergence to hold together.

That equivocations will work is never guaranteed, particularly when they are premised on "displacements" that sustain asymmetrical equivocations. There seems to be a temporal dynamism (see Bonelli, Chapter 8 in this volume) that make the results of equivocations perhaps less stable than "matters of fact," yet the conditions required to obtain the latter from "matters of concern" appear rather restrictive, which leads me to ask whether multiplicity as diffraction is not already a product of a particular way of dealing with multiplicity as divergence. The looming threat of arrests under the current hunting ban is very telling in this regard. If we take the threat as part of the procedures used to stabilize caribou multiple in the face of the disturbances produced by atîku, and compare it with the more civil procedures used in the Dutch hospital to singularize the multiplicity of atherosclerosis, a difference becomes evident in terms of what is required for multiplicity as diffraction to be set up. In effect, it would appear that in order for diffraction to be the working ground of cosmopolitics, divergence would have to be reined in. This, to my mind, remits to the role that coloniality still plays in inadvertently shaping contemporary political imaginations, even those that embrace the idea of a world multiple.

Notes

1 Within this literature, Nadasdy (2007) speaks of ontological differences but in his treatment and discussion of them it is hard to see how they differ from cultural differences.
2 I stress "seems self-evident" to indicate that this understanding of what is implied by pointing to the four-legged being is not universally valid, as will become evident in the next section.
3 Since 2009, I have been involved in a collaborative research project about the "atîku crisis" with a group of Labrador Innu elders and hunters.
4 See Government of Newfoundland and Labrador. 2016. "Summer Census Shows George River Caribou Herd at Critically Low Level," News Release, August 26. http://www.releases.gov.nl.ca/releases/2016/ecc/0829n02.aspx accessed November 16, 2016.
5 See CBC. 2012. "Scientist calls for stop to aboriginal George River caribou hunt," CBC News, August 20. http://www.cbc.ca/news/canada/newfoundland-labrador/story/2012/08/20/nl-720-caribou-hunting-ban-proposal.html accessed November 16, 2016.
6 See Government of Newfoundland and Labrador. 2013. "Hunting Ban Announced on George River Caribou Herd," News Release, January 28. http://www.releases.gov.nl.ca/releases/2013/env/0128n08.htm accessed November 16, 2016.

7 See CBC. 2013. "Innu may hunt caribou despite ban," CBC News, January 29. http://www.cbc.ca/news/canada/newfoundland-labrador/story/2013/01/29/nl-innu-caribou-hunt-129.html accessed November 16, 2016.
8 Partial co-occurrence in bodily presence enables the equivocation inherent to the assumption that, in pointing to a four-legged being when asked show me a caribou or an atîku, Innu and Euro-Canadians are pointing to the same "thing."
9 See CBC. 2013. Op. cit. n.7.

References

Andrew, Alexander (Nikashant Antane) and Damian Castro. 2016. *Atiku Napeu—The Caribou Man*. Innu Nation and Memorial University of Newfoundland. Documentary video, 48: 03. https://www.youtube.com/watch?v=SDGM0AKob8o

Armitage, Peter. 1992. "Religious Ideology among the Innu of Eastern Quebec and Labrador." *Religiologiques* 6: 64–110.

Blaser, Mario. 2016. "Is Another Cosmopolitics Possible?" *Cultural Anthropology* 31 (4): 545–570.

Burkhart, Brian Yazzie. 2001. "What Coyote and Thales can Teach Us: An Outline of American Indian Epistemology." In *American Indian Thought: Philosophical Essays*, edited by Anne Waters, 15–27. Malden, MA: Blackwell Publishing.

Cajete, Gregory. 2000. *Native Science: Natural Laws of Interdependence*. Santa Fe, NM: Clear Light Publishing.

Castro, Damian. 2015. "Meating the Social: Caribou Hunting and Distribution in Sheshatshiu, Labrador." PhD dissertation, Memorial University of Newfoundland.

Deloria, Vine, Barbara Deloria, and Kristen Foehner. 1999. *Spirit & Reason: The Vine Deloria, Jr., Reader*. Golden, CO: Fulcrum Publishing.

Henriksen, Georg. 1973. *Hunters in the Barrens: The Naskapi on the Edge of the White Man's World*. St John's, Newfoundland: Institute of Social and Economic Research.

Henriksen, Georg. 2009. *I Dreamed the Animals: Kaniuekutat. The Life of an Innu Hunter*. New York: Berghahn.

Hummel, Monte and Justina C. Ray. 2008. *Caribou and the North: A Shared Future*. Toronto: Dundurn Press.

Innes, Larry. 2001. "Staking Claims Innu Rights and Mining Claims at Voisey's Bay." *Cultural Survival Quarterly* 25 (1): 12–16.

Latour, Bruno. 2004. "Whose Cosmos, Which Cosmopolitics? Comments on the Peace Terms of Ulrich Beck." *Common Knowledge* 10 (3): 450–462.

—. 2007. "Turning around Politics: A Note on Gerard de Vries's Paper." *Social Studies of Science* 37 (5): 811–820.

Law, John. 2004. *After Method: Mess in Social Science Research*. London: Routledge.

Mol, Annemarie. 2002. *The Body Multiple: Ontology in Medical Practice*. Durham, NC: Duke University Press.

Nadasdy, Paul. 2007. "The Gift in the Animal: The Ontology of Hunting and Human–Animal Sociality." *American Ethnologist* 34 (1): 25–43.

Newfoundland and Labrador Wildlife. 2010. "George River Caribou Management." Presentation. http://www.env.gov.nl.ca/env/wildlife/pdf/GRCH_2010_Consultations.pdf

Samson, Colin. 2003. *A Way of Life That Does Not Exist: Canada and the Extinguishment of the Innu*. London: Verso.

Spaeder, Joseph J. and Harvey A. Feit. 2005. "Co-management and Indigenous Communities: Barriers and Bridges to Decentralized Resource Management: Introduction." *Anthropologica* 47 (2): 147–154.

Speck, Frank G. 1977. *Naskapi: The Savage Hunters of the Labrador Peninsula.* Norman, OK: University of Oklahoma Press.

Stengers, Isabelle. 2005. "The Cosmopolitical Proposal." In *Making Things Public: Atmospheres of Democracy*, edited by Bruno Latour and Peter Weibel, 994–1003. Cambridge, MA: MIT Press.

Vale. n.d. "Voisey's Bay Development: Impacts and Benefits Agreements". Accessed April 24, 2018. http://www.vbnc.com/iba.asp

Viveiros de Castro, Eduardo. 2004. "Perspectival Anthropology and the Method of Controlled Equivocation." *Tipití: Journal of the Society for the Anthropology of Lowland South America* 2 (1): 3–22.

Chapter 5

Maps in action

Quotidian politics through boundary translational matrix for world multiple in contemporary Inuit everyday life

Keiichi Omura

Almost every summer or winter since 1989, I have stayed with Inuit hunters at Kugaaruk in the Nunavut Territory in the Canadian Arctic, and not once have I seen a hunter carrying a topographic map on hunting trips or when visiting neighboring villages. Because these hunters have *Inuit Qaujimajatuqangit* (IQ: Inuit knowledge)—particularly knowledge about hunting or traveling routes, orientation techniques, and geographical and climatic knowledge—they can freely and safely travel their land, called *nuna*, using snowmobiles, outboard boats, or four-wheelers, for a radius of 150 km around their settlement. They are proud of their ability to travel without a map or GPS, going so far as to say, "This is my GPS," pointing to their head.

Nevertheless, they are fond of reading and using topographic maps in daily conversation. Most skillful hunters possess a printed or digital 1:250,000 scale map, published by the Canadian Government's Centre for Topographic Information. I have often observed hunters using these maps when discussing things such as hunting routes, the distribution and movement of wild animals, and the conditions of ice floes. They retrace their routes on these maps after returning from hunting trips, and use them to exchange information about routes and snow and sea ice conditions before leaving to hunt or visit neighboring villages. Elders enjoy these maps while reminiscing.

These maps also play an important role in Inuit dealings with scientists and government officials concerning wildlife management, environmental development planning, and land claim negotiations. When the Inuit were negotiating the Nunavut Land Claim Agreement with the Canadian Government, subsistence territory maps produced from topographic maps provided some of the best evidence of Inuit land use and occupancy (e.g., Freeman 1976). In short, topographic maps have taken a firm hold in contemporary Inuit life as effective communication and negotiation tools with the outside world, as well as for IQ cultivation.

Why are Inuit hunters fond of topographic maps, even though they never use them while hunting and traveling? How does a topographic map function as a medium of interaction with the outside world and among the Inuit? This chapter explores the potential of topographic maps as a *boundary translational matrix*, through which the Inuit lifeworld nuna and outside worlds are divergently regenerated but attuned to each other and loosely assembled as a world multiple. Based on this analysis, it also demonstrates the importance of quotidian politics through translation with map as a primordial politics for diverging worlds from an entanglement of different types of practice, in which scales such as local/global, micro/macro, provincial/universal, or indigenous/modern are not yet differentiated.

IQ narration as re-enactment of engagement with the environment

Almost twenty-five years ago, I began to research IQ, which the Inuit have cultivated and continue to generate as a synthesized body of knowledge, practice, and beliefs through their subsistence practices over the past thousand years. It consists of Inuktitut (the Inuit language), ecological knowledge, subsistence techniques, social norms and values, and the art of social intercourse with humans and non-humans. It is defined as "the Inuit way of doing things: the past, present, and future knowledge, experience, and values of Inuit Society" (IQ Task Force 2002, 4).

My initial interviews with elders and skillful hunters did not go well. My questions, directed at generalized knowledge, included generalizing terms such as "always" and "usually," which my interviewees considered problematic (Omura 2005). I was often cautioned against making easy generalizations when I asked them, "Do you usually (always) take this route to go there?" On each occasion, they explained to me how a route they took at a particular time was different from the previous one, even though these routes appeared almost the same to me. It seemed inaccurate to them to generalize about the routes without considering the differences in detail.

Arctic anthropologists (Briggs 1968, 1970, 1991; Freeman 1976; Morrow 1990) have found a dislike of easy generalization to be common across Inuit groups, and the attitude has been connected to cultural ideals (Briggs 1968, 1970; Omura 2002, 2005). An ideal person is regarded as "having reason" (*ihumaqaqtuq*), an autonomous decision-maker who keeps equanimity in the face of social and physical difficulties and frustrations, and voluntarily conforms to norms of social behavior. This ideal person values both his or her own autonomy and the autonomy of others, and he or she has a realistic and pragmatic view of the environment without any preconceived ideas about other people and the environment on the basis of generalizations. To uniformly and rigidly define or generalize the nature of others or environments is considered childish (*nutaraqpaluktuq*), as any existence has multiple potentialities which cannot be reduced to a unitarily rigid definition.

Accordingly, most elders and skillful hunters I interviewed were unwilling to generalize their experiences and wished to provide a full picture. After I learned to ask them to tell me their experiences in detail, they began to share their knowledge in anecdotal form. Reconstructing and retracing the routes on which they and others actually traveled each year on a 1:250,000 scale map, they vividly related stories about their experiences on each hunting trip using many gestures (Omura 2005, 2007). For example, they continually retraced movements on the map with their fingers or a pen, saying "by this route," "there," "in this direction." Then, when they identified the place where they hunted caribou, fished, or left caches, they explained the process of pursuing the caribou on the map or, raising their faces from the map, used gestures to explain how to catch and dry fish, make storage bags for caribou fur, and build stone caches.

This tendency has also been discussed by Robert Rundstorm (1990) in a study of maps drawn by the Inuit. At the request of explorers and anthropologists, the Inuit drew maps which have a reputation for elaborately expressing subtle details and differences in geographical features. They often compare favorably with modern topographic maps (Spink and Moodie 1972). Rundstorm argued that Inuit map-making practices can be considered an extension of their custom of recounting in detail the environment encountered along a route, miming with gestures the forms of geographical features, after returning from subsistence activities or visiting trading posts. The Inuit maps recorded in explorers' journals and in ethnographies, Rundstorm concluded, were direct pen-and-paper results of these gestural performances. The accuracy of the maps drawn by the Inuit impressively demonstrates that their narration of IQ was basically a re-enactment of past practices and experiences.

This is also true for the IQ narratives about animals such as polar bears, seals, caribou, and fish (Omura 2007). In my interviews, elders and hunters often re-enacted their experiences with gestures, as if the animals were in front of them. They did not describe animals as independent detached entities; rather, they discussed wildlife as being in a constant relationship with them through practical engagements such as hunting. Certainly, they also provided more generalized knowledge of wildlife in terms of the distribution, seasonal migration patterns, and detailed ethological knowledge. This information, however, was only provided when I asked direct questions; they did not voluntarily give descriptions of wildlife as entities independent of human beings.

Tactical ideology as the guiding principle for IQ

Characteristics of the IQ narratives discussed above can be summarized on the basis of Michel de Certeau's (1984) distinction between "strategies" and "tactics," with IQ being based on "tactics" rather than "strategies" (Omura 2005). According to de Certeau, a strategy is a mode of practice in which the subject, standing at a viewpoint detached from and commanding a sweeping view of the environment, controls or manages the environment objectified from that viewpoint. This strategy is exactly what Inuit elders and hunters avoid. Generalizations require reducing complex phenomena to simple principles without regard for detailed contexts, and this is possible only when the subject is isolated from the environment and objectifies it from a detached viewpoint. On the other hand, tactics are a mode of practice in which an individual, enmeshed in the environment and therefore unable to objectify it, copes with it, taking advantage of opportunities according to circumstances, without attempting to control it. This tactical practice is exactly what Inuit elders and hunters reconstruct and re-execute through re-enactments.

However, this does not mean they lack a strategic perspective and never behave according to strategic principles. To travel successfully, it is necessary to use strategic knowledge, such as cardinal directions and place-name networks. For example, when talking about hunting, the Inuit I interviewed demonstrated accurate knowledge of the spatial relationships of over 300 places, which they had organized into a place-name network based on cardinal directions composed of two axes and four directions (Omura 2005, 2013). Whenever traveling by land and sea, they use these reference points to determine their present position and determine cardinal directions from the wind and the orientation of snowdrifts. This strategic knowledge is indispensable in understanding IQ anecdotes, because the IQ narration is located within a place-name network based on a strategic understanding of the geographical environment. Indeed, when I asked people to teach me a way to memorize place names, elders and hunters were able to recite numerous place-name chains organized into networks along the routes. The Inuit also have tongue twisters for these place names, from which children learn the network (Correll 1976). They also have the strategic knowledge of wildlife, such as taxonomy, and knowledge of distribution and migration patterns. Such knowledge is indispensable in understanding IQ narration.

However, this strategic knowledge is seen as basic elementary knowledge, which is indispensable for children, and some foreigners like me, in learning IQ, like a multiplication table in mathematics, with the place-name tongue twisters serving as teaching devices. For this reason, such knowledge is never discussed by Inuit adults; rather, discussions among them are a verbal re-execution of tactical practices. Although Inuit elders and hunters execute both strategic and tactical practices, tactics are preferred to strategies, according to their cultural ideal, when demonstrating IQ. This can be seen as the opposite of modern science (de Certeau 1984). Both strategies and tactics coexist in scientific practice; for example, scientists and anthropologists have to show ingenuity when developing experimental procedures or fieldwork, assembling experimental devices, or conducting interviews or participant observation. They also have to cope with changing situations in their experiments and fieldwork, taking advantage of opportunities. However, only the results of the strategic practices are presented as outcomes, with many tactical practices hidden from the public.

Thus, in contrast to modern scientists guided by a strategic ideology, Inuit elders and hunters adhere to a tactical ideology in which strategies are disregarded or seen as childish. Therefore, IQ contrasts with modern science, as has been reported in many anthropological studies (Freeman 1985, 1993; Freeman and Carbyn 1988; Nakashima 1991; Omura 2005, 2007; Stevenson 1996). If modern science is quantitative, purely rational, analytical, reductionist, and based on a dualistic worldview in which nature is regarded as separate from the human realm, then IQ is qualitative, empirical, subjective, intuitive, context bound, holistic, ethical, and based on a monistic worldview in which humans and non-humans are viewed as not separate from each other, but sharing a common foundation.

So, why is tactical ideology the cultural ideal for the Inuit and the guiding principle behind IQ? To address this question, I examine the Inuit subsistence system, as it is through their subsistence activities that Inuit come to know nuna and cultivate IQ.

The Inuit subsistence system as nuna-generating machine

Since sedentarization under assimilationist policies of the Canadian Federal Government in the 1950s and 1960s, the Inuit have become integrated into the modern nation-state and the world system of the capitalist economy, which has resulted in significant sociocultural shifts. Education, medicine, welfare, law, and currency have gradually permeated Inuit society and accelerated their integration with the Canadian nation-state. They have become more dependent on the world system through wage labor and the selling of fur and Inuit art sculptures. Moreover, they have also been exposed since the 1970s to mainstream North American consumer culture through mass media. The Inuit today work in offices, at construction sites, and in grocery stores, live in houses with central heating, and own and use snowmobiles, four-wheelers, and outboard-motor boats. They also play with iPads and iPods, enjoy the internet and cable TV, and shop online as well as at local grocery stores.

Yet, subsistence has not lost its significance. Inuit hunters now use high-performance rifles and various vehicles in hunting, and need cash to obtain and maintain this equipment. Nevertheless, one can hear statements like "Inuit who do not commit to subsistence are not Inuit" (Omura 2002). Despite the fact that the purchase of processed foods is common, the meat of wildlife obtained by subsistence is preferred as "true food" (niqinmarik), which is indispensable to ethnic identity, and the distribution of such meat still functions to sustain social relationships (Kishigami 1995, 2007; Stewart 1995; Wenzel 1991).

This subsistence does not simply consist of the technical and economic activity of obtaining resources for survival (Bodenhorn 1989; Fienup-Riordan 1983, 1990; Kishigami 2007; Nuttall 1992; Omura 2012, forthcoming b; Stairs and Wenzel 1992; Stewart 1995; Wenzel 1991). Instead, it involves a complex circulation formed by the order of nuna, which actively creates ecological relationships between autonomous non-human persons—i.e., wildlife—and equally autonomous human beings (Omura 2012, forthcoming b).

When an Inuk hunter employs subsistence techniques such as hunting, fishing, and trapping to relate him or herself to wild animals, the wild animal and the hunter fall into a food supplier/recipient relationship. The food (or other subsistence supplies) received as a result is then shared among people. This sharing creates and defines the extended family group, which is the foundation of sociopolitical relationships among the Inuit. This food-sharing activity is normalized among the Inuit because the ontology they strive to achieve requires reciprocity between the Inuit and wildlife.

According to Inuit ontology, wildlife possesses a *tagniq* (spirit) that remains after their bodies perish (Bodenhorn 1989; Fienup-Riordan 1983, 1990; Stewart 1995; Wenzel 1991). However, this spirit can only be reincarnated in another body if—and only if—the Inuit collectively consume all the flesh; therefore, the animal spirits voluntarily offer their bodies to the Inuit to become shared food so as to be reincarnated. The wildlife/human relationship is seen as reciprocal since the wildlife sustains the Inuit and the Inuit facilitate reincarnation through collective consumption of the animal. Under the guiding principles of this ontology, the Inuit must always share the food provided to help the wildlife that is its source. This sharing thus becomes a norm: if food is not shared, the wildlife cannot reincarnate, and people become afraid that the wildlife will stop offering their bodies as food. Consequently, the Inuit are obliged to distribute the meat of wildlife among themselves in order to keep receiving such food.

Note that it is the wildlife, not the Inuit, who impose this food-sharing norm. Therefore, every Inuit follows the same norm and shares food without being asked, which enables them to establish cooperative relationships. Food-sharing also prevents any single Inuit from entering into a "dominant supplier/subordinate receiver" relationship with another, which means that no one enjoys an advantage or faces a disadvantage of being the provider or recipient. From this condition of equality, the Inuit establish trust relationships that depend on wildlife's intentions. This trust stems from a mutual expectation that no individual is going to betray others and monopolize food under the condition that as Inuit, they follow the food-sharing norm as "recipients" always subordinate to wildlife. By rejecting the ruler's role and handing over the power of enforcement to wildlife, the Inuit avoid dominant/subordinate relationships and build trust relationships based on cooperation among equals.

However, this move has its costs. As the Inuit must be subordinate to wildlife at all times, the domestication or domination of wildlife became impossible, because if domesticated, wildlife could no longer impose food-sharing norms on the Inuit. Rather, the Inuit who domesticate them would impose norms on other Inuit and thus bring back the dominant/subordinate relationship that they once eliminated. Therefore, for the Inuit to have equal and trust-based relationships with each other, the wildlife must remain dominant over them. This means that the Inuit cannot make choices that lead to the management or domestication of wildlife and must commit themselves to techniques of enticement, the tactics of the subordinate: hunting, fishing, trapping, and gathering.

Overall, therefore, most Inuit subsistence techniques are tactical and oriented to approaching wildlife from an inferior position. In techniques such as trapping, luring, and weir and net fishing, the hunters utilize the desires, habitual behaviors, and seasonal migration patterns of wildlife to entice them to appear in front of them. Likewise, the hunters study seal behavior and ambush them at their breathing holes in the sea ice. Even when hunting caribou and whale, hunters use their knowledge of distribution and migration patterns to predict where they might be. Before they had rifles, the Inuit used lines of rock cairns (*inukshuk*) and knowledge of caribou behavior to lead the caribou within range of a spear or bow and arrow. In this way, hunters tactically use their strategic knowledge of wildlife behavioral patterns.

The food-sharing norm also promotes the sharing of subsistence techniques and knowledge. Because this norm compels every Inuit to share the food they acquire, subsistence techniques can be shared without the possibility of betrayal or usurpation. The norm discourages the Inuit from practicing single-person fishing and hunting, as well as from monopolizing knowledge or techniques. The collaboration and sharing elaborate their subsistence practices and increase their chances of engaging in a relationship with individual wildlife as recipients of food subordinate to the order of sharing, relative to the supplier of food and commander of the food-sharing norm. Once this relationship is established through hunting or fishing, subsistence comes back to the starting point, and the entire process repeats. This cyclical process perpetually reproduces the relationship between the Inuit and wildlife, which executes the reincarnation of the wildlife spirit. Here, wildlife spirit refers to the relationship that connects the wildlife and the Inuit. In Inuit ontology, this relationship survives through Inuit food-sharing, and then is reproduced in other wildlife and other Inuit.

This cyclical process allows a tight entanglement of enticement/order inter-actions between the Inuit and wildlife, and trusting and cooperative interac-tions among the Inuit. By and through such practices, two categories surface: namely, Inuit, whom one must trust and cooperate with; and wildlife, who are the object of enticement and the imposers of order. Within this asymmetrical relationship with wildlife, the Inuit create an extended family that facilitates cooperation among equal individuals. Of course, the relationships generated through this circular process are not limited to a specific kind of wildlife but are open to many species, all of whom are connected to one another, being articulated as groups embedded in the network of their ecological relationships. This implies that the Inuit extended family becomes blended as an articulation point in a vastly extended, interconnected ecological network of relationships, within which many other groups of wildlife are also demarcated. This vast network, ordered by and interwoven with both ecological and social relation-ships, is the Inuit lifeworld, nuna.

Thus, the Inuit subsistence system creates, differentiates, and relates extended families and wildlife species from the chaos where there is no human or nature, and then produces the order for their entire lifeworld. Therefore, the Inuit subsistence system can be said to be the generator of their nuna. Practicing subsistence is an economic activity for obtaining necessary resources for survival and circulation, but it simultaneously implies being ecologically related to wildlife, having social intercourse with other Inuit, and conducting ethical and social activities to materialize the ideal world represented in their ontology. Precisely for this reason, Inuit subsistence lies at the core of their political, economic, social, and cultural domains, and binds these spheres. This system establishes the entire order of nuna at once, and thus it deserves to be called the Inuit way of life.

Inuit ontology and ideology in the subsistence system

To maintain a relationship of equality among themselves, Inuit must rely on tactics if they are to appeal positively to other Inuit and wildlife, because tactics are a technique of the weak for appealing to their superiors or partners on equal footing without commands. However, as mentioned, this does not mean that the Inuit never behave according to strategic principles. It would be impossible to succeed in enticing wildlife and negotiating with each other without any strategic practices. If they did not understand wildlife distribution and migration patterns, or follow advanced hunting plans using strategic knowledge, they would be unable to track and find wildlife. Likewise, if they had no strategies to persuade others, it would be difficult to establish consensus and build collaborative relationships among themselves. However, to maintain the nuna, strategic practices have to be used only in preparation for tactical practices; strategy becomes invisible behind tactics. In other words, to maintain the relationship of trust among themselves and the relationship of domination/ subordination between wildlife and Inuit, strategies are used in a preparatory stage and tactics are used in the final stage.

Therefore, a tactical ideology has become the guiding principle for engaging with others and it makes sense that Inuit hunters avoid talking about strategic knowledge in their narratives. If they stressed their ability to grasp the intentions of others, instead of their paying attention to and thereby appealing to others' autonomous will from an inferior or equal position, hunters could appear driven by ambition to occupy a superior position to others. To deny this ambition, they must avoid showing strategic knowledge as much as possible.

In short, the Inuit endeavor to confine their strategies within the preparatory process of the engagement and complete it with tactics at the final stage, to place themselves in the role of the weak party and create an equal relationship among themselves, so that their ontology is realized and thus their nuna is regenerated through the circulation of subsistence. This is a mirror image of technoscience, which is led by a strategic ideology in which tactics are restricted to only serving to prepare a suitable environment for strategies. Inuit ontology and tactical ideology are examples not of a faulty understanding of the world, nor of the concealment of truth, but of a guiding principle for materially and semiotically realizing an ontology and therefore regenerating nuna in the future.

Map-using practices in contemporary Inuit society

It should now be clear why Inuit hunters are fond of reading and using topographic maps in daily conversation, even though they never use them when hunting and traveling. Topographic maps save hunters the trouble of explicitly explaining their strategic knowledge of the routes, the place-name network, or the geography, allowing them to devote themselves to re-enacting tactics. They can thus make their strategic practices more invisible and tacit, and simultaneously highlight tactics more effectively.

Moreover, topographic maps function as an effective device for learning. Inuit hunters are virtually forbidden to teach or instruct each other directly, but rather are encouraged to help each other learn because they must never occupy a superior position to anyone, which violates the norm of equal and trust-based relationships. Direct instruction is seen as insulting another's autonomy and is rarely observed, even between adults and teenagers (Omura 2016). It is assumed that teenagers will learn what they need to know as they mature. This is the reason that Inuit map-making practices developed as an extension of their custom of re-enacting past practices and experiences (Rundstorm 1990). Formerly, they drew maps not to teach or instruct other hunters in strategic knowledge, but to re-enact their traveling activities, from which other hunters could learn.

As they now have topographic maps, they can explain more easily how to reach a place by using a map when re-enacting travel. I often observed elders and hunters performing such re-enactments to indirectly show other hunters how to reach places unknown to them, or when discussing matters such as ice and snow conditions and the distribution and movement of wildlife. Inuit can share information about present conditions in nuna by telling each other what they saw and did in each place while pointing to the location on a map, without mentioning strategic knowledge. The topographic map provides them with a common, virtual stage. This may be why the word for map in Inuktitut is *nunanguaq*: an imitation of nuna.

For example, when I asked elders and hunters to plot place names on a map, they first identified the location of places familiar to them by reading the coast, rivers, and contour lines. Then, they plotted one place name after another along the route while following it with their finger or a pen as if they were traveling again. While doing so, they often narrated what they had done and seen in each place. It can be inferred that the topographic features of each place reminded them of past experiences there. This may be why elders enjoy reading maps by themselves. Setting the virtual stage for their recollections, topographic maps evoke memories.

I have never observed the Inuit using topographic maps for any other purpose. Although it is fairly common for them to discuss the conditions of nuna using a map before going hunting or leaving for neighboring villages, they never plot a route on a map or discuss plans and prospects, but only show each other what they saw and did in each place while tracing the route they had followed in the past. It is likely that they depart with a route in mind with information acquired through such discussion. However, they never explain or discuss it. They use topographic maps not for such strategic purposes as making plans and assessing prospects, but as a stage for re-enactment.

Therefore, topographic maps enable hunters to maintain their subsistence system more effectively while following their ideology even more faithfully than they could otherwise. Through the re-enactments on the map, hunters unfamiliar with certain parts of nuna can readily abstract strategic knowledge, while others can update strategic knowledge about, for example, wildlife distributions and migration patterns. Using maps, they can share, accumulate, and elaborate both strategic and tactical knowledge—that is to say, how they tactically utilize their strategic knowledge—so that they can increase their chances of engaging in a relationship with individual animals while keeping their trust-based relationships.

Moreover, topographic maps assume an important role as devices to make tacit, strategic knowledge readily conveyable and visible without directly mentioning it to non-Inuit, called *qaplunaat* (white people), who may live far from nuna and are unfamiliar with IQ or the reality of hunters' lives. It would be impossible for the Inuit to maintain their subsistence if conditions for its sustainability were unfulfilled as a result of external politico-economic aggression: for example, if they were deprived of their indigenous right to subsistence because of public opinion in dominant Canadian society; if they were banned from subsistence activities by the government; or if the environment became damaged by activities such as mining or commercial fishing to an extent that threatened the population, habitat, and health of wildlife. The Inuit understand these dangers and positively engage with actors such as regional and federal governments, transnational corporations, mass media, NGOs, and even the United Nations.

In such engagements, Inuit hunters are faced with a dilemma. They need to present their strategic knowledge as evidence for their claims about the sustainability of their subsistence because what has the power of persuasion as effective evidence in such negotiations is not the detailed description of each subsistence activity, but generalized patterns of the activities and the distribution and migration patterns of wildlife; however, if they explicitly use this strategic knowledge as evidence for their claims, they would be violating their own tactical ideology. It would follow that they were claiming to have the right to freely *take* food from wildlife through their intellectual ability without respecting wildlife's autonomous will. What they want to claim is the right to *receive* food from wildlife and to affirm both the relationship of trust between themselves and the dominant/subordinate relationship between the wildlife and the Inuit, thus maintaining nuna.

Topographic maps are thus effective devices as they convert the hunters' re-enactment of their tactics into strategic knowledge. Only by drawing the routes and places where they saw or acquired wildlife on the maps can hunters show their strategic knowledge without explicitly mentioning it. By overlapping all the lines and marks inscribed by all the hunters on the map, the hunters can display their generalized strategic knowledge and use it as evidence for their claims.

Negotiating with actors outside nuna also amplifies the Inuit tactical ideology because the Inuit become aware of contrasts between their own tactical way of generating IQ-nuna, and how actors outside nuna generate their world through their knowledge-generating and decision-making practices (Omura 2002, 2005, 2013). Inuit make full use of the contrast to construct a positive self-image for themselves. Indeed, the Inuit often emphasize the egalitarian and tactical aspects of *Inuinnaqtun* (Inuit way of life) when contrasting it with the hierarchical, strategic aspects of *qaplunaaqtun* (white men's way of life). While maintaining links with the outside world in order to safeguard their subsistence, they simultaneously bolster their positive identity not only through their endeavor to establish a positive Inuit governance system in the Nunavut Territorial Government based on equanimity and the tactical aspects of their way of life (cf. Omura forthcoming a; IQ Task Force 2002), but also by conducting their daily activities in the Inuit way (e.g., repairing a snowmobile without consulting a manual or traveling without GPS) (Omura 2002, 2005).

Therefore, the topographic map functions as a convenient and effective device for converting the hunters' re-enactments of their tactics into strategic knowledge and thereby disseminates knowledge among the Inuit and conveys it to actors outside nuna, without breaking trust-based relationships among the Inuit by releasing them from the need to explicitly mention their strategies. The maps thereby contribute to maintaining and even stabilizing their nuna, enabling the Inuit to elaborate inward and extend outward their relationships with others, including humans and non-humans, by faithfully following the tactical ideology. First, these maps allow for the sharing of strategic knowledge among hunters without explicitly mentioning it. This allows the hunters to constantly engage in the relationship of "recipients/ suppliers of food and command" with individual wild animals without breaking trust-based relationships among themselves. The maps also serve as aids for Inuit hunters when presenting evidence for their claims to sustain their subsistence without explicitly mentioning strategies, which in turn amplifies their tactical ideology.

Maps in action: Quotidian politics through boundary translational matrix for world multiple

By considering this role of topographic maps in Inuit IQ-nuna-generating practices in relation to one in the world-generating practices of actors outside nuna, especially scientists and bureaucrats, which has been elucidated by Latour (1987, 1999) and Nadasdy (2003), it can be shown that topographic map is a tool indispensable for negotiation between these two world-generating practices, where these practices encounter, attune to, and maintain the balance of power with each other, while divergently regenerating their respective worlds.

For the actors outside nuna, the topographic map also functions as an effective device for world-generating practices because of its ability to convert tactics into strategy, which enables them to gather, distill, and exploit IQ for the strategic purposes of managing and controlling both the Inuit and wildlife (Nadasdy 2003). It is no exaggeration to say that, as Latour (1987, 1999) showed with technoscientific practices, as a typically modern way of knowing and generating worlds, topographic maps are indispensable for the strategic practices of actors outside nuna, in which the data inscribed on materials such as maps and charts are transported to the center for calculation in order to generate, manage, and control the world. The maps are also indispensable when asking the Inuit to stand by negotiated agreements; without the maps, it would not be possible to identify which areas are closed or open to Inuit subsistence activities. In this sense, topographic maps also function as devices to sustain the modern way of knowing and generating worlds while extending the worlds outward and incorporating outside worlds under their management and control.

Therefore, the topographic map can be considered a boundary translational matrix for entangled worlds, which converts the Inuit hunters' tactical practice re-enactments into strategic knowledge, and thereby regenerates both the Inuit nuna and the outside world, but also loosely assembles them as a world multiple. The topographic map corresponds to a "boundary object" (Star and Griesemer 1989; Star 2010) that enables people from different worlds to collaborate without consensus. However, it is not merely an object to be flexibly interpreted in different worlds, but also a matrix through which the Inuit and actors outside nuna can disjunctively develop their respective worlds while attuning to and maintaining partial connections with each other.

In this process, the Inuit intentionally occupy an inferior position both in their relationship to wildlife and in their relationship with actors outside nuna so as to autonomously maintain equal and trust-based relationships among themselves. They use maps so as not to be swallowed by outside worlds and to maintain the autonomy of nuna while simultaneously maintaining partial connections outside. The process of attunement with the use of maps thus could be seen as a political process, in which the balance of power between the Inuit endeavor to maintain and protect the autonomy of nuna and the ambition of actors in the outside worlds to incorporate nuna under their management and control is maintained through translational negotiation.

Topographic maps continue to serve as effective political tools to generate and extend complicated networks composed of technoscience, the nation-state, and the capital economy to colonize the world (cf. Latour 1987, 1999; Nadasdy 2003). In this sense, the topographic map is a product of the modern world that was originally developed to conquer other worlds. However, as in the case of the Inuit map-using practices, topographic maps can be utilized as political devices to maintain and protect the Inuit lifeworld and autonomy against the pressures of exploitation, management, and control by outside networks while maintaining a link with them. The Inuit tactically use these objects from the outside world by converting the tool for strategy into a tactical tool for their own purposes in everyday life.

This political process occurs in quotidian routines of translation between tactics and strategy, which are indispensable for political negotiations between the Inuit and actors outside nuna, prior to the moment when the Inuit nuna and their outside worlds diverge from the entanglement of two types of map-using—tactical and strategic. Only after the political process develops in this quotidian routine can nuna and the outside worlds diverge. Likewise, these worlds could not continue to exist divergently while maintaining partial connections without ceaseless political negotiations between the people who will diverge into the Inuit and the actors outside nuna only after the worlds diverge through the negotiations.

In this sense, the politics in quotidian routines of translation is not between different pre-existing worlds. Rather, it is the politics for diverging worlds from an entanglement of different types of practice, in which scales such as local/global, micro/macro, provincial/universal, or indigenous/modern are not yet differentiated. It is this quotidian politics through translation that generates scales from entanglements of different types of practice, with the topographic map as a virtual, hetero-scale matrix. Thus, the quotidian politics through translation is a primordial politics, through which worlds are divergently generated, attuned to each other, and loosely assembled as a world multiple.

References

Bodenhorn, Barbara. 1989. "The Animals Come to Me, They Know I Share: Inuipiaq Kinship, Changing Economic Relations and Enduring World Views on Alaska's North Slope." PhD dissertation, Cambridge University.

Briggs, L. Jean. 1968. *Utkuhikhalingmiut Eskimo Emotional Expression*. Ottawa: Department of Indian Affairs and Northern Development, Northern Science Research Group.

—. 1970. *Never in Anger: Portrait of an Eskimo Family*. Cambridge, MA: Harvard University Press.

—. 1991. "Expecting the Unexpected: Canadian Inuit Training for an Experimental Lifestyle." *Ethos* 19 (3): 259–287.

de Certeau, Michel. 1984. *The Practice of Everyday Life*. Translated by S. F. Rendall. Berkeley, CA: University of California Press.

Correll, Thomas. 1976. "Language and Location in Traditional Inuit Societies." In *Report: Inuit Land Use and Occupancy Project* Vol. 2, edited by M. M. R. Freeman, 173–186. Ottawa: Department of Indian and Northern Affairs.

Fienup-Riordan, Ann. 1983. *The Nelson Island Eskimo: Social Structure and Ritual Distribution*. Anchorage: Alaska Pacific University Press.

—. 1990. *Eskimo Essays: Yup'ik Lives and How We See Them*. New Brunswick, NJ: Rutgers University Press.

Freeman, M. R. Milton, ed. 1976. *Report: Inuit Land Use and Occupancy Project*. Ottawa: Department of Indian and Northern Affairs.

Freeman, M. R. Milton. 1985. "Appeal to Tradition: Different Perspectives on Arctic Wildlife Management." In *Native Power: The Quest for Autonomy and Nationhood of Indigenous Peoples*, edited by Jens Brøsted, Jens Dahl, Andrew Gray, Hans Christian Gulløv, Georg Henriksen, Jørgen Brøchner Jørgensen, and Inge Kleivan, 265–281. Bergen, Oslo, Stavanger, Tromso: Universitetsforlaget as.

—. 1993. "Traditional Land Users as a Legitimate Source of Environmental Expertise." In *Traditional Ecological Knowledge: Wisdom for Sustainable Development*, edited by Nancy Williams and Graham Baines, 153–161. Canberra: Center for Resource and Environmental Studies, Australian National University.

Freeman, M.R.Milton and Ludwig N. Carbyn, eds. 1988. *Traditional Knowledge and Renewable Resource Management in Northern Regions*. Edmonton: Boreal Institute for Northern Studies, University of Alberta.

IQ Task Force. 2002. *The First Annual Report of the Inuit Qaujimajatuqangit (IQ) Task Force*. Iqaluit: Government of Nunavut, Department of Culture, Language, Elders and Youth.

Kishigami, Nobuhiro. 1995. "Extended Family and Food Sharing Practices among the Contemporary Netsilik Inuit: A Case Study of Pelly Bay." *Bulletin of Hokkaido University of Education 1B*, 45 (2): 1–9

—. 2007. *Kanada Inuitto no shoku-bunka to shakai Henka (Food Culture of the Canadian Inuit and Social Change)*. Kyoto: Sekaishisōsha

Latour, Bruno. 1987. *Science in Action: How to Follow Scientists and Engineers through Society*. Cambridge, MA: Harvard University Press.

—. 1999 *Pandora's Hope: Essays on the Reality of Science Studies*. Cambridge, MA: Harvard University Press.

Morrow, Phyllis. 1990. "Symbolic Actions, Indirect Expressions: Limits to Interpretations of Yupik Society." *Etudes/Inuit/Studies* 14 (1/2): 141–158.

Nadasdy, Paul. 2003. *Hunters and Bureaucrats: Power, Knowledge, and Aboriginal–State Relations in the Southwest Yukon*. Vancouver and Toronto: UBC Press.

Nakashima, Douglas. 1991. "The Ecological Knowledge of Belcher Island Inuit: A Traditional Basis for Contemporary Wildlife Co-Management." PhD dissertation, McGill University.

Nuttall, Mark. 1992. *Arctic Homeland: Kinship, Community and Development in Northwest Greenland*. Toronto: University of Toronto Press.

Omura, Keiichi. 2002. "Construction of Inuinnaqtun (Real Inuit-Way): Self-image and Everyday Practices in Inuit Society." In *Self and Other Images of Hunter-Gatherers*, edited by H. Stewart, A. Barnard, and K. Omura, 101–111. Osaka: National Museum of Ethnology.

—. 2005. "Science against Modern Science." In *Indigenous Use and Management of Marine Resources*, edited by N. Kishigami and J. Savelle, 323–344. Osaka: National Museum of Ethnology.

—. 2007. "From Knowledge to Poetics: The Sophia of Anti-essentialistic Essentialism in Inuit Traditional Environmental Knowledge." *Japanese Review of Cultural Anthropology* 7: 27–50.

—. 2012. "The Ontology of Sociality: 'Sharing' and Subsistence Mechanisms." In *Groups: Evolution of Human Societies*, edited by K. Kawai, 123–142. Kyoto and Melbourne: Kyoto University Press and Trans Pacific Press.

—. 2013. *Kanada inuito no minzokushi: Nichijōteki jissen no dainamikusu* (*Ethnography of Canadian Inuit: Dynamics of Everyday Practices*). Osaka: Osaka University Press.

—. 2016. "Socio-Cultural Cultivation of Positive Attitude toward Learning: Considering Difference in Learning Ability between Neanderthals and Modern Humans from Examining the Learning Process of Inuit Children." In *Social Learning and Innovation in Contemporary Hunter-Gatherers: Evolutionary and Ethnographic Perspectives*, edited by Hideaki Terashima and Barry S. Hewlett, 267–284, Tokyo: Springer.

—. forthcoming a. "A Step to Multiple Worlds: Considering the Potentialities of Indigeneity through an Analysis of the IQ Issues in Nunavut Territory, Canada." In *Challenges to Indigeneity: History, Polity and Recognition*, edited by Sachiko Kubota and Nicolas Peterson. Canberra: Australia National University Press.

—. forthcoming b. "Conditions for Well-being: Sustainability of Inuit Subsistence System in Contemporary Globalized World." In *Wisdom Engaged: Traditional Knowledge for Northern Community Well-Being*, edited by Leslie M. Johnson. Edmonton: University of Alberta Press.

Rundstorm, A. Robert. 1990. "A Cultural Interpretation of Inuit Map Accuracy." *Geographical Review* 80 (2): 155–168.

Spink, John and D. W. Moodie 1972. *Eskimo Maps: From the Canadian Eastern Arctic*. Cartographica Monograph 5. Toronto: University of Toronto Press.

Stairs, A. and G. Wenzel. 1992. "'I am I and the Environment': Inuit Hunting, Community, and Identity." *Journal of Indigenous Studies* 3 (1): 1–2.

Star, Susan Leigh. 2010. "This is Not a Boundary Object: Reflections on the Origin of a Concept." *Science, Technology, & Human Values* 35 (5): 601–617.

Star, Susan Leigh and James R. Griesemer. 1989. "Institutional Ecology, 'Translations,' and Boundary Objects: Amateurs and Professionals on Berkeley's Museum of Vertebrate Zoology." *Social Studies of Science* 19: 387–420.

Stevenson, Marc. 1996. "Indigenous Knowledge in Environmental Assessment." *Arctic* 49 (3): 278–291.

Stewart, Henry. 1995. "*Gendai no netsiriku inuitto shakai ni okeru seigyōkatsudō*" ("Subsistence Activities in Modern-Day Netsilik Inuit Society.") *People and Cultures of the Tundra—Proceedings of the 9th International Abashiri Symposium*, 36–67. Abashiri: Hokkaido Museum of Northern Peoples.

Wenzel, George. 1991. *Animal Rights, Human Rights: Ecology, Economy and Ideology in the Canadian Arctic*. Toronto: University of Toronto Press.

Chapter 6

Climate change and local knowledge in Eastern Arctic Inuit society

Perceptions, responses, and practice

Shunwa Honda (Henry Stewart)

Introduction

During the past decade alone, innumerable results of research concerning scientists' and Inuit perceptions of and commentary regarding climate change have been published. However, there is much disparity among perceptions of climate change, both between and within the two parties. There is conspicuous divergence in perceptions of and commentary regarding climate change between Nunavut (Canada) and Greenland, between north and west Greenland, and between local Inuit and Inuit activists. Although there is general agreement, particularly within the scientific community, that the contemporary climate is warming at a rapid rate, particularly in the Arctic regions, a significant contrast of assessment may be noted concerning the severity and extent of climate change.

This contrast is not derived from any one factor, but from several intertwined factors, including global perspective of scientific research in contrast to specific or local orientation of knowledge. Opposing political and economic agendas also contribute to contrasting assessments. In this chapter, I discuss these divergences and discrepancies among the various parties, both from the perspective of local knowledge/scientific knowledge, as well as from a sociocultural perspective.

An examination of divergences and discrepancies evinces the existence of more than just a contradistinction of "one-world" to "multiple worlds." I argue that the assumption of an Inuit one-world is in fact constituted of a melange of multiple Inuit worlds. The multiplicity of the Inuit world is clearly represented in the dichotomous perceptions of climate change between north and west as well as urban/non-urban Greenland. How local knowledge is mobilized in Nunavut also clearly shows a world different from that of Greenland.

I show that the dimensions and importance of local knowledge are very different for Greenland, especially west Greenland and Nunavut. In the context of perception and response to climate change, I discuss the status and political ramifications of local knowledge in Greenland and Nunavut with reference to "multiple worlds."

The problem

Contemporary and ongoing climate change and its ramifications have received much scientific attention over the past few decades. In particular, it has been shown that the Arctic is especially vulnerable to even minor climate change (e. g., IPCC 2007; Ulmer 2015). However, there are conflicting arguments concerning the severity, duration, and cultural/economic ramifications of this trend (e.g., Stern et al. 2016). Climate change is known for the entirety of human occupation in the Arctic, and the Inuit have coped with and adapted to an ever-changing environment.

In research concerning the effects of recent climate change on the culture and society of the Inuit (e.g., Crate and Nuttall 2009; Ford et al. 2012), perceptions of climate change between scientists and the Inuit evince not only a disagreement between these two parties, but also internal disagreement. Scientific discourse emphasizes the severity of climate change in the Arctic (e.g., Overland et al. 2014), a position reiterated in the discourse of Inuit activists and representative organizations (Hand 2015; ICC 2015). The dispute over natural climate change versus anthropogenic causation continues (e.g., Carleton and Hsiang 2016; Matthews et al. 2004; Stern 2016), but the consensus is that climate change before the twentieth century was primarily due to natural causes, while change since the mid-twentieth century has been compounded by anthropogenic factors that magnify and increase the speed of change (Hegerl and Stott 2014; IPCC 2007).

Terminology

Eastern Arctic

In this chapter, Eastern Arctic refers to Nunavut and Greenland (*Kalaallit Nunaata*), with only passing reference to Nunavik (Quebec) and Nunatsiavut (Labrador).

Sociocultural regions of Greenland

The ice sheet that covers 82 percent of the Greenland land mass spreads extensively to the ocean, leaving only isolated areas along the coastline suitable for human occupation. Historically, the ice sheet obstructed communication and interaction among these areas, resulting in three sociocultural regions: north Greenland (*Avanaa*: Siorapaluk to Sisimiut); west Greenland (*Kitaa*: Baffin Bay/Davis Strait coast); and east Greenland (*Tunu*: Atlantic coast).

Extending 2,650 km from north to south, environmental conditions differ significantly among these three areas, with north Greenland dominated by high Arctic climatic conditions, west Greenland characterized by milder (mid-) Arctic to low Arctic conditions, and east Greenland ranging from high to mid-Arctic conditions.

Environmental factors and differing historical trajectories attributable to geographical isolation have resulted in pronounced cultural, linguistic, and subsistence activity differences among the three regions. In each region, those differences are manifested in diverse economic activities and subtle ethnic variations. These factors are reflected in an almost diametrically opposed reaction to climate change, a variance not conspicuous in Nunavut.

Kalaallit/Greenlander/Inuit

Born-in-Greenland residents are administratively designated as *Kalaallit* (Greenlanders in English). Greenland's official designation is *Kalaallit Nunaat* (Land of the Kalaallit). The national language, Kalaallisut, deriving from the term Kalaallit, carries with it the implication of being a west Greenland dialect. From a historical point of view, both Kalaallit and Kalaallisut (Greenlandic) imply a particular association with south (west) Greenland (Kleivan 1984, 620; Langgård 2010, 177). Following the common usage in scientific and popular literature, I use the term "Inuit" in reference to all indigenous residents of the Eastern Arctic.

Local knowledge

I use local knowledge, traditional knowledge, indigenous knowledge, and traditional ecological knowledge with slightly different nuances. Local knowledge is an umbrella term that covers traditional knowledge, indigenous knowledge, traditional ecological knowledge, and in Nunavut, Inuit *Qaujimajatuqangit* (IQ), a concept that corresponds generally to traditional knowledge or traditional ecological knowledge (Omura 2005b; Pearce et al. 2015, 235; Wenzel 2004). Local knowledge is passed down through generations in a circumscribed area. It may be indigenous knowledge, or that of street children of India, homeless of New York, or water management of terraced rice fields in Oita Prefecture, Japan.

Regardless of which term is used, it must be borne in mind that local knowledge is formed on the basis of a restricted geographical area, focused on particulars rather than generalizations (Dowsley and Wenzel 2008, 182–3). This point is particularly important, as climate conditions vary greatly over the Eastern Arctic, an area covering millions of square kilometers.

Traditional ecological knowledge, traditional knowledge, IQ, and other forms of local knowledge are extremely local in character, and consequently difficult to integrate into extensive interregional scientific observations. Several researchers (e.g., Knopp 2010; Mistry and Berardi 2016) have proposed integration, but such examples are local in nature, such as including local knowledge into scientific observation of local bioenvironmental conditions.

Climate in science

The conventional definition of climate is a time-mean state, an average of a set of properties over a specified interval of time for a given area. Usually the theoretical limits of weather prediction, a few weeks, distinguishes weather from climate, which refers to relatively long-term meteorological conditions over an extensive area (Barron and Moore 1994, 2).

Climate change refers to any change in climate over time, whether due to natural variability or human activity. In scientific terminology, climate is an objective, statistical phenomenon suitable for modelling (Mistry and Berardi 2016, 1275). Local knowledge is literally local and long-term observation, and thus may not be amenable to scientific climate modelling based on relatively short time observations indicating change over large geographical areas (Dowsley and Wenzel 2008, 183).

It must be noted that climate change is not synonymous with "climate warming." Climate warming is often sensationalized as an unprecedented meteorological phenomenon, where media in particular tend to overdramatize events such as melting of the ice sheet, exceptionally hot summers, torrential rains, frequently occurring typhoons or hurricanes (Fernández-Llamazares et al. 2015, 11). Such sensationalism lacks historical perspective, as evidenced in geologically recorded climate change such as glacial/interglacial periods and other environmental transitions.

The context of climate change has a pronounced influence on the perception of all forms of knowledge, not excepting scientific knowledge, where nature and culture/society are markedly distinguished (Mistry and Berardi 2016, 1274–5; Sowa 2013, 75). Anthropological analysis of knowledge theories attempts to remove the boundary between "traditional knowledge" and "scientific knowledge," but much that has been written concerning climate change in the Arctic —be it inadvertently or not—reinforces this boundary (Johnson 2009, 7).

Climate/weather (sila) in Inuit society

Weather and climate, subsumed under the term *sila*, are not differentiated in the Inuit languages (Riedlinger and Berkes 2001, 317). The meaning of sila runs deeper than in scientific discourse because it is also understood as the breath of life, the reason for seasonal and other changes, and the fundamental principle underlying the natural world and its comprehensive "mind" (Hastrup 2012, 227). It is an all-pervading, life-giving force connecting a person with the rhythms of the universe, and integrating the self with the natural world, including "wisdom" or "the forces which push or pull a person through life" (Johnson 2009, 6; Leduc 2007, 2010, 19–48; Nuttall 2009, 299).

Climate in migration and cultural change of the Eastern Arctic

As a background to understanding regional environmental, economic, and political circumstances in the Eastern Arctic, I briefly discuss the cultural history with reference to climate change. That discussion in turn relates to differing subsistence patterns and cultural diversification, and the importance of local knowledge, specifically traditional ecological knowledge/indigenous knowledge. This forms the basis for a critical comparison of reaction to and accommodation of climate change between the Inuit within Greenland and within Nunavut. Through this comparison, I demonstrate the contrast in perception and application of local knowledge between north/west Greenland Inuit and the Inuit of Nunavut.

The Eastern Arctic covers a vast area, and the history of human occupation extends over more than 4500 years. Therefore there is a broad range of regional variation resulting in local cultural distinctiveness. The cultural history of the Eastern Arctic may be divided into the Palaeo-Eskimo[1] and Neo-Eskimo or Inuit periods, both periods being subdivided into regional groups.

Palaeo-Eskimo

The Palaeo-Eskimo group is the result of one, possibly two population migrations. The Palaeo-Eskimo sequence, in chronological order, is Independence/Pre-

Table 6.1 Cultural chronology of Eastern Arctic cultures

	Greenland	Nunavut
Palaeo-Eskimo		
Independence I	4500–3800 years BP*(2500–1800 BC)	
Saqqaq	4500–2800 years BP(2500–1800 BC)	
Pre-Dorset		3800–2800 years BP(2400–1600 BC)
Early Dorset	2800–2000 years BP(800–0 BC)	2800–2000 years BP(800–0 BC)
Mid-Dorset	Greenland completely depopulated (2000–1300 years BP(0–700 AD))	2000–1500 years BP(0–500 AD
Late Dorset	1300–700 years BP(700–1300 AD)	1500–800 years BP(500–1200 AD)
Neo-Eskimo (Inuit)		
Thule Inuit	800 years BP–present(1200 AD–present)	800 years BP–present(1200 AD–present)
European immigrants		
Norse (Viking)	1000–1450 AD	
Europeans and entrepreneurs	1721–presentColonial rule by Denmark	Seventeenth century–present Fur traders, colonial rule

* years BP (years Before Present): 1950 set as radiocarbon (^{14}C) dating commencement date. Subtracting 2000 years gives approximate BC/AD dates.

Dorset/Saqqaq and Dorset. Whether the last phase of the Palaeo-Eskimo, the Dorset culture, was a culture that developed *in situ* out of the Pre-Dorset or was a separate migration has been the focus of much debate. Past research postulated *in situ* development of Palaeo-Eskimo cultures by a single migration from the west (Maxwell 1976). New material culture traits distinctive to the Dorset (Savelle and Dyke 2014, 268–70) and differing patterns of distribution (Milne et al. 2012) suggest an abrupt population replacement by a second migration into the Eastern Arctic during the Dorset era, concurrent with climate change (Ryan 2016, 769).

Neo-Eskimo (Thule Inuit)

The Neo-Eskimo or Thule Inuit population, which originated about 1000 years BP in the Bering Strait area dispersed to the Eastern Arctic at about 800 years BP during the Medieval Climatic Optimum (1100–700 years BP) (e.g. Gronnow 2009; Savelle and McCartney 1990), is the genetic and cultural ancestor to the Inuit (e.g., Rubicz and Crawford 2016, 36).

In past research, the Thule Inuit migration was attributed primarily to the availability of whales moving into the Arctic Ocean, which was free of summer ice during the Medieval Climatic Optimum (McGhee 1969/70). The availability of whales in the Arctic Ocean was one incentive to migrate, but other factors such as social conflict, warfare and population pressure in the Bering Strait region, and the attraction of new resources to the east were important factors (Friesen 2016, 682–3).

There is no conclusive evidence to judge arguments supporting (LeMoine and Darwent 2010, 293; Helgason et al. 2006) and opposing (Gilbert et al. 2008, 1789; Moltke et al. 2015, 65) the occurrence of Palaeo-Eskimo Dorset and Thule Inuit interaction.

Norse

In addition to the above Inuit movements, during the Medieval Climatic Optimum the Norse (Vikings) colonized southern Greenland during the late tenth to mid-fifteenth centuries and Newfoundland, Canada in the eleventh century (Wallace 2003). They brought sheep, goats, cattle, horses, pigs, and dogs to begin a pastoral society that flourished until the onset of the Little Ice Age (ca 650—150 years BP) (Dugmore et al. 2007).

During the Norse colonial period, it appears that the Inuit population of south Greenland had migrated to the north because deteriorating (warming) climate conditions were not suited to sea-ice seal hunting and other Inuit subsistence practices. Thus, south Greenland appears to have been vacant when the Norse arrived in the late tenth century.

Norse interaction with either the Dorset or the Thule Inuit was limited (Golding et al. 2011; Gullov 2008), and there is no evidence that genetic mixture occurred (Moltke et al. 2015, 55, 66).

Factors contributing to the demise of the Norse colonies in the sixteenth century include termination of trade with Europe and resource competition with the Inuit, but climate cooling was also a contributing factor (Arneborg 2015).

As the climate cooled, when whales could not enter the Arctic Ocean because of summer sea ice, Thule culture disintegrated into dispersed mobile seal- and caribou-hunting Inuit groups as recorded in early ethnographies (McGhee 1996).

The history of human occupation and cultural diversification of the Arctic is often presented in correlation to cycles of climatic warming and cooling, and sometimes portrayed as having a one-on-one cause-and-effect relationship to culture change (e.g. McGhee 1969/70). Although climate change does in fact influence culture change and migration (deMenocal and Stringer 2016; Timmermann and Friedrich 2016), such a simplistic correlation obscures multiple agents, or obfuscates reality.

It must also be noted that succession and replacement of cultural traditions in the Eastern Arctic did not progress uniformly. Areas manifest regional accommodation to environmental conditions, including but not limited to climate change. Cultural diversification and development may also occur under similar environmental conditions, as is clearly evidenced in the Bering Strait region (Giddings 1967). Many areas of the Eastern Arctic experienced temporary depopulation or total abandonment, even for periods of several centuries. The whole island of Greenland was entirely uninhabited between 2000 and 1250 years BP (Darwent and Foin 2010, 317), and north Greenland and other areas of the high Arctic saw several periods of depopulation and resettlement (Friesen 2016, 673; Park 2000, 200; Ryan 2016, 769). This phenomenon may not be attributed to climate variation alone, as virtually the same culture thrived under similar ecological conditions in other areas (Gronnow and Sorensen 2006, 65–7).

Now let us see how local climatic variation relates to perception and accommodation to environmental change.

Perceptions of climate change in local knowledge

Many Arctic indigenous peoples realize that climate variation is the norm. Local knowledge indicates that climatic and other environmental conditions are always in a state of flux (Bjorst 2012, 109; Buijs 2010, 41; Berkes and Jolly 2001, 1–2; Hayashi 2013, 286; Ingold 1999, 70; Johnson 2009, 14; Omura 2005a, 79; Willerslev 2012, 2).

Inuit evaluation intimates that climate change may not be as catastrophic as media reports suggest. I do not deny that changes in sea-ice conditions and variation of quarry distribution have made it difficult for the Inuit to pursue traditional subsistence activities (e.g. Berkes and Jolly 2001; Huntington and Fox 2005). Serious and continuing erosion of shorelines in northwest Alaska, and late formation and early spring melting of sea ice, are but a few of the detrimental changes in the Arctic over the past few decades (ACIA 2005; Fast and Berkes 1999; Kishigami 2010, 93).

There are many testimonies to suffering and loss resulting from "unprecedented climate," but such testimonies must be judged from a historical and social perspective, a perspective conspicuously absent in most popular media, as well as some scientific "climate change" discourse (Fernández-Llamazares et al. 2015, 2). The bulk of media focuses upon the negative aspects of climate change on north Greenland Inuit and Nunavut, sometimes bordering on sensationalism (Mason 2016). Inuit representative groups such as the Inuit Circumpolar Council take advantage of this coverage to pursue a discourse of a culture and way of life in danger of extinction.

The Inuit Circumpolar Council and other indigenous agencies contend that hunting skills and knowledge (local knowledge = traditional ecological knowledge, indigenous knowledge) will not be transmitted to the young generation because of the limitation imposed upon hunting by climate warming. Sheila Watt-Cloutier, past Chair of the Council, stated that the very survival of the Inuit is at stake. The Council filed a petition to the Inter-American Commission on Human Rights, in which climate change due to unchecked emissions of greenhouse gases from the United States is in violation of the right to life and physical security, personal property, health, practice of culture, and traditional land use (Aminzadeh 2007; Hand 2015; Osofsky 2007; Watt-Cloutier 2005).

Conversely, over the centuries, the Inuit have experienced and survived repeated climate change. As previously noted, the Arctic has experienced climate change throughout its history of human occupation. Stated otherwise, the Inuit have experienced repeated, and at times, climate change even more drastic than that occurring now.

The effects of past climate change in the Arctic could be ameliorated by migration to more favourable environments (D'Andrea et al. 2011), but following sedentarization policies and population growth the option of migration is no longer viable. The Inuit today are sedentary, living a Euro-American lifestyle, and do not wish to return the seasonal camp life of a century ago. As migration to more favourable areas is no longer an option, coping with contemporary climate change necessitates a drastic change of livelihood and/or removal to completely different habitat.

Perceptions of climate change

There are contrasting perceptions of climate change among the Inuit of different regions, as evidenced in the differing reactions between west Greenland, where climate change (warming) is welcomed with some reservation, and north Greenland/Nunavut, where climate change (warming) poses a threat to subsistence activities (Ford et al. 2012, 817).

What cultural, social, and economic factors underlie the divergent perceptions and interpretation concerning climate change apparent between north and west Greenland, and between Greenland and Nunavut? Also, how does this divergence reflect on local knowledge?

One apparent factor is the difference in the importance of "traditional" subsistence activities between the two regions. In north Greenland and Nunavut, subsistence activities rooted in traditional practices are still important, both economically and culturally. Economically, tradition-based subsistence activities are a means of food procurement and a source of monetary income (sale of game meat, animal fur, etc.). Culturally, subsistence activities serve as an ethnic symbol in politically and economically marginalized north Greenland and Nunavut (Honda 2017).

Conversely, the Government of Greenland, seated in west Greenland, welcomes climate change, albeit with some reservation (Nuttall 2008a, 2010, 29). Climate change resulting in ice sheet retreat and less sea ice benefits efforts towards economic independence from Denmark and domestic food self-sufficiency. Warmer climatic conditions enhance sheep farming, vegetable production in west Greenland, and the fishing industry (fish and fish products constitute 88 percent of Greenland's exports in 2013; Naalakkersuisut n.d.), as well as facilitating extraction and export of natural resources such as petroleum and rare minerals (Nuttall 2016; Poppel et al. 2017). These economic opportunities may eventually form an economic base allowing Greenland economic independence (Nuttall 2012).

Half of Greenland's public spending is funded by block grants from Denmark of 3.5 billion DKK (496 million USD) (University of Greenland 2014, 47). Increased revenue from resource development could enhance Greenland's economic independence, which would allow demands for greater autonomy, possibly even nationhood (Nuttall 2008b; 2016).

Mineral and petroleum deposits in and around Greenland (Mortensen 2013) have been known for decades, but glaciers and sea ice have made it difficult to extract and ship these resources to consumer centres. Recent changes in sea ice conditions and glacier retreat facilitate development and promise to open sea-lanes (Marchenko 2014).

The discussion of climate change in west Greenland may be summarized as follows. First of all, north Greenland and Nunavut are negatively affected, and thus have become a victim icon in the international media. Conversely, in west Greenland, where more than 80 percent of the population are concentrated, there are expectations of economic development and nation-building stemming from climate change (warming) (Nuttall 2010, 29; 2012, 113–22).

Another point is that traditional ecological knowledge/indigenous knowledge has less importance in the livelihood of the Inuit of west Greenland. Here, local knowledge concerning modern agriculture and offshore fishing, global markets, and economic fluctuations is of foremost importance. This form of local knowledge has accumulated for the most part since the Danish

Government's modernization policies began in the 1950s and 1960s (Sejersen 2007, 27) continuing to the present (Sejersen 2015).

These points stand in conspicuous contrast to the situation of north Greenland and the Eastern Canadian Inuit of Nunavut, where there is no possibility of agriculture, and extraction of comparatively small mineral/petroleum deposits is hindered by sea ice. There is little promise of economic development, thus climate change is considered a threat to still important subsistence activities.

Climate, politics, local knowledge

This conflict of interest puts the Greenland Government in a double bind. On one hand, the Government must be sympathetic to the plight of the north Greenland Inuit, who, although they contribute little to the national economy and comprise a very small percentage of the population, are the symbol of the "real Greenland, land of hunters" (Graugaard 2009, 27–8). This stance is in contradiction to development of mineral and petroleum resources that contribute to carbon dioxide emissions.

On the other hand, resource development, while contributing to greenhouse gases, could become the backbone of the national economy and contribute greatly to economic prosperity and efforts towards increased autonomy. This would run against the sentiments of the north Greenland Inuit and the Inuit Circumpolar Council, thus the Government must take a political stand against climate warming while simultaneously taking advantage of the warming trend to bolster the economy.

Another contrast between west Greenland and Nunavut is the importance attached to traditional ecological knowledge and indigenous knowledge. Traditional ecological knowledge and indigenous knowledges that have no, or very little, importance in west Greenland conversely are an integral part of Nunavut society and politics, a point noted also by Hayashi (2014, 154–7). Table 6.2 lists factors influencing the differentiation in attitudes toward traditional ecological knowledge and indigenous knowledge in these two areas.

I have argued that colonialization in the Eastern Arctic may be analysed into two forms, the harshly rigorous Anglo-Saxon form and the more *laissez-faire* Nordic form (Stewart 2005, 214–217; Stewart and Xie 2008, 103–104). This contrast in forms of colonial domination has left its imprint on the status and political importance of local knowledge.

Early colonial policy in Greenland was to have the Inuit retain traditional lifestyles in order to avoid dependence on the colonial regime (Gad 1973, 264; 1984, 260; Stewart 2016, 53). Formal education in local schools was begun soon after the beginning of colonization in the eighteenth century, with the text books printed in Greenlandic (Kalaallisut) (Kjærgaard 2015, 117–8).

Greenland achieved Home Rule in 1979 and Self-Government in 2007, enjoying a high degree of autonomy including limited international diplomacy (Ackren and Jakobsen 2015; Takahashi 2013).

Table 6.2 Comparison of the political, social, and economic situation of west Greenland and Nunavut (Honda 2014, 176)

	West Greenland	Nunavut
Colonial regime (historical)	Paternalistic, *laissez-faire*	Harsh, arbitrary
Geographical relation to colonial ruling state	Geographically separate: relatively little intervention	Contiguous: constant necessity for negotiation with Government
Political status	Strong ethnic self-government with theoretical possibility of independence	Territorial status, little possibility of increased autonomy
Relations with other Indigenes	Greenland Inuit sole Indigenes	Contiguous borders with numerable other Indigenes
Importance of TEK	Little importance to modern industry	Essential to ethnic identity and cohesion, land claims, a political lever
Economic development potential	Large reserves of mineral and petroleum	Little mineral or petroleum reserves
Physical environment	Less sea ice and climate warming conducive to economic development	Early spring ice melt, late ice formation detrimental to subsistence activities

In contrast to the relatively paternalistic colonial domination of Greenland by Denmark (Denmark Ministry of Foreign Affairs 2010; Jensen 2008), under the harsher regime of Canada Inuit were sent to boarding schools far from home (Fournier and Crey 1997) and educated in English. It was not until the late twentieth century that it became possible to have some education in Inuktitut, the language of the Eastern Arctic Inuit. Nunavut was recognized as a territory by the Canadian Government in 1999, but it is a public government with much less autonomy than the Greenland Self-Government. Territories in Canada exercise only delegated powers under the authority of the Parliament of Canada (Loukacheva 2007, 109).

In north Greenland, "traditional" subsistence activities retain cultural importance, as evidenced in many of the articles referenced here. However, there is a striking difference between north Greenland and Nunavut concerning the manipulation of traditional knowledge.

Against this political and social background, traditional ecological knowledge and indigenous knowledge, specifically Inuit IQ, is not only a medium through which traditional knowledge is transmitted from generation to generation, but is also a proclamation of Inuit societal values that serves as a forceful message of distinctive Inuit ethnicity. In the overwhelmingly Euro-Canadian society, IQ functions as political tool to emphasize the social values of Inuit society in negotiations with the Federal Government and neighboring indigenous groups (Honda 2014).

The political and social distance between Greenland and Denmark is not only administrative, but also geographical. There is 3,500 kilometers of ocean between the two. In contrast, Nunavut is geographically part of Canada and contiguous with many other indigenous populations, as well as majority society. This contiguity necessitates repeated negotiation, where distinctive ethnicity serves to form a background to Inuit "otherness." Inuit ethnicity and a philosophy of existence as codified in IQ is an effective instrument at the negotiation table.

Conclusions

I have discussed perceptions, responses, and utilization of Inuit local knowledge as it pertains to climate change, with an emphasis on inconformity between scientific and local discourse. A difference in local perceptions was noted on a regional level, both between north/west Greenland and Greenland/Nunavut. Behind this regional inconformity are social, economic, and political differences. West Greenland accepts and embraces climate change as an economic boon, while north Greenland and Nunavut perceive climate change as a threat to traditional lifestyle subsistence activities.

Media and Inuit representative organizations tend to see climate change as an unprecedented disaster. In contrast, many local Inuit state that the climate is changing, but that change is the norm, as climate is always changing. Also, locals do not always feel that change is significantly more drastic than in the past.

I repeat here that there are situations where climate change is an unquestionable threat to subsistence and lifestyle, even to the destruction of habitation area. However, we must abstain from extrapolating local phenomena into generalities.

Another inconformity may be noted in the difference in the function of local knowledge between Greenland and Nunavut. In Nunavut, traditional ecological knowledge has been codified, not only as a reservoir of traditional knowledge, but under the denomination of Inuit IQ also as a philosophy of environmental custodianship. As such, in Canada IQ functions as a fulcrum in political and inter-indigene negotiations. In Greenland, geographically separated from the majority society of the suzerain Denmark, and with no contiguity with other indigenous peoples, there is little incentive to mobilize local knowledge in the political arena.

On the macro level, we see polarization between scientific observations and local observations. On the micro level, however, the assumed "Inuit one-world" is in reality a melange of multiple worlds. When pursuing research to coordinate diverse interests of these multiple worlds, more effort should be directed to expound upon the diversities and resultant socio-economic phenomena within the multiple facets of the Inuit world.

Acknowledgments

I am grateful to Prof. Robert Chr. Thomsen (Aalborg University) for his pertinent comments on this chapter, some of which, because of space limitation, I was not able to respond to.

Note

1 Friesen (2015), following the initiative of the Inuit Circumpolar Council (ICC 2010), proposes that Paleo-Inuit is a better term when referring to pre-Thule cultural traditions. This proposal is a solution to circumvent the contentious term "Eskimo." However, in order to emphasise the fact that pre-Thule Arctic populations were genetically and culturally distinct, I use the term Paleo-Eskimo. As the Thule population and culture is directly ancestral to the Inuit, I refer to this period as Thule Inuit to emphasise this relationship.

References

ACIA (Arctic Climate Impact Assessment). 2005. *Arctic Climate Impact Assessment Scientific Report*. Cambridge: Cambridge University Press.

Ackren, Maria and Uffe Jakobsen. 2015. "Greenland as a Self-governing Sub-national Territory in International Relations: Past, Current and Future Perspectives." *Polar Record* 51 (4): 404–412.

Aminzadeh, Sara. 2007. "A Moral Imperative: The Human Rights Implications of Climate Change." *Hastings International and Comparative Law Review* 30: 231–265.

Arneborg, Jette. 2015. "Norse Greenland: Research into Abandonment." In *Medieval Archaeology in Scandinavia and Beyond: History, Trends and Tomorrow*, edited by Mette Kristiansen, Else Roesdahl, and James Graham-Campbell, 257–271. Copenhagen: Aarhus University Press.

Barron, Eric and George Moore. 1994. *Climate Model Application in Paleoenvironmental Analysis*. Short Course No. 33. Tulsa, OK: Society for Sedimentary Geology.

Berkes, Fikret and Dyanna Jolly. 2001. "Adapting to Climate Change; Social-Ecological Resilience in a Canadian Western Arctic Community." *Conservation Ecology* 5 (2): article 18. http://www.ecologyandsociety.org/vol5/iss2/art18/

Bjorst, Lill. 2012. "Climate Testimonies and Climate-crisis Narratives: Inuit Delegated to Speak on Behalf of the Climate." *Acta Borealia: A Nordic Journal of Circumpolar Societies* 29 (1): 98–113.

Buijs, Cunera. 2010. "Inuit Perceptions of Climate Change in East Greenland." *Études/Inuit/Studies* 34 (1): 39–54.

Carleton, Tamm and Solomon Hsiang. 2016. "Social and Economic Impacts of Climate." *Science* 353 (6304): 1112–1128.

Crate, Susan and Mark Nuttall (eds.) 2009. *Anthropology and Climate Change: From Encounters to Actions*. Walnut Creek, CA: Left Coast Press.

D'Andrea, William, Yongsong Huanga, Sherilyn Fritz, and N. Anderson. 2011."Abrupt Holocene Climate Change as an Important Factor for Human Migration in West Greenland." *Proceedings of the National Academy of Sciences* 108 (24): 9765–9769.

Darwent, Christyann and Jeremy C. Foin. 2010. "Zooarchaeological Analysis of a Late Dorset and an Early Thule Dwelling at Cape Grinnell, Northwest Greenland." *Danish Journal of Geography* 110 (2): 315–336.

deMenocal, Peter and Chris Stringer. 2016. "Human Migration: Climate and the Peopling of the World." *Nature* 538 (7623): 49–50.

Denmark Ministry of Foreign Affairs. 2010. "Factsheet Denmark-Greenland." http://www. netpublikationer.dk/um/10180/index.htm accessed July 20, 2018.

Dowsley, Martha and George Wenzel. 2008. "The Time of the Most Polar Bears: A Co-management Conflict in Nunavut." *Arctic* 61 (2): 177–189.

Dugmore, Andrew J., Christian Keller, and Thomas H. McGovern. 2007. "Norse Greenland Settlement: Reflections on Climate Change, Trade and the Contrasting Fates of Human Settlements in the North Atlantic Islands." *Arctic Anthropology* 44 (1): 12–36.

Fast, Helen and Fikret Berkes. 1999. "Climate Change, Northern Subsistence, and Land-based Economies." In *Securing Northern Futures: Developing Research Partnerships*, edited by Denis E. Wall, Patricia A. McCormack, and Milton M. R. Freeman, 9–19. Edmonton, AB: Canadian Circumpolar Institute.

Fernández-Llamazares, Álvaro, María Elena Méndez-López, Isabel Díaz-Reviriego, Marissa F. McBride, Aili Pyhälä, Antoni Rosell-Melé, and Victoria Reyes-García. 2015. "Links between Media Communication and Local Perceptions of Climate Change in an Indigenous Society." *Climate Change* 131 (2): 307–320.

Ford, James D., Kenyon Bolton, Jamal Shirley, Tristan Pearce, Martin Tremblay, and Michael Westlake. 2012. "Mapping Human Dimensions of Climate Change Research in the Canadian Arctic." *AMBIO* 41: 808–822.

Fournier, Suzanne and Ernie Crey. 1997. *Stolen from our Embrace: The Abduction of First Nations Children and the Restoration of Aboriginal Communities.* Vancouver: Douglas & McIntyre.

Friesen, Max. 2015. "On the Naming of Arctic Archaeological Traditions: The Case for Paleo-Inuit." *Arctic* 68 (3): iii–iv.

——. 2016. "Pan-Arctic Population Movements; the Paleo-Inuit and Thule Inuit Migrations." In *The Oxford Handbook of the Prehistoric Arctic*, edited by T. Max Friesen and Owen Mason, 673–692. Oxford: Oxford University Press.

Gad, Finn. 1973. *The History of Greenland II 1700–1782.* Kingston, Ontario: McGill-Queen's University Press.

——. 1984. "History of Colonial Greenland Arctic." In *Handbook of North American Indians Vol. 5*, edited by D. Damas, 556–576. Washington, DC: Smithsonian Institution Press.

Giddings, James. 1967. *Ancient Men of the Arctic.* New York: Alfred A. Knopf.

Gilbert, M. Thomas P., Toomas Kivisild, Bjarne Grønnow, Eske Willerslev et al. 2008. "Paleo-Eskimo mtDNA Genome Reveals Matrilineal Discontinuity in Greenland." *Science* 320 (5884): 1787–1789.

Golding, Kirsty A., Ian A. Simpson, J. Edward Schofield, and Kevin J. Edwards. 2011. "Norse–Inuit Interaction and Landscape Change in Southern Greenland?: A Geochronological, Pedological, and Palynological Investigation." *Geoarchaeology* 26 (3): 315–345.

Graugaard, Naja. 2009. *National Identity in Greenland in the Age of Self-Government*. Working Paper 09/5. Peterborough, ON: Centre for the Critical Study of Global Power and Politics, Trent University.

Gronnow, Bjarne (ed.) 2009. *On the Track of the Thule Culture from Bering Strait to East Greenland*. Copenhagen: National Museum of Denmark.

Gronnow, Bjarne and Mikkel Sorensen. 2006. "Paleo-Eskimo Migrations into Greenland: The Canadian Connection." In *Dynamics of Northern Societies*, edited by Jette Arneborg and Bjarne Gronnow, 59–74. Copenhagen: Aarhus University Press.

Gullov, Hans. 2008. "The Nature of Contact between Native Greenlanders and Norse." *Journal of the North Atlantic* 1 (1): 16–24.

Hand, Jacquie. 2015. "Indigenous Private Legal Action Against Climate Change in the Arctic." In *Current Developments in Arctic Law Volume* □, edited by Timo Koivurova and Waliul Hasanat, 15–16. Rovaniemi: University of the Arctic Thematic Network on Arctic Law, University of Lapland.

Hastrup, Kirsten. 2012. "The Icy Breath: Modalities of Climate Knowledge in the Arctic." *Current Anthropology* 53 (5): 227–230.

Hayashi, Naotaka. 2013. "Cultivating Place, Livelihood, and the Future: An Ethnography of Dwelling and Climate in Western Greenland." PhD dissertation, University of Alberta.

——. 2014. "The Construction of Indigeneity: A Case Study of Sheep Farming in Southern Greenland." *Japanese Journal of Cultural Anthropology* 79 (2): 143–163.

Hegerl, Gabi and Peter Stott. 2014. "From Past to Future Warming." *Science* 343 (6173): 844–845.

Helgason, Agnar, Gísli Pálsson, Henning Sloth Pedersen, Emily Angulalik, Ellen Dröfn Gunnarsdóttir, Bryndís Yngvadóttir, and Kári Stefánsson. 2006. "MtDNA Variation in Inuit Populations of Greenland and Canada: Migration History and Population Structure." *American Journal of Physical Anthropology* 130: 123–134.

Honda, Shunwa. 2014. "Persistence of Traditional Subsistence Ideology in Nunavut Inuit Society: A Comparison of Modern Economic Activities between Nunavut and Greenland." In *Japan and Canada in Comparative Perspective: Economics and Politics; Regions, Place and People*, 164–182. Japan Studies Association of Canada.

——. 2017. "Whaling and Local Arctic Communities." International Arctic Social Sciences Association (ICASS IX), presentation, Umeå, Sweden.

Huntington, Henry and Shari Fox. 2005. "The Changing Arctic." In *Arctic Climate Impact Assessment*, 2–20. Cambridge: Cambridge University Press.

Ingold, Tim. 1999. "On the Social Relations of the Hunter-gatherer Band." In *The Cambridge Encyclopaedia of Hunters and Gatherers*, edited by Richard Lee and Richard Daly, 399–440. Cambridge: Cambridge University Press.

ICC. 2010. "The Use of the Term 'Inuit' in Scientific and Other Circles." Resolution 2010-01. Anchorage, Ottawa, Nuuk, Anadyr: Inuit Circumpolar Council. http://www.inuitcircumpolar.com/-the-use-of-the-term-inuit.html accessed July 20, 2018.

ICC. 2015. UNFCCC COP 21 Position Paper. Anchorage, Ottawa, Nuuk, Anadyr: Inuit Circumpolar Council. http://www.inuitcircumpolar.com/uploads/3/0/5/4/30542564/icc_position_unfccc_cop_21_final.pdf accessed July 20, 2018.

IPCC. 2007. *Climate Change 2007: The Physical Science Basis*. Cambridge: Cambridge University Press/Intergovernmental Panel on Climate Change.

Jensen, Niels. 2008. "Between Paternalism and Indifference." *Social Work & Society News Magazine*. https://www.uni-vechta.de/fileadmin/user_upload/Soziale_Arbeit/Dokumen ten/Kutscher/Socmag_Archiv/November2008/November2008-Jensen__Niels_Rosen dahl-Between_paternalism_and_indifference.pdf accessed July 20, 2018.

Johnson, Noor. 2009. "Inuit Traditional Knowledge and the Politics of Adaptation: Broadening Conceptions of Agency in Climate Change Governance." Paper presented at the 2009 Amsterdam Conference on Earth System Governance. http://www.earth systemgovernance.org/ac2009/papers/AC2009-0068.pdf accessed July 20, 2018.

Kishigami, Nobuhiro. 2010. "Climate Change, Oil and Gas Development, and Inupiat Whaling in Northwest Alaska." *Etudes/Inuit/Studies* 34 (1): 91–107.

Kjærgaard, Kathrine. 2015. "Religious Education, Identity and Nation Building: The Case of Greenland." *Nordidactica* 2: 114–130.

Kleivan, Inge. 1984. "History of Norse Greenland, Arctic." In *Handbook of North American Indians Vol. 5*, edited by D. Damas, 549–555. Washington, DC: Smithsonian Institution.

Knopp, J. A. 2010. "Investigating the effects of environmental change on Arctic char (*Salvelinus alpinus*) growth using scientific and Inuit traditional knowledge." *Arctic* 63 (4): 493–497.

Langgård, Karen. 2010. "West Greenlander's View of East Greenlander Over Time: The Discourse of *Atuagagdiutit* from 1861 to the First World War and in Greenland Literature." In *Cultural and Social Research in Greenland: Selected Essays 1992–2010*, edited by Karen Langgård, 175–201. Nuuk: Forlaget Atuagkat.

Leduc, Timothy. 2007. "Sila Dialogues on Climate Change: Inuit Wisdom for a Cross-cultural Interdisciplinarity." *Climatic Change* 85 (3): 237–250.

——. 2010. *Climate, Culture, Change: Inuit and Western Dialogues with a Warming North*. Ottawa: University of Ottawa Press.

LeMoine, Genevieve and Christyann Darwent. 2010. "The Inglefield Land Archaeology Project: Introduction and Overview." *Danish Journal of Geography* 110 (2): 279–296.

Loukacheva, Natalia. 2007. *The Arctic Promise: Legal and Political Autonomy of Greenland and Nunavut*. Toronto: University of Toronto Press.

Marchenko, Nataliya. 2014. "Northern Sea Route: Modern State and Challenges." Paper presented at ASME 2014 33rd International Conference on Ocean, Offshore and Arctic Engineering, San Francisco, CA June 8–13, 2014.

Mason, Arthur. 2016. "Arctic Abstractive Industry." *Cultural Anthropology* website. https://culanth.org/fieldsights/945-arctic-abstractive-industry accessed May 1, 2018.

Matthews, H. Damon, Andrew Weaver, K. J. Meissner, N. P.Gillett, and M. Eby. 2004. "Natural and Anthropogenic Climate Change: Incorporating Historical Land Cover Change, Vegetation Dynamics and the Global Carbon Cycle." *Climate Dynamics* 22: 461–479.

Maxwell, Moreau. 1976. "Introduction." In *Eastern Arctic Prehistory: Paleoeskimo Problems*, Memoirs of the Society for American Archaeology No. 31, edited by Moreau S. Maxwell, 1–5. Washington, DC: Society for American Archaeology.

McGhee, Robert. 1969/70. "Speculations on Climatic Change and Thule Culture Development." *Folk* 11 (12): 173–184.

——. 1996. *Ancient People of the Arctic*. Vancouver: UBC Press.

Milne, S. Brooke, Robert W. Park, and Douglas Stenton. 2012. "Dorset Culture Land Use Strategies and the Case of Inland Southern Baffin Island." *Canadian Journal of Archaeology* 36: 267–288.

Mistry, Jayalaxshmi and Andrea Berardi. 2016. "Bridging Indigenous and Scientific Knowledge." *Science* 352 (6291): 1274–1275.

Moltke, I., M. Fumagalli, T. S. Korneliussen, J. E. Crawford, P. Bjerregaard, M. E. Jørgensen, N. Grarup, H. C. Gulløv, A. Linneberg, O. Pedersen, T. Hansen, R. Nielsen, and A. Albrechtsen 2015. "Uncovering the Genetic History of the Present-Day Greenlandic Population." *American Journal of Human Genetics* 96: 54–69.

Mortensen, Bent. 2013. "The Quest for Resources: The Case of Greenland." *Journal of Military and Strategic Studies* 15 (2): 93–128.

Naalakkersuisut (n.d.) "Economy and Industry in Greenland."Nuuk: Government of Greenland. http://naalakkersuisut.gl/en/About-government-of-greenland/About-Greenland/Economy-and-Industry-in-Greenland accessed July 20, 2018.

Nuttall, Mark. 2008a. "Climate Change and the Warming of Politics of Autonomy in Greenland." *Indigenous Affairs* 1/2: 44–51.

——. 2008b. "Self-rule in Greenland: Towards the World's First Independent Inuit State?" *Indigenous Affairs* 3/4: 64–70.

——. 2009. "Living in a World of Movement: Human Resilience to Environmental Instability in Greenland." In *Anthropology and Climate Change: From Encounters to Actions*, edited by Susan Crate and Mark Nuttall, 292–310. Chicago, IL: Left Coast Press.

——. 2010. "Anticipation, Climate Change and Movement in Greenland." *Etudes/Inuit/Studies* 34 (1): 21–38.

——. 2012. "Imagining and Governing the Greenlandic Resource Frontier." *Polar Journal* 2 (1): 113–124.

——. 2016. "The Making of Resource Spaces in Greenland." *Cultural Anthropology* website. https://culanth.org/fieldsights/942-the-making-of-resource-spaces-in-greenland accessed May 1, 2018.

Omura, Keiichi. 2005a. "'Repetition of Different Things': The Mechanism of Memory in Traditional Knowledge of the Canadian Inuit." In *Construction and Distribution of Body Resources*, edited by Kazuyoshi Sugawara, 79–104. Tokyo: Tokyo University of Foreign Studies.

——. 2005b. "Science against Modern Science: The Socio-Political Construction of Otherness in Inuit TEK (Traditional Ecological Knowledge)." In *Indigenous Use and Management of Marine Resources* (Senri Ethnological Studies 67), edited by N. Kishigami and J. M. Savelle, 323–344. Osaka, Japan: National Museum of Ethnology.

Osofsky, Hari. 2007. "The Inuit Petition as a Bridge?: Beyond Dialectics of Climate Change and Indigenous Peoples' Rights." *American Indian Law Review* 31: 675–697.

Overland, James, Muyin Wang, John E. Walsh, and Julienne C. Stroeve. 2014. "Future Arctic Climate Changes: Adaptation and Mitigation Time Scales." *Earth's Future* 2 (2): 68–74.

Park, Robert. 2000. "The Dorset: Thule Succession Revisited." In *Identities and Cultural Contacts in the Arctic*, edited by Martin Appelt, Joel Berglund, and Hans Christian Gulløv, 192–205. Copenhagen: Danish Polar Center.

Pearce, Tristan, James Ford, Ashlee Cunsolo, and Barry Smit. 2015. "Inuit Traditional Ecological Knowledge (TEK), Subsistence Hunting and Adaptation to Climate Change in the Canadian Arctic." *Arctic* 68 (12): 233–245.

Poppel, Birger, M. Fægteborg, M.O. Siegstad, and H. T. Snyder. 2017. "The Arctic as a 'Hotspot' for Natural Resource Extraction and Global Warming." In *The Economy of the*

North 2015, edited by Solveig Glomsrød, Gérard Duhaime, and Iulie Aslaksen, 129–136. Oslo: Statistics Norway.

Riedlinger, Dyanna and Fikret Berkes. 2001. "Contributions of Traditional Knowledge to Understanding Climate Change in the Canadian Arctic." *Polar Record* 37: 315–338.

Ryan, Karen. 2016. "The 'Dorset Problem' Revisited: The Transitional and Early and Middle Dorset Periods in the Eastern Arctic." In *The Oxford Handbook of the Prehistoric Arctic*, edited by T. Max Friesen and Owen Mason, 761–782. Oxford: Oxford University Press.

Rubicz, Rohina and Michael Crawford. 2016. "Molecular Genetic Evidence from Contemporary Populations for the Origins of Native North Americans." In *The Oxford Handbook of the Prehistoric Arctic*, edited by T. Max Friesen and Owen Mason, 27–50. Oxford: Oxford University Press.

Savelle, James and Arthur Dyke. 2014. "Paleoeskimo Occupation History of Foxe Basin: Core Area Model and Dorset Origins." *American Antiquity* 79 (2): 249–276.

Savelle, James and Allen McCartney. 1990. "Prehistoric Thule Eskimo Whaling in the Canadian Arctic Islands." In *Canada's Missing Dimension: Science and History in the Canadian Arctic Islands*, edited by C.R. Harington, 695–723. Ottawa: Canadian Museum of Nature.

Sejersen, Frank. 2007. "Indigenous Urbanism Revisited: The Case of Greenland." *Indigenous Affairs* 3: 26–31.

——. 2015. *Rethinking Greenland and the Arctic in the Era of Climate Change: New Northern Horizons*. London: Routledge.

Sowa, Frank. 2013. "Indigenous Peoples and the Institutionalization of the Convention on Biological Diversity in Greenland." *Arctic Anthropology* 50 (1): 72–88.

Stern, Nicholas. 2016. "Current Climate Models are Grossly Misleading." *Nature* 530 (7591): 407–409.

Stern, Paul C., John H. Perkins, Richard E. Sparks, and Robert A. Knox. 2016. "The Challenge of Climate-change Neoskepticism." *Science* 353 (6300): 653–654.

——. 2005. *"Senjuminundo: kako, genzai, mirai"* ("The Indigenous Movement: Past, Present and Future.") In *Senjumin no sekai* (*Studies in Cultural Anthropology: The World of Indigenous Peoples*), edited by Henry Stewart, Keiichi Omura, and Hiroaki Kuzuno, 253–270. Tokyo: Foundation for the Promotion of The Open University of Japan.

Stewart, Henry. 2016. *"Dento teki na seikatsu"* ("History of Greenland: Traditional Lifeways.") In *Aisulando, guriinlando, hottukyoku o shirutame no 65 shou* (*Iceland, Greenland and the Arctic in 65 Lessons*), edited by Minoru Ozawa, Teiko Nakamaru, and Minori Takahashi, 49–53. Tokyo: Akashi Shoten.

Stewart, Henry and Xie Lie. 2008. *"Hakubutsukan ni okeru senjuu minzoku hyoushou"* ("Representation of Indigenous Peoples in Museums Abroad.") *Journal of The Open University of Japan* 25: 95–107.

Takahashi, Minori. 2013. *Jiko kettei ken o meguru seijigaku* (*Political Science Regarding the Right to Self-determination*.) Tokyo: Akashi Shoten.

Timmermann, Axel and Tobias Friedrich. 2016. "Late Pleistocene Climate Drivers of Early Human Migration." *Nature* 538 (7623): 92–95.

Ulmer, Fran. 2015. "One Arctic." *Science* 348: 6232.

University of Greenland. 2014. *To the Benefit of Greenland*. Nuuk: Committee for Greenlandic Mineral Resources to the Benefit of Society.

Wallace, Birgitta. 2003. "The Norse in Newfoundland: L'Anse aux Meadows and Vinland." *Newfoundland and Labrador Studies* 19(1). https://journals.lib.unb.ca/index.php/nflds/article/view/140/237 accessed July 20, 2018.

Watt-Cloutier, Sheila. 2005. "Petition to the Inter American Commission on Human Rights Seeking Relief from Violations Resulting from Global Warming Caused by Acts and Omissions of the United States." http://www.inuitcircumpolar.com/inuit-petition-inter-american-commission-on-human-rights-to-oppose-climate-change-caused-by-the-united-states-of-america.html accessed May 1, 2018.

Wenzel, George. 2004. "From TEK to IQ: Inuit Qaujimajatuqangit and Inuit Cultural Ecology." *Arctic Anthropology* 41 (2): 238–250.

Willerslev, Rane. 2012. "The New as Always the Same: A Critical Perspective on Yukaghir Hunting Adaptations to Climate Change." *Bulletin of the Hokkaido Museum of Northern Peoples* 21: 1–18.

Part II

Space-time multiplicities

Chapter 7

Landscapes, by comparison

Practices of enacting salmon in Hokkaido, Japan

Heather Anne Swanson

Comparison is a practice that folds multiple worlds together. It is not only an analytical act, but also a landscape-making and body-making force. Focusing on the case of salmon fisheries management in Hokkaido, Japan, this chapter explores how the comparative practices of this island's government officials, agricultural advisors, and fisheries managers have become a powerful but often overlooked part of the production of its human–nonhuman arrangements, as well as knowledges about them. I focus on the comparisons of these people because their imaginative and practical work has been central to a profound reconfiguration of the island, one that has included the usurpation of Ainu territory and its conversion into a part of the Japanese nation-state. Attention to the materiality of their comparisons sheds light on the processes through which indigenous lands become agricultural and natural resources, and how those processes materially adhere in bodies. The landscape-making practices on which I focus here are not the only ones at play in the iterative emergence of Hokkaido: countless other human and nonhuman activities have had, and continue to exert, a strong influence on the island. In foregrounding particular development projects, I seek to contribute to broader efforts to understand the layering of histories in colonized and industrialized places and the challenges of living with the ongoing legacies of modernist projects (such as Stoler 2016).

Since the mid-nineteenth century, natural resources management in north-ern Japan has been profoundly shaped by how people both within and beyond the region have compared Hokkaido's landscapes to those of other places. After the Meiji Restoration of 1868, Japanese officials sought to claim, colonize, and "develop" Hokkaido's lands and waters in order to make the new Japanese nation-state more legibly "modern" to Euro-American audiences.[1] Their com-parisons, however, were not between Japan and an undifferentiated "West"; instead they engaged in heterodox modes of analogic thinking that reached out to such diverse places as the American West, the Russian East, New Zealand, and Chile. Today, Hokkaido residents' comparisons between their forests, fields, and waters, and those of others around the world, continue to dramatically affect the region's environmental management and physical landscapes. By examining such comparisons, this chapter aims to show how comparisons pull material pieces of multiple worlds together in ways that iteratively remake the island's watershed ecologies and the bodies of its salmon.

Studying multiplicity

This chapter, like many in this volume, is deeply indebted to Annemarie Mol's (2002) work on how the practices of enacting atherosclerosis in various parts of a Dutch hospital (i.e. in its operating room, pathology lab, and walking clinic) at once differ and "hang together" (84) such that the disease is neither singular nor plural. Echoing the work of Strathern (1991, 35), Mol describes atherosclerosis as an entity that is "more than one and less than many" (Mol 2002, 55). Such theoretical insights about multiplicity are entangled with a particular methodological approach—extensive ethnographic attention to the distinct practices through which atherosclerosis is "done differently" in varying situations (ibid. 35). Mol's attention to differences across communities of practice shows us how modes of enactment emerge in everyday life.

Marianne Lien and John Law (2011) have sought to extend this approach specifically to salmon—the same fish that are at the center of this chapter. As they develop the concept of a *salmon multiple*, Lien and Law explore how Norwegian salmon—along with nature/culture divides—are enacted differently across textbook definitions, government documents, farm feeding routines, and methods for containing farmed fish. Like Mol, their methods are attuned to the practices through which farmed salmon are enacted variously as biomass in fish farm business management, alien invaders in conservation policies, and responsive beings that need to be fed in daily practices of fish care.

While informed by these methodological approaches to multiplicity, this chapter also differs from them in two important ways. First, it begins not with practices per se, but with *bodies* and *landscapes*. Second, instead of asking about the practices through which multiple salmon emerge, it asks about the practices *already inside* the bodies of specific salmon. These two moves are inspired by Donna Haraway's (2008) opening question in her book, *When Species Meet*: "Whom and what do I touch when I touch my dog?" (3). Haraway's query directs our attention to the historically specific multiplicities *within* her dog, named Cayenne, and in doing so, it highlights how multiplicity occurs not only *across* different enactments of phenomena, but also simultaneously within beings.

While the kind of multiplicity that Haraway describes is not in conflict with that of Mol, Lien, and Law, it does call out for different methodological practices. For Haraway, beings are knots of relations, and one of her core methods for engaging them is to trace the strands of those knots. When she touches her Australian shepherd, Haraway finds herself compelled to explore the histories of dog breeding and genetics, animal training and cross-species communication, Australian settler colonialism, and American pet ownership, which shape both the bodies and behaviors of Haraway and her dog. For

Haraway, when we touch any entity, it is already multiple; nothing is ever singular. From this perspective, the challenge, then, is to better understand the material-semiotic multiplicities that we and others inherit and how we might best live with them.

By adopting a Haraway-inflected approach, I bring somewhat unorthodox material and temporal sensibilities to questions of multiplicity. Specifically, I frame multiplicity as *an embodied historical accretion*. Thus, I also bring a different set of methods to multiplicity. Instead of relying primarily on ethnographic methods to look at multiplicity in a flat temporal space (as Mol [2002] does in *The Body Multiple*), I use historical and archival methods to examine how multiple—and multitemporal—modes of practice inhere in material bodies and landscapes.

Landscapes, travel, and comparisons

This chapter also differs from much work on multiplicity in terms of its *objects* and its approaches to their *spatial relations*. It specifically examines salmon bodies as they emerge *in relation to Hokkaido's landscapes*. I use the term landscape here to refer to an assemblage of more-than-human relations in a given place, and I consider it an important object for analysis in the midst of the widespread ecological damage that some call the Anthropocene (Swanson et al. 2015). Landscapes—with their nonhuman ecological relations and layers of human histories—make visible the imbrication of the "natural" and "cultural," and pull scholars toward modes of analysis that refuse to parse scholarship into the social and biological. The historical approach I use in this piece—which attempts to bring together cultural, ecological, and evolutionary histories—is a humble step in this direction.

As the following sections demonstrate, Hokkaido salmon cannot be understood separately from the landscapes they inhabit. Although salmon spend much of their adulthood feeding in the ocean, they start and end their lives in small freshwater rivers that are intimately connected to the lands that surround them. During their freshwater phases, salmon are incredibly sensitive to the changes in water and stream morphology that land alteration generates. Dams can divert water for irrigation and block salmon migration, agricultural runoff can pollute rivers, and logging-related erosion can cause rivers to fill with silt, smothering the fishes' eggs. If any such alterations occur, they reshape salmon behaviors, modify patterns of fish survival, and rework the genetics of salmon populations. Landscape processes—and any changes to them—are thus literally written into the bodies and genes of these fish. These are bodies and landscapes characterized by a historical accumulation of practices.

The multiplicity of Hokkaido landscapes and fish, however, is not merely that of temporally sequenced accretions; it is also the multiplicity of each set of development and fisheries management practices, which enfold other places through their acts of comparison. When one thinks of landscapes, comparison is not typically the first thing that comes to mind. Landscapes still tend to conjure an overly simplistic sense of the "local." We often think of landscapes as more-or-less self-contained entities rooted in particular places. But landscapes—like cultures—do not precede encounters; they emerge out of them.

In his book *Routes*, James Clifford (1997) discusses an excerpt from an autobiographical story by author Amitav Ghosh, in which Ghosh comes to realize that the rural Egyptian town he visits—ostensibly a traditional and settled place—has long been as cosmopolitan as an airline transit lounge. Its people, Ghosh shows, are constantly caught up in cross-cultural encounters as they travel to Libya, Jordan, and Syria as laborers, to Yemen as soldiers, and to Saudi Arabia as pilgrims. But this is not just a story of late twentieth-century globalization; such encounters are nothing new for the people of this rural village. For generations, these people have travelled widely, and their so-called "local" and "traditional" community has been built through cross-cultural encounters.

Landscapes are similarly made through travels that link together geographically far-flung places. For millions of years, pollen grains have floated on wind currents and migratory birds have transferred diseases from one continent to another. But while long-distance encounter itself has long been a part of landscape formation, the epic changes that some call the Anthropocene and others call modernity have generated radically new kinds of encounters. For both Egyptian villagers and landscapes, encounter itself may be a constant, but the specifics of encounters are not.

Since the beginning of the nineteenth century, landscapes around the world have been thrust into new kinds of encounters on an unprecedented scale. Some of the stories of these encounters are familiar to us. We know, for example, how the links forged between landscapes of production and consumption have transformed both; think of extractive relations between European nations and their colonies, as well as rural areas newly connected to the metabolisms of industrial cities. We also know stories of the human-introduced species that, when they encounter new ecologies, end up completely remaking them; think of the European rabbits in Australia that have decimated a good portion of the continent's native plant life.

To what we have not yet paid enough attention, however, is how these new forms of landscape encounter are often deeply intertwined with practices of *comparison*. As Gergely Mohacsi and Atsuro Morita (2013) demonstrate in a special issue dedicated to *traveling comparisons*, travel and comparison are fundamentally linked, "chang[ing] and transform[ing] each other in unexpected ways" (ibid. 176). Comparisons are part and parcel of human encounters. When people meet other people, objects, or ideas that travel, they tend to make comparisons through which translations, borrowings, and differentiations come into being. As scholars in science and technology studies and anthropology increasingly explore such comparisons as material-semiotic practices "in which scales and contexts are manipulated and folded into each other" (ibid. 178), my intervention is to extend such work to landscapes. Comparisons, I aim to show, become embedded not only in objects such as machines (Morita 2013), but also in landscapes, with profound effects on human and nonhuman relations.

Comparing with and from Hokkaido

When I arrived in northern Japan in 2007 to conduct anthropological field-work, I quickly discovered that one could barely do anything in Japan without engaging with comparisons; they were an explicit and ubiquitous part of every-day life. Although the comparisons I encountered were varied, the most common were between what people called "Japan" and "the West." Such categorical comparisons were at once pervasive and material. Even simple quotidian tasks, such as ordering breakfast at a restaurant or using a public restroom, required selecting a configuration that was labeled either "Japanese" or "Western." Comparison was everywhere.

When I dove into my formal research on salmon in Hokkaido, I was similarly struck by comparisons. Salmon, like so much else in Japan, were enacted in ways that were radically transnational and comparative. I encountered members of a salmon fishing cooperative who designed their business practices in comparison with models from Russia; salmon scientists who tried to distinguish their theories of sustainability through comparisons with those of Canadians; and a university fisheries school modeled after an American land grant college. Everywhere I went, people noted relations between their own fisheries practices and those of people in Norway, France, New Zealand, and Chile. These were "place-based" practices of salmon management, but thoroughly cosmopolitan ones.

Allow me to turn to a bit of Japanese history to explain. After the arrival of U.S. Commodore Perry's ships in the mid-nineteenth century, Japanese elites—fearful of European or American domination—embarked on a mas-sive project to transform Japanese lands from a collection of feudal domains into a globally powerful and internationally legible nation-state. To avoid colonization, Japanese elites decided they had to become a legible state in the eyes of Europeans. Officials saw comparison as essential to this project; they did not yearn to *become* Euro-American, but they needed to *become comparable* to Europe—militarily, politically, and culturally—in order to be recognizable as a modern power. For Japanese government officials, the process of modernization was, above all, experienced as a process of learning how to make transnational comparisons and to articulate themselves within them. Sending numerous missions abroad and inviting countless foreign experts to Japan, government officials built their new state in a comparative dialogue between what they came to experience as "Japan" and the "West."

The leaders of the new Japanese state saw its imperial expansion as a critical component in such projects, and the first place they colonized was Hokkaido. Although Japanese merchants had traded with the island's indigenous Ainu people for centuries, Japan did not stake an official claim to the island until 1869. The colonization of Hokkaido was a comparability project from the get-go; it was an attempt to demonstrate that Japan was an inappropriate place for Western colonization through a display of Japan's own colonial powers. But the colonization of Hokkaido required a complex set of comparisons. The Japanese state desired to bring Hokkaido into its fold, but the island's terrain and history put it at once inside and outside the body of "Japan proper." This northern territory was very different from the main Japanese islands: it was too cold for growing rice, inhabited by indigenous peoples, and covered with what ethnic Japanese settlers considered to be frightening wilderness (Mason 2012).

Nineteenth-century government officials thus sought other models for colonizing the area. The nearby Russian Far East provided a climatic equivalent, but they did not think Russia a suitable source of inspiration—it was not the type of place to which they wanted to link Hokkaido through explicit comparison.[2] Despite Russian knowledge about cold-weather farming, drawing a comparison between themselves and a late-developing empire on the margins of Europe was unappealing. As a result, the officials tasked with Hokkaido's development opted instead to stress the parallels between what they saw as the unambiguously "modern" American West and their own colonization efforts. Using the American West as a model, Japanese officials began to characterize Hokkaido as a frontier where they could test and refine the most cutting-edge Euro-American ideas of the times—including forms of scientific agriculture and modern natural resource management. From the start, the folding of Hokkaido into the Japanese state was a comparative project in which landscape could not be ignored; the grounds of comparison were often literal ground.

Embedded comparisons

Today, many travelers continue to experience Hokkaido's landscapes as on the edge of Japan. In the late 1990s, the author of a popular travelogue described Hokkaido as "the least 'Japanese' of all the main islands. It's Texas and Alaska rolled into one. It's Siberia. Switzerland. The last frontier and the end of Japan. [...] Hokkaido even *looks* like the American West" (Ferguson 1998, 365). It is a common sentiment: my Japanese friends in Honshu told me that they consider vacationing in Hokkaido as an experience that embodies some of the exoticness of international travel, but without the hassles of dealing with passports and foreign languages.

One of the reasons for this is that comparisons between Hokkaido and the American West have been literally built into the island's landscapes. In the next section of this chapter, I present four material objects that help us to understand such comparisons and the ways that they have come to be embedded in Hokkaido's landscapes and fish. How, I ask, does paying attention to the details of the comparative stories enfolded within Hokkaido's salmon and their environs help us to understand multiplicity in a different way?

Figure 7.1 A Hokkaido farm
Photo by author

Object 1: Hokkaido farm

In 1871, the Japanese Government sent Kuroda Kiyotaka on a study tour of the U.S. and Europe. Kuroda, a former samurai from Kyushu who had helped to overthrow the Shogunate, was appointed to head the *Kaitakushi*, or Hokkaido Colonization Commission, the organization charged with opening the Hokkaido frontier. Kuroda was intrigued by American settlement practices, and he considered American advice essential to Hokkaido's development. During his stay in the U.S., Kuroda managed to convince General Horace Capron, the sitting federal Commissioner of Agriculture, to resign his post and travel to Hokkaido that same year to serve as an advisor to the Kaitakushi.

During his two years in Hokkaido, Capron sparked a revolution in the island's agriculture and land use by introducing American crops and livestock. The lists of the species that made their way across the Pacific by steamship at his request are impressively long. Some came in the form of cuttings: cherries, nectarines, plums, peaches, apricots, raspberries, currants, black gooseberries, strawberries, rhubarb, quinces, and grapes (Russell 2007, 129). Others arrived as seeds: onions, turnips, carrots, cabbage, lettuce, tomatoes, beets, celery, spinach, corn, peas, beans, and potatoes. Still others arrived on the hoof: Devon and Durham cattle, Berkshire and Suffolk pigs, Cotswold, Merino, and Southdown sheep, and Arabian horses (ibid. 132, 134). Their numbers were not small. For example, by the end of 1873, more than 32,000 young fruit trees had been shipped to Hokkaido (ibid. 129). Overall, these animals and plants provided a foundation for the large-scale industrial agriculture that both the Americans and the Kaitakushi imagined for Japan.

Capron was only one of a cadre of American men that the Japanese Government hired to survey the island, map its geology and rivers, lay out the grid system for its capital city, build mechanized sawmills, foster the development of mining industries, and assist with road, bridge, and railroad construction (Duke 2009; Fujita 1994). Another of these foreign pioneers was Edwin Dun, an Ohio rancher, whom Capron selected to introduce modern livestock production to northernmost Japan. Tokyo officials understood the symbolism of powerful horses and meaty cattle. Moreover, for the island's colder and more marginal climates, livestock rearing seemed more promising than rice farming. Dun, with years of practical experience in the U.S. Midwest, became their guide. He brought more than 100 cattle and 100 sheep to Japan, including some from his own farm (Hokkaido Prefectural Government 1968, 44–5). But once he arrived in Hokkaido, he faced a serious challenge: the island was no pastoral paradise. Its grasses were poor, its farms lacked fences, and wolves prowled its mountains.

Thus, Dun and the Kaitakushi set out to make the landscape safe and hospitable for modern animal husbandry. They introduced Kentucky bluegrass, red top, timothy, and clover; they built miles of split-rail fences; and they exterminated wolves and dogs with strychnine, a chemical poison widely used for predator control in the Western U.S. (Fujita 1994; Walker 2004, 2005). Through such practices, they helped build industrial-scale beef, dairy, and military horse industries in Hokkaido by turning miles of hills and plains into parcels of pasture, while decimating Ainu dog populations and laying claim to Ainu lands through comparisons with U.S. practices of American Indian disenfranchisement (Medak-Saltzman 2015). Although the Kaitakushi did not follow all of Capron's, Dun's, or the other Americans' advice, they took much of it seriously. In doing so, their countless comparisons with the American West materially remade Hokkaido: parts of U.S. agriculture were literally incorporated into the island's landscapes.

Object 2: Hokkaido University

Although the American advisors clearly sparked significant changes in Hokkaido's social and natural landscapes, they did not stay long enough to see their projects to fruition. Most of them returned home at the end of their one- to three-year contracts. But another institution—the Sapporo Agricultural College (SAC)—kept the comparisons between Japan and the U.S. alive, ensuring

Figure 7.2 Bust of William Smith Clark displayed on the Hokkaido University campus
Photo by author

that the American-inflected logics of modern scientific agriculture and natural resource management would continue to transform Hokkaido's lands and waters for decades to come.

In 1875, Kuroda asked the Japanese ambassador in Washington, DC to secure the services of an American educator capable of establishing a first-rate agricultural college in Hokkaido. The Japanese Government managed to recruit a consultant of the highest caliber, William Smith Clark, then-President of the Massachusetts Agricultural College, which is now the University of Massachusetts, Amherst. In summer 1876, Clark arrived in Hokkaido along with two other professors from Massachusetts Agricultural College, and they immediately established SAC (Fujita 1994). The curriculum that Clark created for SAC emphasized practical agricultural education in tandem with scholarly pursuits. In the school's early years, courses included geometry, English, German, elocution, and political economy, along with drainage and irrigation, manures

Figure 7.3 A Hokkaido salmon canning label from 1877
Source: The Archives of Hokkaido

and crop rotation, vegetable pathology, stock farming, and veterinary science (Nitobe 1893). Notably, students also took classes titled "History of Colonization" and "Political History of Europe," with much of the instruction in English (see Nitobe 1893, 35–42 for complete list of courses). The Sapporo Agricultural College's efforts to create citizens of the world also extended to the cafeteria, where the college used meals as a tool to craft students who would be at home with one foot in the East and one in the West. In addition to Japanese-style rice-based meals, students were introduced to "Western" foods such as chicken, coffee, bread, butter, and ice cream, served on flat plates.

A primary goal of the college was to craft men who were skilled in the arts of comparison and could thus become Japan's first generation of modern, cosmopolitan nation-builders.[3] The initial SAC instructors, New Englanders steeped in the gospels of Protestant Christianity and liberal education, believed that the students needed to be inculcated with a certain kind of desire—a yearning for continual improvement at the scales of both the self and the nation. That desire required comparison—between what was characterized as the backward East and the modern West, or between what Japan was and what it could be. For SAC students, "modernity" itself came to be experienced as a practice of cross-cultural comparison.

As a result of their "Western" educations in Sapporo, the school's graduates were exceptionally skilled in such comparisons. They became Japan's translators, making a place for themselves and their new nation in an increasingly global world. The SAC students went on to become diplomats and statesmen. One rose to the position of prime minister and another became Under Secretary-General of the League of Nations. With skills gained at SAC, they introduced

Figure 7.4 A Columbia River salmon canning label from 1881
Source: Oregon State Archives

Hawthorne to Japan, developed a Shakespearean theater, authored bilingual dictionaries, and founded English language newspapers. Their accomplishments were also sometimes troubling: some graduates drew on their agricultural planning knowledge to guide Japan's colonization of Taiwan and Korea (Willcock 2000, 1015).

Notably, SAC also directly influenced Hokkaido's development. More than a third of the school's pre-1900 alumni remained in Hokkaido permanently, becoming the leaders of its businesses and institutions. The logics they preached and practices they performed set off a cascade of landscape changes. They drained the marshlands around the Ishikari River, converting them to agricultural land. They cut forests and processed wood products in sawmills and pulp plants. They built coal and gold mines. But most importantly, they institutionalized the comparative spirit and visions of modernist development demonstrated by the American advisors. Today, SAC remains Hokkaido's most important educational institution, although its name has been changed to Hokkaido University. On its webpage, the university continues to cite "frontier spirit" as the first of its four guiding principles. This is not mere rhetoric. Echoes of SAC's original philosophies remain, especially in the university's agricultural and fisheries departments, which train the majority of the island's natural resource scientists. The making of comparative subjects continues.

Object 3: Salmon canning label

As the new Japanese elite developed their comparative sensibilities, they did so in a nineteenth-century world filled with the comparisons of others. They were forced to contend with widespread comparisons that invoked the binary categorizations of the savage and civilized as well as the West and rest. Yet in addition to such racial and civilizational comparisons, they also encountered many others, including comparisons specifically related to salmon. While American advisors to Hokkaido initially stressed agricultural improvement, Japanese officials also focused on the island's abundant fisheries. As a result of comparative consideration of the U.S. salmon industry, Hokkaido administrators saw the island's seafood as a potentially lucrative export.

In 1866, two brothers built a small salmon cannery near the mouth of the U. S. Columbia River, tucked in a corner of the American West. Almost immediately, it spawned a new industry. With salmon safely preserved in metal vessels, Columbia River fish could be shipped to markets anywhere in the world. By 1873, customs records show that Columbia River salmon were already being directly exported to England, China, and Australia (Penner 2005, 10). The Columbia River salmon industry created a buzz among entrepreneurs on multiple continents—one that Hokkaido administrators heard—and, by the mid-1870s, Hokkaido bureaucrats had decided that they wanted a comparable canned salmon industry. But they quickly encountered a problem: the texture, taste, and color of Hokkaido salmon were slightly different from those of the Columbia River fish, which had already become a *de facto* global standard. Hokkaido's officials had to grapple with the fact that their fish would be compared to a Columbia River "norm" and that—if they were going to sell their salmon for a good price—they needed to compare well.

The Kaitakushi sent their first attempts at canned salmon to American ambassadors and European merchants for their opinions on how Hokkaido's salmon measured up to those from the U.S. Aiming to impress foreigners, the Hokkaido factory wrapped its first cans in bright red bilingual labels, with directions for use in both English and Japanese. Despite such efforts, no one liked Hokkaido's canned fish. A British merchant noted: "As to the sample of tinned salmon sent, the reports both from London and the Continent are unsatisfactory. The salmon [...] could not be brought into competition with the preserved salmon from America" (Ahrens 1877b).[4] Another merchant drew explicit attention to the kinds of consumer comparisons with which Japanese salmon had to contend:

> We think that the people of Europe, who have become accustomed to the appearance and taste of the Oregon Salmon, would not consider the Hokkaido fish as equal to it either in quality or value. The Hokkaido Salmon is no doubt very good food, but the Oregon fish would probably be much preferred, and it might be difficult, at least in the beginning, to introduce, or to obtain a fair price for, the Japanese product. [...] We would suggest that you should yourself make a comparison between the Oregon and the Hokkaido fish, remembering that the toughness or firmness (hardness) of fibre which in Japan is considered a merit in fish, is not so considered in foreign countries.
>
> (Walsh 1877)

The Kaitakushi took this merchant's advice and began directly comparing their product with canned fish from the Columbia River in order become more competitive. After all, the stakes were high. The Dutch Ambassador to Japan had discouraged the Kaitakushi from trying to sell Hokkaido's fish in Europe, advising that the fish would likely find "a better and more profitable market in British India and Java" (Bauduin 1879). But the Kaitakushi did not want either their fish or Japan's citizens condemned to second-class colonial status.

The Kaitakushi thus commissioned reports and sent Japanese emissaries to observe all aspects of the Columbia River salmon industry. By tinkering with their own practices, these Hokkaido officials soon brought their own canned salmon into line with that of the Columbia River industry, and sales rocketed. By 1932, approximately 80 percent of Japanese-exported canned salmon was bound for the high-prestige market of England, while the remainder headed to France, Holland, Belgium, and South Africa (Canned Foods Association of Japan 1934, 31–2). In 1934, the Canned Foods Association of Japan reported steady increases in exports, "indicative of the fact that Japanese canned salmon has maintained its good reputation in foreign lands" (ibid. 33).

Figure 7.5 Indian water wheel in the Chitose River—the wheel is located toward the bottom left of the image, half submerged beneath a wooden frame

Photo by author

Object 4: The Indian water wheel

As illustrated in the previous example, powerful comparisons can set *de facto* standards, which one is then forced to negotiate. Yet, while Hokkaido officials and their salmon production schemes were caught in comparisons not of their making, their own comparative efforts were not mere attempts to fashion Hokkaido after Euro-American models. Consider the Indian water wheel, a device used today to capture salmon in Hokkaido's Chitose River. Its analysis demonstrates why comparative practices cannot be reduced to imitation, but must instead be viewed as complicated and creative practices of bricolage.

Ito Kazutaka, a member of SAC's first graduating class, revolutionized Hokkaido's fisheries by instituting the salmon ranching system that remains the backbone of today's salmon industry. In 1886, at the request of the Japanese Government, Ito traveled to North America to study U.S. and Canadian fisheries practices, particularly those related to fish cultivation, with an eye to improving those of Hokkaido. During his 12-month whirlwind tour, Ito traversed the continent, visiting more than 15 states and provinces.[5] By the time Ito returned to Hokkaido, his notebooks were filled with meticulous and detailed line drawings of hatchery incubators and fish capture devices—and his mind was racing with new ideas. At the time, modern fisheries science in North America was still embryonic, so Ito's job was less to help Hokkaido "catch up" with the West than it was to help the island's industries join the mounting wave of late-nineteenth-century fish culture. During his trip to North America, Ito saw much that interested him, but he did not choose a unified model or make a singular comparison. Instead, he compared and contrasted fragments from each place he visited. Rather than trying to measure up to a pre-existing standard for fish culture, he was attempting to craft something novel.

When he visited the Columbia River, Ito had observed fish wheels, which were used at the time to harvest salmon. Although he very accurately understood the functioning of the fish wheels, Ito misunderstood their origin; he assumed they were an American Indian technology when they were instead an invention of Euro-American fishermen. When he returned to Hokkaido, Ito combined the design of Columbia River fish wheels with a Honshu style weir to create an innovative method for harvesting fish for the hatcheries he was also building. He called the device he built an Indian water wheel, explicitly citing its American reference point, to highlight that it was a product of comparative thinking. A version of the device remains in use today.

The Indian water wheel was part of the wider salmon cultivation system that Ito developed using multiple comparisons simultaneously. In the U.S. state of Maine, Ito saw a fish hatchery and considered it a useful tool for scientific fisheries management. Combining inspiration from the Maine facility, the Columbia River fish wheel, and the Honshu weir, among others, Ito became a pioneer in the development of sea-ranching. Under the influence of his work, staff at Hokkaido's salmon hatcheries raised young fish until they were ready to migrate to the sea and then released them into rivers and the ocean, as if turning cattle out to pasture. As adults, the salmon returned to the rivers of their birth to spawn. Staff at the hatcheries could then take a small portion of the returning fish, propagate their eggs, and begin the cycle again.

Hatcheries were redolent of Japanese modernity: technologically impressive, comparable and legible to the West, and demonstrative of Japanese innovation, they were a scientific management practice that would ostensibly improve nature. Hatcheries were popular in Hokkaido, and between 1888 and 1908 the fish cultivation program there grew to a network of 50 hatcheries—a faster expansion than that seen on the U.S. West Coast (Kobayashi 1980, 97). From archival materials, Ito seems to have positioned comparative thinking as central to fisheries innovation and modernization. In addition to setting up Hokkaido's first hatchery, he also founded a fisheries society that focused on sharing and comparing information from around the world about evolving fish technologies.

Ito's spirit of comparative innovation has persisted in Hokkaido's fish hatchery sector, which is now the world's most productive sea-ranching program. At present, it produces more than a billion juvenile salmon annually (Fukuzawa and Hirabayashi 2018), as Ito's comparisons continue to shape salmon bodies and populations.

Landscape multiple

These salmon are creatures of comparison; comparisons are literally the stuff of their flesh. Some comparisons have made their way into salmon bodies through landscape change and new ideals of natural resource management. Consider the effects of the Kaitakushi's agricultural projects and of the logics promulgated by SAC. The irrigation dams, denuded stream banks, drained marshes, and agricultural pollution that have flowed from their comparisons have dramatically reduced the ability of salmon to spawn in Hokkaido's rivers. Other comparisons have made their way into the bones and scales of salmon through Japanese desires for an internationally competitive salmon industry and the hatcheries systems associated with such intensive harvest regimes. Technologies such as weirs and fish wheels have blocked salmon from swimming upstream and spawning on their own, funneling them instead into holding pens for hatchery use. By modifying salmon reproduction, the comparative practices of hatcheries have left a direct imprint on the genetics and morphology of these fish.

Today, Hokkaido's landscapes and salmon populations look nothing like they did in the 1860s. Nearly all of the island's rivers are diked or dammed, their bottoms lined with concrete rather than the small stones that salmon need to lay their eggs. Over multiple generations, cement ponds and pelleted feed have provided evolutionary pressures on salmon that are inherently different from those of undercut banks and free-flowing, insect-filled rivers.

These changes in Hokkaido's landscapes and salmon populations cannot be understood as generic forms of *modernity, progress,* or *environmental degradation*. Rather, I posit that they must be understood in relation to the specific comparisons through which they have come into being.

Since the nineteenth century, Hokkaido's landscapes and its inhabitants have been remade by Japanese desires to transform the island and its fish into a landscape that is at once legibly "modern" and distinctly "Japanese." Such a process has required comparisons that are specific, material, and concrete. In the case of Hokkaido, many of those comparisons have been with the American West and, in the case of salmon, with the Columbia River. These comparisons are layered upon others—especially those of Ainu people who harvested, managed, and traded the region's salmon for hundreds of years within a different set of comparative practices with people, places, and objects from Honshu, Kamchatka, Siberia, and China. While traces of those comparative practices remain, they have been irrevocably torqued by subsequent comparisons of nation-making and modernization. Through such practices of comparison, the evolutionary futures of Hokkaido's landscape relations, along with those of its fish, have been altered in ways that cannot be undone. Thus, one cannot understand their configurations and forms without attending to the ongoing material persistence of layers of comparative practices.

Comparisons, seen through Hokkaido's landscapes, are always inside the material stuff of the world, even as it is iteratively compared anew. Histories of comparative practices are sedimented into the island's landscapes and accreted in fish bodies. This is the *enfolded multiplicity* that animates this chapter. Practices of comparison have pulled the American West and the Columbia River into Hokkaido's landscapes in a material way. When we look at how comparisons are embedded in this context, we see how even these landscapes of state-led development are themselves multiple; they are made not by some pure, internal, Japanese logic, but by a set of comparative encounters that continually bring bits of other places, practices, and logics inside that which is called Hokkaido.

Returning to Haraway's query—who and what do I touch when I touch a Hokkaido salmon? Among countless other relations, I touch the histories of comparison that I have outlined in this chapter, and through them, the places that those comparisons bind together. Through attention to historical detail, landscape changes, and salmon bodies, I have sketched a nascent method for exploring landscape multiplicity. In turn, I offer this focus on the relationship between landscapes and multiplicity as one approach for studying the *world multiple*.

Notes

1 This process included renaming the island, which was previously called Ezo by ethnic Japanese and which continues to be called Ainu Moshir by many Ainu people. It also involved the established and widespread colonial practices of ignoring the territorial claims of the island's indigenous residents.

2 The Japanese Government officially classified Russia as a second-rate country and thus sent few officials and students there (Togawa 1995, 215).

3 The first woman did not attend the school until 1918, after its name had been changed to Hokkaido Imperial University.

4 See Ahrens (1877a) for another example of a European recommendation that the Japanese learn about salmon canning practices in Oregon.

5 The information on Ito in this section is from the displays and conversations with staff at the *Chitose Sake no Furusato-kan* (Chitose Salmon Aquarium) in Chitose, Hokkaido, as well as from the book *Ito Kazutaka to tsunagaru hitobito* (Ichiryu Kai 1987). See also Ito's original report *Hokkaido-cho dainibu suisanka beikoku gyogyo chosa fukumeisho* (1890).

References

Ahrens, H. 1877a. *Oshu e itaku yushutsu no Kaitakushi sake kanzume ni kan suru houkokusho, Ahrens shokai* (Report on the consigned export of the Hokkaido Colonization Commission's canned salmon to Europe, Ahrens Company.) Archival material. File: H. Ahrens 008. Northern Studies Collection, Hokkaido University, Sapporo, Japan.

—. 1877b. *Kaitakushi gaikokujin kankei shokan* (Correspondence related to the Hokkaido Colonization Commission's foreign employees.) Archival material. File: H. Ahrens 008. Northern Studies Collection, Hokkaido University, Sapporo, Japan.

Bauduin, Albertus Johannes. 1879. *Nemurosan sake kanzume no honro mikomi market ni tsuki kaitou* (Response to the inquiry about the market possibilities for canned salmon from Nemuro,) *Kaitakushi gaikokujin kankei shokan* (Correspondence related to the Hokkaido Colonization Commission's foreign employees.) Archival material. File: Bauduin, Albertus Johannes 045. Northern Studies Collection, Hokkaido University, Sapporo, Japan.

Canned Foods Association of Japan. 1934. *Marine Foods Canning Industry in Japan*. Tokyo: Canned Foods Association of Japan.

Clifford, James. 1997. *Routes: Travel and Translation in the Late Twentieth Century*. Cambridge, MA: Harvard University Press.

Duke, Benjamin C. 2009. *The History of Modern Japanese Education: Constructing the National School System, 1872–1890*. New Brunswick: Rutgers University Press.

Ferguson, Will. 1998. *Hokkaido Highway Blues: Hitchhiking Japan*. New York: Soho Press.

Fujita, Fumiko. 1994. *American Pioneers and the Japanese Frontier: American Experts in Nineteenth-Century Japan*. Westport, CT: Greenwood Press.

Fukuzawa, Hiroaki and Yukihiro Hirabayashi. 2018. *Preliminary 2017 salmon enhancement production in Japan*. NPAFC Doc. 1762. Hokkaido National Fisheries Research Institute, Japan Fisheries Research and Education Agency. https://www.npafc.org/status-of-stocks

Haraway, Donna J. 2008. *When Species Meet*. Minneapolis, MN: University of Minnesota Press.

Hokkaido Prefectural Government. 1968. *Foreign Pioneers: A Short History of the Contribution of Foreigners to the Development of Hokkaido*. Sapporo: Hokkaido Prefectural Government.

Ichiryu, Kai. 1987. *Ito Kazutaka to tsunagaru hitobito* (*The people connected to Ito Kazutaka*). Ito Suai.

Ito, Kazutaka. 1890. *Hokkaido-cho dainibu suisanka beikoku gyogyo chosa fukumeisho* (Report from the survey of American fisheries by the Hokkaido prefecture's fisheries department, second section). Sapporo: Hokkaido Prefecture Fisheries Department, Second Division.

Kobayashi, T. 1980. "Salmon Propagation in Japan." In *Salmon Ranching*, edited by J. E. Thorpe, 91–107. New York: Academic Press.

Lien, Marianne and John Law. 2011. "'Emergent Aliens': On Salmon, Nature, and Their Enactment." *Ethnos* 76 (1): 65–87.

Mason, Michelle. 2012. *Dominant Narratives of Colonial Hokkaido and Imperial Japan: Envisioning the Periphery and the Modern Nation-State*. New York: Palgrave Macmillan.

Medak-Saltzman, Danika Fawn. 2015. "Empire's Haunted Logics: Comparative Colonialisms and the Challenges of Incorporating Indigeneity." *Journal of Critical Ethnic Studies* 1 (2): 11–32.

Mohacsi, Gergely and Atsuro Morita. 2013. "Traveling Comparisons: Ethnographic Reflections on Science and Technology." *East Asian Science, Technology, and Society* 7: 175–183.

Mol, Annemarie. 2002. *The Body Multiple: Ontology in Medical Practice, Science and Cultural Theory*. Durham, NC: Duke University Press.

Morita, Atsuro. 2013. "Traveling Engineers, Machines, and Comparisons: Intersecting Imaginations and Journeys in the Thai Local Engineering Industry." *East Asian Science, Technology, and Society* 7: 221–241.

Nitobe, Inazo. 1893. *The Imperial Agricultural College of Sapporo, Japan*. Sapporo: Imperial College of Agriculture.

Penner, Liisa. 2005. *Salmon Fever, River's End: Tragedies on the Lower Columbia River in the 1870s, 1880s, and 1890s: Articles from Astoria Newspapers*. Portland, OR: Frank Amato Publications.

Russell, Harold S. 2007. *Time to Become Barbarian: The Extraordinary Life of General Horace Capron*. New York: University Press of America.

Stoler, Ann Laura. 2016. *Duress: Imperial Durabilities in Our Times*. Durham, NC: Duke University Press.

Strathern, Marilyn. (1991 [2004]). *Partial Connections*. Walnut Creek, CA: AltaMira Press.

Swanson, Heather, Anna Tsing, and Nils Bubandt. 2015. "Less than One but More than Many: Anthropocene as Science Fiction and Scholarship-in-the-making." *Environment and Society: Advances in Research* 6 (1): 149–166.

Togawa, Tsuguo. 1995. "The Japanese View of Russia before and after the Meiji Restoration." In *A Hidden Fire: Russian and Japanese Cultural Encounters, 1868–1926*, edited by J. Thomas Rimer, 214–227. Stanford, CA: Stanford University Press.

Walker, Brett L. 2004. "Meiji Modernization, Scientific Agriculture, and the Destruction of Japan's Hokkaido Wolf." *Environmental History* 9 (2): 248–274.

—. 2005. *The Lost Wolves of Japan*. Seattle, WA: University of Washington Press.

Walsh, Hall. 1877. *Kaitakushisei sake kanzume shishoku hinhyo* (Evaluation from the tasting of the canned salmon produced by the Hokkaido Colonization Commission,) *Kaitakushi gaikokujin kankei shokan* (Correspondence related to the Hokkaido Colonization Commission's foreign employees.) Archival material. Northern Studies Collection, Hokkaido University, Sapporo, Japan.

Willcock, Hiroko. 2000. "Traditional Learning, Western Thought, and the Sapporo Agricultural College: A Case Study of Acculturation in Early Meiji Japan." *Modern Asian Studies* 34 (4): 977–1017.

Chapter 8

Spectral forces, time, and excess in Southern Chile

Cristóbal Bonelli

To investigate some of the questions raised by the editors of this volume, I focus on one of the inspirational conceptual sources at stake. The editors invite us to think about multiplicity by substituting the word *body* with the term *world*. This substitution becomes possible when we think of both words as sharing a similar logical level: They operate in everyday language as classes of things, generic abstractions that we can mobilize to think about situated socio-material realities. Moreover, the substitution of these words spectrally echoes the book *The Body Multiple: Ontology in Medical Practice* by Annemarie Mol (2002), in which she experiments with tracing, or following, the multiple ways in which an object is relationally practiced. From the heart of Western biomedical techno-science, *The Body Multiple* invites us to reconsider static, predefined, and coherent notions of the body. Rather, Mol suggests that the body's ontological status depends upon heterogeneous practices, insofar as the body is enacted in multiple ways through different epistemic practices.

Given Mol's argument, we might wonder: What is at stake when we are invited to substitute the word "body" with the generic word "world"? Contributors to this volume have offered one answer: "world" should not be considered a coherent place *out-there* that precedes everyday practice. Rather, it should be understood as a highly contingent, conceptual, and empirical place where the juxtaposition of different "practical achievements" (cf. Stengers 2011; Woolgar and Lezaun 2013) generates unpredictable ontological configurations between humans and nonhumans. Therefore, taking up the challenge to think about such configurations in the world multiple entails analytically reconsidering what counts as political, and thus reconsidering the relation, rather than the final and absolute substitution, between the "politics of what" and the "politics of who." The "politics of what" questions what kind of reality is produced through the co-existence of humans and nonhumans, while the "politics of who" underscores issues around who has, or does not have, the right to speak and to act (Mol 1999).

Reconsidering, rethinking about, or somehow analytically refreshing the imbricated relation between the "politics of who" and the "politics of what" becomes particularly relevant if we consider contexts characterized by violence and authoritarianism. In this chapter, my concern is to interrogate violent socio-material situations that involve both the "politics of what" and the "politics of who." One such context is my home country of Chile, where one of the cruellest military dictatorships in Latin America prevailed between 1973 and 1990 under the leadership of Augusto Pinochet. Here, I posit the deployment of this dictatorship as a series of cruel and violent attempts to enact the modern "one-world world" project (see Law 2015 and Chapter 1 in this volume), which I suggest inherently implied attempts to also impose a *one-time temporality*.

Indeed, I position the deployment of this dictatorship as a failed attempt to do away with the juxtaposition of heterogeneous practical achievements. Put differently, I show how the practical achievements of such a project intended to produce a one-world world could not fully erase singular socio-material traces and temporalities of previous forms of co-existence between humans and nonhumans. In this respect, I suggest that the singularities of human practices matter crucially when thinking about *the world multiple*: Human singularities are not classes of things. Instead, they are specific and embedded in socio-material realities. As such, they resist any kind of substitution or generic epistemic abstraction.

In what follows, I challenge notions of the one-world world and demonstrate how embracing the concept of the world multiple necessarily entails careful ethnographic exploration of socio-material entanglements that express "more than one" temporalities. To do this, I build on Mol's scholarship by proposing a third kind of politics, *the politics of when*. I offer this heuristic as a way to attend ethnographically to temporal socio-material singularities that emerge within environments strongly affected by state terrorism. By so doing, I aim to demonstrate how different processes of *worlding* do not share a pre-established temporal dimension that allows for the secular co-existence of different practical achievements, which are prone to be co-ordinated or even assembled into a common world (Latour 2007). Moreover, I want to shed light on how the unpredictable ontological configurations between humans and nonhumans taking part in the world multiple might also be predicated upon what I suggest are spectral socio-material forces.

Inscriptions—time—excess

In this chapter, I mobilize ethnographic examination of different *life-times* through stories that are based on two ethnographic snapshots that capture the subject of my long-term fieldwork in Southern Chile.

Image one

Consider a woman who wishes to inscribe the name of her husband, *Miguel Cuevas Pincheira*, on the bridge where Miguel was killed before being thrown into a river—the same bridge where the human body of Miguel disappeared more than 40 years ago.

Image two

Consider the inscription of the dictator's name, *Augusto Pinochet*, upon a massive rock located in a Pewenche indigenous community in the same region —a rock that is considered by many local inhabitants to be sacred—a rock that, as I will show, has resisted destruction.

In order to investigate temporalities stemming from the violent attempt to enact one-world world realities, I contrast the name of *Miguel Cuevas Pincheira* with that of *Augusto Pinochet*. Miguel is one of the dictatorship's victims, and his name is one that persists as an expression of the singularity of a disappeared human. In contrast, *Augusto Pinochet* is the name of the dictator, and his is a name associated with deleting a communal indigenous singularity.

What I foreground in this chapter is how violent practices that attempt to impose one-world realities and one-world temporalities encounter socio-material expressions of spectral resistance. In particular, I show how personal names and things are related, and how the configurations between names and things can express not only a multiple topological time "folded" into things (Serres and Latour 1995), but also the singular excess latent in every being. My aim is to explore processes of socio-material resistance through considering the analytical challenges at stake when the relation between a name's inscription and the notion of *excess* is considered. My use of this term resonates with Marisol de la Cadena's (2015) definition of excess as that which overcomes the limit of what can be understood and thought by modern knowledge practices (see also Chapter 2 in this volume). De la Cadena (2015) focuses on the state as a quintessential guarantee of modern practices and suggests that engaging with that which exceeds modern knowledge would imply the transformation of the state itself, and therefore the disruption of history—and historical time—as the main register of the real. Building on these ideas, I posit an additional dimension of excess: that which emerges from the material inclination of humans and nonhumans to continue to co-exist and enhance themselves. Such material inclination has been the subject of longstanding philosophical discussions and has been conveyed in Western philosophy by Spinoza, and other philosophers, through the word *conatus*,[1] which indexes the way in which "each thing, as far as it lies in itself, strives to persevere in its being" (Spinoza 1996, part 3, prop. 6).

Specifically, I show how this insistence on existing, which is inherent in different beings, exceeds and resists the cruel and violent attempts of the modern one-world world project to limit our understanding of the world and temporality to a single sphere. I also show that the ways through which the co-existence between humans and nonhumans perseverates depends strongly on an enduring relevance of relations. It depends on the emergent outcome of a situated relational materi-alism (Abrahamsson et al. 2015) for which human practices are pivotal. Finally, I also suggest the need to resist a certain conceptual post-human rhetoric that runs the risk of concealing the human in its attempts to destabilize human exceptionalism. What can we learn about the human in places where human lives have been literally interrupted or anonymized? Which *politics of when* spring from socio-material entanglements in places strongly affected by state terrorism? I suggest that the world multiple, understood as the intersection and overlapping of different practical achievements, always entails a socio-material spectral dimension that exceeds the practical achievements of the one-world world project and its one-world temporalities.[2]

Miguel Cuevas Pincheira

On September 20, 1973, around 10:00 p.m., Miguel Cuevas Pincheira, a 41-year-old shoemaker, agricultural worker, father of five, and member of the Chilean

Figure 8.1 Miguel Cuevas Pincheira
Acuña (2015)

Socialist Party, was violently arrested at his home in Santa Bárbara, Southern Chile. A group of more than ten people (including custom officers and local civilians) forcefully entered Miguel's house, found him in bed, and brutally removed him from his home in full sight of his family members. Miguel's wife, Norma Panes, has been searching for him—or his body—ever since the evening he was arrested and became one of those colloquially known in Chile as "the disappeared."[3] According to reports given by witnesses to the Chilean Commission for Truth and Reconciliation (*Comisión de Verdad y Reconciliación*), which was created in the 1990s during the first democratic government after Pinochet, Miguel and others arrested that night were tortured, killed, and finally thrown into the waters of the Bío Bío River from a bridge that connects Santa Bárbara and the province of Quilaco.[4]

Thirty-seven years later, I met Norma at her home in Santa Bárbara. Having spent 18 months conducting fieldwork within rural Pewenche indigenous communities, I wanted to learn more about how Pinochet's dictatorship had been deployed in the region. Many of the people with whom I spoke were from the Queuco Valley, where I used to live, and they referred to Pinochet's dictatorship as the "cruellest period ever." Further, some told me that their communities were still under a "curfew" period (Sp. *Acá todavía vivimos en toque de queda*), which evoked the times of Pinochet's dictatorship, which I, as a member of the Chilean community, had thought to be over.[5] Moreover, recent processes of land reclamation in the Queuco Valley had been violently interrupted; controversial executions had occurred in the early 2000s, and many people were or had been imprisoned because of the reclamations.

During my visit, Norma told me how traumatically violent the first months of the dictatorship had been in the region, and provided me with details about how the perpetrators "came together in a caravan of death to carry out the worst atrocities ever."[6] She also told me that some Pewenche families had never reported crimes committed against them because "fear still persists, and people have not been able to break those internal repressive fences they have within themselves."[7] Additionally, Norma does not know what happened to Miguel's body. She said, "I have been fighting for 37 years, trying to know what they did with Miguel. [...] If they threw him into the river, we will never find his body. Even God was against us that night because there were heavy rains and terrible winds. I don't know where they killed Miguel. Probably they killed him on the Quilaco bridge." Although she is uncertain about the exact location where Miguel was killed, she and other families decided to build a memorial at the Quilaco bridge several years ago.

With a shaky voice, Norma added, "That memorial is dead, and I want to fix it. We have a cross, but the memorial does not have the names; the memorial is dead because it does not have the name of Miguel. [...] and this allows his murderers to go about freely."

***

Figure 8.2 Memorial at the Quilaco bridge
Photo by author

Norma's words raise several important questions. What could the name *Miguel Cuevas Pincheira* do for Norma, her community, or the broader state if it were inscribed upon the place of Miguel's death? If we recall the old Spinozian concern about "what a body can do," and how bodies can be defined by their persevering socio-material capacities to affect and be affected (see Deleuze 1992), we could suggest that names can be considered bodies with similar capacities. Even though the human, physical body of Miguel disappeared, his name is still a body insofar as it is capable of affecting the world and turning the memorial into a socio-material witness. What is the vital relevance of the inscription to which Norma refers? How do we conceptually foreground the dignity at stake in Norma's desire for such an inscription? What do these intimate, ethnographic moments reveal about temporalities in places where different worldings are violently interrupted? Finally, what kind of intimate worlding does a named inscription, such as the one Norma desires, entail?

Drawing on the concepts I discussed in this chapter's introduction, I suggest the inscription of Miguel's name upon the Quilaco bridge can be considered a practical achievement triggered by Norma. For her, anonymising Miguel at the memorial by omitting his name entails the risk of supporting a certain kind of impunity. Given that justice within modern liberal democracies depends on epistemic practices performed by the bureaucratic machinery of tribunals, whose decisions are based on written texts, is justice possible without such written inscriptions? What I foreground is that particular moment in which the singular name of Miguel is socio-materially inscribed by Norma upon her socio-material surroundings—that is, upon the memorial. From that moment forward, Miguel's life-time immanently resists, and is capable of destabilizing, the period of curfew implied by a memorial without names.

Inscription—exscription—excess

I have claimed that the inscription of Miguel's name is a practical achievement triggered by Norma, but it is also made possible by the forced exile of a personal name from its physical body. I suggest the inscription of Miguel's name on the memorial is not just a symbolic abstraction of Miguel, but is also an instantiation of his lyric and irreplaceable singularity, which resonates with what Harrison (2003) noted when he analyzed inscriptions of the names of American victims of the Vietnam War on national monuments. The achievement initiated by Norma is an expression of Miguel's inclination to persevere in existence, but it may also be understood as a form of socio-material resistance against the dominant-colonialist processes of signification. Such resistance is triggered by Norma's perseverance in finding a place to commemorate her husband's name. What is more, the inscription of his name, I suggest, entails a particular relational process of *exscription* (Nancy 1991, 2001, 2008) that reveals a dimension of Miguel's name that exceeds language, considering that signs are not always closed to the inscription of their meanings.[8] Processes of exscription emerge in relation to what is inscribed as meaning, allow us to analyze a dimension of signs beyond equivocal interpretation, and index an extra-linguistic domain that exceeds language. That which emerges as the place from which every inscription is possible is referred to by Nancy as sense.[9] From this, I argue it might be plausible to think about excess as an ontological dimension that exceeds language, and not just as something that overcomes the limit of what can be understood by modern knowledge practices. This particular understanding of excess as an expression of sense is relevant in the Chilean context because it potentially expropriates inscriptions enacted from the one-world world practices; sense exceeds the historical register of the state and allows us to consider a dimension that is not governed by equivocal processes of signification.

Since signs are not always limited to their ascribed meanings, Norma's inscription of Miguel's name is an example of how names can exceed language. In the moment of its inscription, Miguel's name expresses a constitutive part of his singularity that resists generic abstraction and overcomes analogy. I suggest this is possible because there is a spectral dimension of Miguel that cannot be touched or erased by violent practices of the one-world world project.

Specifically, I speak of the corporality of a ghost with whom Norma has co-existed for decades, a corporality that is "neither present nor absent, but spectral" (Derrida 1994, xix).[10] In this sense, the inscription of the name upon the memorial could be considered a *spectral practical achievement*. By making this statement, I highlight how each thing, as far as it lies in itself, strives to persevere in its being despite the violent interruption of worldings, such as arrest and murder in the case of *Miguel Cuevas Pincheira*. In fact, the name *Miguel Cuevas Pincheira* allows the apparition of a singular space that precedes symbolic dimensions, a spacing "without which any symbol could symbolize" (Nancy 2001, 54). Thus, the inscription of Miguel's name makes it possible not only for Norma to remember Miguel without being pervaded by destructive memories, as clinical psychologists have taught us (Castillo 2013); it also crucially operates, to echo Nancy, as an *exscription of sense* of Miguel's extra-linguistic singularity.

In providing an account of this dramatic situation affecting Norma and Miguel, I highlight the need to develop conceptual tools that allow us to think about how the juxtaposition of practical achievements can entail unpredictable ontological configurations that resist univocal temporalities, such as those imposed by Pinochet and the one-world world project. Indeed, Norma's act of writing the name of her disappeared husband upon the bridge enables us to reflect on the materiality of a name, and how it could be understood as a body with the capacity to affect (Deleuze 1992). In this case, a name has the ability to exscribe the singularity of Miguel. This capacity makes explicit how temporalities are never predefined, but rather strongly depend upon the insistence on existing of different spectral forces that both exceed and resist the cruel and violent attempts of the modern "one-world world" project. This capacity also makes explicit how the world multiple can be seen as the practical outcome of heterogeneous practices that also involve a form of undeletable spectrality.

In order to better contemplate the world multiple as the juxtaposition of practical achievements without losing sight of how material things persevere in their being, I shift focus to the name of *Augusto Pinochet*. In particular, I examine the way in which this name was inscribed in one of the valleys of Alto Bío Bío as an instantiation of dominant-colonialist processes of signification. In so doing, I highlight the processes of inscription at stake in any juxtaposition, but also consider the ethical relevance of thinking in terms of *conatus* and *exscription* in places where the one-world world project has been violently enacted.

Augusto Pinochet

During Pinochet's violent dictatorship, his administration built many roads that enabled the exploration and subsequent extraction of natural resources and the construction of hydroelectric dams. Recently, I have written about the particular ways in which these roads transformed social and material relations in the country (Bonelli and Gonzalez 2016). Here, my focus is on how this infrastructural unfolding also resulted in the killing of people like

Figure 8.3 Augusto Pinochet
Source: Library of National Congress of Chile

Miguel and in the deployment of a dominant-colonialist processes of signification. Consider the image in Figure 8.4.

The rock in the photograph is situated alongside a rural road connecting the Queuco Valley with Ralco, which is about 70 kilometers from the Quilaco bridge where Miguel was killed. Residents of the valley have characterized this rock as possessing a great force, or *newen*, and as a powerful shamanic meeting place, or *renü*. It is known as a place where people used to establish communication with beings from other dimensions. This characterization may seem strange to people who view rocks as inert, anonymous objects that have no force or agency and are usually separated from human capacities to perceive the world.[11] However, in Pewenche analytics, newen is a force immanent to all beings inhabiting the indigenous world (Bonelli 2015; Course 2013). For instance, different entities, such as a place, person, tree, river, or even a rock, can manifest this intrinsic earthly force, which varies in intensity from entity to

Figure 8.4 Pinochet's rock and/or renü
Photo by author

entity. There are entities whose force is practically imperceptible, which makes it difficult to interact with them. Other entities, such as the rock in the photograph, possess such force that their presence never goes unperceived. Specifically, the rock's newen permitted the inhabitants' ancestors—probably those with certain shamanic qualities—to see the future, to obtain visions relevant to the valley communities.[12]

In recent decades, however, residents of the valley have noted the newen of this rock has been altered. In fact, it is no longer known only as a place with newen, or as a renü. Instead, it is now known as "Pinochet's Rock." In daily life, "Pinochet's Rock" serves as a reference point for Pitril's residents and separates what are now known as Lower and Upper Pitril. The rock also expresses drastic socio-material alterations in the valley. In the words of Renato, one of Pitril's residents:

> This rock has a history; it's not just another rock. It's a sacred rock where there was *newen*. [...] It's a really big rock, two machines couldn't move it [...] It remained on the side of the road, they couldn't move it, because that rock was a *renü* where there was a lot of newen, where those with a lot of spiritual knowledge would go to learn how we were going to be in 50 years, in 60, or today [...] When they built the road there, the machines started to break it, break it, break it, and trucks flipped over and people died, and they

Figure 8.5 Inscription upon Pinochet's rock and/or renü
Photo by author

> couldn't move it. The rock stayed so pretty, and it stayed there [in place] [...]
> And they made Pinochet's thing, the inscription that says: "Opening of the
> road. President Augusto Pinochet." It's like a monument that they made to
> Pinochet for everything he did, for the road, for the minimum wage he paid
> the people to build the road.

Renato's reference to Pinochet, the road, and the rock can be considered an
example of how infrastructures visibly express wider political projects (Larkin
2013). However, I would suggest the persistence of the rock tells us about
something more than the infrastructural expression of state power. Rather, the
rock is an expression of a sort of Pewenche material force that resists through
being: it perseveres because of its *newen*.[13]

This situation evokes Marisol de la Cadena's description of indigenous
protests over mining projects at Ausangate Mountain in Peru, a mountain
considered by the indigenous to constitute a nonhuman entity—an earth-being
known as *tirakuna*—that has the capacity to "drive people crazy, and even to
kill them" (2010, 339). In Peru, as in Southern Chile, people evoke entities
that exceed or fall outside of modern one-world understandings of the nature–
culture division *tout court*. Runakuna people in Peru consider the Ausangate
Mountain to have the agency and power of a human, and the *renü* of Chile

empowers people with the capacity to see the future. Yet what I wish to emphasize here is that the rock's materiality could be understood as a distinct ethnographic event; its materiality reveals something about the immanent inclination of the rock to continue to exist. I argue it does so without necessarily invoking indigenous mobilizations that question the univocality and objectivity of modern politics, which considers both rocks and mountains inert.

At first glance and within linear logic, one could think that the temporality of the *renü* or sacred rock was fully deleted "by reason or force" (to use the motto on the Chilean coat of arms); that is, by the chronologic temporality brought with the roads of development. However, I suggest that the enduring qualities of the rock, illustrated through its continuing existence, *exscribes* the name of the dictator, and in so doing materially resists full encapsulation and appropriation by the logocentric, possessive desire of Pinochet. In other words, the exposure of Pinochet's name to the *newen* of the rock exceeds the inscription of the dictator's name. It also potentially expropriates the inscription enacted from one-world world practices and one-world temporalities. By resisting destruction, this rock fights back against geological naturalism, in which any particular rock could be substituted by any other rock. Through its mere continued presence, the rock demonstrates how the name Pinochet fails to travel as an "immutable mobile" (Latour 1987)—as a body that moves around but also holds its shape. What this rock teaches us is that a certain material force, its newen, escapes brutal attempts at appropriation enacted by the logocentric and extractivistic one-world world project. In fact, similarly to the persistence of Miguel's name at the bridge, the singularity of this rock as *newen* cannot be fully deleted. It has a particular politics of when, which is strongly predicated upon the spectral socio-material qualities of the rock.

To be clear, I am not suggesting the spectral socio-material quality of the rock presupposes an everlasting essence outside of all relations. Some proponents of the object-oriented ontology project might make such a claim. Indeed, Harman has proposed:

> The science of geology does not exhaust the being of rocks, which always have a surplus of reality deeper than our most complete knowledge of rocks but our practical use of rocks at construction sites and in street brawls also does not exhaust them [...] rocks themselves are not fully deployed or exhausted by any of their actions or relations.
>
> (Harman 2013, 32)

Such a claim would imply the deletion of Renato from the scene, along with all those Pewenche inhabitants who insist on speaking about the enduring *newen* of different entities. When considering how this rock perseverates in its being, we must instead take into account a form of the world multiple that entails heterogeneous relations, such as those with Renato. Moreover, the material resistance of the rock also teaches us how the practical achievements of the one-world world project failed to fully erase the singular socio-material traces of previous co-existences between humans and nonhumans.

Conclusions

In this chapter, I have implied a redisposition of different narratives, names, things, and images, which resonates with the Deleuzian understanding of ethics as nothing but experimentation (Deleuze 2007). Consequently, this text could

Figure 8.6 Bricolage

be considered an inherent and partial part of the world multiple (Jensen, 2017); it produces its singular intersections of different spectral practical achievements and overlaps with their singular temporalities. Thus, I conclude by discussing the following visual bricolage, which is itself a practical achievement enacted by this text.

What does this bricolage do? What are its capacities for affecting the ways we think about politics, time, and processes of worlding? Surely, it invites us to consider how the world multiple can be a partial and never-ending entanglement of different practical achievements. When we consider the named inscriptions of Augusto Pinochet on the rock and Miguel Cuevas Pincheira on the memorial, this bricolage allows us to think about the limitations of the one-world world project as something that attempts to impose dominant-colonialist temporalities and processes of signification. Indeed, this bricolage could rather be understood as expressing the complexities of how the world multiple entails material entanglements of various temporalities emerging upon bodies that persevere in their being.

However, if we examine this bricolage while remaining aware of how our ethnographic accounts can inscribe forms of concealment, we notice what is conspicuous by its absence. This bricolage runs a risk of concealing Norma and Renato, people whose practices are pivotal in this context for considering the ways in which entities insist on existing and on resisting any kind of substitution or epistemic abstraction. In my ethnographic account, the presence and actions of Norma and Renato are crucial for thinking through the politics of who has, or does not have, the right to speak and act. Without Norma, Miguel cannot speak; without Renato, the rock cannot speak. Moreover, their presence and actions are also quintessential elements for interrogating the politics around what kind of reality is produced through the co-existence of humans and nonhumans. Finally, I draw attention specifically to how their presence and actions are necessary for understanding what I call the *politics of when*: those socio-material qualities that result in the multiple temporalities inherent in any process of worlding. Such temporalities, and the particular ways in which Miguel and the rock perseverate, differ in important ways that provide a foundation for thinking about how things persevere in their beings.

For instance, even if Miguel's name and the *newen* are both spectral socio-material forces that insist on existing, the name is inherently human and indexes a human singularity in intimate relation to Norma. The political practices around the name and the *newen* also differ. Their imbrication in political issues depends strongly upon the relations in which they partake; their materialities work in concert and are relational (Abrahamsson et al. 2015). As Renato told me, Pinochet is not univocally remembered as an instantiation of evil. Some people are grateful to him because his dictatorship brought salaried jobs and "comfort" to their communities. Additionally, Pewenche people living around the rock are not persevering with those practices that allowed the rock to be a shamanic place where the future could be foreseen. Nevertheless, I have tried to establish that ethnographic attentiveness to the socio-material perseverance of the rock through its *newen* allows us to destabilize the practical achievements of the one-world world project and to imagine another existence potentially prone to being re-enacted. Indeed, paying ethnographic attention to the singular excess latent in every being is a way to explore how different worldings entail different temporalities. However, it is also a way to verify, as Jorge Luis Borges wanted, that *there is a dignity that the victor cannot reach*. For this reason, I advocate embracing the spectre's socio-material dignity in contexts strongly affected by state terrorism, as it is one of the places from which we are able to make time differently and from which we can give due respect to the singularity of human lives.

Acknowledgments

I am grateful to Marisol de la Cadena, Magnus Course, Marcelo Gonzalez Galvez, Marianne de Laet, John Law, Annemarie Mol, Marcelo Pakman, Oscar Reyna, Jeltsje Stobbe, Gerard Verschoor, Else Vogel, and Marina Weinberg for having read and commented on previous versions of this text. I am also grateful to the editors of this book for their invaluable suggestions for improvement. Part of the writing up of this article was supported by the Interdisciplinary Center for Intercultural and Indigenous Studies (CIIR, Conicyt/Fondap/15110006) and by the National Research Center for Integrated Natural Disaster Management (CIGIDEN, Conicyt/Fondap/15110017.

Notes

1 I am grateful to Andrés Haye for having brought this to my attention.
2 Acuña, Patricio Torres. 2015. "Miguel Cuevas Pincheira (La historia va mas allá que la palabra)." Paperblog, July 25. http://es.paperblog.com/miguel-cuevas-pincheira-la-historia-va-mas-alla-que-la-palabra-patricio-torres-acuna-3312979/ accessed July 20, 2018.
3 The word *desaparecido* (disappeared) in Chile and other Latin American countries is a noun used to denote people kidnapped by government agents for political reasons, generally tortured, and then killed (see Sluzki 1990).
4 Memoria Viva. n.d. "Miguel Cuevas Pincheira." http://www.memoriaviva.com/Desa parecidos/D-C/cue-pin.htm accessed July 20, 2018; see Acuña (2015) Op. cit. n.2.
5 For a critical reflection on temporality and imperial formations, see Stoler (2008).
6 Verdugo, P. 2015. *Los zarpazos del Puma. La caravana de la muerte*. Santiago: Catalonia.
7 All interviews were originally held in Spanish. Translations are my own.
8 In relation to the concept of exscription used by Nancy, I took inspiration from the Marcelo Pakman's (2014) work on psychotherapy and imagination.
9 This elaboration of sense resonates with Deleuze's (1969) immanent understandings of sense as a virtual dimension that exceeds language and affords the actualization of what exists.
10 For an analysis of Derrida's concepts in relation to political violence in Argentinean literature, see Mandolessi (2016). For an exploration of techno-science experiments

and the temporalization of scientific objects in relation to Derrida's spectral logic of time, see Schrader (2010).

11 As Povinelli (1995) discusses in a similar case, the Pewenche description is in this sense fully converted into belief and therefore often subordinated to discourses that only evaluate it in terms of patrimonial value but never as a description of "reality."

12 For a deeper analysis regarding these prophetic visions, see Bonelli (2016).

13 For a productive ethnographic contrast regarding the patrimonialization practices of a stone in Coatlinchan, Mexico, see Rozental (2016). In that place, the removal of a similar stone from a local context has triggered ecological consequences, which make apparent how pre-Hispanic objects are "actors within interdependent social, environmental, and material relationships that might better be described through ecological frameworks" (ibid. 183).

References

Abrahamsson, Sebastian, Filippo Bertoni, Annemarie Mol, and Rebecca Ibáñez. 2015. "Living with Omega-3: New Materialism and Enduring Concerns." *Environment and Planning D: Society and Space* 33 (1): 4–19.

Bonelli, Cristóbal. 2015. "Eating One's Worlds: On Foods, Metabolic Writing and Ethnographic Humor." *Subjectivity* 8 (3): 181–200.

—. 2016. "*Palabras de piedra, materiales proféticos y políticas del dónde.*" *Antipoda. Revista de Antropología y Arqueología* 26: 19–43.

Bonelli, Cristóbal and Marcelo Gonzalez. 2016. "*¿Qué Hace un Camino? Alteraciones Infraestructurales en el Sur de Chile.*" For special issue "Ontologies, Cosmopolitics and Systems of Knowledge in South America" edited by S. Schavelzon. *Revista de Antropologia* 59 (3): 18–48.

de la Cadena, Marisol. 2010. "Indigenous Cosmopolitics in the Andes: Conceptual Reflections beyond 'Politics.'" *Cultural Anthropology* 25 (4): 334–370.

—. 2015. *Earth-Beings: Ecologies of Practice Across Andean Worlds.* Durham, NC: Duke University Press.

Castillo, Isabel. 2013. *El (im)posible proceso de duelo.* Santiago: Ediciones Universidad Alberto Hurtado.

Course, Magnus. 2013. "The Birth of the Word: Language, Force, and Mapuche Ritual Authority." *Hau: Journal of Ethnographic Theory* 2 (1): 1–26.

Deleuze, Gilles. 1969. *Logique du sens.* París: Éditions de Minuit.

—. 1992. "Ethology: Spinoza and Us." In *Incorporations*, edited by J. Crary and S. Kwinter, 625–633. New York: Zone.

—. 2007. "On Spinoza." In *Lectures by Gilles Deleuze.* http://deleuzelectures.blogspot.com/2007/02/on-spinoza.html accessed July 20, 2018.

Derrida, Jacques. 1994. *Specters of Marx: The State of the Debt, the Work of Mourning, and the New International.* New York, London: Routledge.

Harrison, Robert Pogue. 2003. *The Dominion of the Dead.* Chicago, IL: University of Chicago Press.

Jensen, Casper Bruun. 2017. "New Ontologies? Reflections of some 'Turns' in STS, Anthropology, and Philosophy." *Social Anthropology/Anthropologie Sociale* 25 (4): 525–545.

Larkin, Brian. 2013. "The Politics and Poetics of Infrastructure." *Annual Review of Anthropology* 42: 327–343.

Latour, Bruno. 1987. *Science in Action: How to Follow Scientists and Engineers Through Society*. Milton Keynes, UK: Open University Press.

—. 2007. "Turning around Politics: A Note on Gerard de Vries's Paper." *Social Studies of Science* 37 (5): 811–820.

Law, John. 2015. "What's Wrong with a One-World World?" *Distinktion: Journal of Social Theory* 16 (1): 126–139.

Mandolessi, Silvana. 2016. "*Narrativas espectrales en la literatura postdictatorial en Argentina*." In *Narrativas del Terror y la Desaparición en América Latina*, edited by Liliana Feierstein and Lior Zylberman, 193–207. Buenos Aires: EDUNTREF.

Mol, Annemarie. 1999. "Ontological Politics: A Word and Some Questions." In *Actor Network Theory and After*, edited by John Law and John Hassard, 74–90. Oxford: Blackwell.

—. 2002. *The Body Multiple: Ontology in Medical Practice*. Durham, NC: Duke University Press.

Nancy, Jean Luc. 1991. *The Inoperative Community*. Minneapolis, MN: University of Minnesota Press.

—. 2001 [1993]. *Le sense du monde*. París: Galilée.

—. 2008. *Corpus*. New York: Fordham University Press.

Pakman, Marcelo. 2014. *Texturas de la imaginación. Más allá de la ciencia empírica y del giro lingüístico*. Barcelona: Gedisa.

Povinelli, Elizabeth. 1995. "Do Rocks Listen? The Cultural Politics of Apprehending Australian Aboriginal Labour." *American Anthropologist* 97 (3): 505–518.

Rozental, Sandra. 2016. "In the Wake of Mexican Patrimonio: Material Ecologies in San Miguel Coatlinchan." *Anthropological Quarterly* 89 (1): 181–220.

Schrader, Astrid. 2010. "Responding to *Pfiesteria piscicida* (the Fish Killer): Phantomatic Ontologies, Indeterminacy, and Responsibility in Toxic Microbiology." *Social Studies of Science* 40 (2): 275–306.

Serres, Michel and Bruno Latour. 1995. *Conversations on Science, Culture and Time*. Ann Arbor, MI: University of Michigan Press.

Sluzki, Carlos. 1990. "Disappeared: Semantic and Somatic Effects of Political Repression in a Family Seeking Therapy." *Family Process* 29 (2): 131–143.

Spinoza, Baruch. 1996. *Ethics*. London: Penguin.

Stengers, Isabel. 2011. "Comparison as a Matter of Concern." *Common Knowledge* 17 (1): 48–63.

Stoler, Laura. 2008. "Imperial Debris: Reflections on Ruins and Ruination." *Cultural Anthropology* 23 (2): 191–219.

Woolgar, Steve and Javier Lezaun. 2013. "The Wrong Bin Bag: A Turn to Ontology in Science and Technology Studies?" *Social Studies of Science* 43 (3): 321–340.

Chapter 9

Temporalities in translation

The making and unmaking of "folk" Ayurveda and bio-cultural diversity

Moe Nakazora

The world multiple in Indian medicine

"Unity in diversity" has been one of the most powerful and frequently used political slogans in post-independence India. Among Indian intellectuals, it has also served as a convenient explanatory model for "what India is." It implies that in India there are different castes, religious communities, and language groups, having multiple viewpoints (against *a* world) that should be co-ordinated and brought into unity. Against this prevalent assumption, postcolonial scholars have insisted that cultural differences as such did not exist in Indian society *a priori*, but have been made and remade in colonial and postcolonial encounters. For instance, different caste groups were formulated in the encounter of colonial technologies of governance (such as statistics) and hierarchical relations in local Hinduism that used to be more fluid and dynamic.

If we direct our eyes to Indian medicines, a similar observation could be made. India has been regarded as a model case for medical pluralism (Leslie 1992), with biomedicine and diverse traditional medical "systems" co-existing. Despite such assumption of medical pluralism, if we closely look at the trajectory of Ayurveda, we could recognize that not systems, but translations and relations, are in the foreground (Zhan 2009).

Around the turn of the twentieth century, the modernization of Ayurveda was attempted by adopting the institutional framework of biomedicine such as hospitals, universities, and pharmaceuticals. The idea of such reform, called *misra* (integrated) Ayurveda, was that for Ayurveda to be understood properly, any concepts and techniques must be explained using the terminology of modern science. What was interesting was the logic that the supporters of misra Ayurveda used to avoid Ayurveda appearing subordinate to biomedicine. They claimed that contemporary Ayurveda had been corrupted and had deteriorated, as could be seen in its lack of anatomical knowledge, which mainly resulted from its merger with Buddhist disciplines, Unani (Muslim) medicine, and other folk forms of knowledge. They insisted that to recover "scientific" Ayurveda, they should re-establish Ayurvedic education based on ancient texts by mimicking the institutional framework of biomedicine. In fact, for them, such an effort is not "mimesis" but "recovery," since any institutional devices and findings of biomedicine had been "already expected" in ancient Ayurvedic texts.

For instance, the leading figure of misra Ayurveda, Dwarkanath, writes in translating between *slaismika ojas*, one of the most important life energies in Ayurveda, and the protein properdin as follows:

> As James B. Conant noted, "from the history of science, we know that any theories can be overturned not by contradictory facts but by better theories." Based on this, the contemporary research (on the effect of properdin for natural resistance against infections) does not contradict with the existing Ayurvedic concept of *slaismika ojas*. Rather it only *rearticulates* the old theory later. Properdin is not *slaismika ojas* itself, but their similarity is surprising. Both are the part of the wider scheme of *kapha*.

In this short paragraph, the particular Ayurvedic concept of slaismika ojas was connected with properdin, but at the same time re-differentiated. What is noteworthy is Dwarkanath's strategy of re-differentiation to show the superiority of Ayurveda *in translation* (Zhan 2009). He emphasizes the similarity and difference between slaismika ojas and properdin by saying that the latter "only re-articulates" the former. This comparison is consistent with the overall misra Ayurveda project, claiming that ancient Ayurveda had "anticipated" any findings of biomedicine. In particular, here the *temporal* differences between Ayurveda and biomedicine, rather than spatial or epistemological differences, were articulated in translations.

Such attention to the temporal dimension by revivalists of Ayurveda encouraged me to think about a possible direction for envisioning "the world multiple." In my thinking, temporality guides us away from understanding "multiple worlds" within a conventional framework of cultural relativism and liberal multiculturalism that assumes the existence of different social worlds distributed in spatially different locations. Thus, in this chapter, I attempt to describe layers of multiple realities happening simultaneously in the same place as encounters of practices with different temporalities in contemporary India. As I will show in the next section, the recent global politics of biodiversity has brought various practices such as "folk" Ayurveda, plant taxonomy, and local anthropology into direct contact in India. Here, attending especially to the temporal dimension, I focus on a particular project in a rural state in North India, Uttarakhand, to elucidate how such practices are connected and re-differentiated, and what forms of knowledge *emerge in translation*.

Biodiversity in translation

The recent global pharmaceutical politics regarding biodiversity and traditional medicine like Ayurveda have made unexpected connections among different actors in India. In the late 1980s, many life-science corporations showed renewed interest in natural resources and indigenous knowledge in the hope of finding leads that might lead to the development of new drugs. Since then, there has been greater interest in the intellectual property rights of indigenous people and farmers. The 1992 UN Convention on Biological Diversity mandated that drug companies accessing indigenous resources and knowledge must share with the source nations and communities any economic benefits that accrue. Although it is in many ways a fragile mandate, the Convention's idiom and institutional framework have had noteworthy effects on the practices of the parties involved. In line with the tenets of the Convention, approval of bioprospecting by scientists has required benefit-sharing agreements with the resource owners and, as a consequence, numerous nongovernmental organizations (NGOs) and indigenous activists have emerged aiming to prevent illegitimate exchange.

More recently, state actors and NGOs of "resource nations" have launched documentation and digitalization projects to catalogue "valuable" indigenous knowledge. In India, in the late 1990s, the Government and NGOs succeeded in overturning several patents granted by the patent offices of the European Union and the United States for neem, turmeric, and basmati rice, which were recognized as having originated in India. Since the revocation of granted patents involves huge costs and takes time, to give patent examiners improved access to background information (prior art) of Indian traditional knowledge, it was thought prudent to make a database of traditional knowledge that would make it easier to spot misappropriation during the initial phases of patent examinations (Saxena, Roy, and Tripathi 2002, 340–3). According to the Indian National Biodiversity Act (2002)—national legislation enacted in line with the Convention on Biological Diversity—in India the "traditional knowledge" to be databased includes codified (documented) as well as uncodified (not documented but may be orally transmitted) information, the assumption being that the knowledge-holders for each category are different: Ayurvedic doctors and traditional folk healers (*Vaidya*), respectively. The Act specified that the central government is responsible for databasing already documented knowledge, and state governments are responsible for recording/collecting/eliciting and databasing oral knowledge.

As Gaudillière (2014) pointed out, these databasing projects led to complex translation activities among seemingly incommensurable knowledge traditions, including Ayurveda, plant sciences, and international law. My previous research (Nakazora 2015a), focusing on a state government project in Uttarakhand called the People's Biodiversity Register, elucidated how such translating activities have produced new connections and separations among diverse practices involved in the project.

For instance, in Uttarakhand, plant taxonomists at the Forest Research Institute were allocated the task of formalizing orally transmitted folk medical knowledge. Notably, their initial activities took place in the herbarium rather than in "fields." Since colonial times, Uttarakhand has been explored by botanists, a number of them famous, and as a result the Forest Research Institute herbarium, the second-largest herbarium in India, now preserves 330,000 specimens. Importantly, most of these specimens were collected with the assistance of Vaidyas. Based on that fact, what the scientists attempted first of all was to carefully examine specimen labels, where information not apparent in the specimens themselves—such as the location of collection, the local use of plants, and the parts—can be found. In this way, scientists tried to find "original Uttarakhand" plants, then later to remove "colonial mistakes" by conducting interviews with present Vaidyas (Nakazora 2016).

As I have written elsewhere (ibid.), this "herbarium specimen-based" databasing methodology has led to unexpected translations, that is, connections and differentiations between scientific and indigenous knowledge. In the process of comparing their herbarium specimens with the fieldwork, scientist discovered that *garhwali* local names that Vaidyas use were relatively stable *compared with* scientific names. While most of the local names (84 out of 86) remained the same between the time when specimens were originally collected and the present, the scientific names had changed many times due to new methods of classification—from morphological to reproductive characteristics to generics and back—over the past century. As I have described in detail elsewhere (Nakazora 2016), this realization of the variability of scientific names *in comparison to* local names motivated the scientists to propose "parataxonomy," the setting of scientific and traditional taxonomies alongside one another, sometimes allowing for translation of one to the other for the new databasing project, rather than relying on the "universal" and "robust" methodology of science.

From biodiversity to bio-cultural diversity: Toward new translation

In spite of such a reflexive process in translation, this project was criticized by various actors in India, which has led to more translating activities in Uttarakhand. Many Indian anthropologists have been especially critical of the project's focus on indigenous knowledge concerning "natural" resources, especially medicinal plants that have economic and ecological values. They pointed out that such reduction occurred because medicinal plants were the only element in indigenous medical "systems" commensurate with modern science (Mishra 2018). To represent and protect the "whole system" of folk medicine, they further proposed adopting a "cultural property" scheme rather than one of "intellectual property."

Joining this proposal by local anthropologists, the transformation of global environmental discourse from "biodiversity" to "bio-cultural diversity" has also motivated various local NGOs and state governmental institutions in India to database "folk medicine" as a "holistic system." The concept of bio-cultural diversity implies that "the diversity of life is made up not only of the diversity of plants and animal species, habitats and ecosystems found on the planet, but also of the diversity of human cultures and languages," thus nature and culture are seen as "dual aspects of a single entity, bio-cultural diversity" (Maffi 2012). Although such ideas were rare when I was carrying out research for my PhD in 2011 and 2012, during a visit to my fieldwork site in 2014 I heard scientists and NGO staff discuss the concept of "bio-cultural property" and I learned they were gradually initiating documentation of "folk medicine" as a "whole" system.

Nevertheless, the category of "folk medicine" is an arbitrary construction of colonial and postcolonial medical history in India, as explained at the beginning of this chapter. In an attempt to (re-)make professional and scientific Ayurveda by borrowing the institutional framework of biomedicine, the gap between Ayurveda and a host of indigenous practices with which it had once been closely associated has widened, and has been essentialized as a gap between the professional and folk sectors of Indian medicine (Brass 1972, Leslie 1992). This arbitrary construction of categories of Ayurveda/folk medicine in relation to biomedicine, however, seems to be forgotten among those discussing bio-cultural diversity, who assume that folk medicine is a rigid system existing *a priori*. In Uttarakhand, the work of the prominent anthropologist P. C. Joshi gives particular form to this naturalization.

When I started field research related to medicinal plants in Uttarakhand, most people mentioned P. C. Joshi as "the first person one must contact to ask for advice." Indeed, copies of his medical anthropological works on tribal medicine in Uttarakhand are well circulated in the local NGO network, *Sambandh* (cf. Langford 2003)[1]. While his works are based on fieldwork he conducted in collaboration with local NGOs, they simultaneously and reflexively constitute the activities of NGOs by giving concrete images of "folk medicine." Among his papers, his medical anthropological study of a people identified generically as Khos (Jaunpuri, Jaunsari, and Rewai speakers) (Joshi 1993) is especially famous. This essay was explicitly situated within a medical anthropological frame informed by Loren Eisenberg and Arthur Kleinman's distinction between disease and illness (Kleinman 1988).

In his paper, Joshi classifies the knowledge of illness in Jaunsar into spiritual and naturalistic categories, sketching a classificatory distinction between *doṣ*, illness that is due to "superhuman" or "supernatural" forces, and *bīmārī*, illness that is due to "the state of imbalance in the body in terms of 'hot–cold,' 'wind,' and 'air' humours" (Joshi 1993, 257). According to Joshi, people treat *doṣ* with supernatural treatment (*jhāḍ-phūṅk*), while for *bīmārī* they rely on medicinal plants (*jadi buti*). Joshi further delineates a typology of supernatural beings, which includes *devata* (gods) and *devi* (goddesses) associated with various kinds of illness. The devi include the *matri*, who are "culturally postulated fairy beings" divided into two categories, pure (*succi matri*) and impure (*maśān matri*). Other types of doṣ are *dag* (witches), *dankin* (the evil eye), and *bis-būtī* (a set of mysterious ingredients possessing supernatural powers passed down through families).

Thus, Joshi depicts Khos medicine as a bounded and consistent system having rigid "folk" classifications regarding disease/illness, natural treatment (jadi buti)/supernatural treatment (jhāḍ-phūṅk), and names of spiritual beings. This clear-cut classification was also used in the new project in Uttarakhand to document the "whole" system of "folk medicine." Here, we will follow the documentation process of such a project to explore the particular separation and connection emerging in translation.

Treatment as effect

In March 2015, with staff of Alaknanda Ghaati Shilpi (AAGAAS) Federation and an anthropologist, Sharma, I visited 17 Vaidyas in six villages around Pipalkoti in Chamoli district. Although the questionnaire was based on Joshi's classifications of Jaunsari medicine above, the targeted villages were not tribal areas, but villages where the dominant castes are Garhwali Brahmans and Rajputs. The scenes of the interviews with Vaidyas, who seemed to have knowledge of jhāḍ-phūṅk and *mantra* as well as that of medicinal plants, were where the differences *emerged*, rather than being eradicated, between the project assumption of "folk Ayurveda" and Vaidyas' views of their treatment *in translation*. Such emergent differences eventually inspired the Vaidyas to generate new ideas about their knowledge, as I will show in the next section.

Raghuveer Singh Negi is a 45-year-old Vaidya who resides in a village located 7 km away from the nearest town, Pipalkoti. A farmer as well, he has continued herbal treatment and pulse treatment as the only Vaidya in the village for 21 years. First, Sharma, the anthropologist, asked questions about the content of jhāḍ-phūṅk and differences among spiritual beings (*sayyad*, *bhūt*, *bhairav*), following Joshi (1993). His answers are below:

> It is like this. He's got fever. His heart is now apart from him. He's fallen into bad conditions. Jhāḍ-phūṅk is for these situations. Also, sayyad (Muslim's ghost) attacks someone. You can call such being as bhūt. More or less they are the same. You can call him as sayyad, bhūt, or bhairav (the ghost closely related to Lord Shiva). Jhāḍ-phūṅk is for them. Also, it is for *bīmārī*.

Then, asked about the differences between bhūt, *chaya*, and *piśāc*, Raghuveer replied, "It is only a way of saying. They are the same. In old language, it is chaya, while in new language, it's piśāc. In Muslim's language, it is sayyad." The villagers surrounding Raghuveer during the interview also started to say "they are the same! The different names, but the situation itself is the same," and "Uttarakhand is adobe of god (*deva-bhūmi*), and naturally there reside various gods." Here, Jaswant, a member of staff of AAGAAS Federation, said "they are only kinds of fruits in the same basket," implying that although differences exist, they are not so important.

Moreover, when Sharma changed the question and asked "what is chaya?" Raghuveer's answer was "Chaya is *when* we cannot eat or drink anything." Then the surrounding people again started to say, "In the midnight, I was reading a book, and then, I suddenly started to cry without any reason," and [addressed to myself] "Because you are a foreigner, you must climb up to the mountain with colorful clothes, but we do not do such things. We wear black dresses (for protection)." This kind of conversation typically ended up with someone proposing, "Let's share our experiences of our encountering ghosts," followed by the recounting of various episodes in which they fought bravely and wisely with the ghosts in sudden encounters (field notes, March 13, 2014).

In this typical interview situation, we should note Raghuveer's indifference about the classifications of supernatural beings, which was central in P. C. Joshi's paper. Such indifference was gradually adopted even by the NGO staff who were supposed to make a classification list, and it finally led to various narratives about people's experiences of encountering ghosts. Thus, in this process of documentation, the questions of the project team about how Vaidyas define and classify spiritual beings, based on the assumption of folk medicine as a holistic and consistent system, have been transformed by Raghuveer and/or the surrounding people, and further by the NGO staff who attempted to mediate different visions of knowledge. When they say "Chaya is [. . .] *when* we cannot eat or drink anything," or "We wear black dresses when we go up to the mountain," they relate a name of a particular spiritual being with the environment where it *arises* or *happens*, and with the treatment of and protection for it. Here, their translations show that spiritual beings are not one element of an abstract system, but a particular environment and situation existing only in connection with the specific treatment and protection that they adopt.

I would like to explore further such a vision of knowledge as emerging in contact zones through the example of an interview with a female Vaidya, Swami Devi. Swami Devi, as well as being a prominent Vaidya, serves as the principal of an elementary school in the village, near Pipalkoti.

> Chaya attacks someone. People get afraid. That is related to fear. Imagine you go somewhere, and something attacks you. Your body starts to get fear. At that moment, Chaya happens. Bhūt, piśāc, sayaad, there are many beings.

Swami replied to Sharma's questions at the principal's office, where a number of powdered medicines had been made from medicinal plants. Then she proceeded to explain the usage of medicinal plants rather than that of jhāḍ-phūṅk, saying that she rarely performs jhāḍ-phūṅk these days, as she has more focus on medicinal plants (field notes, August 17, 2014).

In this interview, like Raghuveer Singh, Swami Devi does not connect chaya with specific meaning. Rather, recognizing it as an event that *happens*, she relates it with "fear" which people feel when it happens.

Raghuveer Singh's narrative—"jhāḍ-phūṅk is for them (doṣ). Also, it is for bīmārī"—denied the project team's distinction between natural treatment (jadi buti) and bīmārī/supernatural treatment (jhāḍ-phūṅk) for doṣ. Also, Swami Devi articulated that these days she uses jadi buti *instead of* jhāḍ-phūṅk for her treatment. My own research has made clear that this attitude is widely shared among Vaidyas in Uttarakhand. Most of them are now better at the treatment of jadi buti, which they recognize not as a completely different category of treatment from jhāḍ-phūṅk, but as the contemporary alternative to it. They often recall the gradual conversion of most Vaidyas from jhāḍ-phūṅk to jadi buti, saying "our guests tended to have more interests in medicinal plants rather than in jhāḍ-phūṅk." Interestingly, such "guests" include not only those who visit them to learn their treatment, but also botanists who have been contacting them since colonial times and, more recently, the staff of government institutes and NGOs seeking to document their knowledge.

Different knowledge

The contact zones revealed the Vaidyas' concept of "knowledge" was very different from the assumptions about knowledge prevalent in the project on folk medicine. What is important for Vaidyas is not the preservation of the particular system of "folk medicine," but the effect of daily treatment, that is, how it works on a particular person, environment, and events (cf. Langford 2003). In fact, in search of effective treatment, Vaidyas keep incorporating different elements from multiple sources.

Vaidyas in Uttarakhand become Vaidyas by gaining knowledge from multiple sources. For example, one Vaidya said that he learned pulse treatment from a Vaidya from other regions of India, while another Vaidya learned about jadi buti treatment from his friend's uncle because his grandfather, who taught him jhāḍ-phūṅk, did not have proper knowledge of jadi buti. Furthermore, despite the project team's assumption that folk medicine is orally transmitted informal knowledge, distinct from formal Ayurveda, Vaidyas often mention written texts as their knowledge source. The knowledge sources include classical Ayurvedic texts, which they say their grandparents or parents once had, being lost at some point; as well as contemporary popular Ayurvedic books. For the former they express their desire for "authentic" Ayurveda; while about the latter they say "in such books, we can easily learn which medicinal plants are good, and what kind of effect they have." Here, we see how their search for effective treatment denies the boundary of knowledge systems that the project assumes between formal Ayurveda and folk medicine. The study of Vaidyas in this region by Langford (2003) further suggests how Vaidyas cross the boundary between Ayurveda and biomedicine, represented by the concept of *kīḍe*. According to Langford, Vaidyas call the invisible in biomedicine, including cells and bacillus, kīḍe, without mentioning the definition and classification of it. What is more important for them is how it causes diseases or where it exists, that is, its effect and environment. ("When red kīḍe is generated, people become healthy. He doesn't fall ill. When white kīḍe prevails and push red kīḍe out, people get ill.") (Langford 2003, 286–87.)

The project's documentation process exposed a conflict between the project's assumption of "folk Ayurveda" as a bounded system of knowledge and the Vaidyas' concern that their treatments be effective. However, it should be noted that the project also provided Vaidyas with occasions to discuss what their "knowledge" is, where they attempted to mediate and translate such expressed differences. In the following section, we will follow what forms of knowledge emerge in such mediation, especially paying attention to the temporal dimension.

Generating new temporalities

Translation is a part of this situation, in that many of the present Vaidyas recall classical texts their ancestors once had as "the authentic Ayurvedic knowledge that has been lost." They also say that "once our ancestors had the mantra which could cure all the diseases." On the other hand, in the context of the herbal projects of the Uttarakhand Government, they insist "the government should provide the proper trainings of medicinal plants for us." How do these desires for the past and future relate to each other? Consider the following conversation, which took place during the project.

VAIDYA 1: In India, the Veda culture is written in Sanskrit. Ayurveda is one of them. However, India was ruled by the empires like Mughal and Britain. Because of that, the Veda culture had been gradually lost. The British introduced biomedicine. The government did not support Ayurveda. *Then, Ayurveda lost its importance and even the doctors do not have legitimate knowledge* [author's emphasis]. From now on, the government has to do much for Ayurveda and medicinal plants. There is a variety of medicinal plants around us. Our gods and goddesses said that there is no medicinal plant from which we cannot develop medicine, and further that there is no disease which cannot be cured from such medicines. Ayurveda was transmitted from India to China, and Chinese still practice it. These days 30 percent of Veda techniques are supported by Chinese [. . .] In China, people very carefully cultivate medicinal plants and gain much profit from them. On the other hand, we Indians are [. . .]

VAIDYA 2: In India too, it is not that people do not practice it. We do practice it. *The thing is, we do not have proper knowledge anymore.* For example, in one ritual, it is expected that only one cook is in charge of cooking, while others clean and set the table. The scientific reason for this is that if only one cook is in charge of cooking, the amount of salts and spices can be perfectly set. And if those who set the table also clean the room, we can solve the sanitation problem. Though these things are in our conduct and attitudes, we do not completely understand them.

VAIDYA 3: Ayurveda is a part of Veda. There are more things than we can see. These are spiritual. For example, one woman is suffering from a difficult delivery. If we tie one particular medicinal plant around her waist, her baby easily comes out. This is surprising [. . .] Ayurveda is magic.

VAIDYA 2: As I said just now, tradition exists inside us. For example, during delivery, women are supposed to go near a barn of cows. There is a scientific reason for this, that is, the urine of cows prevents the breeding of bacteria. These are practiced, but they are accepted as tradition. Scientific reasons behind it are never thought about. That is a problem.

VAIDYA 4: There used to be the great god, *Charaka*.[2] He made Ayurveda. He named all the medicinal plants, recorded everything, and finally wrote *Charaka Samhita* including the procedures for making medicines. But nowadays there are not so many people who understand the content.

VAIDYA 5: We should educate the society and change the system. Recently babies after delivery are not left near a barn of cows, but are passed to relatives or other people. In hospitals, new babies often suffer from jaundice, but there were no such things happening in villages before. While modern medicine prevails, Veda is gradually lost. *The government should educate people.*

VAIDYA 6: Vaidyas need medicinal plants. Medicinal plants grown in lower lands are easily collected, while those in higher lands are not. In addition to this, recently the forest department have given many restrictions on collecting medicinal plants.[3] The state government has told us to cultivate medicinal plants. However, it is costly, and further, here people have not had such training.

VAIDYA 7: *Many of these projects are conducted away from mountains. They should do them for us too.*

In this conversation, although various topics are mentioned, the common underlying assumption is that authentic Ayurveda for them *used to* exist. Such "authentic Ayurveda" is described in different ways: Ayurveda based on scientific logic, Ayurveda as magic, or Ayurveda in classical texts like *Charaka Samhita*. That is, they imagine the "whole knowledge" differently. However, they all point out the absence of such knowledge "here and now" by saying that no-one (including themselves) practices it properly. Namely, what they practice is, for them, not folk medicine as a system but *partial* (incomplete) Ayurveda.

Then, they ascribe their "loss" to colonial rules and the resultant government's (over-)support for Western medicine, and further to Uttarakhand's unique situation in light of the recent state government's restriction on the collection of medicinal plants. Not only that, they also propose various ways of recovering knowledge, such as "the government should educate society," or "they should organize projects on medicinal plants." For them, Ayurveda is knowledge (*jñān*), which used to exist but does not any more, not "here and now," and thereby should be recovered *in the future*.

It should be noted that in this temporal scope of knowledge of Vaidyas, "recovering authentic Ayurveda" is somewhat similar to the revivalists' logic of Ayurveda in postcolonial India, introduced at the beginning of this chapter. However, while the revivalists generated a sense of temporality to support adopting the institutional framework of biomedicine—an effort intended to recover Ayurveda while insisting on Ayurveda's superiority ("Ayurveda had expected the findings of modern science")—here Vaidyas' claims reflect their translation between their daily sense of treatment as *effect* and the project's requirement for their Ayurvedic knowledge. Namely, their everyday search for more *"effective* treatment" intersected with the project's search for folk Ayurvedic "knowledge" as property, leading to the specific temporal scope of knowledge existing in the past and future (not in the present): Their Ayurvedic knowledge, which the project searched for, used to exist and will be recovered in the future, and for the purpose of the recovery, in the present, they attempt to incorporate various (seemingly *effective*) elements from multiple sources in their daily practice, and they need the government's support. As you can see in the remark about cultivation projects of medicinal plants being one variation of the "government supports," their translation reflects the entanglement of previous biodiversity projects which focused on "medicinal plants." Therefore, the temporal scope of knowledge Vaidyas express in the project is the product of situated translation.

Ethnographic engagement?

How does a newly emerging vision of knowledge emerging in contact zones creatively relativize the original project assumption? Hirokazu Miyazaki's (2004) *The Method of Hope* is suggestive for thinking about differences among knowledge practices from the viewpoint of temporal orientations.

The Method of Hope describes how the sense of a lack of authentic self-knowledge leads Suvavou people in Fiji to archives as sites of inquiry. When Miyazaki as an anthropologist visited the archives, there were not only academic researchers but also Suvavou themselves, and the consultants/lawyers who were there in search of documentary evidence to support demands for compensation for the loss of ancestral lands—an effort so far without success. Suvavou people share the assumption that archives are the sites that preserve "truth" about themselves, while there is no authentic knowledge in Suvavou. According to Miyazaki, it is this sense of detachment from their own knowledge that makes people continue to inquire and to seek truth in the archives. In other words, recognition of partiality and the uncertainties of their knowledge in the present orients them to imagine the achievement of gaining truth *in the future.* By paralleling such knowledge practice with the knowledge of anthropologists and philosophers, Miyazaki relativizes the latter in terms of its past orientation.

The vision of knowledge of Vaidyas expressed *in translation* during the project, especially its new temporal scope, also relativized the assumption of "bio-cultural property." The idea of "bio-cultural property" implies the right of particular subjects toward knowledge that they have labored to produce *from the past to the present.* The basic idea of property rights regarding indigenous knowledge is as follows:

> Genes and cultural information have been produced and reproduced by farmers and indigenous people for thousands of years. However, just like female unpaid work, in spite of its effectiveness, their labor has not been recognized. On the other hand, when such information is processed and transformed in developed countries, its values were recognized in legal and political methods.
>
> (Kloppenburg 1991, 16)

In addition, "Those who added labor to natural resources should be given proprietary right and compensation" (ibid. 18).

As I have written elsewhere about intellectual property rights (Nakazora 2015b), the underlying property concept has been partially adopted from John Locke's, only it focuses on the economic right or rewards for what one labored to produce or the values that one added to natural resources in the past. That focus, combined with taxonomic and ethnological methods based on anthropology, generates the idea of an indigenous knowledge system that is a product of the past labor of the people and that can be extracted "here and now." It could be said that, in contrast to Vaidyas' sense of partiality regarding their "present" knowledge and their search for more *effective* knowledge, the peculiar temporality of the project assumption emerged *in their translations and encounter.*

Considering such temporal differences, can we think of different ways of translating from the project practice that assumes Vaidyas' knowledge as a rigid folk system that they have labored to produce from the past to the present? Miyazaki's ethnography (2004) offers a way of introducing a new temporality to anthropology and philosophy through Suvavou people's knowledge practice. For me, this chapter itself is an enactment of intersecting but different traditions of translation in anthropology and science and technology studies, which could be renewed through visualizing different temporal engagements between Vaidyas and the project of bio-cultural diversity.

I would like to explore the issue of temporality by considering several "experimental" projects in anthropology, science and technology studies, and information technology engineering. These researchers are trying to alter the basic architecture of databases in order to open up the possibility of a dynamic archive that captures knowledge in motion as performance. They are also trying to make the metadata—the categories of classification—amenable to rewriting by users (Waterton 2010). This is the case, for example, with the Australian science and technology studies researcher Helen Verran, who has worked with information technology engineers and Yolngu people to archive the indigenous knowledge of the latter in a format similar to their original oral tradition, using video and interactive media (Verran et al. 2007). As Waterton summarizes,

> what these scholars are doing is trying to make space for the *generative* within the archive, within the confines of the 'database' that has histori- cally been thought of as a container, but which they are transforming so that it becomes more like a site, a ceremonial ground where movement, difference, negotiation relating to knowledge can take place.
>
> (Waterton 2010, 666)

This work by anthropologists of science is suggestive in that the technical details such as the categories of classification are crucial in transforming temporal orientations and the politics of the project, thereby realizing better dialogue and connectivity among different knowledge traditions. For my informant botanists in my previous research on the biodiversity databasing project (Nakazora 2016), the proposition of "parataxonomy" was one of such experiments with the database, reflexively adopting discourses of postcolonialism in India. Parataxon- omy means the setting of scientific and traditional taxonomies alongside one another, sometimes, but not always, allowing for translation of one into the other. It was considered to be a technical way to realize a "postcolonial" database and to move forward from organizing indigenous knowledge on *medicinal plants* through the "universal" and "robust" methodology of science.

   This chapter has focused mainly on the emergent phase of "bio-cultural diversity," in which protecting not only the diversity of plants and animal species, but also that of human cultures and languages, is said to be crucial for the planet. Just as the Anthropocene concept creates new relations across the divide between the "two cultures" of the natural and social sciences (Swanson 2016) by making a new imaginary of entanglement of human and nonhuman, the introduction of bio-cultural diversity in India made a space for anthro- pological knowledge to be incorporated in environmental projects. Anthropo- logical knowledge was adopted when databasing the "whole" system of folk medicine as "cultural property." Here, following the actual translation process, I observed how the Vaidyas' vision of their knowledge differs from that assumed in the "holistic" folk medicine concept of the project, especially in terms of temporalities. Based on this finding, could we propose an alternative form of documentation as *techno-cultural* process which adjusts to people's *making* of effective knowledge *toward the future* rather than representing folk medicine as an existing system? As a scholar of the anthropology of science, when engaging in the technical details of translation, I believe there should be the possibility of anthropology not as analysis, but as response.

Notes

1 Langford (2003) also noted that she was passed a copy of P.C. Joshi's paper by a local NGO staff. She shows how her informant Vaidyas' narratives on their treatment are different from Joshi's typological understanding of tribal medicine. This chapter follows her findings, though focusing more on how such differences emerge in translation at the particular project. Also, it explores the way in which the differences are partially mediated by Vaidyas themselves, paying attention to temporal dimension.

2 It is more accurate to call Charaka a saint rather than a god.

3 Partly due to the *Chipko* movement—the Gandhian environmental movement supporting the conservation of forests, which prevailed all over Uttarakhand in 1970—there have been strict restrictions on the collection of wood and plants especially above an altitude of 1,000 meters.

References

Agrawal, Arun. 2002 "Indigenous Knowledge and the Politics of Classification." *International Social Science Journal* 54 (173): 287–297.

Brass, Paul. 1972. "The Politics of Ayurvedic Education: A Case Study of Revivalism and Modernization in India." In *Education and Politics in India: Studies in Organization, Society, and Policy*, edited by Susanne Hoeber Rudolph and Lloyd I. Rudolph, 342–371. Cambridge, MA: Harvard University Press.

Gaudillière, Jean-Paul. 2014. "An Indian Path to Biocapital?: The Traditional Knowledge Digital Library, Drug Patents, and the Reformulation Regime of Contemporary Ayurveda." *East Asian Science, Technology, and Society* 8 (4): 391–415.

Joshi, P. C. 1993. "Culture, Health and Illness: Aspects of Ethnomedicine in Jaunsar-Bawar." In *The Central Himalayan Panorama*, edited by S. K. Biswas, 253–280. Calcutta: Institute of Social Research and Applied Anthropology.

Kleinman, Arthur. 1988. *The Illness Narratives: Suffering, Healing, and the Human Condition*. New York: Basic Books.

Kloppenburg, Jack. 1991. "No Hunting! Biodiversity, Indigenous Rights, and Scientific Poaching." *Cultural Survival Quarterly* 15 (3): 14–18.

Langford, Jean. 2003. "Traces of Folk Medicine in Jaunpur." *Cultural Anthropology* 18 (3): 271–303.

Leslie, Charles. 1992. "Interpretations of Illness: Syncretism in Modern Āyurveda." In *Paths to Asian Medical Knowledge*, edited by Charles Leslie and Allan Young, 177–208. Berkeley, CA: University of California Press.

Maffi, Luisa. 2012. *Biocultural Diversity Conservation*. London: Earthscan.

Mishra, Arima, ed. 2018. *Local Health Traditions: Pluralism and Marginality in South Asia*. New Delhi: Orient BlackSwan.

Miyazaki, Hirokazu. 2004. *The Method of Hope: Anthropology, Philosophy, and Fijian Knowledge*. Stanford, CA: Stanford University Press.

Nakazora, Moe. 2015a. "Pure Gifts for Future Benefit?: Giving Form to the Subject in a Biodiversity Databasing Project in India." *NatureCulture* 3: 106–121.

—. 2015b. "Between Commensurability and Incommensurability: Emergence of Ayurveda in the Contact Zones with Biomedicine, Alternative Medicine, and Intellectual Property Right Regime" (*Honyakukanousei to fukanousei no aida: seibutsuiryou, daitaiiryou, chitekishoyuukenseido tono settushokuryouiki ni okeru ayuruveda no seisei.*) *Jinbungakuhou* 107: 111–142.

—. 2016. "Infrastructural Inversion and Reflexivity: A 'Postcolonial' Biodiversity Databasing Project in India." In *Infrastructures and Social Complexity*, edited by P. C. Harvey, B. Jensen, and A. Morita, 309–322. Abingdon: Routledge.

Saxena, Aakanksha, Sudeep Roy, Kumar Parijat Tripathi, Akansha Saxena, Manoj Mishra, Sanhita Gupta, J. Singh and Ashok Sharma. 2002. "Indian Traditional Knowledge: New Attempts for Fortification and Globalization." *Journal of Medicinal and Aromatic Plant Sciences* 30: 340–343.

Swanson, Heather. 2016. "Anthropocene as Political Geology: Current Debates Over How to Tell Time." *Science as Culture* 25 (1): 157–163.

Verran, Helen, Michael Christie, Bryce Anbins-King, Trevor Van Weeren, and Wulumdhuna Yunupingu. 2007. "Designing Digital Knowledge Management Tools with Aboriginal Australians." *Digital Creativity* 18 (3): 129–142.

Waterton, Claire. 2010. "Experimenting with the Archive: STS-ers as Analysts and Co-constructors of Databases and Other Archival Forms." *Science Technology & Human Values* 35 (5): 645–676.

Zhan, Mei. 2009. *Other-Worldly: Making Chinese Medicine through Transnational Frames.* Durham, NC: Duke University Press.

Chapter 10

Healing in the Anthropocene

Stacey Langwick

In Tanzania, plant life and human life extend through one another, grow out of each other, and shape the scope of perceptual possibility.[1] The cycles of plant life —that is, their progressions, spaces, sensitivities, and struggles—drive the rhythm of everyday human labor and conversation. Assessments of the height of the corn, the color of its leaves, even the microregions where, in a given season, it is growing well involve careful discernments. These observations fuel fears of hunger and hopes of satiation. Reflections on plants shared with kin and those with whom one stands at a *daladala* stop or chats in the market while surveying the produce, articulate both individual and communal anxieties. The state of plants and the elements on which their growth depends (rain, sun, labor) are often an answer to the question "*Habari yako?*" [English, "What's your news?"] posed by a far-away friend or relative. Plants and planting not only shape social and material bodies, but also intervene in how they are experienced.

Even in large, densely populated urban areas, many Tanzanians pay attention to how elemental forces are shaping crops around the country. If one can, one owns a farm somewhere outside the city. Others know how high the corn is in their *nymbani kabisi*, that place one points to when asked where you and your people are from. Still others, who find themselves landless in Dar es Salaam, crowd the sides of the road and the medians with *mchicha* (amaranth) that they will sell for a little cash, as well as use to feed themselves and those for whom they care. Weeds and wild plants are also attended to, selectively left in gardens and fields. The patterns and placement of their growth are noted and revisited. Complaints of a stomach ache reveal that friends are aware of where medicinal plants can be found in the grassy patch near the house or along the road.

Gestures toward and with plants draw others into a shared poetics of space. For instance, one hot afternoon when walking between a strip of shops and stalls of vegetable sellers, my colleague Romana bent down and plucked the leaves of a scrubby, short *Euphorbia hirta* plant pushing up through the dry, packed earth. The singular weed growing in this heavily trafficked environment created a brief pause, drawing her and me into recognizing it and its striving. As she rubbed the sticky white fluid between her fingers for a moment, she remembered its reputation as helpful with digestive and respiratory complaints.

Such shared forms of attention to the dynamics of the co-creation of bodies and landscapes through plants provides orientation as well as sustenance and healing.

To draw attention to the specific ways that plants and people cycle through each other, I focus later in this chapter on the life of *mlonge* (*Moringa oleifera*) as it collaborates with Tanzanians through a local non-governmental organization (NGO) dedicated to the thriving of people in precarious conditions—those with AIDS, street children, orphans, pregnant teens who have found themselves abandoned, and others. Mlonge draws people together, establishing new collectives. It co-creates an eventful space as it challenges boundaries between food and medicine, traditional and modern, gift and commodity, and subsistence and commercial products. The politics of mlonge's worlding project is in these challenges to modernity's divides (Latour 1993). This argument highlights moments of collective labor among plants and people, rather than of human labor to harness the capacities of plant and their labor. It requires developing a way of accounting for plants' agency beyond that of resource (for knowledge, medicine, nutrition, shelter, etc.).

When plants exceed humans' instrumentalized knowing and use, then they also exceed a philosophy that calls us to search for essential ontologies, universal beings, and the qualities or properties of existence. They are not disciplined by first principles. Plants rather lead us to forms of knowing open to multiple histories, times, spaces, and senses as well as their incommensurabilities and frictions. To the world multiple. I am inspired by Michael Marder's (2013, 2016) insistence that our articulations of "life" include plant life more explicitly (and carefully). He argues for an attunement of our intellectual attention to the effects of specific relations between plants and humans. Such accounts challenge the reductions that enable the "one world" conceptions that are inherent in metaphysics. As Marder destabilizes metaphysics by thinking with plants, he opens up ethnographically rich spaces to philosophical thought. With his provocation, I take up the charge of this volume to account for the world multiple.

Particularly important to my thinking is Marder's (2015a) challenge to the notion that seeds stand for the potential of the plants' actual becoming, that seeds are that which lies in wait before actualization. The problem with the epistemological commitments that inhere in this story of the seed is that "The delay [read: the event] that constitutes the time required for seasons to change, plants to grow, and humans to develop appears to be redundant" (ibid., 10). In contrast, it is this moment to which many Tanzanians, and perhaps all who coax the substance of their survival from the earth, pay such very close attention. It is here that the drama unfolds. This spatial and temporal moment glossed over as delay—a waiting for the overdetermined, self-evident actualization of the seed—is the unfolding of life in all its relationality and unpredictability. The possibilities of what forms of life and vitality develop cannot be exhausted between self-evident actualization or death, but rather it is in this so-called "delay" that plants make their desires and needs understood. This is where they respond to heat, light, soil, wind, coolness, darkness, water, and dryness. They grow response-able. For those who scientifically investigate therapeutic plants, it is also here, in plants' responses to "stress"—to too much dryness or moisture, too much light or darkness, too much wind, or too many pests, or insufficient nutrients—that a plant's secondary metabolites develop and intensify (Langwick 2015). These are the plants' protective mechanisms and they emerge in response to elemental forces, in response to the immediate conditions of extension and growth. The therapeutic potential of a plant is dependent exactly on what is happening in these "delays." The time of the seed and its sprouting is event-ful. It is not a mere redundancy to be glossed over. It is that which matters—scientifically, but 'not only' (de la Cadena, Chapter 2 a in this volume). And there are other delays that create critical spaces of growth, vitality, and possibility, that matter therapeutically—for instance, in the practices of tending to and feeding the soils, the turning over of the stalks or other plant matter that litters the field after the harvest, returning it to the earth, generating relationships of decomposition as well as aerating dense, clay soil (Puig de la Bellacasa 2015; Langwick 2018).

A collective, carefully refined attention to plants, and particularly to the many contingencies and possibilities of their growth, not only challenges the assumption that one can be sure what a seed will do, what it will turn into, and what it will produce, but also shapes anxieties about the environment in Tanzania. Forms of life driven by the dramatic social and material changes of the past 150 years in Africa—including missionization, colonialism, postcolonial development, international aid, industrial agriculture, and the expansion of biomedicine—have changed environments and what it means to flourish within them. The elemental forces that shape the unfolding of plant life and human life have multiplied. Both demand not only careful observation, but also keen judgement and persistent response. Holding open the time of growth as an event requires more than critique. It raises the questions: What forms of vitality, of growth, are possible in Tanzania? Who and what can grow more amply, vitally, and productively in contemporary conditions, and how?

During the past decade in Tanzania these questions have come to be caught up in the intensification of a broad-based public concern about toxicities. Tanzanians are experiencing fundamental shifts in the landscape, including changing water patterns, denuded hillsides, infertile soil, and new pests. Simultaneously, they are feeling the impact of rising rates of diabetes, hypertension, AIDS, and cancer. The health of the landscape and the health of the body are read together; they present as the same struggle as people and plants intervene in each other's unfolding.

The articulation of pervasive toxicity renders immediate the experience of Tanzanians living in the Anthropocene, a term first crafted by geologists in an effort to capture the profound impact that humans, and more specifically capitalist forms of production, have had on the Earth. When Tanzanians speak of the toxicities that are now central to life, they are pointing to the products and by-products of histories of human expansion, imperialism, and capitalism that have burdened water, air, and soil and have transformed the very relations of life. In the Kilimanjaro and Arusha regions of northern Tanzania, where I have carried out my most extensive work since 2012, the landscape and the lives of plants, animals, and others within it are marked by mining, large-scale industrial agriculture (including coffee, sugar, flowers, and green beans), the introduction of industrial meat production, state-supported use of first DDT and then other pesticides, as well as a rise in the use of cars, electricity, and other elements of urban development. The most mundane aspects of life are seen as presenting a threat to health, such as the plastic bags, buckets, and Tupperware that are ubiquitous due to their particular helpfulness in homes that may not have running water or refrigeration. As impacts of similar trends are investigated in different pockets of the globe, some toxins have been identified and isolated. They have come to be seen individual even as they are found entangled with others. Such efforts to disaggregate toxic threats can provide an important space for specific responses—from municipal bans on plastic bags, to internationally funded environmental efforts eliminate particularly dangerous pesticides and herbicides, to public health initiatives to intervene in the causes of kidney disease.[2] Yet the question remains: What forms of life can endure in these troubled spaces? Tanzanians are clear that the toxicity of contemporary life is not only the result of the deleterious effects of development, or the toxic waste of irresponsible capital expansion, or even modern conveniences such as aluminum pots and pans and plastics, but also of the very life-saving technologies that represent the promise of the modern world. The latter include anti-retroviral drugs (ARVs), hypertensive drugs, and the fruits and vegetables now available most months of the year at the local market.

Plants have become collaborators in striving for an answer to the question: What forms of vitality and growth are possible through these multiple effects glossed as toxicity? By attending to the ways that people and plants literally live through one another, the possibilities and contingencies of the space of development and growth—between the seed writ large and the plant—is held opened up as the critical space. An eventful space. How will toxic landscapes change what sorts of plants and people develop? What will they become in the midst of these multiple, not always knowable, stimuli? What sort of living through each other might develop the abilities needed to inhabit these spaces? Or transform them?

One place that enables us to track this concern, as well as see the effects of such collaborations, is the rise of contemporary herbalism in Tanzania, or the rise of what one of my Tanzanian colleagues called *dawa lishe* [Kiswahili: *dawa*, medicine; *lishe*, the causative conjugation of the verb to eat *kula*, nutritious]. Dawa lishe refers to plant therapies that heal by feeding us—nourishing, strengthening, supporting bodies, bringing vitality, stimulating growth, enabling endurance (Langwick 2018). Dawa lishe is a playful phrase merging the more official categories of medicine (dawa) and fortified or nutrient dense foods (*chakula lishe*). It refers to products that live in the interstices between medicine and food. Indeed, these products are throwing a wrench into regulatory frameworks that have neatly divided the institutional roles of those who surveil food and those who surveil medicine (both traditional and modern) to ensure safety and quality, standards and consistency, and at times efficacy.

Producers of dawa lishe are simultaneously articulating the toxicity of everyday life as a problem and cultivating a diverse set of ways to live through this toxicity. Their practices lead us to a variety of answers to the questions above. As Natasha Myers's (2015, 2017, 2019) work has so evocatively argued, "Many of the origin stories for that era we seem bent on calling the Anthropocene hinge on profound shifts in the ways people have staged their relationship with plants" (Myers 2017, 126). Radical forms of extraction on larger and larger scales have supported the industrialization and urbanization that marks modern history. From the domestication of corn, to plantation agriculture, to the Green Revolution, to the powerful pull of petrified plants from deep under the Earth's crust for fossil fuels, plants have enabled modern political economies. Their capacities have been enlisted to extend slavery, colonialism, and what Michelle Murphy (2017) calls the "industrial exuberance" of post-World War II economies (see also Lyons 2016; Todd 2016; Tsing 2015). Central to these forms of worlding through plants has been the slow but steady separation of engagements in the name of agriculture and those in the name of medicine. Dawa lishe in all its playfulness, then, is also a refusal of this divide and a counter to those "solutions" that rest in its continuation. Therapeutic foods and nutritious medicines are emerging as generative material through which to think the pervasive, unpredictable, hidden, unacknowledged (often denied), and hard-to-isolate effects of industrialization and capitalism. They articulate toxicity as they innovate ways of intervening in the body's capacity to shape and be shaped by the ecologies of which it is part.

The fact of toxicity and the problem of thriving is localized, but it is not only local. The forces that have created these dynamics did not begin only within Tanzania or East Africa, and interventions include subject-objects born of movement between and across continents. Many of the specific plants that have emerged as central to new commercialization of herbal therapies have complicated histories. They have been shaped by the pressures of precolonial wars and expansions, ancient Indian Ocean trade, Islamization of the coast, missionization of the nineteenth century, nationalism, post-independence development, and the industrialization of agriculture. These plants have travelled and continue to move. They are part of a process of worlding and they suggest ways and relations through which the world might be re-made.

One of the plants central to this new commodity production of therapeutic herbals in Tanzania is mlonge (moringa). There are thirteen species in the plant family Moringaceae. Some are indigenous to East Africa, although they are usually thought to have started farther north than Tanzania. The most widely cultivated species in Tanzania and elsewhere is *Moringa oleifera*, which was native to the foothills of the Himalayas in northwestern India. *Moringa oleifera* likely traveled to Tanzania along numerous routes, over both land and sea. Gujarati traders arrived in Tanzania in numbers in the nineteenth century. In addition, Indians were brought to East Africa as indentured laborers, many of them to work on the Kenya–Uganda railway. Even before these migrations, however, *Moringa oleifera* may have already found its way to Tanzania along earlier trade routes, whether down from Egypt, or up from South Africa, or through centuries of Indian Ocean exchange.

In more recent times, *M. oleifera* has extended through international nutrition and water purification projects. The tree's willingness to grow with little water and in sandy soils has endeared it to those attempting to mediate the difficulties of life in drought-prone areas. Ethnobotanical and nutritional studies have also revealed it to be densely nutritious. *Moringa oleifera* has been enrolled in projects both large and small. The effects of some are difficult to trace, such as the outreach effort sponsored by the Church World Service and led by a member of Second Congregational Church in Palmer, MA in 2000, which involved distributing 20,000 M. *oleifera* tree seeds along the route walked by Burton and Speke in 1857–58 in their search for the source of the Nile. The sheer number of these small-scale efforts has had an effect on the landscape, even if their after-lives are harder to identify individually than those of larger-scale initiatives, such as the abandoned plantation of M. *oleifera* outside Tanga. The acres of trees at that site are the result of a development project that failed because the labor of picking the small leaves by hand required more people than the project could support.

Moringa oleifera has taken up residence in Tanzania relatively quietly— through gifts whose purpose might have never been fully understood, or have been forgotten as land and people have moved on. Therefore, many inhabitants may not recognize the tree in their midst as food or medicine. It is not unusual for mlonge to remain tucked away in home gardens, used to mark boundaries between plots, for shade, or to supplement animal feed. Some entrepreneurs take advantage of this gap, and buy the leaves and seeds cheaply from people in rural areas and package them for the growing middle class (Figure 10.1). Moringa powder (from the leaves) and oil (from the seeds) are sold next to organic produce in upscale farmers' markets in the capital city. Moringa is also included in an energy drink (with rosella, baobab, and aloe) produced by the Mabibo lab in the National Institute for Medical Research in Tanzania.

The charisma of moringa, and that of other dawa lishe plants, is energizing a different emphasis in language around the work of medicines (e.g., for more on charisma see Satsuka, a in this volume). In addition to the more familiar verbs —to remove (*kutoa*) and to protect (*kulinda*)—that are used to describe what medicines do, the efficacy of herbals such as moringa is best described as working to strengthen, enhance, nourish, support, boost, or encourage the

Figure 10.1 Moringa Leaves powder packaged and sold by the Institute of Traditional Medicine, a division of Muhimbili University of Health and Allied Sciences, the primary teaching and research hospital in Tanzania

Photo by author

body. These verbs are not emerging as responses to legal distinctions between food and medicine as they might in the United States and Europe (although government policy is coming to reinforce these distinctions), but rather from an explicit effort to reframe the role of medicine. This project requires reimagining what efficacy is. Attention is trained on how the bodies of plants and people intervene in each other and collaborate toward growth, working together to establish nourishing spaces.

Moringa is one of the plants that drew me to Helen Nguya early in 2014. I was conducting research in a herbal clinic that stocked a therapy produced by the non-governmental organization she founded, Training, Research, Monitoring and Evaluation on Gender and AIDS (TRMEGA). They call the mixture *Imarisha Afya Yako*, in English this is a command: "Stabilize (or Strengthen) Your Health" (Figure 10.2). The formula combines four plants, one of which is moringa. This treatment can be bought for TZS 10,000 (approximately USD 5), and at times Helen gives it away to TRMEGA members. In many ways, however, this prepared medicine is a precursor to the more intense relationships with the plant that TRMEGA fosters. Imarisha is relatively easy to add to a person's routine even if they are debilitated by AIDS and unable to leave their bed. A teaspoon can simply be added to water and drunk three times a day. If people see results with this medicine, then they may be more open to the labor required to care for the trees, to garden—both because they see the benefits, and because they will likely have more strength to do so. Helen first saw the effects of mlonge through Jane (Figure 10.3). Jane crossed paths with Helen during a particularly difficult moment in her life. She not only had AIDS, but she had also stopped her ARVs, had lost her husband, had no

Figure 10.2 Imarisha Afya Yako [Strengthen Your Health], a herbal formula containing moringa produced by TRMEGA

Photo by author

Figure 10.3 A mlonge tree (*M. oleifera*) in the demonstration garden at TRMEGA headquarters in Maji ya Chai, Arusha

Photo by author

income, and had started becoming too weak to rise from bed and care for her
children. In contrast, Jane is now one of the most dynamic and generative
members of TRMEGA. She lives on and works in one of the TRMEGA
community gardens. She leads several support groups, and is regularly catalyzing
new ones.

As a child, Helen Nguya tended to the fields with her grandfather and came
to know her grandmother's love of herbs, especially those connected to birth as
her grandmother was a well known traditional midwife. Later, Helen studied
agriculture and nutrition. She worked for a number of agricultural organizations. For ten years, she developed and supervised the Catholic Church's social
service projects in the northern zone of Tanzania. During her tenure with the
church, she received an opportunity to study for a Master's degree abroad. Her
thesis, like much of her work, focused on rural development, in particular
strategies for rural development that would best address those with HIV/AIDS.
She came to feel that the most significant problem for people living with AIDS
was "stigma" (she uses the English word). "AIDS patients are sick and they are
not able to do anything, but others do not help them out of the condition
because of the stigma." The problem is that others do not help. To work

against the stigma that paralyzes people with AIDS, TRMEGA focuses on connecting people to each other and to plants. Many people come to her through a local private HIV clinic run by the Catholic Church. Patients visit monthly for their check-up and to receive their ARVs. Nurses and others at the clinic may mention TRMEGA when they are talking with new patients or with patients who do not seem to be responding to the ARVs as well as they had hoped.

As Saidia,[3] one TRMEGA member, described:

> When I was at [the clinic], there was a woman talking to us about nutritious food and about the mlonge medicine. I was listening because my CD4 was not going up. Now she was talking to us and advising us to use the mlonge tree, especially the green leaves, for tea. I was listening closely. I was thinking [...] my CD4 count is not going up, perhaps it would increase if I was using the mlonge that she is talking about, do you understand me? I waited while listening. Later I called her aside and told her that my CD4 was not increasing and asked how she could help me. That sister told me, "No problem! Wait until after you see your doctor, then we will go together." You understand me? She brought me here. We came together to Mama Nguya's. She paid for my transportation fee when we came here. It was last year. This is the second year that I am a member.

What does it take to be introduced to a plant? To welcome it into one's body and routine? Who makes the introduction is important. Saidia describes how her introduction to moringa came through someone working in a church-based, biomedical clinic for people with AIDS. The introduction is facilitated through other gifts: first the transportation fees and then the moringa itself.

> Mama Nguya welcomed me warmly when we came. When she received me, I explained my problem to her: my CD4 count was not increasing. It was not adding. I told her about my condition, the worries that I had. For sure, my health was not good! When I came, this mother took two canisters of moringa and gave them to me and instructed me to use them. When I started, I was using moringa. I mix it in the porridge and drank one cup, because I was not used to it yet. I was drinking one cup. The instruction was to drink three times a day, but I was drinking one cup a day, you understand me? While I continue with my ARVs, I drank. Some days she was calling me asking me how I was doing. I would tell her that I was doing well then after a while, she ask me are you drinking it [the moringa] properly. I said am drinking it properly, but I am drinking one cup, she told me, "No you need to drink it morning, afternoon, and evening." She told me to try my best. I continued drinking [moringa], and going for the treatment [ARVs], then one day the doctor told me that I was doing well! "Don't worry, you are now doing well." It is for sure that

since I started using this moringa, my CD4 could increase. The doctor wrote six hundred and something on my paper the other day. Before I was taking the moringa regularly, I did not have such a high CD4 count. It was 200, 300; it was not climbing up to 600. Certainly the biggest benefit of joining TRMEGA is learning about medicinal plants. I only knew the hospital medicine, and whenever someone talked to me about the herbal medicine I was not understanding.

Moringa as it is conceived of here intervenes in a body with ARVs. Its work is evaluated through its ability to support the efficacy of the ARVs. Rather than suggesting that moringa is an alternative to ARVs, moringa is an intervention into the working of the ARVs. The issue Saidia describes is that she is taking the ARVs she is being given, but her CD4 count is not rising. Moringa collaborates with ARVs, with her body on ARVs; it is conceived as an intervention to enable the ARVs to work (better). Moringa also comes with Helen Nguyga, her calls, her efforts to check in and follow up, her encouragements to continue and insistence on the recommended amounts, her attention to other discomforts, and the joys of regular contact. Helen comes to know Saidia, to hear about her daily struggles and problems, to be able to help her to build a relationship to moringa and to build the life that might support this relationship. Moringa's efficacy depends on these entanglements and it highlights that ARV efficacies do so as well.[4]

> I take ARVs, but if a person comes and tells me to take other [hospital] medicines, I will not take them. If I get sick I run here to Mama Nguya. Even the other day I was sick, I was having trouble. When I go to the toilet, I strain. I went and told the doctor. The doctor told me it was the ARVs, do you understand? I came back to Mama Nguya. I told her whenever I go to the toilet, I strain and it is not coming out. Mama Nguya gave me the medicines here (I don't know how they are called). So now it is soft; the medicine softens! So, this Mama, I have made her like my second God. [Laughter] Whenever I get sick I go to her.

Ultimately, TRMEGA hopes to encourage people not only to seek out herbal medicines, but also to draw plants around themselves and their homes. Their work does not delineate a clear inside of the body to be the focus of therapeutic treatment as much as it catalyzes and encourages relations between plants and people. It invites a space for their integration and mutual interruption. Not only commercialized herbals but the trees themselves cement relations and remake space as they become part of revitalizing land and people.

Walking through the TRMEGA gates, one is most immediately struck by the dense, lush garden (Figure 10.4). There are two small buildings and a covered gathering space, but mostly there is garden. Helen, and other members of

Figure 10.4 Slow Food sign marking the demonstration garden at TRMEGA headquarters in Maji ya Chai, Arusha, Tanzania

Photo by author

TRMEGA who have now become leaders, work to teach people how to plant herbs around their homes. Helen dreams,

> I wish I had the ability to mobilize the whole community to plant moringa trees. Then they could use the leaves as a vegetable in their meals. First, it is a drought-resistant plant. So, when it is not yet sunny, they will get vegetables and there are a lot of nutrients in the leaves. In addition, the roots are beneficial. The barks are beneficial and the seeds are beneficial. But most importantly, where you see that it is dry and people don't have enough vegetables, moringa is there. Yet, people don't know about this. We have a neighbor behind our house who had a problem and saw this tree. [Helen points to the moringa tree in her own demonstration garden.] She had a similar tree at home, and was curious. She asked: Why did you plant that tree? Why did you put a label on it? What is it for? We told her that it was very good tree and informed her of its uses. That neighbor's husband was a pastor. So, the pastor came to our house, and I explained everything about moringa to him. I also gave him a book [about moringa] and asked him to read it. When he brought the book back, he apologized

for he had taken a photocopy of it. I told him that was fine. During World AIDS Day this past year, he came [to the celebration at TRMEGA] and participated. He testified to something which really surprised me. He said that since he learned about moringa, he started healing people at his house. He has been very successful. He also said that since he had grown older, he had been experiencing pain in his legs. He was having trouble walking. Then he knelt and stood up exclaiming that now all the pain had vanished. Now, that is only one person. What if we had educated all people about it? It could really help as it is something that just grows [*kitu kinaota tu*].

Moringa is something that "just grows." It is not a fussy or demanding plant; that is, it is able to endure variable amounts of sun and water. This phrase also references a vitality that exceeds human relations with it, something that can be folded in, brought in relation, a vital force that might be ingested and lived through. Proximity and presence, however, are not enough. Healing is about intervention. An unfolding together—not simultaneously or in parallel, but through each other. The work of this through-ness is evident in each turn in Nguya's story about her neighbor, as it is marked by TRMEGA's work and support. Nguya revels in the "surprise" that her neighbor not only started eating moringa and feeling its benefits, but also healing others. TRMEGA strives to enable people to cultivate compact, productive gardens that can significantly add to the vitality of the home and body.

Once people are strong enough, Nguya and other TRMEGA members talk with them about saving. TRMEGA teaches members how to put a little profit aside and then to join together, establishing small savings groups. The hope is that these will then support "income-generating" projects. By not only making medicines, but teaching people to know and care for plants, as well as sharing seeds, cuttings, and saplings, these efforts work toward cycles of commodification and subsistence. Plants are at times articulated as a gift from God, but this perhaps is only in search for a way to speak of these relationships with things that "just grow." One that cannot be captured in any easy or stable distinction between commodity and gift. Plants and people are in extended collaboration, and this collaboration is understood to make the world before and after any particular economic or social formation.

TRMEGA intervenes in specific constellations of toxicities. TRMEGA works with "vulnerable people" who often feel the impacts of the dumping of capitalist waste more acutely. This impact may be because they live on less desirable lands that sit below large-scale industrial farms and are affected by agricultural runoff and disruptions in the flow of water. Or it may be because the low price of the pesticides that leaked from the large-scale flower farms into local markets seduced them to use particularly strong toxins on their vegetable gardens. Treatments for AIDS, like those for other chronic diseases, also introduce chemicals into the body daily. While these are understood as life-

Figure 10.5 Teaching tool developed by Helen Nguya, founder and director of TRMEGA, after being inspired by those used to promote mlonge in Nigeria

Photo by author

saving, they are also seen as harsh (*kali*). As a Kiswahili proverb notes, that which cures can also kill. Simply taking ARVs—that is, introducing even life-saving chemicals into the body—may not make one's CD4 climb, as Saidia reported. Rather, living within the toxicity of a daily regime of ARVs means finding ways to strengthen the body through and within this regime. Moringa, and other plant-based therapies, collaborate in that. They strengthen individual bodies. When we see the specific dynamics of how human vitalities are fostered and extended through plants, however, we see that it is also more. Moringa strengthens the body when taken up in projects that strive to work against stigma by suggesting new ways of noticing, knowing, and engaging plants. Moringa is efficacious as it builds social and material bodies, making multi-species lifeworlds denser—lusher in every possible way.

TRMEGA's community gardens have come to be supported by Slow Food through its 10,000 Gardens in Africa project.[5] Helen serves as the northern zone convivium leader in Tanzania. By linking TRMEGA's work with therapeutic plants to Slow Food, Helen privileges alignments with food sovereignty movements over public health concerns with access to medicine. The connection to Slow Food offers many practical relations. When, in the TRMEGA office, Helen talks of moringa to a new member or to a visiting anthropologist, she reflexively turns to a wall-hanging she made elaborating the nutritional benefits of moringa, the design of which she attributes to Nigerian colleagues (Figure 10.5). Helen also travels every two years to Terre Madre, a large Slow Food gathering in northern Italy. Due to this connection, Carlos Petrini, Slow Food founder and president and an FAO Special Ambassador, visited her Maji ya Chai community garden in 2016. Yet, the affiliation with Slow Food articulates more than the circulation of visual graphics and information, or even transnational networks. Slow Food enables a way of situating the politics of plants. Demands for food sovereignty are used to question the sorts of sovereignty that might be opened up through medicine and healing (and those that may too often be closed down through some ways of rolling out biomedicine). New trajectories of impact, autonomy, and possibility are being experimented with as dawa lishe is folded into food sovereignty projects.

Food sovereignty tends to focus on the right to define food and agricultural systems. This argument challenges the economic and ecological trends in industrial food production. It raises questions about that which is planted and by whom, and how it is distributed. TRMEGA draws on these efforts and, by bringing them into conversations about healing, extends them. TRMEGA is opening up notions of sovereignty to questions about the practices, collaborations, and relations that structure the forms of vitality and growth to be fostered in Tanzania. They strive to establish a space for debate over who and what can grow more amply, vitally, and productively in contemporary conditions, and how.

This is where Marder's effort to articulate the unfolding of the seed as an eventful, creative, unpredictable space of becoming has been helpful. Seeds labor around, with, and through humans. People intervene in, extend, and shape plant life as they garden, share seeds, move plants, and generate and respond to the charisma of particular species. Issues of sovereignty are embedded not only in what seeds are available, but also in the comings together that structure a seed's becoming (and that of the other entities that are at stake in this process). Sovereignty is then located in having the ability to shape the relations involved in the unfolding of plants and human bodies together. For those in TRMEGA this is not just an environmentalist argument, even though collaborations across international ecological networks are generative. This is a deeper philosophical position rooted in other ways of imagining and enacting bodies and environments—in other worldings. TRMEGA members live with plants not only as raw materials (be it for medicines, food, shelter, biochemical diversity) but also as co-creators of the physical and conceptual spaces in which strength and vitality are formulated. TRMEGA gardens are a space in which to argue about and experiment with the relations between plants and people (ecological, corporal, economic, philosophical) that structure that which we see as healing and define as a healthy body and a healthy ecology. Through these gardens and the dawa lishe they produce, TRMEGA poses questions about what we might call therapeutic sovereignty.

Notes

1 I am inspired here by the emerging field of critical plant studies (Stark 2015) and by Gabrys's (2012) thinking about the way that people's engagement with plants (forests, in her case) works in part by unfolding a "process of perceptual possibility."
2 Outside of environmental and medical science, other responses also emerge targeting particular toxic threats. For example see Brad Weiss (1996) describing the emergence of a new malady, plastic teeth, a disease of infants and children in Tanzania.
3 All members and patients are given pseudonyms.
4 As many medical anthropologists have shown us, medicines are not "seeds" of potential, their efficacy is not self-evident. The technologies of the clinical trial that works to articulate the agency in individual medicines require translation into lives and social worlds. One of the more compelling articulations of this fact is Vinh-Kim Nguyen's (2009) notion of "experimentality," in which he suggests that public health projects must remake social worlds in the image of the lab in order to facilitate the efficacy for pharmaceuticals as they move from clinical trials into clinical interventions.
5 Slow Food Foundation for Biodiversity, 10,000 Gardens in Africa, https://www.fondazioneslowfood.com/en/what-we-do/10-000-gardens-in-africa-2/

References

Gabrys, Jennifer. 2012. "Sensing an Experimental Forest: Processing Environments and Distributing Relations." *Computational Culture* 2. http://computationalculture.net/article/sensing-an-experimental-forest-processing-environments-and-distributing-relations accessed July 20, 2018.

Latour, Bruno. 1993. *We Have Never Been Modern.* Cambridge, MA: Harvard University Press.

Langwick, Stacey. 2015. "Partial Publics: The Political Promise of Traditional Medicine in Africa." *Current Anthropology* 56 (4): 493–514.

—. 2018. "A Politics of Habitability: Plants, Healing, and Sovereignty in a Toxic World." *Cultural Anthropology.*

Lyons, Kristina. 2016. "Decomposition as Life Politics: Soils, Selva, and Small Farmers under the Gun of the U.S.–Columbian War on Drugs." *Cultural Anthropology* 31 (1): 56–81.

Marder, Michael. 2013. *Plant-Thinking: A Philosophy of Vegetal Life.* New York: Columbia University Press.

—. 2015a. "The Sense of Seeds, or Seminal Events." *Environmental Philosophy* 12 (1): 87–97.

—. 2015b. "What's Planted in the Event? On the Secret Life of a Philosophical Concept." In *The Green Thread: Dialogues with the Vegetal World,* edited by Patricia Vieira, John Ryan, and Monica Gagliano, 3–17. Lanham, MD: Lexington Books.

—. 2016. *Grafts: Writings on Plants.* University of Minnesota.

Murphy, Michelle. 2017. "Alterlife and Decolonial Chemical Relations." *Cultural Anthropology* 32(4): 494–503.

Myers, Natasha. 2015. "Conversations on Plant Sensing: Notes from the Field." *NatureCulture* 3: 35–66.

—. 2017. "Photosynthetic Mattering: Rooting into the Planthroposcene." In *Moving Plants,* edited by Line Marie Thorsen, 123–9. Rønnebæksholm Press.

Myers, Natasha. 2019. "From Edenic Apocalypse to Gardens Against Eden: Plants and People in and After the Anthropocene." In *Infrastructure, Environment, and Life in the Anthropocene*, edited by Kregg Hetherington. Durham, NC: Duke University Press, in press.

Nguyen, Vinh-Kim. 2009. "Government-by-exception: Enrolment and Experimentality in Mass HIV Treatment Programmes in Africa." *Social Theory and Health* 7 (3): 196–217.

Puig de la Bellacasa, Maria. 2015. "Making Time for Soil: Technoscientific Futurity and the Pace of Care." *Social Studies of Science* 45 (5): 691–716.

Stark, Hannah. 2015. "Deleuze and Critical Plant Studies." In *Deleuze and the Non/Human*, edited by John Roffe and Hannah Star, 180–196. Berlin: Springer.

Todd, Zoe. 2016. "Relationships." Theorizing the Contemporary, Cultural Anthropology website, January 21. https://culanth.org/fieldsights/799-relationships accessed July 20, 2018.

Tsing, Anna Lowenhaupt. 2015. *The Mushroom at the End of the World: On the Possibility of Life in Capitalist Ruins*. Princeton, NJ: Princeton University Press.

Weiss, Brad. 1996. "Plastic Teeth Extraction: An Iconography of Gastrosexual Affliction." In *The Making and Unmaking of the Haya Lived World*, 155–178. Durham, NC: Duke University Press.

Part III

Exploring quotidian politics

Chapter 11

Out of nothing

(Re)worlding "theory" through Chinese medical entrepreneurship

Mei Zhan

> Taoism knew no "ethos" of its own; magic, not conduct, was decisive, for man's fate.
>
> (Weber 1951 [1915], 200)

Events

In fall 2013, I spent a semester in Shanghai teaching "Debating Globalization" for the University of California Education Abroad Program. Aside from teaching, I spent much of my time eyeing new fieldwork possibilities beyond the colleges and hospitals of "TCM"—the institutionalized form of traditional Chinese medicine that emerged under the Chinese party-state's directives in the 1950s—with which I had worked for over two decades. There were plenty of obvious novelties around as metropolitan Shanghai was bursting with breathtakingly fast and mercurial changes from day to day. As winter approached, however, my explorations took a somewhat unexpected turn. A "fan club" of traditional Chinese medicine, consisting of local college students and young professionals, decided to stage a conference on global opportunities and challenges.[1] They asked that I give the keynote speech on *tianrenheyi* (天人合一)—"heaven and human are one"—an idea of the dynamic oneness of humans and cosmos with pre-Daoist roots and enjoying a surge of popularity in recent years (Zhan 2012).

Perhaps itself a sign of the multiplicitous and contrary ways in which heavens and humans are one, the conference took place on a heavily polluted day when the entire city was enveloped in impenetrable smog. The speakers and audiences included owners of startup firms and private clinics of Chinese medicine, classics scholars, foreign-trained practitioners practicing in Shanghai, college students and faculty, and more. Many self-consciously and strategically positioned themselves outside of the "establishment" (体制, *tizhi*)—the system of state-owned and state-operated institutions including the majority of universities, hospitals, and large enterprises—even though their actual institutional affiliations and histories might suggest a more complex story.[2] This disparate cast of actors spent the day immersed in earnest discussions of the future of China's rapidly privatizing healthcare landscape and how traditional Chinese medicine would fit within it.

Whether implicit or explicit, science and biomedicine are unavoidable topics in any discussion involving traditional Chinese medicine. This time, however, many participants went far beyond trying to measure—or, to be exact, measure up to—the scientific validity of Chinese medicine. Invoking, but without dwelling on, comparisons and commensurabilities of East and West, tradition and modernity, superstition and material science, they argued that traditional Chinese medicine could not move forward without coming back to the ground. Building on the theme that "heaven and human are one," several speakers spoke of their own experiences in medicine and entrepreneurship, and in doing so accentuated that tianrenheyi was not just a matter of philosophy, religion, or science, but rather a way of life. The discussions became quite heated at times, and the moderator, a college student and Chinese medicine enthusiast, navigated them with poise and poetry. As the conference drew to a close to the soothing sound of a folk melody, she gestured at the smog outside while delivering a set of hopeful remarks: by re-embracing its primal spirit (元神, yuanshen) that focuses on the transformative oneness of all worldly beings, traditional Chinese medicine will find its way out of the haze and back to life.

Today, as I write about the emergence of "classical" (古典, gudian) or "ancient" (古, gu) Chinese medicine—a set of heterogeneous and effervescent experiments reanimating the "primal spirit" of traditional Chinese medicine—I think back to that event in 2013.[3] It was significant, especially in hindsight, in the conceptualization of my current project. But its significance did not lie in it being a moment of discovery or revelation in which a novel ethnographic subject unveiled itself to the curious but unknowing anthropologist. Rather than a starting point, this event was part of deep entanglements and continuous unfoldings through which particular worldly analytics become imaginable, thinkable, and doable—analytics that demanded further thoughtful engagements staying close to the ground.

In the book *Event: Philosophy in Transit*, the philosopher Slavoj Žižek discusses the effect of "event" in transforming paradigms of universality (to be exact, Hegelian "concrete universality") (2014, 5–6). Žižek defines "the basic features of an event" as "the surprising emergence of something new which undermines every stable regime" (ibid.). The rising popularity of ancient "religions" such as Buddhism and Daoism is among his examples of paradigm-shifting events. He writes, "If the sociologist Max Weber were alive today, he definitely would have written a second, supplementary volume to his founding text The *Protestant Ethic and The Spirit of Capitalism* (1904), entitled *The Taoist Ethic and The Spirit of Global Capitalism*" (ibid., 66). I am not convinced that Weber would have written such a volume (although Karl Marx, who famously argued that religion is the opium of the people, might have). Nor do I think of events exclusively in terms of epistemic ruptures and paradigm shifts. What about events that are far more mundane? Life is full of those, after all. What about *their* worldly transformative potentials?

In this chapter, I explore a set of entwined world-making events that unfold against each other—in social theory, and in scientific, entrepreneurial, and ethnographic knowledge production. World-making might sound grand. But my point is precisely the opposite. These events traverse any ready-made spatiotemporal scales against which their significance can be reliably measured. With a focus on the emergence of classical Chinese medicine through entrepreneurship (with which my own ethnographic project is entangled), I discuss the ways in which classical medicine engages even as it challenges Weberian, Marxist, and Maoist paradigms on materialism, religion, rationality, capitalism, and entrepreneurship—not in the sense that these theories are wrong or misplaced (especially in "non-Western" worlds as one might argue), but that their functions are not those of Theory at all. Rather, they are un-worlded and re-worlded: brought back down to the ground as critical resources for everyday knowledge-making and world-making.

Cosmos of capitalism

Max Weber did not think highly of Daoism (Taoism). In both *The Protestant Ethic and the Spirit of Capitalism* (1930 [1905]) and *The Religion of China* (1951 [1915]), he argued that Occidental religions tended to be transformative whereas their Eastern counterparts were contemplative. The Puritans, on one hand, saw themselves as "the tool of divine will" (Weber 1930, 68) by which other-worldly calling materialized in this-worldly transformations: the emergence of the capitalist *geist*, the rise of rationalism and intellectualism, and a "cosmos of the modern economic order" (ibid., 123). On the other hand, contemplative religions—Daoism (Taoism), Buddhism, and Hinduism in particular—were steeped in mysticism and hence inconsequential, ineffectual, or inhibitive in the production of this-worldly modern capitalism (Weber 1951 [1915], 1958 [1916]). The problem with contemplative religions (along with the likes of Catholicism and Lutheranism), in short, was that they were not able to generate a dynamic ascetic relation between other-worldly calling and this-worldly conduct.

According to Weber, Confucianism, for example, was entirely this-worldly and therefore lacked the dynamism required of worldly transformations (1951 [1915]). Daoism, formed when intellectual escapism into the other-world was coupled with the this-worldly trade of the magicians (ibid., 192), was even worse. The uncanny coupling of intellectual retreat and magical crafts laid the ground for unscrupulous profit seeking which was legitimated by pseudo-rationality (ibid., 199). Daoism, Weber went on, generated "a superstructure of magically 'rational' science" in "chronometry, chronomancy, geomancy, meteoromancy, annalistics, ethics, medicine, and classical mantically-determined statecraft." Chinese medicine was especially insidious for disguising magic and quackery as a system of rational practice (ibid.).

Much has been said about how Weber got the facts wrong when it comes to Chinese religions—and, for that matter, Chinese medicine. Indeed, relying on the works of early Sinologists, especially J. J. M. de Groot, Weber got them horribly wrong. Having never set foot in China, Weber nevertheless constructed a sweeping view of Eastern religions which then served as the perfect foil for the transformative spirit of capitalism. One might argue that *they* all did it—it was a time when colonialism held the world hostage and armchair social science was the norm; or that Weber's errors were merely empirical, and his allegorical use of the East should not detract from his general theory of rationalism and capitalism.[4] But either embracing (or dismissing) Weber's discussion of Eastern religions on the grounds of outdated research and/or colonial prejudice misses the larger points that reverberate in social inquiry today, including our analytical tools for understanding the cosmos of modern economic order, knowledge production, and ways of being in the world.

To begin, Weber's framing of Chinese religions—as well as that of J. J. M. de Groot and Marcel Granet before him—remains influential in defining the parameters of academic discussions of Daoism, Confucianism, and Buddhism as subjects of comparative "religion" or "philosophy" rather than as possible analytics in their own terms—analytics that might contest the ubiquity and stability of these epistemic categories in the first place. Weberian intellectual heritage thus continues to set the terms for comparing epistemes, ontologies, and ethics through translation—comparative terms that also produce epistemes, ontologies, and ethics as distinctive and universalistic domains of inquiry. However, if we could allow ourselves to hold "religion" in suspense for a moment, we could see Weber's analytical moves in a different light. It was by focusing on *specific forms* of relationality (or the lack thereof, as in Confucianism) between this-world and other-world that Weber bolstered his argument that Calvinism alone was able to provide the true transformative spirit: in acting as the tool of the divine will between the two worlds—each incomplete on its own—it was the Calvinist who led the way for the historical emergence of modern capitalism. In other words, Weber's cosmos of capitalism rested as much on distinctively modernist binary structuring—this-world and other-world, transformation and contemplation, the divine and the secular, the spiritual and the material, theory and empirical data—as it was enmeshed in specific histories of relationship, entanglement, and differential becoming that would trouble these binaries.

In exploring these tensions in Weber's cosmos, I turn to postcolonial and feminist critiques of theory-making and world-making. As I have argued elsewhere (Zhan 2009, 2012), the worlding of particular kinds of theories—or rather, the worlding of Theory itself—entails the (sometimes violent) unworlding of other ways of thinking, doing, and being in the world by banishing them to the earth— that is, by rendering them imaginable, thinkable, and representable *only* as secondary objects of comparative analyses. Heidegger, for example, claimed a Greco-European intellectual genealogy while staying mum on his associations with other traditions of thoughts—in particular Daoist analytics—in his postwar rehabilitation and philosophical works (Zhan 2012). More importantly, contemporary critical theory is not immune to Weber's and his colleagues' strategy. As the literary critic Petrus Liu points out, Michel Foucault's *The History of Sexuality*, a definitive study in poststructuralist theory, remains faithful to a Greco-French genealogy that recruits China (and Japan and India) as the example of a non-Christian society that "functions as the constitutive outside of the modern European homosexual's self-definition, as the negative space against which it becomes possible for individuals who are, presumably, genetically unrelated to the Greeks to speak of a 'we' and 'our society'" (Liu 2015, 28). For Liu, this kind of theoretical Othering has disabled non-liberal queer theory and politics that cannot be imagined within the secular intellectual and social genealogy of liberalism. In other words, the abstraction of Theory, which obscures its own histories, associations, and translations, sets a limit on our sociopolitical imaginations and actions.

In feminist anthropology and feminist science and technology studies, too, there is a long-felt frustration with Theory as a masculine construct that renders women's labor and activity secondary at best (e.g., Haraway 1991; Hartsock 1983; Rosaldo 1974; Rose 1983; Strathern 1980; Yanagisako and Delaney 1994). Marxist-feminist responses to the masculinity of Theory-making vary a great deal, from advocating feminist empiricism (Rose 1983) to insisting that feminists too must aspire to do Theory from their own standpoint (Hartsock 1983). The shortcomings of feminist empiricism and standpoint theory have long been made obvious, but their critiques still stand and have inspired others to continue pushing for critical analytics committed to immanence and entanglement—from Donna Haraway's "mobile positioning" and "passionate detachment" (1991), to Karen Barad's "diffraction," which displaces Theory with a methodology that foregrounds "dynamic topological reconfigurings/entanglements/relationalities/(re)articulations of the world" (2007, 141).

The world is not made up of things that exist outside of, or prior to, relations. Invoking the quantum physicist Niels Bohr's work on complementarity, Barad argues that the world is a dynamic process of intra-activity and materialization. She writes,

> This ongoing flow of agency through which part of the world makes itself differentially intelligible to another part of the world and through which causal structures are stabilized and destabilized does not take place in space and time but happens in the making of spacetime itself. It is through specific agential intra-actions that a differential sense of being is enacted in the ongoing ebb and flow of agency. [. . .] The world is an open process of mattering through which mattering itself acquires meaning and form through the realization of different agential possibilities.
>
> (2007, 140–1)

Not this-worldly or other-worldly. No origin stories. No genealogy. No transcendence into the abstract. Even though Chinese medicine and Daoism are not comparable to quantum physics in their "thing-ness," I find that Barad's argument for immanent relationality, contingency, and continuous unfolding in knowledge- and world-making practices resonates with ongoing experiments in reinventing classical Chinese medicine. As I will discuss below, like Barad, these experiments ask us to find ways to stay close to the ground, and be ready to let go of—to empty out—conceptual presumptions, analytical habits, and worldly predispositions. So back to the ground and back to nothingness we go. In what follows I discuss the emergence of the new, heterogeneous classical Chinese medicine through entrepreneurial practices positioned outside of the establishment. Rather than a religious revival or a wholesale rejection of socialism and Marxist materialism, classical Chinese medicine makes novel everyday associations and refigurations of materialism (in its Marxist and other incarnations), science, rationality, pre-Daoist and Daoist concepts, transforming these ideas and animating them as critical resources for thinking, doing, and being in the world.

(Re)worlding "theory" through *wuxing* (五行)

The entanglement and contingency of this-world and other-world, idealism and materialism, are part and parcel of translating, understanding, and remaking traditional Chinese medicine. To delve deeper into these worldings, let us revisit Weber once more. At the center of his critique of the "magically 'rational' science" of Daoism is the concept of *wuxing*—or rather, the "sacred number five" operating in terms of "five planets, five elements, five organs, etc." (Weber 1951 [1915], 199). How could there be only "five (!) human organs" (ibid., 198; original exclamation mark)? Yet by applying the sacred number five across a wide range of phenomena—from organs, to seasons, to tastes—the "Chinese 'universist' philosophy and cosmogony transformed the world into a magic garden" where "the ethical rationality of the miracle is out of the question" (ibid., 200).

Having come of age in the 1980s when China entered the Reform Era, I—and my peers, some of whom now spearhead medical entrepreneurship—were taught by high school and college textbooks that Marx was the materialist theorist of the proletariat whereas Weber was the idealist theorist of the bourgeoisie. Of course, closer engagements with and examinations of Marx and Weber would present a far more complex story, much of which is unfortunately beyond the limits of the current chapter. But even the short excerpts quoted above show that Weber's discussion of wuxing and Daoism invoked a straightforward materialist analysis: that the Chinese simply got the elemental constitution of the world wrong, and that their system of magical rationality was grounded in erroneous empirical observations.

Whereas Weber's rebuke of wuxing focused on the "sacred number 'five' (五, *wu*)", others have struggled to define *xing* (行). Wuxing—consisting of wood, fire, water, metal, and earth—has been translated into English as "five phases," "five elements," or "five agents". Scholars of traditional Chinese medicine today argue that wuxing is part of the holistic *qi-yinyang-wuxing* cosmological system that is the manifestation of *dao*, the ineffable nonbeing—nothingness that generates rather than negates—from which all beings continuously emerge and unfold (e.g., Furth 1999; Jullien 1999; Kuriyama 2002). In the context of medical and everyday understandings and practices of body, illness, and well-being, wuxing is applied to a wide range of relationships and affinities including the *zangfu* system (a functional-visceral system, often considered erroneously by the likes of Weber to be an inaccurate version of the anatomical organ system), the meridian system, emotions, seasons, directions, deities, and so forth. These particular phases/agents/elements are named in a "cosmogonic order" (Furth 1999) through cycles of generation and control. In spite of extensive studies of wuxing, its standard translation remains in question: "element" privileges substance, "agent" points to what might be called thing-power (Bennett 2010), and "phase" emphasizes relation and change. "Element" and "phase" are the two most commonly used translations today.

The term "five elements" was introduced by the Jesuits and early scholars of Chinese medicine, philosophy, and religion, who thought of wuxing as comparable but inferior to the four-element system of ancient Greece (Furth 1999). In the place of "air," the Chinese erroneously came up with wood and metal as the basic constitutive elements of the world (Lloyd 2012). This elemental approach to wuxing is critiqued as an ontological error by the historian Geoffrey Lloyd, who argues that wuxing is about phases and processes, not substances. "*Shui*, the term conventionally translated 'water', is 'soaking downwards'. *Huo*, 'fire', is 'flaming upwards'. So where the Jesuits—and before them Aristotle himself, come to that—would have seen *things*, the Chinese saw *events*" (2012, 22–3).

Interestingly, the strongest resistance to the processual and eventful view of wuxing perhaps comes from TCM practitioners. Trained at TCM institutions through standardized curricula, many of them argue that wuxing needs to be discussed as "material entities" first and then as correlations between these elements (Hsu 1999, 202). To understand this kind of staunch defense of materialism—or rather, materialism grounded in the ontological priority of substance and things—we need to understand the importance of materialism in China as a mode of investigation (and political struggle) and its place in the institutional history of TCM.

It is impossible to talk about traditional Chinese medicine today without referencing TCM, especially the ways in which it is shaped by conversations in dialectical and historical materialisms. Materialism constituted the theoretical and methodological foundation of TCM during its institutionalization and scientization in the 1950s and 1960s, which required inventing a body of basic scientific theory—or, to be precise, Theory itself (Farquhar 1994; Scheid 2002; Zhan 2009, 2016). Some analytics were excluded from TCM theory for having religious, spiritual, or superstitious connotations, and others were re-theorized through the scientistic framework of dialectical and historical materialisms.

To be clear, Chinese (Maoist) dialectical materialism is not an inferior version of its European counterpart. As Žižek has cautioned, Mao's reading of Marx is not a relocation of the original work in a more backward country, or a misidentification of the peasantry as the main revolutionary force (2007). Rather, Mao's main contribution lies in his elaboration of the notion of contradiction and his insistence that Theory should be given a key role in political struggle instead of being treated as superstructure (ibid., 7). As Mao famously stated, "all knowledge originates in direct experience" (2007 [1937], XX), and experience must make the quantitative and qualitative leap to theory.

Mao's emphasis on materialism and theorization is carefully digested by the compilers of TCM textbooks. Beginning in the 1950s, the Chinese party-state brought together traditional and biomedical professionals in inventing a core of scientistic theory consistent with dialectical materialism, purging esoteric elements, and supporting laboratory experiments that sought to establish and verify the material basis of Chinese medical concepts (Zhan 2014). Efforts in compiling standardized textbooks for state-run TCM colleges began as early as 1954 (Scheid 2002). Classical texts such as *Zhouyi* disappeared from the curriculum and were referenced only in fragments (Farquhar 1994). Classical concepts were reformulated and embraced as the basic philosophical or theoretical foundation of traditional Chinese medicine. The secularization and scientization of traditional Chinese medicine was seen as progress predicted by the theory of dialectical and historical materialisms. As stated in a textbook compiled and adopted by the Shanghai College of Traditional Chinese Medicine:

> Chinese medicine and pharmacology was developed in continuous struggle. This is reflected in the struggle between materialism and idealism in academic thoughts, which is in turn a reflection of class struggles in the society. In the early stages of the development of medicine, the struggle between materialism and idealism is represented by the struggle between yi (medicine) and wu (witchcraft). Witches belonged to the ruling class of slavery societies [...] whereas medicine comes from the people's experience. In spite of their overlaps: medicine is medicine after all, and witchcraft is witchcraft after all.
>
> (1974, 8–9)

Accentuating the importance of overcoming possible interpretations that might contradict materialism, the textbook further argued for the imperative to "use dialectical materialism and historical materialism as our weapons to criticize the garbage of idealism and metaphysics and absorb the rational elements in their concrete contents" (ibid., 12).

Yet wuxing proved problematic in the face of such secularization, purification, and fragmentation: its specification and categorization of myriad particular "things" (within the Marxist-Maoist framework) in the world—rocks and spirits included—raised more questions concerning its status as a materialist theory.

The standardized introductory textbook for the Shanghai College of Traditional Chinese Medicine offered the following explanation and qualification of wuxing:

> Wuxing Theory, which argues that all things in the universe are made up of materials and that there are connections between various things, is an ancient form of rudimentary materialism and spontaneous dialectic thinking. However, Five Element Theory insists that all things must be divided or grouped into five [...] This clearly cannot truthfully reflect the objective world. When analogy and deduction are used to understand internal organs, tissues, mental activities, and the properties of herbs, medicine becomes trapped in idealism and metaphysics.
>
> (ibid., 28–9)

The textbook named wuxing as a "theory" (*lilun*). However, the subsequent discussion was far less clear-cut. Like Weber, the textbook pointed out that the numbers of wuxing literally did not add up. Like the Jesuits, the textbook articulated an ontology of materiality in which "things" pre-exist "relations" and are enumerable only as such. However, the compilers' inquiries into wuxing were not simply about figuring out whether it was numerical, dialectical, materialistic, idealistic, or metaphysical. At issue here were the particular analytics employed in wuxing: that analogies and deductions are inappropriate or inadequate tools for the material world. In pointing this out, the textbook subtly shifted the discussion from one about *Theory* to *method*.

Toward a cosmography of entrepreneurship

In 2016, the Chinese Ministry of Science and Technology announced a list of Basic Standards for cultivating the "scientific quality" of ordinary Chinese citizens. The list begins with an overview of "scientific worldview and spirit, innovative attitude, and scientific analytic"—including yinyang, wuxing, tianrenheyi, and other cosmological concepts identified as "ancient Chinese naive materialism and holistic methodology that have contemporary significances" (Chinese Ministry of Science and Technology 2016, 5). Spreading quickly through social media, the Basic Standards drew on discourses of dialectical and historical materialisms, and at the same time re-oriented "science" toward embracing classical cosmological analytics. Some are troubled by the surprising inclusion of what they see as outdated knowledge, superstition, and quackery within the scope of scientific worldview and analytic. Chinese social media platforms—Weixin (similar to WhatsApp) and Weibo (similar to Twitter) in particular—were flooded with commentaries that ridiculed these new Standards. Others, meanwhile, have taken the opportunity to push forward entrepreneurial experiments in classical cosmographic concepts and practices that reimagine and actualize holistic and immanent ways of thinking, doing, and being in the profoundly disharmonious and ever-shifting modern world. They see the new Standards as in part the results of their own efforts in promoting classical concepts and pushing back against the establishment, which began, as discussed in the opening sections of this chapter, in the early 2010s.

These entrepreneurial experiments reject the materialist theoretical framework of TCM in favor of what they call the "primal spirit" of Chinese medicine. Aiming to "bring medicine back to life," the quotidian activity of these academies, clubs, and reading groups—consisting of young men and women with backgrounds in international trade, banking, information technology, and other institutions in China's "new economy"—emphasizes immersion in classical texts, ancient herbal formulas, and (pre)-Daoist analytics. This is not a retreat into mysticism or selling spirituality as a lucrative commodity (even though it does sell, sometimes). Rather, this is a larger and deeper quest that calls into question inherent contradictions in modern techniques of rationalization, and brings forth into the world critical possibilities for immanent modes of thinking, doing, and being that do not rely on the dualism of Weber's bi-worldly model or Marxist-Maoist orthodoxy.

There is not a definitive origin of this new classical Chinese medicine. Nor is it uniform in terms of organizational structures, conceptualization of medicine and healthcare models, or entrepreneurial aspirations. Some begin as online chat groups and then add bricks-and-mortar shops, clinics, and branches offline. Some start as small clinics, book clubs, reading groups, or wellness clubs, and then set up online shops and chat groups. Some online groups are stable over several years. Others come and go with the rise of particular interests and cosmological events (for example, shifting patterns of wellbeing associated with particular lunar years). Some entrepreneurs follow a business model in which the enterprise expands by setting up branches (especially clinics) across Chinese cities. Others refuse to expand even when given the opportunity (one entrepreneur, for example, told me that he wanted his clinic to be like an American boutique law firm). Some provide services to members who would like a space for mindful reading, learning, meditating, and eating. Others concentrate on identifying pristine lands for growing natural herbs and for peaceful retreats. Some dwell on exploring classical and sometimes obscure texts, especially the ones fragmented in and excluded from TCM textbooks. Others, in contrast, focus on herbal formulas—not only as a material collection of herbs but also as analytics in their own terms. The seasonal use of *guizhitang* (cinnamon twig decoction), which requires adjustment of specific ingredients according to specific events such as seasonal changes, is an especially popular topic (Zhan 2017). The reinventions in classical medicine through entrepreneurship, as many cultural forms in contemporary China go, are decidedly experimental.

Perhaps the most important feature of classical medicine outside of the establishment is that it self-consciously and strategically distances itself from the institutional and ideological apparatus that sustains TCM.[5] First, many of the entrepreneurs and practitioners leading the entrepreneurial experiments in classical Chinese medicine were born during or shortly after the Cultural Revolution (1966–76). They came of age during the political upheavals and market liberalizations in the 1980s. Having been educated in the scientistic curricula of the Chinese educational system, they are deeply wary of canonical Marxist-Maoist teachings. Some argue that there is no "pure" traditional Chinese medicine within the establishment because of decades of scientization and standardization in the vein of dialectical materialism and historical materialism. Refusing to subscribe to a developmental or evolutionary narrative, they are suspicious of those practitioners trained in TCM institutions in the 1960s and 1970s, in spite of the fact that seniority and longevity alone is often taken as a sign of experience and therefore superior to expertise in Chinese medicine. At the same time, they actively seek out younger TCM practitioners who are open to other modes of learning, scholars who are self-taught and/or trained by masters, and "lost" senior masters who either refuse to participate in TCM or cannot find their footing within the establishment. A popular saying among these entrepreneurs is that "truly skilled healers are found among the grassroots" (gaoshou zai minjian).

Second, many of the entrepreneurs, practitioners, and enthusiasts of classical medicine are suspicious of "materialism" and "fetishism". In the Chinese language, both "materialism" (唯物主义) and "fetishism" (拜物主义) contain the character 物 ("thing" or "material"). Although Marx makes a clear distinction between the two theoretical concepts—one grounded in the material and the other attributing superhuman power to it—in everyday Chinese discourse they tend to be conflated. During my fieldwork on medical entrepreneurship, I heard my interlocutors repeatedly differentiate their practice from intellectual, political, and entrepreneurial pursuits of "things." At the student-organized conference I mentioned at the beginning of this chapter, Dr. Cheng, owner of a private clinic that he founded after training at a TCM college, working for a biotech company, and completing an MBA program, criticized the evils of "things" in these provocative words:

> Tianrenheyi is not a system of theory or a philosophical thought. It is a way of life. In my experience, those who pay the most attention to this true spirit of Chinese medicine are grassroots enthusiasts (in China) and foreigners. The biggest disbelievers are TCM college students. Sometimes it is easier for me to explain Chinese medicine to foreigners. For example, when I teach the diagnosis of "floating pulse", it requires that you experience and feel the Spring season. A lot of foreigners get it. But when I talk to the Chinese, they have a hard time with it. They are so focused on the stock and capital investment markets that they can't feel the seasons. So, I don't worry about how to explain tianrenheyi to foreigners. I worry about how to explain it to the Chinese whose thinking is too mechanical.

"Floating pulse" is one of the pulse patterns in pulse diagnosis and syndrome differentiation in Chinese medicine. When the healer feels the patient's pulse on the wrist, floating pulse feels like "wood floating on water." It is commonly associated with beginning stages of wind-heat syndromes (some but not all common colds, for example, fall under this category). According to wuxing, floating pulse corresponds with Spring, the season of youthful growth and the rise of yang—the warming, ascending principle of yinyang. In spite of the fact that Dr. Cheng certainly and almost deliberately exaggerated in his praise of "foreigners," I find his use of a set of entwined analytical moves thought-provoking. He challenges materialist "theory" as relevant categories for understanding classical Chinese medicine, which requires sensorial and conceptual immersions of the practitioner's entire being—not only in clinical practice but also in life. Singling out the obsession with "things" as an evil that defines Chinese modernity and postsocialism, Dr. Cheng also saw thinking through and doing medicine outside of the establishment as an alternative path that departs from the unethical and dehumanizing pursuit of wealth and profit.

Dr. Cheng's sentiments are shared by many of those who champion classical Chinese medicine through entrepreneurship. Taking a step back from habitual discourses and forms of "TCM," "medicine," "science," and "healthcare," they search for an opening, however elusive and transient, through which the hegemony of modernist institutions and discourses of knowledge can be critically engaged or even challenged. Themselves the product of both socialist and entrepreneurial China, they nevertheless come to question the meanings and forms of modernity. It is a common sentiment that by engaging in classical medicine, it is possible—though by no means guaranteed—that one might reclaim some dignity (尊严) from the hegemonic state, the cut-throat market, and the dehumanizing aspects of modern life.

The interpretation, translation, and enactment of (pre)-Daoist analytics through entrepreneurship, then, is not simply a matter of mistaken ontology, rudimentary materialism, or quackery. It is about the patterning of relations that traverse abstract and concrete, theory and phenomenon, substance and process. Both Weber and Žižek framed their questions around which "religion" would most effectively connect this-worldly capitalist practice and other-worldly calling. Following this line of inquiry and through a Kuhnian move, Žižek also assumed that the connection between Buddhism/Daoism and capitalism is only a recent event, a surprising emergence undermining a stable regime. These Eurocentric assumptions obscure the multiplicitous and dynamic oneness of thinking, doing, and being in the world.[6] The question is therefore not whether "Daoism" (or any kind of "ism" for that matter) would provide the geist or ethos leading China down the path of modern global capitalism. What is at issue is this: even as we get pulled toward Theory—its promise to create and rationalize seemingly distinctive epistemological, ontological, and ethical domains—world-makings in and through classical medicine retain and articulate the critical possibilities for imagining multiplicitous and undivided ways of thinking, doing, and being in the world. These possibilities cannot be found or resurrected by a simple return to the pre-modern world or its ways of knowing and being. In order to keep these possibilities alive, we need to co-imagine a critical methodology oriented toward continuous unfolding and differential becoming. Life itself is full of events. As Franz Boas argued in his vision for a "cosmography," each phenomenon, no matter how big or small, is worth studying not because it is explainable but because it is true (Boas 1940, 639–47, discussed in Zhan 2014). The effect of events lies less in their dramatic ability to transform paradigms of universality than in everyday transformations of universality itself.

Acknowledgments

I thank the participants and especially the organizers of the World Multiple conference, Atsuro Morita, Keiichi Omura, Grant Otsuki, and Shiho Satsuka, for including me in the conversations. This chapter has also benefited greatly from comments by George Marcus, Grant Otsuki, Lisa Rofel, Shiho Satsuka, and Sylvia Yanagisako.

Notes

1 "TCM" refers specifically to the institutionalized form of traditional Chinese medicine that came out of the 1950s. I use "traditional Chinese medicine" to refer to a much broader and heterogeneous set of discourses and practices.
2 Lisa Rofel and Sylvia Yanagisako remind us of insights from feminist anthropology that the division between "public" and "private" should never be taken for granted as uncontested boundaries. The same analytics, they argue, should inform our treatment of public/private in capitalist relations (Rofel and Yanagisako 2018). I heed their call in my treatment of the "establishment," which does not equate with the state, the government, or the public domain. I think of the establishment as ongoing hegemonic institutional and ideological projects and processes produced through shifting positionalities, relations, and entanglements.
3 As Lisa Rofel (2007) points out, the word "experiment" foregrounds the fact that the complex socialities of contemporary China cannot be explained with "socialism" or "capitalism" as stable points of reference. As the Chinese engage these discourses, they also push against their adequacy in capturing the contingency and complexity of social lives and political actions.
4 For comparison, see Stanley Tambiah's (1973) and David Gellner's (1982) critiques of recent sociological interpretations of Weber's facts and his larger project in his study of the religions of India.
5 This is by no means a uniform discourse or position. For example, Liu Lihong, who rose to fame by championing classical medicine, is based in and supported by TCM institutions and overseas connections. In recent years, Liu has worked extensively with private Chinese medicine enterprises and organizations in advertising his brand of educational programs and recruiting students. This is a poignant example that "*tizhiwai*" must not be taken literally; nor does it naturally lead to egalitarian forms of medical knowledge and practice.

6 As Shiho Satsuka puts it, the binary between this-world and other-world is mute as they are inseparable in everyday life (personal communication, March 21, 2018).

References

Barad, Karen. 2007. *Meeting the Universe Halfway: Quantum Physics and the Entanglement of Matter and Meaning*. Durham, NC: Duke University Press.

Bennett, Jane. 2010. *Vibrant Matter: A Political Ecology of Things*. Durham, NC: Duke University Press.

Boas, Franz. 1940. *Race, Language and Culture*. New York: The Free Press.

Chinese Ministry of Science and Technology. 2016. *Basic Standards for the Scientific Quality of Chinese Citizens* 《中国公民科学素 • 基准》. http://www.most.gov.cn/mos tinfo/xinxifenlei/fgzc/gfxwj/gfxwj2016/201604/t20160421_125270.htm

Farquhar, Judith. 1994. *Knowing Practice: The Clinical Encounter of Chinese Medicine*. Boulder, CO: Westview Press.

Furth, Charlotte. 1999. *A Flourishing Yin: Gender in China's Medical History, 960–1665*. Berkeley, CA: University of California Press.

Gellner, David. 1982. "Max Weber, Capitalism and the Religion of India". *Sociology* 16 (4): 526–543.

Haraway, Donna. 1991. *Simians, Cyborgs and Women*. London: Routledge.

Hartsock, Nancy. 1983. "The Feminist Standpoint: Developing the Ground for a Specifically Feminist Historical Materialism". In *Discovering Reality: Feminist Perspectives on Epistemology, Metaphysics, Methodology, and Philosophy of Science*, edited by Sandra Harding and Merrill B. Hintikka, 283–310. Boston, MA: D. Reidel Publishing Company.

Hsu, Elisabeth. 1999. *The Transmission of Chinese Medicine*. Cambridge: Cambridge University Press.

Jullien, Francois. 1999. *The Propensity of Things: Toward a History of Efficacy in China*. New York: Zone Books.

Kuriyama, Shigehisa. 2002. *The Expressiveness of the Body and the Divergence of Greek and Chinese Medicine*. New York: Zone Books.

Liu, Petrus. 2015. *Queer Marxism in Two Chinas*. Durham, NC: Duke University Press.

Lloyd, Geoffrey. 2012. *Being, Humanity, and Understanding*. Oxford: Oxford University Press.

Mao Tse-Tung. 2007 [1937]. *On Practice and Contradiction*. Introduction by Slavoj Žižek. New York: Verso.

Rofel, Lisa. 2007. *Desiring China: Experiments in Neoliberalism, Sexuality, and Public Culture*. Durham, NC: Duke University Press.

Rofel, Lisa and Sylvia Yanagisako. 2018. *Made in Translation: A Collaborative Ethnography of Italian–Chinese Global Fashion*. Durham, NC: Duke University Press.

Rosaldo, Michelle Z. 1974. "Woman, culture and society: A theoretical overview." In *Woman, Culture and Society*, edited by Michelle Rosaldo and Louise Lamphere, 17–42. Stanford, CA: Stanford University Press.

Rose, Hilary. 1983. "Hand, Brain, and Heart: A Feminist Epistemology for the Natural Sciences". *Signs* 9 (1): 73–90.

Scheid, Volker. 2002. *Chinese Medicine in Contemporary China: Plurality and Synthesis*. Durham, NC: Duke University Press.

Shanghai College of Traditional Chinese Medicine. 1974. *The Basics of Chinese Medicine*. Shanghai College of Traditional Chinese Medicine Press.

Strathern, Marilyn. 1980. "No Nature, No Culture: The Hagen case." In *Nature, Culture and Gender*, edited by Marilyn Strathern and Carol MacCormack. Cambridge: Cambridge University Press.

Tambiah, Stanley. 1973. "Buddhism and This-worldly Activity." *Modern Asian Studies* 7 (1): 1–20.

Weber, Max. 1930 [1905]. The Protestant Ethic and the Spirit of Capitalism. Translated by Talcott Parsons. London and New York: Routledge.

—. 1951 [1915]. *The Religion of China: Confucianism and Taoism*. Translated and edited by Hans. H. Gerth. Glencoe, IL: The Free Press.

—. 1958 [1916]. *The Religion of India: The Sociology of Hinduism and Buddhism*. Translated by Hans H. Gerth and Don Martindale. Glencoe, IL: The Free Press.

Yanagisako, Sylvia and Carol Delaney. 1994. "Introduction." In *Naturalizing Power: Essays in Feminist Cultural Analysis*, edited by Sylvia Yanagisako and Carol Delaney. New York: Routledge.

Zhan, Mei. 2009. *Other-worldly: Making Chinese Medicine through Transnational Frames*. Durham, NC: Duke University Press.

—. 2012. "Worlding oneness: Daoism, Heidegger, and Possibilities for Treating the Human." In Special issue on China and the Human, edited by D. L. Eng, T. Ruskula, and S. Shuang. *Social Text* 29 (4): 107–128.

—. 2014. The Empirical as Conceptual: Transdisciplinary Engagements with an "Experiential Medicine." *Science, Technology, & Human Values* 39 (2): 236–263.

—. 2016. "Cosmic Experiments: Remaking Materialism and Daoist Ethic Outside of the Establishment." Special issue on Non-Secular Medical Anthropology. *Medical Anthropology* 35 (3): 247–262.

—. 2017. "Into the Woods," presented at the panel "Elements," co-organized by Daniel Fisher and Mei Zhan, American Anthropological Association Annual Meeting, Washington, DC, November 29–December 3 2017.

Žižek, Slavoj. 2007. "Introduction: Mao Zedong, the Marxist Lord of Misrule". In *Mao: On Practice and Contradiction*. New York: Verso.

—. 2014. *Event: Philosophy in Transit*. New York: Penguin Books.

Chapter 12

Traveling and indwelling knowledge

Learning and technological exchange among Vezo fishermen in Madagascar

Taku Iida

Rural areas are frequently sites of heated environmental dispute, as is the case in Madagascar. This island is a "biodiversity hotspot" (Ganzhorn et al. 2001), where management of the natural environment and its resources has served to attract foreign tourists, encourage investments from overseas, and win international grants-in-aid, all of which stimulate the domestic economy. As a result, Malagasy rural villages are no longer isolated societies representing a homogeneous "culture," but have become arenas of negotiation and competition among people of different cultures and values, notably between *gasy* (Malagasy) and *vazaha* (whites, or Europeans in particular) (Gezon 2006; Kaufmann 2008; Keller 2015; Muttenzer 2010; Sodikoff 2012; Walsh 2012). Consequently, rural Madagascar provides a wealth of materials for the exploration of knowledge and technology exchange between local and non-local populations.

While technology, as represented by such things as engineering skills and machines, travels easily across cultural borders (Morita 2013), knowledge itself (as distinct from information) is not always so easily transferrable. The *rootedness* of knowledge—"indigenous knowledge"—is a key topic of this volume. The transfer of knowledge is not characterized as a specific phenomenon, possibly because the word "knowledge" itself carries too many connotations. The Malagasy people live in a world of heterogeneous knowledge, the exploration of which will clarify the differentiation of "information" and "knowledge" as we proceed.

The study's focal group is the Vezo fishermen who inhabit the southwestern coast of Madagascar. Since the colonial age, European writers have shown that the Vezo people practice a way of life based on capturing, consuming, and marketing fish (Koechlin 1975), and that the Vezo construe their identity through these skills (Astuti 1995). The term *Vezo* is often used to connote proficiency at fishing and sailing and to express admiration for those skills (Iida 2005). This in turn reflects the importance of Vezo physical skills and inherited knowledge for life along the coastal waters. Vezo people express the same idea with the expression *mahay rano* ("know [coastal] water").

Mahay is frequently translated as the verb "to know," but this fails to capture its nuance. One well known Malagasy–English dictionary translates it instead as an adjective meaning "able, clever, competent" (Richardson 1982). As a verb phrase, an appropriate translation would be "to have or acquire skills." One can be called mahay after succeeding at a difficult task. By contrast, knowing what is already common knowledge is rarely described as mahay.[1] In this sense, the Malagasy word mahay relates primarily to procedural knowledge (knowing how), describing a subject's actions and perceptions, rather than to declarative knowledge (knowing that), which relates only to what the subject perceives (de Mey 1982; Piaget 1974). For Malagasy people, the emphasis is on what they can do, procedural knowledge, rather than on what they perceive, or declarative knowledge.

This does not mean that Malagasy people have no notion of declarative knowledge, especially in urban settings, where formal education is relevant. In urban life, mahay's derivative fahaiza (in Vezo dialect; fahaizana in standard Malagasy) is used to indicate declarative knowledge, while mahay is rarely used to indicate a state of possessing such knowledge. Therefore, the meaning of fahaiza as declarative knowledge is subsidiary; rather, mahay and fahaiza are more closely related to tacit knowledge (Polanyi 2009).

Even for non-Malagasy people, the concept of knowledge cannot be detached from personal action or subjective knowledge. Nevertheless, in cases of knowledge exchange, knowledge transfer, or social knowledge, "knowledge" is frequently perceived or assumed to be inherent, as if crystallized out of living bodies. But Vezo people (or rural Malagasy generally) also learn ways to modify their knowledge from foreigners.

To explain the contradictory character of knowledge pursuit, this paper examines how Vezo fishermen learn new jobs introduced by Westerners; how Vezo boys learn from adults; and how fishermen take advantage of factory-made materials and instruments in order to earn their living. This study also elucidates what kinds of "knowledge" circulate beyond social boundaries and what kinds do not; and how people maintain their own world in the global network of information exchange.

The data and anecdotes in this chapter were collected as part of my field research in the village of Ampasilava[2] from 1994 to 2016. The village of Andavadoaka, approximately 5 kilometers from Ampasilava, is home to Blue Ventures, a British-based NGO promoting coastal and oceanic environmental conservation. Its European/American staff has been an important source of information about foreign countries and practices for the Vezo people. For this reason, our description begins with the relationship between Ampasilava villagers and Blue Ventures workers.

Success and failure in transplantation of knowledge

Blue Ventures was established in Andavadoaka in 2003 (Harris 2007). Initially, the NGO's major activity was coral reef mapping with the help of volunteer divers from Europe and America (Lorimer 2010). The resident officers' task was to organize diving trips and accumulate scientific data (Gillibrand et al. 2007; Nadon et al. 2007); the local Vezo people were excluded from involvement. This insensitivity towards native people was shortly exposed as "colonial," as "participatory" and "integrated" conservation schemes were becoming popular or even standard at about that time (Cinner et al. 2009; Rakotoson and Tanner 2006).

Building a good relationship with the Vezo people was not easy. While Blue Ventures provided some benefits (educational support in and out of school, a reproductive health program, opportunities for additional income), they also asked for collaboration (permanent or temporary closure of fishing grounds, collection of scientific data, an experimental aquaculture program), which sometimes created conflict. However, Blue Ventures continues to be based in Andavadoaka and to work with the local community.[3]

Most Ampasilava villagers favor the activities of Blue Ventures, despite some complaints. One important reason for this is the acquisition of new knowledge. For example, one woman was surprised to learn, through Blue Ventures' activities, about women's independence in urban areas and in other countries; while one man was shocked to watch a video showing corals spawning. Without the presence of Blue Ventures, villagers would not have had access to such a variety of new perspectives. According to a friend in Ampasilava, "meeting [with strangers] brings about new ideas, and makes the unseen familiar as if it were the ever-seen."[4]

The Vezo people gain not only new information but also practical skills from Blue Ventures, such as those used to cultivate the marine algae *Kappaphycus cottonii*, which is exported and processed to extract the thickener carrageenan used in both edible and non-edible products from yogurt and chocolate to shampoo and shoe polish. Blue Ventures introduced the farming of *Kappaphycus* to Ampasilava in 2013 in order to mitigate the impacts of fishing on coral reefs. This case provides an excellent example of knowledge transfer.

Kappaphycus grows naturally in shallow waters, but in aquaculture environments it is grown on the surface of deep waters, kept afloat and in place with a cord. The fisher-cultivators are allocated sandy-bottomed areas where few fish live, and fishing activities are extensive. Each plant is left afloat in the water for 20 days before the harvest, then fisher-cultivators use a knife to cut a part of the algae that has been untied from the cord. The part that fisher-cultivators put in the water in the beginning remains tied to the cord; for that reason they call it "capital (*tahiry*)," the same as an initial deposit at the bank.

Kappaphycus farming is a simple process, requiring going to the area, tying, checking, and harvesting algae. After the harvest, the farmer-cultivator must dry the algae; at this stage, the risk of loss to waves and tides is particularly high. Nonetheless, the skill is easy to acquire. The native fisher-cultivators were thus exposed to unfamiliar knowledge which they then easily absorbed.

A more complicated case presents a second example of knowledge transfer. In 2014 through 2016, Blue Ventures hired several fishermen from each village to record large-size catches such as turtles and sharks and to accumulate a biological data set (Humber et al. 2011). Economic advantages of the project included job opportunities for villagers and cost reduction for Blue Ventures. However, the most important effect was the villagers' participation in scientific activities.

Rossy (pseudonym, born around 1961), my closest friend in Ampasilava, was asked by Blue Ventures in 2014 to record all catches of shark, including the total length and weight of the shark, the harvester, and the vernacular name of the species. He saved the record, including digital photographs, in a smartphone app provided by Blue Ventures.

Nowadays, around the world, people spend considerable time becoming accustomed—literally, *to accustom one's own body*—to new electronic devices. This was also true for my friend Rossy, who often had to ask his younger brothers, sisters, sons, and daughters to help him find the initial screen. Through a process of trial and error, he will eventually master its use. But will Rossy and the other fishermen be able to meet Blue Ventures' expectations?

Rossy receives a small monthly remuneration for his job at Blue Ventures, but not everyone wants to do what he does, partly because most fishermen prefer to concentrate on fishing and related matters such as net preparation, and partly because they do not understand the meaning of it. The most significant difference between farming algae and data collection relates to this assignment of meaning. The algae cultivator takes charge of a *process* of production, estimating the outcome for himself, and deciding for himself whether some aspect of the process needs improvement. The data collector, in contrast, cannot even judge whether his job is successful or not. His work is a fragment of the process; Blue Ventures scientists are the only ones with an overview of the project.

Another difference between the two jobs is the role of apparatus. In the case of data collection, the fisherman has to know how to command the app and to recognize how it responds. Since the app was designed by someone else (a professional designer), the user must acquire another's idea to make it work—it isn't intuitive or instinctive. In this particular case the apparatus communicates the fisherman's job to the scientists automatically, regardless of the fisherman's intent or effort. One could say that the apparatus plays a more important role than the fisherman.

In contrast, in the case of algae cultivation, the fisherman does not need a complex apparatus. He manipulates the algae, cords, and a canoe, which react according to their physical attributes but do not form a command–response chain, like a black box. The fisherman only needs to know mechanical techniques, in the sense of "actions intentionally combined with instruments to produce a mechanical effect" (Mauss 2007, 24–31). Paddling a canoe and tying algae with cords are mechanical techniques in this sense. Such instruments function according to physical actions and reactions between objects. The Vezo people are good at these kinds of visible, concrete dynamics, but not at invisible, abstract electronics.

In summary, algae cultivators only have to know the behaviors of simple objects and tools, whereas data collectors use a complex apparatus based on its designers' ideas and the work orders of Blue Ventures' scientists. Cultivators can work independently, while data collectors are dependent on an apparatus that works regardless of visible dynamics. In the case of data collection, the apparatus shares the role of record and communication, and this strange job for the Vezo is characterized by comparatively less human contribution.

Personal knowledge and learning

To further discuss these contrasting jobs of foreign origin in relation to knowledge, let us examine how Vezo children learn from adults. Children take much time to acquire practical kinds of knowledge, or procedural knowledge as opposed to declarative knowledge. For them, learning is not an event that occurs at a certain time and place, but a continuous process encompassing different times and places. Canoe sailing is a good example (Figure 12.1).

Figure 12.1 A Vezo canoe being launched to the sea
Photo by author

Instead of an outboard engine, sailors fix the sail and the mast according to the direction and strength of the wind. If they make a mistake, the canoe might be hit hard by the wind and capsize. To control the vessel, the captain must manipulate the physical actions and reactions among instruments, water, and wind.

Vezo boys usually begin learning to sail at around the age of ten, as the boat is indispensable for reaching other coastal villages. First, an adult teaches him how to make knots to fix the sail and masts to the canoe. If he makes mistakes, the adult points them out, but the boy sometimes does not understand. If that is the case, the session is ended, as the adult's aim is not to complete the boy's training but to set out the canoe. This session is repeated every time the boy goes out to sea with adults, and he only masters the knotting skill after a long period. His progress and eventual mastery is within the context of trans-generational collaboration.

Thus, knowledge is not transferred directly but replicated imprecisely. Personal knowledge, especially procedural knowledge, consists of partial units so intricately interconnected and bound to personal experiences and beliefs that systemicity is damaged if one tries to uproot it. Procedural knowledge lingers briefly in the body. However, something is certainly transferred between the individuals. I call it "information" in line with Gregory Bateson, who defined information as "a difference causing difference" (1972). Here, information might be intellectual, like declarative knowledge, or sensory, like awareness of winds or of the feel of knots. However, it cannot be as integral as procedural knowledge, which consists of memories comprising the five senses and actual episodes.

Information as a peculiar stimulus results in a different state of mind from the individual's previous one. Whether intellectual or sensory, information is so fragmentary that it cannot convey complexity or totality of knowledge. However, the individual who is stimulated by information received will develop *knowledge* or have previous knowledge modified. Thus, knowledge that is developed in the recipient differs from that of the donor. We habitually call this process a *transfer of knowledge*.

My argument encompasses three points. Firstly, knowledge is primarily personal because it is inseparable from the individual's body and mutually connected with other parts of the memory. Knowledge, especially procedural knowledge, is not a single entity but consists of plural modules that are connected systematically to one another: experiences, memories, and beliefs. Secondly, information is a mobile factor affecting knowledge and forming new knowledge. Unlike bodily knowledge, information is free from a systemic connection with senses and other memories, and this is why it travels from one individual to another. Throughout the learning process, a Vezo boy receives much sensory and intellectual information, including an adult's instructions, reactions from the ropes and the canoe body, the motion of the canoe and the sail, and so forth. He combines this information with his own knowledge, and finally establishes a module, a working unit of knowledge, such as how to make a proper knot. Thirdly, so-called knowledge transfer is nothing but incomplete knowledge replication stimulated by communication. The pieces of information that a Vezo boy develops into new knowledge derive from adults' knowledge. However, they are reduced to fragments and thus different from their original, pre-transfer form (how they are constructed in the donor's mind). We must keep in mind that "knowledge transfer" is just a metaphorical expression, at least in the Vezo society.

Dialogue with physical attributes: Tire nets and night-diving equipment

Consideration of the difference between knowledge and information leads us to a reconfiguration of the problem. If knowledge is essentially personal and information is essentially fragmentary and mobile, then what Vezo fishermen do cannot be regarded as an implantation of Western knowledge. Rather, they develop their own knowledge by using information of Western origin as material or catalyst. The smartphone app for shark data collection is an example of the body embedding information. However, before discussing the nature of information, we will look at how skilled Vezo fishermen take advantage of factory-made materials in order to make innovations in their livelihood.

In 2008, I came across some curious fishing gear nearly 200 kilometers away from Ampasilava. There, fishermen and their wives were weaving a beach seine with thick black fiber taken from secondhand tires. Underneath the tire tread is a layer of steel mesh. Cut the layer along the wire, and you get a thick, rubber-coated steel fiber. This is a good material for weaving a seine because it can withstand the abuse it suffers when in use better than the traditional seine. It is rather heavy to manipulate, but fishermen and their wives recognize its utility despite that.

I observed the next example for the first time in 2009. As cheap Chinese products spread in rural areas of Madagascar, fishermen adopted some of them for fishing. One such is the LED torch. It is both brighter and smaller than those that the fishermen had used before, so they tried to use it under the sea at night. Because some fish species sleep at night and are easy to catch, or because others are active and easy to find, spearing at night was regarded as more efficient than spearing in the daytime. For this reason, fishermen waterproofed the torches by covering them with condoms, which are plentiful and cheap at shops in the village, because donor organizations are keen to decelerate population growth. Fishermen created a bricolage by appropriating international rationing and considering with fresh eyes the product's physical attributes.

Examples of innovation through bricolage will be further discussed in the following section. Let us now turn to the issue of social knowledge transfer.

Despite the personal and systemic essence of knowledge, we can easily find cases of transferring tacit as well as explicit knowledge. According to Ikujiro Nonaka, a researcher in business management studies, knowledge is deeply embodied in individuals, and therefore tends to deteriorate if left unshared. To stimulate the sharing process, Nonaka proposed creating opportunities for mutual interaction (Nonaka and Takeuchi 1995). A formally organized company—a business—is in a position to require such an action. But how do people share tacit knowledge successfully in a less formally organized society without strong leaders, such as a Vezo fishing village? And do they do it intentionally? While one can conclude that Vezo fishermen do not intend to share knowledge, they actually do so as a result.

To explain this, let us begin with the peculiarity of the Vezo fishing innovation. While fishing innovation is significant for the development of Vezo life, it is completely different from innovation in industrialized countries. In a highly industrialized country such as Japan, inventive fishing gear is usually developed jointly by fishing-equipment companies and fisheries' cooperative associations. Fishermen buy the gear for themselves in return for a fair price. However, for fishermen in Madagascar, the scale of investment is so small that no industrial companies are involved in product development for fisheries. The fishers themselves, both males and females, invent and build what they need through the use of the knowledge and materials at hand. The use of second-hand tires to weave seines and the combination of LED torches with condoms are good examples.

The Vezo fishermen achieve innovation at a low monetary cost by combining already-shared cheap and second-hand goods. In such conditions, individuals do not have to rely heavily on social knowledge transfer, but this does not mean that transfer is not significant. Individual knowledge development is a more intentional matter in a small society, where face-to-face communication is dominant and manufacture is deeply embedded in everyday life. In such conditions, imitation of neighbors' skill is unintentionally included in individuals' skill development. Vezo fishermen are keen to acquire a wide variety of fishing skills in this way, and by this means also to become famous in the village. In their endeavor to gain skills, they engage in dialogues with the physical attributes of materials, rather than with their fisherman colleagues.

Sharing knowledge: Shark nets, spearguns, and squid angling

When individuals master a wide variety of skills in both fishery and gear-making, a bricolage of fishing innovations spreads widely and quickly, but individual skill acquisition, rather than the social transfer of knowledge, is the relevant factor. To show this clearly, I provide additional examples of fishing innovations.

In about 1991, just before I began my field research, local fishermen were faced with serious resource depletion caused by the introduction of highly productive monofilament nylon nets. Shark nets were welcomed as an innovative fishing method to overcome a decade of fishing families' poverty. According to the fishermen who netted shark for the first time in the village, they had not learnt the method from anyone else, but they had heard that shark fins sell at a good price and that large gill nets can catch shark easily. Large and strong monofilament was unavailable at that time, so they untwisted a rope used for a canoe rig to make meshes. When weaving the nets, they appropriated their own technique for making small gill nets to catch smaller fish. To select the place, they considered the habits of shark, and to ensure success, they tied small fish to the net to attract shark. The fishermen thus combined knowledge from various contexts. As in other cases, this Vezo innovation was achieved at low cost by using materials at hand and body techniques already mastered. Verbal communication also plays a definitive role here: the fishermen had heard about the idea of netting shark, without which they wouldn't have acted.

Other innovations occurred similarly. In the beginning of 1998, juvenile fishermen who were good at diving began to use handmade spearguns. Having observed similar instruments used by European touristic divers, a fisherman got the idea to make the gun barrel from wood. The trigger mechanism was difficult to make from wood, but the fisherman solved this problem by applying the principle of leverage. The spear is launched by the elasticity of the stretched rubber band that was made from a secondhand tire. The end of this band is connected with a wire from an umbrella rib, because this part has to be strong enough to be fixed together with the metallic spear. The spear is made of a steel stick, which is tied to the gun barrel with a long string to avoid loss. A burr made of a spoon handle is attached to the top to keep the prey.

This innovation is based on the fishermen's diving skill as well as their skill at crafting wood, rubber, and metal. Most Vezo boys learn how to process wood by making their own toys, especially canoe models. Sewing rubber has now become a basic crafting skill for Vezo who own ox carts, and those who were lucky to receive diving fins from European tourists. Most Vezo fishermen had already mastered all the skills necessary for crafting a speargun, and so the idea spread quickly by word of mouth. Sharing of the idea occurred over a brief period, while implementing it utilized a set of crafting skills that fishermen had acquired previously, over a long period.

A final example of innovation occurred in 2003, when fishermen were beginning to catch squid that had been worthless before. To line the squid, the fishermen used lures provided by a buyer who ships products in a freezer carrier. The company started to ship frozen products regularly in 2002, thereby modernizing the system of fish distribution. However, the introduction of squid lures had an unexpected effect. Fishermen did not use the lures in their original form, but dismounted the hook and replaced the original plastic body with a wooden one of the fishermen's own making. They did this because the original body was too heavy for Vezo fishermen, who do not use fishing rods or spinning reels. When lining squid, they move their canoe ahead by paddle and haul in the line by hand, thus causing the lure to swim and hop. Because the hauling is slower than spinning by reel, the body has to be lighter than the original. The fishermen not only made the wooden bodies for the lures themselves, but also painted them and added glass eyes to attract squid.

Information mediates knowledge

For the Vezo fishermen, verbal means are inadequate for the transfer of knowledge, because for them important knowledge is procedural rather than declarative, and procedural knowledge has a systemic character. The fishermen actually develop their own knowledge in relation to specific experiences, and fragments of their individual knowledge are closely interconnected and bound to personal memories and beliefs (cf. Omura 2005). In what follows, I will identify four types of information that the Vezo use: human speech and motions; the physical attributes of materials; the forms and structures of tools and instruments; and inscriptions on media. This distinction of information is useful to show how the Vezo make their own world in the global network of information and material exchange.

The cases I adduce so far show that there are two kinds of basic information that develop personal knowledge: human speech and motions, and the physical attributes of materials. Speech and motion, by which all humans communicate to others, are especially significant when children learn from adults. However, older fishermen learn how to manipulate gear, water, and wind, with consideration to how their own actions evoke reactions from the materials. This is why material attributes are important as information that develops individual knowledge. Physical attributes constitute the central concern for skilled fishermen, as evidenced by the rapid spread of the unusual use of old tires, condoms, umbrella rims, and the like.

The above two types are not the only kinds of information that develop individual knowledge. When we see a child competently playing a video game, we think that he or she is having a "dialogue" with the controller and the monitor. The information that he or she receives indeed comes from the controller and the monitor, but it does not necessarily relate to their physical attributes. These types of artificial instruments can thus provide information in a different way than natural things do.

The Vezo canoe is a good example. It is true that canoe builders carefully select the material (wood species), but plastic canoes would also serve the fishermen's use. In contrast, even when wood is suitable for a canoe, it might not function if the proportion of the hull to outrigger is not correct. Here, the human-designed form and structure of the canoe is more critical than the material. In general, the forms and structures of tools and instruments designed for human utility reflect the producer's knowledge. In other words, while perception of the attributes of natural things is a personal matter, using artificial tools is more social.

The interesting character of artificial tools as information relates to their portability and mobility. While it is probable that those who have seen a speargun can then replicate one, it is much less likely that those lacking that first-hand experience would be able to. As visible evidence, artificial tools provide plenty of information, as in the proverb "seeing is believing." In addition, information associated with a tool transcends language, cultural, or national boundaries. The Vezo thus invented their own speargun after the European model. As exampled by this, and by new swimming techniques resulting from the introduction of the diving fin, new tools generate both new personal knowledge and acculturation.

As Atsuro Morita (2014) has observed, machines or artificial instruments in general are relational and performative objects, because they make the user compare the contexts of where they were produced and where they are used. They actually migrate while still maintaining their original context. This applies as well to simpler tools.

The case of introducing smartphones is similar, but neither its material nor form stimulates the development of knowledge: the texts and images shown on the monitor according to the program do that. Such texts and images, whether digital or not, provide meanings irrelevant to the media that carries them. This final kind of information, which I call inscription, is common for physical attributes and forms or structures in that it has a material base, but it is different in that it is not the medium itself, but inscribed on it. It enables modern science to assemble and standardize heterogeneous information in one space. For example, plans and maps described on paper played a significant role in building Gothic cathedrals (Turnbull 2000). It is true that material tools like templates were also effective to externalize and "share" bodily knowledge, but inscribed information brought about more dramatic architectural development.

An apparatus like the smartphone will take a long time to spread in the village because its mechanism is concealed. It requires the user to understand the icons and the language shown on the monitor, whereas its shape and physical attributes afford no information. The fisherman who recorded the shark harvest had difficulty using the app. I do not say that no Vezo fishermen are sensitive to inscription as information. As stated at the beginning of this chapter, the most interesting information that Blue Ventures provided the fishermen with was the video image of corals spawning. Watching, the Vezo people became convinced that the coral polyp is a kind of animal. Video images are now one of the most important sources by which Vezo fishermen develop their knowledge and acquire new knowledge. The difference between the smartphone and the video image is the visibility of their structures relating to their functions. Vezo fishermen are good at understanding the perceptible, but poor at understanding the imperceptible, such as the function of a smartphone.

Conclusion: Interaction of knowledge systems and the Vezo position on a global scale

While knowledge is embodied in individuals, a knowledge *system* goes beyond individuals and specific localities, with the help of human bodily devices and external vehicles of information. Because Vezo fishermen use heterogeneous information from factory-made materials to develop local knowledge, we cannot distinguish the world of technoscientific knowledge from that of indigenous knowledge. Knowledge systems, therefore, can interact with each other across borders, whether they are political or cultural.

If so, why does it appear that Vezo fishermen live in a world distant from that of Blue Ventures scientists? Apparently, the range of a Vezo fisherman's knowledge cannot be said to coincide with that of a Western scientist, or even that of a teenager in a Japanese city. It is because the Vezo people, who rarely possess smartphones, have less knowledge of how the apparatus responds to commands. However, the Vezo knowledge is so rich concerning objects, natural or artificial, that they adapt these objects to create tools suitable to their way of life. The Vezo fisherman and the Japanese teenager are in different situations where different kinds of information have relevance. Relevance for Vezo fishermen is success in fishing and thus inevitably site-specific. Although the Vezo have a relationship with a scientific knowledge space from which they import new information and materials and to which they export biological data, they maintain lives within their own knowledge system for the sake of local success.

To understand the process of world-making, David Turnbull's (2000) analysis is useful, although what he calls knowledge refers not only to individual know-how but also to the total sum of embodied knowledge possessed by a group of people. According to him, knowledge itself is produced locally but can be delocalized through actions of creating "knowledge space." Certain kinds of social and technical devices, such as Incan knotted string and European navigators' maps, or even the smartphone the Vezo fisherman uses, connect heterogeneous components, people, practices, and places to achieve projects on a superhuman scale. An individual can live in the global technoscience world without foregoing the local (see also Blaser, Chapter 4 and Omura, Chapter 5 in this volume) if he or she uses an electronic and digital device. The Vezo knowledge system is only loosely articulated to industrialized countries and remains autonomous because the Vezo still value site-specific information. In this world-maintaining process, not only the mode of communication but also cultural and economic values and motivations play significant roles, as I have discussed elsewhere (Iida 2010).

Finally, I wish to consider the future of the Vezo people within the context of local politics rather than anthropological trends. To advance its research, Blue Ventures wants Vezo fishermen to become better at interacting with smartphones, but this will take a long time, as previously noted. Visualization will be necessary—not a visualization of the smartphone structure, but a visualization of what Blue Ventures plans to do. In the case of data collection, the role of electronic devices is as important as that of the fishermen, because Blue Ventures is after not Vezo knowledge based on personal experience, but a knowledge capital in the form of samples and measured values investable in their scientific activities. In the cycles of accumulating facts (Latour 1987), fishermen play a partial role and do not have hegemony. The central actor with a wider vision of the process is the scientist, whom the fishermen cannot replace.

In a technoscience network with a long reach, the most important knowledge for the fishermen remains local. As we have seen with the fishermen's work with algae, most of them prefer to remain king of their domain rather than to become an element of a network. Fishery and science are different games. I hope that all readers will respect both worlds of these different games.

Acknowledgments

This work was supported by JSPS KAKENHI Grant Numbers JP13710191, JP14251004, JP14251011, JP17401031, JP25244043, and JP15H02601. The author thanks all those concerned, as well as Ampasilava villagers for providing and converting information for scientific purpose, and Caroline Jennings for making the text simpler and more precise.

Notes

1 When one does not know a fact (declarative knowledge), passive voice is usually used as follows: *tsy haiko* (it is not known to me) or *tsy hai'e* (it is not known to him/her). The noun *fahaiza*, which reflects the meaning of passive as well as active verbs, means both declarative and procedural knowledge.
2 Formerly, Ampasilava belonged to the district of Morombe, in the province of Toliara, which was the largest among the six provinces (*faritany*) in Madagascar. Provinces dissolved into 22 regions (*faritra*) in 2009, according to a constitutional change aiming to establish a higher degree of local autonomy. As a result, Ampasilava and the district of Morombe came to belong to the region of Atsimo-Andrefana (Southwest).
3 Tension between the Vezo people and Blue Ventures grows in particular when a new reserve is proposed. However, it is not as acute as expected, probably because the first attempt at a temporary reserve in 2004 was successful (Benhow et al. 2014).
4 *Fivoria mampisokatse ty hevitse, sady hahazara olo ze mbo tsy hitan-teña hitan-teña.* (Recorded in Ampasilava in 2015.)

References

Astuti, Rita. 1995. *People of the Sea: Identity and Descent among the Vezo of Madagascar.* Cambridge: Cambridge University Press.
Bateson, Gregory. 1972. *Steps to an Ecology of Mind.* New York: Ballantine Books.
Benhow, S., F. Humber, T. A. Oliver, K. L. L. Oleson, D. Raberinary, M. Nadon, H. Ratsimbazafy, and A. Harris. 2014. "Lessons Learnt from Experimental Temporary

Octopus Fishing Closures in South-West Madagascar: Benefits of Concurrent Closures."
African Journal of Marine Science 36 (1): 31–37.

Cinner, Joshua E., Andrew Wamukota, Herilala Randriamahazo, and Ando Rabearisoa. 2009. "Toward Institutions for Community-Based Management of Inshore Marine Resources in the Western Indian Ocean." *Marine Policy* 33 (3): 489–496.

Ganzhorn, Jörg U., Porter P. Lowry II, George E. Schatz, and Simone Sommer. 2001. "The Biodiversity of Madagascar: One of the World's Hottest Hotspots on its Way Out." *Oryx* 35 (4): 346–348.

Gezon, Lisa L. 2006. *Global Visions, Local Landscapes: A Political Ecology of Conservation, Conflict, and Control in Northern Madagascar.* Lanham, MD: AltaMira.

Gillibrand, C. J., A. R. Harris, and E. Mara. 2007. "Inventory and Spatial Assemblage Study of Reef Fish in the Area of Andavadoaka, South-West Madagascar (Western Indian Ocean)." *Western Indian Ocean Journal of Marine Science* 6 (2): 183–197.

Harris, Alasdair. 2007. "'To Live with the Sea' Development of the Velondriake Community-Managed Protected Area Network, Southwest Madagascar." *Madagascar Conservation and Development* 2 (1): 43–49.

Humber, F., B. J. Godley, V. Ramahery, and A. C. Broderick. 2011. "Using Community Members to Assess Artisanal Fisheries: The Marine Turtle Fishery in Madagascar." *Animal Conservation* 14: 175–185.

Iida, Taku. 2005. "The Past and Present of the Coral Reef Fishing Economy in Madagascar: Implication for Self-Determination in Resource Use." In *Indigenous Use and Management of Marine Resources*, edited by Nobuhiro Kishigami and James M. Savelle, 237–258. Osaka: National Museum of Ethnology.

——. 2010. "The Community of Bricolage Practice: Appropriation of Global Flows among Vezo Fishermen in Madagascar." *Japanese Journal of Cultural Anthropology* 75 (1): 60–80 (in Japanese).

Kaufmann, Jefferey C., ed. 2008. *Greening the Great Red Island: Madagascar in Nature and Culture.* Pretoria: Africa Institute of South Africa.

Keller, Eva. 2015. *Beyond the Lens of Conservation: Malagasy and Swiss Imaginations of One Another.* New York: Berghahn.

Koechlin, Bernard. 1975. *Les Vezo du Sud-Ouest de Madagascar: Contribution à l'Étude de l'Éco-Système de Semi-Nomades Marins.* Paris: Mouton.

Latour, Bruno. 1987. *Science in Action: How to Follow Engineers and Scientists through Society.* Cambridge: Harvard University Press.

Lorimer, Jamie. 2010. "International Conservation 'Volunteering' and the Geographies of Global Environmental Citizenship." *Political Geography* 29 (6): 311–322.

Mauss, Marcel. 2007. *Manual of Ethnography.* Translated by Dominique Lussier. New York: Durkheim Press.

de Mey, Marc. 1982. *The Cognitive Paradigm: Cognitive Science, a Newly Explored Approach to the Study of Cognition Applied in an Analysis of Science and Scientific Knowledge.* Dordrecht: D. Reidel.

Morita, Atsuro. 2013. "Traveling Engineers, Machines, and Comparisons: Intersecting Imaginations and Journeys in the Thai Local Engineering Industry." *East Asian Science, Technology and Society* 7: 221–241.

——. 2014. "The Ethnographic Machine: Experimenting with Context and Comparison in Strathernian Ethnography." *Science, Technology and Human Values* 39 (2): 214–235.

Muttenzer, Frank. 2010. *Déforestation et Droit Coutumier à Madagascar: Les Perceptions des Acteurs de la Géstion Communautaire des Forêts.* Genève: Institut de haut études internationales et du développement.

Nadon, M., D. Griffiths, E. Doherty, and A. Harris. 2007. "The Status of Coral Reefs in the Remote Region of Andavadoaka, Southwest Madagascar." *Western Indian Ocean Journal of Marine Science* 6 (2): 207–218.

Nonaka, Ikujiro and Hirotaka Takeuchi. 1995. *The Knowledge-Creating Company: How Japanese Companies Create the Dynamics of Innovation.* New York: Oxford University Press.

Omura, Keiichi. 2005. "Science against Modern Science: The Socio-Political Construction of Otherness in Inuit TEK (Traditional Ecological Knowledge)." In *Indigenous Use and Management of Marine Resources*, edited by Nobuhiro Kishigami and James M. Savelle, 323–344. Osaka: National Museum of Ethnology.

Piaget, Jean. 1974. *Success and Understanding.* Translated by Arnold J. Pomerans. London: Routledge & Kegan Paul.

Polanyi, Michael. 2009 [1966]. *The Tacit Dimension*, Chicago, IL: University of Chicago Press.

Rakotoson, Lalaina R. and Kathryn Tanner. 2006. "Community-Based Governance of Coastal Zone and Marine Resources in Madagascar." *Ocean and Coastal Management* 49: 855–872.

Richardson, J. 1982 [1885]. *A New Malagasy–English Dictionary.* Amersham, UK: Gregg International.

Sodikoff, Genèse Marie. 2012. *Forest and Labor in Madagascar: From Colonial Concession to Global Biosphere.* Bloomington, IN: Indiana University Press.

Turnbull, David. 2000. *Masons, Tricksters and Cartographers: Comparative Studies in the Sociology of Scientific and Indigenous Knowledge.* London: Routledge.

Walsh, Andrew. 2012. *Made in Madagascar: Sapphires, Ecotourism, and the Global Bazaar.* North York: University of Toronto Press.

Chapter 13

Worlds apart? Reflexive equivocations in the Alto Rio Negro

Antonia Walford

In this chapter, I examine how one specific configuration of the world multiple, drawn from Amazonian anthropology, can be used to think through a short period of fieldwork I conducted in the Alto Rio Negro region of the Northwest Brazilian Amazon. While there, I was struck by the way in which the "world of the indians" and the "world of the whites" (*mundo dos índios; mundo dos brancos*) appeared explicitly as such in people's discourse, and how the people I spoke to were often reflecting on and pondering the relationship between the two. In some settings, such reflexive awareness has important ramifications for our understandings of these contexts and of the role of anthropology in them.

A short history of colonial contact in the Alto Rio Negro

According to anthropologist Christine Lasmar (2005), the Alto Rio Negro region of Brazil, which stretches to the border with Colombia and Venezuela, has a long and violent history of colonial contact, starting in the seventeenth century when Portuguese colonizers ventured up the northern reaches of the Rio Negro, capturing indigenous people to sell as slaves in larger cities downriver. This was followed by an influx of missionaries waging so-called "just wars" in order to spread salvation to the indigenous populations. This, along with the disease epidemics that swept through indigenous communities, meant that by the eighteenth century, many of the indigenous groups of the lower and middle Rio Negro were depopulated and several groups had been completely exterminated. The beginning of the twentieth century was marked by the arrival of Salesian missionaries. In the name of "civilizing" the indigenous people, they ordered the tearing down of ceremonial houses (*malocas*) so that they could build nuclear family houses. They also prohibited male initiation rites and the use of adornments (*enfeites*), and they drove away the shamans (Lasmar 2005, 34–6).

In 1980, during the Russel Tribunal in Amsterdam, the Salesians were denounced for committing ethnocide, and they started to re-align themselves with more moderate strands of the Catholic Church (ibid., 37). At the same time, an indigenous political movement was gaining momentum, and in 1987 the Federation of Indigenous Organizations of the Rio Negro (Federação das

Organizações Indígenas do Rio Negro, FOIRN) was created with the express aim of fighting for indigenous territory rights. FOIRN had the support of a Brazilian NGO, Instituto Socioambiental (ISA), and of several prominent Brazilian anthropologists. It achieved success in 1996, when the Brazilian government granted FOIRN permanent ownership of five indigenous territories in the Alto Rio Negro, with a total area of 100,000 km^2. Alongside this, a new demand for indigenous education emerged, and Instituto Socioambiental and FOIRN helped to create several so-called "indigenous schools" (*escolas diferenciadas* or *escolas indígenas*) in different communities on the different rivers, in which indigenous languages and customs were taught to varying degrees. But this was far from a simple victory for the indigenous people, who still live with the legacy of colonialism. As one indigenous Baré person remarked to a member of ISA—at first, you *brancos* told us we weren't allowed to speak our language; now you tell us we have to in order to be *indios*.

São Gabriel da Cachoeira

São Gabriel da Cachoeira (henceforth São Gabriel), the capital of the municipality of the same name in the Alto Rio Negro, sits at the convergence of the Rio Negro and the Rio Uaupés, just outside indigenous demarcated land. In 2013 I spent five weeks in São Gabriel, where I rented a room in a small house that ISA maintains for its employees. I spent the duration of my time interviewing and talking to as many people as possible who were involved in intercultural projects. What follows is not based on in-depth, long-term ethnographic fieldwork, but on preliminary research.

During my stay, I noticed that alongside a constant flux of indigenous people moving along the river between the town and the communities, a steady trickle of non-indigenous people flows into the region, made up of either military personnel, people connected to ISA, or researchers of some sort or another (as was my case). This saturation of the region with a certain sort of person from 'outside'—NGO members, scientists, linguists, anthropologists—is to a certain extent a continuation of the long history of contact, and indeed of the region's colonial history, not least because these outsiders are constantly and explicitly producing and circulating knowledge about the place they are in and the people they are with. At first, then, I was intrigued by what happens when a cultural environment becomes saturated with a sort of "self-knowledge" that is produced by people who come from "outside" it. This is not a new observation by any means, and has been extensively discussed by several anthropologists who have worked in this Amazonian region and others over the past few decades (Chernela 2005, 2011; Hugh-Jones 1988; Jackson 1995a,b; cf. Turner 1999). Jean Jackson, for example, writing over two decades ago, points out (with not a little alarm) that within what she calls "cultural preservation" projects, "Tukanoans are beginning to be instructed by outsiders, both whites and indians, on what it means to be indians" (1994, 384). Imputed within such concerns are now-familiar conflicts between authenticity and superficiality, continuity and change, and tradition and acculturation (e.g., Fabian 1983; Gow 1991).

These debates are complicated considerably in the Alto Rio Negro because the indigenous people there not only are being authored by others, but increasingly are authoring their own books about themselves, through the work of the various indigenous schools.[1] Nevertheless, these activities, and indeed the larger question of indigenous education systems, are still caught up in wider, and ongoing, debates about how it is even possible to teach "indigenous knowledge" from within a system such as a school, which relies on writing rather than oral modes of transmission, and on a temporality and spatiality that is often at odds with indigenous organizational and cosmological practices (cf., de Cunha and Cesarino 2014).

Acculturation or appropriation?

Concerns about indigenous cultural authenticity are often premised on the idea that there is an inherent way to be indigenous, which is in some way contaminated or distorted by contact with outside entities (cf., Theodossopoulos 2013). In the Alto Rio Negro, there seem to be a growing number of people moving from their communities into the town, money is increasingly becoming vital to existence, and people seem to be forgetting traditional ritual knowledge and practices of planting and fishing. In such a context, it is difficult not to reach for terms such as "acculturation" to describe this encroachment of "globalization," "capitalism," or "modernization."

As an alternative to this approach, however, several anthropological studies have instead stressed the creative and appropriative capacity and agency of indigenous people as they negotiate such interactions (Gow 1991; Hugh-Jones 1979, 1988; Kelly 2005). Thus Geraldo Andrello (2010), who has worked for many years in the Rio Negro region, has written about the FOIRN series of mythic narrative books produced in the Alto Rio Negro, in which myths are first recounted by an elder of a particular clan to his son in an indigenous language and then transcribed with the help of an anthropologist. These books contain the genealogical and mythico-cosmological topology of the clan, and are sold not only in São Gabriel, but in São Paulo and beyond. Andrello argues that these books are in fact a contemporary transformation—and therefore continuation—of the ritual *dabucuru* male initiation and naming process, in which before the exchange of ceremonial items, those involved would cite their lineage to their exchange partner and the assembled people, reasserting their place in the cosmos. In fact, DVDs, CDs and books are, from this perspective, not simply western technological objects with which indigenous people are forced to engage; rather, "even market goods of the Whites are appropriated by the thought of the people of the Rio Negro as 'operators' of differentiation between *sibs* and ethnic groups" (Martini 2012, 347). Underpinning these arguments are complex and culturally specific ideas about the importance of differentiation for the constitution of indigenous identity; in fact, the people of the Alto Rio Negro know themselves as *a gente de transformação*—the people of transformation. As Andrello and Ferreira (2014) argue, differentiation and transformation are therefore constitutive aspects of what "to be *indio*" means.

What Andrello and colleagues demonstrate, then, is very much in the spirit of Marshall Sahlins's "indigenization of modernity" (2000, 271). These "other" or Western technologies, far from modernizing the indigenous people, are appropriated in order for them to further indigenize themselves—that is, further differentiate themselves. What "we" understand as acculturation and homogenization, "they" understand as appropriation and differentiation. Rather than reduce the latter to the former, the anthropologist's role is to reveal this equivocation (cf., Viveiros de Castro 2004)—to reveal the multiplicity of relations at play in any interaction. One can of course still take account of the effects of what we might recognize as macro-forces, such as colonialism, globalization, capitalism, and modernity—it is just that these forces do not encompass indigenous realities, they are in fact multiplied and transformed by them, making it necessary to constantly interrogate what we assume we are referring to when we use such terms (cf., Strathern 1988).

Of particular importance to this general argument has been the notion of "controlled equivocation," a term coined by Eduardo Viveiros de Castro (2004) in order to indigenize the anthropological method of comparison and translation itself. Drawing on his long-term research with Amerindian peoples, Viveiros de Castro argues that anthropology can learn from Amerindian cosmologies, in which, for example, members of the same species see themselves as humans, and see their behavior and bodies in terms of human culture. Thus when a human sees blood, a jaguar sees manioc beer; when a human sees "a muddy salt-lick on a river bank, tapirs see their big ceremonial house" (2004, 6; also Viveiros de Castro 1998). It is not that that there is one referent ("blood" or a "salt lick") and two points of view on it; rather, the jaguar and the human are in fact referring, in the same way (as they both see themselves as human), to two very different referents. Therefore, there is "not a plurality of views of a single world, but a single view of different worlds" (2004, 6). This indigenous cosmology has come to be known as "Amerindian perspectivism," developed also by Tânia Stolze Lima (1996, 1999) and subsequently further elaborated by other anthropologists (e.g., Kelly 2010; Vilaça 2005). What Viveiros de Castro suggests, however, is that this Amerindian method of comparison (2004, 7) needs to be allowed to recursively shape the anthropological method. If "indigenous perspectivism is a theory of the equivocation, that is, of the referential alterity between homonymic concepts" (ibid., 5), Viveiros de Castro potentializes this ethnographic realization, arguing that instead of translating indigenous realities into their own conceptual language, anthropologists must recognize and maintain—or "control"—the equivocation (the "referential alterity") that exists between their referential universe and that of the people they are trying to describe.

However, although "controlling equivocations" is how Viveiros de Castro characterizes the anthropological endeavor, one of the observations that I made in São Gabriel was that most of the interactions and discussions I had seemed to center on exactly *who* was controlling these equivocations. It is therefore worth briefly drawing out what it might mean *not* to control equivocations. José Antonio Kelly draws on Viveiros de Castros's insight to draw attention to what he calls the "uncontrolled" equivocations that occurred throughout his fieldwork (2010, 2011). Kelly studied the relations between the Venezuelan state and the Yanomami in the implementation of state healthcare in the Yanomami territory. Analyzing a series of meetings between the medical professionals of the Ministry of Health and the Yanomami, Kelly notes the way in which each seem to be trying to translate each other. Whereas the Venezuelan state, in the name of "cultural authenticity" and the preservation of indigenous identity, is interested in "making indians," the Yanomami are instead looking to the biomedical health system to "become white," that is, to use white culture "at the service of reproducing Yanomami society" (2011, 3). Whereas the doctors see the Yanomami desire for "white man's goods" as demonstrating rampant materialism, the Yanomami are instead interested in the cosmological efficacy of the relation that the act of obtaining these goods manifests in differentiating between those who "give" and those who "receive" (2010, 285). At the heart of this is an equivocation around what "white" and "indian" in fact refer to: "Yanomamis are neither becoming the white people that white people conceive as such, nor do they see themselves as being like the indians that the state would like to restore" (ibid., 289, my translation). Thus the doctors and health officials understand the "becoming white" of the Yanomami as alienation and cultural loss; and the Yanomami criticize the whites for their "meanness" in their provision of biomedical services and their "unreliability" (ibid., 291, my translation). Kelly points out that these uncontrolled or unrecognized equivocations are often taken as either "understandings" (when the Yanomami and the state officials seem to agree) or "misunderstandings" (when there is conflict between them). However, approaching these relations as a question of understanding or misunderstanding presumes that the officials and the Yanomami have a shared system of referential meaning. In fact, Kelly argues, these intercultural relations need to be approached by the anthropologist as evidence of the multiple referential universes that are in play as both sides struggle to translate the other side into something recognizable.

Inspired by this body of work, I would like to add a further observation that appears to me important to consider, drawn from the short time I spent in São Gabriel. This is simply that the people I talked to had their own ideas about how "white worlds" and "indigenous worlds" are related to each other in different ways; in fact, they seemed to be constantly and explicitly reflecting on those very relations. This was an ongoing discussion that could take place in many different contexts, from formal meetings about the implementation of a higher education system for indigenous knowledge, to conversations over beer of an evening. What also became apparent, however, was that it was not just the relationship between indigenous and white referential universes that was at the center of these discussions, but exactly the differences inherent in these relations that were being reflected on and negotiated (cf., Kelly 2010, 295). Therefore, the distinction between the controlled equivocations of anthropological method, and the uncontrolled equivocations that anthropologists encounter in their field sites, become harder to distinguish; people in São Gabriel were controlling and uncontrolling equivocations simultaneously, and as a result, equivocations seem to be able to both shift around and get stuck. This implies that it might make sense to understand intercultural interactions as complex, unstable, and shifting equivocational choreographies, in which people, including anthropologists, are involved in open-ended relational negotiations. I will give two examples to illustrate my point.

Equivocational complexities

Because I stayed in the town of São Gabriel for the duration of my visit, and was associated with ISA in an indirect fashion, most of the people I talked to were involved in one way or another with different sorts of "cultural revitalization" projects. One such project that I became particularly interested in was the Indigenous Environmental Agents project (Agentes Indigenas de Manejo Ambiental, AIMA). Based mostly on the Tiquié river, people designated as AIMA receive a small grant in return for conducting various sorts of research into different themes of cultural importance around the idea of environmental management (*manejo*)—these might involve fish, fruit, agriculture, or constellations. In the case of those AIMA investigating fish, for example, they collect quantitative data such as the length and weight of fish caught, draw exceedingly beautiful illustrations of the fish, and keep daily and very detailed diaries recording whether the river was high or low, who went to fish, what was caught, and so on (cf., Cabalzar and Azavedo, 2012). They also attend a meeting three times a year during which they compare results with each other and show it to the *conhecedores*—elders from different communities known to have ritual and mythical knowledge.

Ronaldo[2] is a young Tukanaon AIMA who I had the chance to talk to on several occasions. He was also training to be a shaman (*kumua*), with his father. When I asked him about his relationship with the conhecedores, Ronaldo told me, "It's very important, the knowledge of the elders because their knowledge sometimes approximates, or comes close, to scientific knowledge." I asked for an example.

> Well, we asked them [the conhecedores] about the constellations [. . .] and we drew a graph [. . .] using the knowledge of the conhecedores. And then [Paulo] got the data from the National Water Agency. And our graph was very similar to the whites' research [*pesquisa do branco*] [. . .] the climate is

changing, the same as the old people are suggesting [. . .] the conhecedores are curious about these changes, and the brancos as well—they have the same knowledge, hey?

But is it the *same* knowledge? I wondered.

"Well, it's also very different from the knowledge of the brancos," he replied immediately. "Because our ancestors thought that man, they have these parts, which represent the lower, the middle, the sub-middle, and the world where we live, that would be the heart," he said, indicating the different parts of his body.

> That's why they bless (*benziam*). This part signifies the support, the thorax —where man lives supported in a *cuia* [gourd bowl]. And so they bless each year, each constellation, each season, they bless. But after the missionaries arrived, they stopped burning the resin in the communities and stopped doing that ritual that controls the weather. And the world started to change, the old people mention this. They never say it directly but I'm certain [. . .] when the thunder comes, my father makes a ritual cigarette and blesses, and he teaches me, always teaches me—in order not to get sick from the lightning he makes a protective cigarette. He smokes it out [. . .] the thunder's manioc beer is poison for us, it transmits disease. The white man, he understands everything very differently from us, he is the brother of the *wai-mahsã*, the enchanted ones [*encantados*], according to the conhecedores. That's why they [the brancos] aren't affected by the diseases that make us sick. For us it is different. One time my daughter had a fever of 42 degrees, and they put an IV drip in her and they couldn't get the fever to go down. My father performed some blessings, and he managed to lower the fever.

My conversation with Ronaldo was peppered with explanations of the relation between os brancos and os índios in this way. But it was also evidence of a constant negotiation of continuity and difference. Ronaldo is carefully negotiating the differences between the pesquisa do branco and the knowledge of the conhecedores, while at the same time maintaining a politico-ontological parity: they understand things very differently, but their knowledge has the same status. He was very comfortable talking to me about the ways in which brancos and índios live in different worlds, which sometimes overlap and sometimes do not. In this sense, he seemed quite at ease "controlling the equivocation" between the two worlds himself, as it were. However—at least as far as this conversation was concerned—Ronaldo frames this difference in terms of his own cosmology: the brancos are related to the wai-mahsã, who are the "enchanted ones" or invisible entities, and that is what makes them different. So at the same time as being aware of the differences, he is also positing what we might think of as an indigenous theory for that difference.

This capacity for equivocations to be both revealed and negated is also apparent when we consider the other side of this particular relation. In their diaries, the AIMA have suggested that there is a lack of fish because the fish are in fact turning into birds. This was a result of one of the AIMA meetings with the conhecedores, during which the conhecedores decided that the lack of fish was because *benzimentos*, or ritual blessings, were not being said frequently enough, and so the fish were turning into birds and then attacking the palm trees. They decided to send some of the AIMA upriver with a specially blessed piece of tree resin to burn at the head of the river, to try to slow or even reverse this transformation. When I asked Paulo, a scientist who collaborated on the AIMA project and had worked in the region for several decades, what he thought about the co-existence of these two very different ways of understanding the problem, he said quite openly,

> Yes, for me this thing of fish transforming in birds is completely out of the question. But it's also [...] what my opinion is, is irrelevant. Because they will not look for me to resolve *that* problem. They will look for me to resolve the problem of the [overfishing with] nets, the *malhadeiras*. They will not come to me to resolve that other part, so my opinion, if I agree or disagree, is totally irrelevant, because I am not a specialist in that kind of stuff."

He went on to tell me that holding two contradictory positions in one's head is not something special about indigenous Amerindians, it's simply "human nature."

Both Ronaldo and Paulo are clear that there is a difference between what they respectively think and act upon. On one side, Ronaldo is both managing the gap between indigenous and white people's knowledge, and giving an indigenous theory for the differences between the two. That is, the equivocation has been shifted to another explanatory level, as it were—he recognizes that brancos and índios understand and live in different worlds, but the reason for that difference is given in the terms of only one of those worlds. He thus explicitly recognizes the misunderstandings between them at one level (or controls the equivocation), but reinstates the equivocation at another (in what we might think of as an uncontrolled fashion). On the other side, Paulo is also very conscious of the differences between his understanding and that of the conhecedores and the AIMA, and is very reluctant to comment on the former, aware it is out of his remit. Even though it is "out of the question" for him to believe personally in what the conhecedores cite as the cause of the problem, he is also very sensitive to the fact that this is *because* there are two very different worlds of knowledge and practice contained within this interaction. At the same time, for Paulo there is still, at base, something called "human nature" that allows such contradictions to be held simultaneously. For Paulo, then, there is both an understanding of different worlds (controlled), as well as a universalizing theory as to how these different worlds might be held in tension with each other (uncontrolled).

My conversations with both Paulo and Ronaldo show, I believe, that there is a common understanding that índios and brancos do and think things differently; at the same time, there is a recursive reiteration of the equivocation, shifting it to another level. What that equivocation consists in is different for each—for Ronaldo, it consists in a *difference* between índios and brancos; for Paulo it consists in a *commonality* between them. Nevertheless, the two of them both control and do not control the referential multiplicity inherent in their relationship to each other, at the same time.

I had other conversations, however, in which the displacement of the equivocation, as I am calling it, to another "level" was not so readily accomplished. In these cases, people evidenced signs of doubt and uncertainty, and sometimes distress. The most obvious examples I encountered involved non-indigenous people who were part of state-implemented systems. The most striking case was Claudio, who worked for the regional Distrito Sanitário Especial Indígena, the unit responsible for the management of indigenous healthcare provided by the Brazilian state. Claudio told me that he had never felt at home in allopathic medicine, so when a chance came up to work in São Gabriel with indigenous health, he jumped at it. "It was exciting!" he said, laughing. "You think you'll arrive here, and you'll be working with plants and ritual blessings (*benzimentos*) [...] that no-one wants dipirona [an over-the-counter analgesic] or wants to be a doctor [...] I arrived not wanting certain things, but the indigenous people wanted certain things from me [...] in fact, they wanted exactly what I was questioning!" he told me, smiling. He had quickly realized that there were certain expectations of doctors, particularly to give out medicines, because the previous doctors had always behaved in certain ways with the indigenous people. But Claudio struggled with this. "I'm not an anthropologist," he said thoughtfully. "I have a responsibility [as a doctor]. But I always asked myself this question: am I a colonizer or not? Up to what point am I here to contribute, and at what point will I look back and see myself as a Salesian missionary? The Salesians came here with the best of intentions, and destroyed everything [...] maybe I am doing the same. I question myself endlessly. Am I colonizing?" He went on, "There has already been contact, there's no way round that—and here I am. My science is not the truth; it makes sense here, it gives results—but it's not the truth." Claudio was adamant that "we need to develop a concept of indigenous health;" he was worried at the extreme "sanitization" and "hygienization" that western medicine insists on. "Western medicine is arriving here," he said with a frown, "whether it's inevitable or not, I don't know."

Claudio was intrigued by the ways in which "his" medicine got entangled in indigenous ways of curing—he mentions how shamans bless soap for children to wash with, or bless medicines they give to people before they take them. He told me, "There are indigenous diseases and white diseases [*doença de índio*, doença de branco], this is something I learned here, it's really true. There are some diseases that don't make any sense in my science [...] I saw a Yanomami girl who simply wouldn't wake up, as if she was in a coma, but she wasn't; others have pains in their arms which move to their chest to somewhere else—it doesn't make any sense to me." He was aware that he was just one option available to indigenous people, and tried to get them to go and see the benzedor (a healing shaman) when there was something he could not deal with. Claudio was very aware of the gap between the mundo dos brancos and mundo dos índios, and at one point he told me that, really, it was all about profound differences—"we see things one way, they see them another," he repeated several times.

On one hand, Claudio's reluctance to give out medicines to the indigenous people when they requested them hints at the sort of uncontrolled equivocations that Kelly alerts us to, in terms of what Claudio presumes this medicine "is" for indigenous people. However, on the other hand, it was clear that Claudio knew there was more than one referential universe in question, and that he was struggling to make sense of this not only intellectually, but also ethically. His doubt resided in the fact that, unlike Ronaldo and Paulo, he was in fact finding it hard to shift the equivocation—that is, he was unable to stop recognizing it—and as a result was filled with uncertainty about his position in relation to it.

Reflexive misunderstandings

I am aware of the partiality of the picture I have painted here with these short encounters. It is more than likely that my observations reflect the fact that I was talking to people in São Gabriel, who were directly involved in projects in which intercultural relations were explicitly the focus, and I may have come to very different conclusions had I spoken to different people. Nevertheless, I want to focus on the idea that the people I spoke to, however unusual they may or may not have been, were in fact very aware of the equivocations potentially occurring between themselves and their others, and were aware that the misunderstandings might be different for each of them. This, it seems to me, is both a banal observation and also a significant one.

It is banal because it can be taken simply as evidence of the argument that Viveiros de Castro, Kelly, and others have already made about the "double" misunderstandings that are constitutive of these sorts of relations. However, it does emphasize the way in which equivocations seem endlessly recursive and can shift around. As Viveiros de Castro mentions, "an equivocation is indissoluble, or rather, recursive: taking it as an object determines another equivocation 'higher up,' and so on ad infinitum" (2004, 11). Given this recursivity, it is therefore not a shock that Paulo and Ronaldo both dwelt on —and in—an equivocation between their worlds, and in dwelling on/in it, instated another equivocation "higher up." However, this does imply that perhaps one cannot control an equivocation without *uncontrolling* another equivocation simultaneously. It is clear, in fact, that *not* being able to do this can in fact cause considerable ethical discomfort, as we see with the case of Claudio. This would imply that understanding these sorts of intercultural contexts necessitates taking account of a much more dynamic and distributed choreography of equivocation than is permitted from a perspective in which control remains the responsibility of the anthropologist, and the uncontrolled is manifest in the unreflexive actions of their interlocutors.

There are two further points to be taken from the way in which the misunderstandings, and indeed the equivocations they mask, are themselves being reflexively negotiated in São Gabriel. The first is that this might provide another dimension to internal anthropological debate on these matters. To return to my original framing, it should be noted that the approach that understands interactions between indigenous Amazonian peoples and non-indigenous peoples as based on ontological multiplicity and difference has provoked some criticism. Much of the critique is broadly levelled at the impossible incommensurability that seems to be implied between "worlds" from within such a framing. The proponents of this critique are concerned that these "worlds"—for example, the "world" of the indigenous people and the "world" of the whites—cannot simply be mutually exclusive domains chugging along beside each other on their separate ontological tracks. The reasons given that are most relevant here include moral and political arguments about collective humanity and the problems of "Othering" (Vigh and Sausdal 2014) and fears about the return of essentialism (Heywood 2012).

One answer is that, of course, relations "between" different "worlds" exist—in fact, such relations are constitutive of what we might think of as "worlds" in the first place, be they human and spirit worlds, or indigenous and non-indigenous ones.[3] But the important point is that what constitutes any given relation might not be the same for all of those implicated in it—and that holds for relations between spirits and humans as much as for ones between indigenous and non-indigenous actors (cf., Viveiros de Castro 2002, 120). However, at least in São Gabriel, these relations do not have to take the shape of either the common understanding of a collective humanity, or an unacknowledged difference between radically divergent referential universes—but rather a reflexive acceptance of equivocation itself as explicitly constitutive of relationality. It is of course possible that this acceptance simply shunts the equivocation (around a shared "human nature," for example) "higher up" or to what I have been calling a different "level." But it is also clear that the explicit acceptance that differences might go "all the way down," even if they cannot be fathomed as such without negating them, very much shapes (at least some) people's interactions with each other and with themselves. What is revealed is people's knowledge that relations can be multiple; and, as the examples I have given demonstrate, this understanding is something that not only indigenous people seem to be working with, but also the non-indigenous people who are negotiating their ethical and intellectual commitments in such interactions. If we take these equivocations themselves as relations between worlds, then we must also accept that they may be much more dynamic and motile than expected. Controlling equivocations might be a case not just of recognizing them, but of managing their motility.

Secondly, the examples I have given also allow for an exploration of a peculiar characteristic of reflexivity. By reflexivity, I simply mean the difference between, on one hand, "a type of communicative disjuncture where the interlocutors are not talking about the same thing, and *do not know this*" (Viveiros de Castro 2004, 9; my emphasis), and on the other, a type of communicative disjuncture when interlocutors are not talking about the same thing and *do know this*. That is, reflexivity might be framed exactly as the shift from uncontrolled to controlled equivocations. The question is, what does this shift change?

In a recent introduction to a special issue, Katherine Swancutt and Mireille Mizard (2016) describe the "reflexive feedback loop" through which "professional visitors—fieldworkers, missionaries, ideologues—transmit elements of their theoretical perspectives to native thinkers. These thinkers, in turn, offer anthropologizing perspectives back to us, indirectly reflecting the diverse ethnographic influences that shape anthropologists' views" (Swancutt and Mizard 2016, 3). Swancutt and Mizard are concerned with how an ethnographic concept such as animism is "jointly reinvented" through this process, and coin the term "hyper-reflexivity" to describe "the circulation of ideas through multiple sites, as the subjects of ethnographic inquiry appropriate and reinvent the abstract formulations of anthropology and other systems of thought" (ibid., 2). As a form of relationship between worlds, these feedback loops seem to resemble a sort of cross-pollination, one in which, as Rane Willerslev writes in the foreword to the special issue, "native ideas feed into and play havoc with scholarly models of animism" (Willerslev 2016, v). Swancutt and Mizard note that it is accentuated reflexivity on both sides of the relation that effects a form of relational transformation between anthropologists and those they study.

Arguing that this cross-pollination has always characterized the ethnographic relationship, and anthropologists just were not aware of it, is to point to the strange way in which reflexivity is and is not transformative. Being aware of your differences in effect becomes a sort of joint venture—which, in fact, it always was. The simultaneous banality and significance, for anthropology, of the shared awareness of their misunderstandings that people in São Gabriel have might similarly be a function of this strange characteristic of reflexivity, which makes you what you are, at the same time as transforming you. In a setting such as São Gabriel, where the opposition between cultural continuity and cultural rupture still appears for many as relevant, such a focus on reflexivity as a means of re-figuring and re-framing that very opposition seems a particularly important avenue to pursue.

Notes

1 There are also an increasing number of master's dissertations in anthropology defended by indigenous people from the region; see for example João Paulo Barreto (2013).
2 I have used pseudonyms, unless directed not to.
3 In a recent book, two prominent proponents of this approach, Martin Holbraad and Morten Axel Pedersen, suggest that the point is to focus not on many separate "worlds," but on the potential for any "world" to be "multiple" (Holbraad and Pedersen 2017, ix)

References

Andrello, Geraldo. 2010. "*Falas, Objetos e Corpos: Autores indígenas no alto rio Negro.*" *Revista Brasileira de Ciências Socias* 25 (73): 5–27.
Andrello, Geraldo and Tatiana A. S.Ferreira. 2014. "*Transformações da cultura no alto rio Negro.*" In *Políticas culturais e povos indígenas*, edited by Manuela Carneiro da Cunha and Pedro Niemeyer Cesarino, 22–55. São Paulo: Editora da UNESP.
Barreto, João Paulo Lima. 2013. "*Wai-Mahsa: peixes e humanos. Um ensaio de Antropologia Indígena.*" Master's Dissertation, Federal University of Amazonas, Brazil.
Cabalzar, Aloísio and Dagoberto Lima Azavedo, eds. 2012. *Manejo dos peixes na bacia do Rio Tiquié: memórias e perspectivas.* São Paulo: Instituto Socioambiental; São Gabriel da Cachoeira; Federação das Organizações Indígenas do Rio Negro.
Chernela, Janet M. 2005. "The Politics of Mediation: Local–Global Interactions in the Central Amazon of Brazil." *American Anthropologist* 107 (4): 620–631.
—. 2011. "Indigenous Rights and Ethno-Development: The Life of an Indigenous Organization in the Rio Negro of Brazil," *Tipití: Journal of the Society for the Anthropology of Lowland South America* 9 (2): 92–120.
de Cunha, Manuela Carneiro and Paulo de Niemeyer Cesarino, eds. 2014. *Políticas Culturais e Povos Indígenas.* São Paulo: Editora UNESP.
Fabian, Johannes. 1983. *Time and the Other: How Anthropology Makes its Object.* New York: Columbia University Press.
Gow, Peter. 1991. *Of Mixed Blood: Kinship and History in Peruvian Amazonia.* Oxford: Clarendon Press.
Heywood, Paolo. 2012. "Anthropology and What There Is: Reflections on 'Ontology.'" *Cambridge Anthropology* 30 (1): 143–151.
Holbraad, Martin and Morten Axel Pedersen. 2017. *The Ontological Turn: An Anthropological Exposition.* Cambridge: Cambridge University Press.
Hugh-Jones, Stephen. 1979. *The Palm and the Pleiades: Initiation and Cosmology on Northwest Amazonia.* Cambridge: Cambridge University Press.
—. 1988. "The Gun and the Bow: Myths of White Men and Indians." *L'Homme* 106–107:138–155.
Jackson, Jean. 1994. "Becoming Indians: The Politics of Tukanoan Ethnicity." In *Amazonian Indians: From Prehistory to the Present*, edited by Anna Roosevelt, 383–406. Tucson, AZ: University of Arizona Press.
—. 1995a. "Culture, Genuine and Spurious: The Politics of Indianness in the Vaupés, Colombia." *American Ethnologist* 22 (1): 3–27.

—. 1995b. "Preserving Indian Culture: Shaman Schools and Ethno-Education in the Vaupés, Colombia." *Cultural Anthropology* 10 (3): 302–309.

Kelly, José Antonio. 2005. *"Notas para uma Teoria do 'Virar Branco.'"* Mana 11 (1): 201–234.

—. 2010. *"'Os Encontros de Saberes': Equívocos entre índios e Estado em torno das políticas de saúde indígena na Venezuela."* ILHA 11 (2): 266–302.

—. 2011. *State Healthcare and Yanomami Transformations: A Symmetrical Ethnography.* Tucson, AZ: University of Arizona Press.

Lasmar, Christine. 2005. *De Volta ao Lago de Leite: Gênero e transformação no Alto Rio Negro.* São Paulo: Editora UNESP.

Lima, Tânia Stolze. 1996. *"O Dois e Seu Múltiplo: reflexões sobre o perspectivismo em uma cosmologia tupi."* Mana 2 (2): 21–47.

—. 1999. "The Two and its Many: Reflections on Perspectivism in a Tupi Cosmology." *Ethnos* 64 (1): 107–131.

Martini, André. 2012. *"O retorno dos mortos: apontamentos sobre a repatriação de ornamentos de dança (basá busá) do Museu do Índio, em Manaus, para o rio Negro."* Revista de Antropologia 55 (1): 331–355.

Sahlins, Marshall. 2000. *Culture in Practice.* Cambridge, MA: MIT Press.

Strathern, Marilyn. 1988. *The Gender of the Gift: Problems with Women and Problems with Society in Melanesia.* Berkeley, CA: University of California Press.

Swancutt, Katherine and Mireille Mizard. 2016. "Introduction: Anthropological Knowledge Making, the Reflexive Feedback Loop, and Conceptualisations of the Soul." *Social Analysis* 60 (1): 1–17.

Theodossopoulos, Dimitrios. 2013. "Laying Claim to Authenticity: Five Anthropological Dilemmas." *Anthropological Quarterly* 86 (2): 337–360.

Turner, Terence. 1999. "Representing, Resisting, Rethinking: Historical Transformations of Kayapo Culture and Anthropological Consciousness." In *Colonial Situations: Essays on the Contextualization of Ethnographic Knowledge.* The History of Anthropology Vol. 7, edited by George Stocking, 285–313. Madison, WI: University of Wisconsin Press.

Vigh, Henrik Erdman and David Brehm Sausdal. 2014. "From Essence Back to Existence: Anthropology Beyond the Ontological Turn." *Anthropological Theory* 14 (1): 49–73.

Vilaça, Aparecida. 2005. "Chronically Unstable Bodies: Reflections on Amazonian Corporalities." *Journal of the Royal Anthropological Institute* 11: 445–464.

Viveiros de Castro, Eduardo. 1998. "Cosmological Deixis and Amerindian Perspectivism." *Journal of the Royal Anthropological Institute* 4 (3): 469–488.

—. 2002. "O Nativo Relativo." *Mana* 8 (1): 113–148

—. 2004. "Perspectival Anthropology and the Method of Controlled Equivocation." *Tipití: Journal of the Society for the Anthropology of Lowland South America* 2 (1): 3–22.

Willerslev, Rane. 2016. "Forward: The Anthropology of Ontology Meets the Writing Culture Debate: Is Reconciliation Possible?" *Social Analysis* 60 (1): v–x.

Chapter 14

Translation in the world multiple

Shiho Satsuka

> Last spring, while it was still cold, I saw bees moving from an old hive to make a new one. [...] I told people, "this will be a good year for matsutake mushrooms." [...] This is a kind of channeling the natural world.
>
> —Mr. Fujiwara Gihei

> After all, we don't really know how and where exactly in the mountains the matsutake inhabits, the very basic things to begin with. It is not researchers who know the matsutake best, but the people who live by the forests. [...] If we can translate what they know into scientific language, it will help advance our knowledge tremendously.
>
> —Dr. Yamada Akiyoshi

In 2015, Japan's Ministry of Agriculture, Forestry and Fisheries (MAFF) launched a large five-year research project on the artificial cultivation of matsutake mushrooms. The matsutake is a highly valued wild mushroom. The mushroom is treasured as an autumn delicacy and is said to represent the ethos of the Japanese culinary tradition: appreciating nature by eating items specific to the season. Its significance is often described as similar to that of the truffle in French cuisine. However, since the 1960s Japan's domestic harvest of matsutake has drastically declined. Matsutake's primary niche has been that of the *satoyama* forest, the secondary forest near agricultural settlements, historically being managed by customary rules and practices to secure green manure and firewood for communities. Since the mid-1950s, the satoyama forest has been deteriorating due to the drastic social and environmental changes that Japan has experienced in the post-World War II period. The population of rural agricultural communities has drained to urban and semi-urban industrial areas. Moreover, the "fuel revolution" shifted the source of household energy from firewood to imported fossil fuels. Many satoyama forests have been left unattended and the matsutake lost its habitat. For the past two decades, most of the mushrooms labeled as "matsutake" in the Japanese market are imported from other countries, mostly from Asia and North America.[1]

While many attempts have been made over the past century, no successful method has been established for the artificial cultivation of matsutake mushrooms. In order to increase the harvest of wild matsutake, scientific experts have advised farmers to condition the entire forest for the fungus to produce mushrooms. With its untamed characteristics, matsutake has gained charisma as a prime example of "a blessing from the mountains" (yama no megumi).

Matsutake has also become a "charismatic species" in satoyama forest revitalization movements. The decline of satoyama not only means the loss of the mushroom's habitat. It symbolizes a "crisis" of agriculture and forestry in Japan, that the population engaging in these primary industries has sharply dwindled, and that the nation relies on imported agricultural and forestry products. Loss of matsutake forests is considered a price that the country has to pay for capitalist development. In this context, making matsutake-producing forests has become a "dream" for many farmers in rural communities. Matsutake has cast a hope of correcting the severe environmental and social consequences of industrialization and simultaneously of revitalizing the forest environment as well as rural communities. With recent advances in DNA sequencing and the development of techniques for fungus inoculation of tree seedlings, the MAFF research project intends to leverage the development of viable matsutake cultivation techniques.

Yet, the idea of matsutake "artificial cultivation" raises questions. If humans find a way to produce matsutake, and if it becomes plentiful, would matsutake still be valued in the market? If matsutake becomes domesticated by humans, would it still retain its unique cultural significance as a "gift from mountain deities" (yama no kami kara no okurimono)? Would it maintain its charismatic status in culinary culture, trade, environmental movements, and science as an untamed precious mushroom?

While I heard these anxieties from outside observers, the researchers I talked to do not seem to share the concerns that their work could result in a decline in the value of matsutake. There seems to be a gap between the popular image of "artificial cultivation" and what the researchers in the field are doing. In particular, the work of Dr. Yamada Akiyoshi, one of the leading matsutake scientists who plays a key role in the MAFF-sponsored research project, led me to think about multidimensional aspects of the scientists' practices. The scientists' research is integral to the matsutake artificial cultivation project. But what Dr. Yamada is doing in his research is "not only" (de la Cadena, Chapter 2 in this volume) about artificial cultivation as a form of human exploitation of mushrooms. His attempt to produce matsutake mushrooms is also an effort to know this fungus.

The fungus's life experience is hard to capture with human senses. The lives of humans and fungi are radically different as they have dissimilar body structures and functions. Their information exchange systems are also different, and scientists cannot resort to human language when communicating with fungi. While Dr. Yamada was aware that his experiments could be used to tame matsutake and control its life for producing valued non-timber forest products, his interest lies in finding a method for communicating with the fungus, a fantastical being he encounters. In other words, by materially stimulating the fungus to grow and observing its reactions by using all his senses, this scientist has been developing skills to attune his senses to the world as experienced by the matsutake. He is trying to translate the life of the fungus into human language, or perhaps, literally documenting its bio-graphy.

Moreover, the charisma of matsutake has led humans to consider the wider web of life in the forest. With the help of the "matsutake meister" (*matsutake meijin*)—a farmer who excels at conditioning the forest for the mushroom—Dr. Yamada has realized that he needs to know how the world is experienced and generated by other beings in the forest—not only by matsutake's host trees, but also by other fungi and plants, bacteria, insects, animals, as well as their detritus and minerals. The meister showed the scientist that although these beings experience the world in materially different ways, there is a way to communicate with them—not with language, but through careful attunement and materially crafted improvisation.

Dr. Yamada's practices suggest that he is dwelling in multiple social worlds simultaneously. While he might be an actor in a number of different world-making circles, due to the limited space here, this chapter focuses on the MAFF project on applied matsutake artificial cultivation research and his personal interest in matsutake lifeways. As Dr. Yamada enacts practices that could belong to different worlding circles, the mode with which matsutake exists in this world is also multiple. Matsutake is an object of applied research in which scientists seek techniques for producing high-value forest products. Simultaneously, matsutake is a charismatic creature that guides humans to be aware of the deep entanglements of multiple beings through which humans, mushrooms, and trees have been co-constituted.

How do we conceptualize the multidimensional aspects of scientists' practices and human–fungi relationships? I argue that by paying attention to the multidimensionality of practices we can better understand the quotidian nature of politics in the contingent process of world making. The notion of "world multiple" is helpful to start this exploration. As John Law (2015) points out in his critique of the "one-world world" doctrine, because the world is not homogeneously experienced, assuming a singular truth about the reality of the world is a doubtful enterprise. The world multiple does not refer to multiple interpretations of one world. Rather, it brings attention to the world as an entanglement of various practices happening simultaneously that could produce different material effects and consequences. In this formation of world multiple, humans are simply one kind of actor among many others. Those various actors constitute what Eduardo Viveiros de Castro (1998) calls "multinatural." In a multinatural perspective, each animal is materially different, thus "nature" takes different shapes. In biological terms, this perspective echoes Jakob von Uexküll's (1982) notion of *Umwelt*, the world experienced by a species for its own unique material structure and function. Amazonian shamans in Viveiros de Castro's publications, as well as the matsutake meister, teach us that humans can still communicate with other beings across radical material differences by tuning their senses and by channeling the world of others. Therefore, I argue that the act of translation is integral—both interspecies as well as intraspecies —in forming the world multiple. By tracing translation processes, we can see how various beings are folded and unfolded into constantly shifting material-semiotic relationships (Haraway 2016).

After briefly explaining his research, I will describe Dr. Yamada's visit with a matsutake meister who is good at interspecies translation, or "channeling" the natural world in his forest. Then, I will move on to the intraspecies translation between the scientist and the farmer-meister. What I observe here is closer to Isabelle Stengers's (2011) cosmopolitical translation than Bruno Latour's (1988, 1993) notion of translation. Building on Latour's notion of translation, which describes the complex process of enlisting various human and nonhuman actors to represent scientific facts, Stengers's cosmopolitical translation adds more dimensions to the world—the virtual, the potential of the "unknown," or the world actualized at certain moments, but not yet realized as a common reality. Cosmopolitical translation urges us to attend to the multiple circuits of requirements and obligations that scientists are actually engaging, not just those that lead to the "obligatory passage point" (Callon 1984; Latour 1988) or the conditional pathway for scientific knowledge to be represented. It directs our attention to what is not represented, yet simultaneously exists and is experienced by scientists. In this sense, I take cosmopolitics not as the politics of representation in a usual sense, but that of the possibility of otherwise. The attention to "otherwise" is integral to understanding the world multiple.

Tracing the life of fungi

A mushroom is the fruiting body of a fungus. Most of the time, a fungus lives in the form of a mycelium, consisting of a network of tube-like filaments called hyphae. A mycelium grows in the ground. During what is called vegetative growth, hyphae grow by extending their tips. Once the mycelium is well established, and the timing is right, the fungus's life cycle shifts to reproductive growth, and it produces a fruiting body. From this fruiting body, the fungus spreads spores in the air and to the ground.

Scientists explain that it is difficult to understand the timing of this shift to reproduction, especially in the case of a mycorrhizal fungus. Matsutake is a mycorrhizal fungus. Unlike saprobic fungi—such as common button mushrooms and shiitake—that grow by taking nutrition from decayed organic matter, mycorrhizal mushrooms require a symbiotic relationship with live host plants. They need to exchange nutrients with their hosts, but how the symbiosis works still poses puzzles for scientists. It is hard to reconstruct the complex interactions in the symbiosis with human hands, as there are so many factors to coordinate. It is about creating not only ideal conditions for one organism, but a particular coordination among a variety of organisms so that they form the necessary relationships for the fungus to produce a fruiting body. Most of the highly valued mushrooms in the world—such as truffle, chanterelle, and porcini —are mycorrhizal. Their high price in the market reflects the difficulty of artificial cultivation.

Dr. Yamada specializes in mycorrhizal mushrooms including matsutake. He runs an applied mycology lab in Shinshu University, located in the Ina valley in Nagano prefecture. According to government statistics, Nagano has been the top matsutake-producing prefecture since 2006. This is a recent shift that highlights the complex ecology in which matsutake lives. Historically, the centers of matsutake harvest and consumption have been western prefectures, such as Kyoto and Hiroshima, but in the last several decades matsutake production in these prefectures has drastically declined. Experts explain that due to global warming, matsutake habitats have been moving to cooler regions. The pine forests in the western and warmer prefectures have been severely damaged by pine wilt disease caused by the pine nematode, which is transmitted by the pine sawyer beetle. Pines in the cooler regions are less affected by the disease. Accordingly, the main harvesting areas have shifted to northern and high-altitude regions. Nagano is a mountainous prefecture embracing all three ranges of the Japan Alps and other high-peaked mountains. Mushrooms have long been an important food source for communities at the foot of the mountains, although local favorites were other kinds of mushrooms, such as gypsy mushrooms and larch boletes.

Within Nagano, the Ina region has the highest yield of matsutake mushrooms. Aided by this geographic advantage, Dr. Yamada has made advances in developing techniques of "artificial cultivation." The field scientists agree that the first step in the artificial cultivation of matsutake is to determine the conditions in which the matsutake forms symbiosis with its host tree. Under the right conditions, the fungus forms a mycorrhiza with a host tree, then the mycorrhiza is extended to make a mat-like network of roots in the soil called *shiro*, and then finally, a mushroom, a fruiting body of fungus, emerges from the shiro.

In order to trace this process, to begin with, Dr. Yamada made sterilized pots of pine seedlings and inoculated matsutake fungus. In each of his pots, there is only one pine seedling and one mycelium with a single DNA identification. Then, he transplanted the matsutake-inoculated pine seedlings into the ground of several experimental fields, some in the existing satoyama forest, others in empty space on the university campus. If a mushroom is produced, by using the genetic information he can find out whether or not the mushroom derives from the inoculated fungus. When this experimental method was established, he expected to be able to identify the conditions in which the fungus produces mushrooms.

It might sound simple, but just to isolate and grow good matsutake mycelium in a laboratory is not easy, as matsutake does not grow well when taken out of its natural habitat. Matsutake's slow growth rate also makes it a tough research object. Even after matsutake mycelium has been cultivated and successfully inoculated at the pine roots, growing the pine seedling in a pot is also challenging, as it requires close monitoring of temperature, moisture, and lighting. Dr. Yamada and his research collaborators have succeeded in establishing this technique, considered to be a big breakthrough in the artificial cultivation of matsutake. He was also trying to establish a technique for transplanting the inoculated pine seedlings to the forest so that he could observe and examine the whole process in which the mycelium grows to produce its fruiting body of mushrooms. By further advancing this method, he aimed to trace the whole life cycle of the fungus by following how it extends the mycelium, how it forms a mycorrhizal root network with the host tree, and how the mycorrhiza grows to form a shiro in the forest ground and produce its fruiting body. Further, the goal is to examine how other fungi, plants, and bacteria in the soil interact with the matsutake fungus.

Dr. Yamada told me that the success rate of growing the transplanted seedlings was much lower than he anticipated. There were many unexpected factors in outdoor experiments that might have affected the intricate interaction among matsutake fungus, its host trees, and other organisms, including the mineral components in the soil as well as weather and climate. There seemed to be a long way to go before a mushroom could be produced directly from the inoculated pine seedlings. He was well aware of the limitations of lab research in communicating with the fungus. After showing me his latest experiments in his lab, he told me, "we don't have enough basic scientific knowledge about matsutake as an organism." The life experience of fungus in general is hard to understand with the conventional biological model based on knowledge about animals or plants. The fungus's reproductive system consists of sexual and asexual stages, and the nucleus exchange occurs at both stages. Also, it is hard to distinguish an individual body of fungus as its cells constantly connect with each other and exchange genetic information within a mycelium. The unit of life is not based on an isolatable individual body. Rather, researchers observe and treat matsutake fungus as a collective, an entangled web of hyphae with different origins and genetic formation, constantly interacting and changing genetic components to extend their life in space and time. He suggested that scientists have not even accumulated enough knowledge about the matsutake's basic habitat. He humbly suggested that people who know the matsutake best are not researchers, but the people who live alongside the forests (as expressed in the epigraph quotation).

While developing the techniques of tracing the fungus life cycle in the lab setting, Dr. Yamada was also gaining insights from the people who are closely watching matsutake in their everyday lives. He had developed good relationships with traders, skilled harvesters, and farmers who condition their forests for matsutake, and he exchanged information and ideas with a number of people in this network. Mr. Fujiwara Gihei, known as a "matsutake meister," was one of the farmers he respected. If Dr. Yamada was trying to translate fungal life into human language through scientific experiments, Mr. Fujiwara was channeling the natural world through bodily and sensual attunement. In order to know the matsutake deeply, Dr. Yamada not only relied on scientific knowledge, but also learned from Mr. Fujiwara by translating his tacit knowledge.

Channeling the natural world

On a warm, sunny day in early June in 2017, I visited Mr. Fujiwara with Dr. Yamada and two prefecture officers—a researcher in a prefecture forest research center with whom Dr. Yamada has been collaborating, and a liaison officer in a local development office. Mr. Fujiwara was in his late seventies and had more than sixty years of experience in matsutake forest conditioning. According to his autobiography (Fujiwara 2011), after finishing middle school, he attended one year of agricultural technical school, and in the 1950s he moved to Tokyo to work in a vegetable market in Tsukiji. He was told at school that there would be no bright future in agriculture. In Tsukiji, he saw a train cargo full of matsutake shipped directly from Hiroshima. The high price of matsutake traded in the market strongly impressed him. In Tsujiki, he felt that the merchants looked down on farmers and he felt humiliated as a farmer from a rural village. Watching matsutake mushrooms traded at incredibly high prices, he dreamed of shipping matsutake from his village to Tokyo. When he returned to his home town, he gained access to some matsutake forests, harvested mushrooms, and started to ship them by train. Year by year, he gradually expanded his forests, and he carefully took care of the forests to make them suitable for matsutake to grow. Through this process, he has cultivated unique skills of tuning his senses to the forest. He was so drawn to matsutake that he stopped farming rice and vegetables. After several decades of economic hardship, his forests were conditioned, and he became able to make a living from his mushrooms.

Mr. Fujiwara is unusual as a successful matsutake harvester. Usually harvesters are very secretive about their mushroom spots. It is said that people do not reveal the location of matsutake even to their parents or children. But Mr. Fujiwara has been allowing people who are serious about learning techniques of forest conditioning—such as scientists, government officials, and farmers from across the country—to come and observe his forest. He has frequently been asked to hold study sessions at his forests.

We met at Mr. Fujiwara's house at the foot of the Akaishi Mountains (the Southern Japan Alps). His forest is located near his house, about a ten-minute drive along a narrow winding road. He parked his four-wheel-drive van in a small open area on a hillside. He climbed up the slope quickly and lightly. It was hard to believe he was close to eighty years old. While walking, he indicated the ground under which the matsutake's shiro exists and pointed out the trees that host the fungus. Along the way, Mr. Fujiwara also explained what he had observed there in previous years: other mushrooms, trees, grass, ferns, insects, snakes, deer, and various kinds of humans—from the children he invited from a nearby elementary school for a matsutake picnic to unwelcome matsutake thieves who sneak in at night. He introduced us to many creatures who conduct their own ways of life in the forests and indicated how their worlds might be connected with each other. For example, just below a ridge, he stopped at bald ground under pines on a sunny steep slope. He explained that he eliminated *warabi* (bracken fern) there. Warabi had attracted wild boars. Boars eat matsutake. They also destroy the matsutake's shiro when they look for food. But boars are not simply an enemy for Mr. Fujiwara. One spring, he saw the shiro had been disrupted by boars. Then he found matsutake mushrooms growing there the following year. He found the boars disturbed the soil just enough to stimulate the shiro to produce mushrooms. He tried to remember what he saw and connected the cut pine roots and surrounding shiro. It was successful. He applied the same treatment in other spots where shiro was not active. The shiro was revitalized. He learned this method from the boars.

During this session, he told us how plants, animals, and insects send him messages through their behaviors. When chestnut flowers blossom well in the spring, he sees many matsutake mushrooms in the fall. In a year when there are not many bamboo shoots, it will not be a good year for matsutake, either. Among these messengers, Mr. Fujiwara was most keen on watching bees. Precipitation is important for matsutake growth. Mushroom pickers constantly look for signs of precipitation. When he sees yellow hornets making their nests at higher places than usual, he knows there will be no typhoons passing through the area. He predicted the precipitation by watching the movements of bees. He said, "Bees have much better 'computers' than humans." Through careful attunement with various beings in the forest, he was "channeling the natural world" (Fujiwara 2011, 16, my translation).

Because he trusted the bees' ability to sense the subtle micro-climate change and relied on bees to read the weather, he bought honey bees and started to practice beekeeping. From the bees' behavior, he learned about air pollution and precipitation, and he used what he learned when conditioning the matsutake forest. Collecting honey was not his primary interest. But he was able to collect much more honey than his friends who are professional beekeepers. He treated the bees in the same manner as he treated matsutake—he did not want them to become stressed. He explained that if one collects honey too frequently, it would put stress on the bees. So, he left the bees alone and collected honey only when the hives were full. Similarly, he restrained himself from over-exploiting the productive ability of the matsutake forest. When he found too many mushrooms had appeared after his treatment, he worried that the forest would become exhausted. So, he conditioned the shiro to produce the "right" amount of mushrooms to maintain the balance (*ii anbai ni*), so that the shiro would continue to grow well and keep its vitality. He said mushrooms were "tips" he received from the fungus as a reward for the work he performed in maintaining its habitat.

Mr. Fujiwara's practices can be analyzed as interspecies translation. He worked as a mediator of worlds, similar to what the late nineteenth- and early twentieth-century biologist Jakob von Uexküll called "Umwelt," often translated in English as a "subjective universe" of an animal (1982, 29).[2] Against the understanding of biology that was hegemonic during his time, Uexküll argued that the behaviors of living organisms are not mere mechanical movements or reactions, but each organism exists in the world subjectively; the behaviors consist of the organism's perception of the surrounding world and its active operation and engagement with its surroundings. Because each organism uses its own unique structure to perceive and reach out to its surroundings, the properties of an object in the environment vary according to the specific physical characteristics of the organism. Therefore, there is no single universal reality experienced in the same manner by every organism. The world consists of materially different experiences of a variety of organisms. The reality of the world for one species might not exist for another species. But it does not mean that each organism lives separately in its secluded world. The behavior of one organism creates the Umwelt of another organism. The world is constantly made and remade by the interactions of various organisms at the multitude of "counterpoints" of Umwelts (ibid., 52).[3]

In central Japan, until the mid-twentieth century, trees in satoyama forests provided important materials for human dwelling practices. Humans selectively cut trees as firewood and construction materials to build their habitat, and they collected leaves from the forest floor to use as fertilizer in food cultivation. Through these activities, humans unintentionally created a suitable niche for the matsutake fungus and pine. For the matsutake fungus, the characteristics of pine appreciated by humans—such as the high percentage of oil in its wood tissue—were not a primary concern. What matters to the fungus's Umwelt is different. Important aspects include the carbohydrate released from the fine tips of a pine's roots, the minerals in the soil the fungus can pass on to the pine in return, and the moisture in the soil that the tree branches and needles control. Humans and the fungus live in their own Umwelts, but they are mediated by the pine. Once the humans stopped going to the forest for fuel and fertilizer, the counterpoint of human, pine, and matsutake fungus was lost. The satoyama forest lost its significance not only for humans, but also for the matsutake fungus. What Mr. Fujiwara has been doing is to recover the counterpoint of pine and fungus, and to bring back the Umwelts of pine, fungus, and human together. By physically reshaping his forest and tuning his senses to the subtle changes in the variety of counterpoints, he has been mediating the subjective living worlds of the matsutake and the human.

Translation in multiple circuits

While walking and talking with Mr. Fujiwara in his forest, Dr. Yamada had already come up with four potential research projects. He translated the information from Mr. Fujiwara's "channeling the natural world" into scientific terms and then into feasible research projects. Dr. Yamada quickly determined that these research projects were in the domain of prefecture research rather than that of his university laboratory. While walking, he explained these projects to the prefecture researcher. The prefecture researcher conscientiously jotted notes in his pocket notebook while walking up and down a narrow trail on a steep hill.

A few months later, I asked Dr. Yamada if he had developed any research projects from the visit that would allow him to address any of his particular interests. He told me, with his eyes sparkling, "There are plenty of research ideas! But I set them aside for now and try not to think about them." He needed to focus on his ongoing research, he said, including the MAFF project. Mr. Fujiwara had given him many clues about what he needed to do in order to understand the basic living experience of matsutake. But for now, he must work in the world of applied research.

The aim of the MAFF project is "to establish a technique to cultivate matsutake in an artificially controlled environment" (MAFF 2015, my translation). Here, "artificial cultivation" means enhancing the reproductive productivity of matsutake fungus in the forest environment with the assistance of human intervention. In this circuit, the tasks of scientists include accumulating information from past expert and folk experiments, identifying the necessary factors for the fungus to establish symbiosis with a tree, abstracting the process from locally specific environments and experimental practices, and determining reproducible steps to establish a technique applicable to a wide range of locations. These are the obligations that scientists in the MAFF project need to fulfill.

Dr. Yamada translated the information learned from Mr. Fujiwara and created a hypothesis about the necessary conditions for matsutake–pine symbiosis. In this process, Dr. Yamada has abstracted the information from locally specific practices that Mr. Fujiwara has developed with his everyday bodily engagement with his forest. He isolated the material exchanges that might have occurred in Mr. Fujiwara's forest into several units, and reorganized these units of the material exchanges to turn them into testable experiments. He encouraged the prefecture researcher to do the experiments and to observe the reproducibility of their material effects. If the expected material effects were reproduced in an experimental setting, his hypothesis would be supported. Based on this information, they would establish a technique that would be applicable across different settings.

One might worry that in this process of scientific translation Mr. Fujiwara's worldview and respectful attitude toward the fungus might be lost. His life-long relationship with matsutake, filled with interspecies care, might be erased in the world of the expert science of applied mycology. In this translation circuit, the farmer's tacit knowledge could be reduced to mere intangible resource, and "artificial cultivation" could mean material manipulation of the fungus to extract its reproductive ability for economic development.

But, along with this circuit, Dr. Yamada was also a part of another circuit of translation. Dr. Yamada's own personal interest was to understand the basic lifeways of the mycorrhizal fungus—how the fungus lives in the world and generates its living environment. This interest derived from his own experience of growing up as a *kinoko shonen*, or mushroom-loving boy, who spent much of his youth wandering in the forests to collect wild mushrooms.[4] He continues to be an avid mushroom hunter. He knows that the hunters are deeply attracted by, and care for, wild mushrooms, and that they devote their lives to getting to know mushrooms—sometimes even risking their lives by eating toxic mushrooms or by getting lost in hard-to-navigate landscapes.

Because humans and fungi have different sensory and motion systems, a human cannot take the fungus's perspective, or hear from the fungus about its experience through language. Humans need to develop skills to tune their senses to the fungus's daily living practices and to communicate with it through material means. What Dr. Yamada is trying to do in his artificial cultivation experiments is to follow the exact steps of the fungus's living experience by materially stimulating and observing its reactions. His method of documenting matsutake's fungal biography includes reading genetic markers; labeling the mycelium with the result of DNA sequencing; tracing how the mycelium grows and how it interacts with pines, other plants, and microbes in the soil; and seeing the correlation with the fungus's living experience and its environment measured by temperature, soil moisture, and mineral components. He translates the world-making practices of the matsutake fungus into information comprehensible to human beings. By developing a scientific method to follow the life experience of the fungus, he tries to create a hinge between the living worlds of fungi and human beings.

In this translation circuit, his practices are extensions of him being a "mushroom boy"—simply being fascinated by, and curious about, the unfamiliar and fantastical life form of other organisms. His curiosity can be easily coordinated with Mr. Fujiwara's careful attunement to and care for the fungus and other beings that compose the world. Or rather, without this sense of fascination with the fungus, a scientist might not be able to effectively translate the tacit knowledge of the matsutake meisters. What Dr. Yamada was doing as "artificial cultivation" in this circuit was communicating and understanding the life of the fungus by tracing the material effects produced in the counterpoint among Umwelts of fungus, pine, and human. The role of the human in this circuit is to mediate between fungus and tree by materially creating a zone of contact and exchange.

Dr. Yamada was simultaneously an actor within these different circuits of translation. These layers of translation circuits are coordinated to generate the world multiple, just like Keiichi Omura's description (Chapter 5 in this volume) of Inuit living at the same time in the world of traditional navigation systems and the world of cartographic maps. These circuits of translation are often in tension, just as Taku Iida describes with a British NGO's attempt to bring Malagasy fishermen into the circuit of translation for environmental stewardship (Chapter 12 in this volume). Dr. Yamada seemed to be well aware of this tension. He was temporarily leashing his interests as "a mushroom boy" and keeping them within the realm that he could coordinate with the MAFF-applied research.

Conclusion

The forest is a world multiple—a world generated as a result of constant encounter, negotiation, and the coordinated efforts of various beings, including humans. As these beings materially encounter and influence each other, they are constantly translating the world-making practices of other beings, reflecting back and negotiating their positions while constantly exerting mutual influence. Following these translation practices allows us to see the formation of this world multiple, which produces "coordination" (Gan 2017; Tsai et al. 2016; Tsing 2015 and Chapter 15 in this volume) among various actors' world-making practices.

The concept of the "world multiple" is helpful in understanding what matsutake scientists and meisters are doing. Led by matsutake's charisma, the meister has developed skills to tune his senses to various beings in the forest. Mr. Fujiwara's engagement with his forest illustrates that a variety of subjective and material worlds exist beyond the human Umwelt. His practices also suggest that while human sensory and cognitive systems have their physical limitations, humans can still "channel" the subjective universes of other beings if they develop skills to carefully tune their senses to the counterpoints of multiple Umwelts.

Then, by translating the meister's tacit knowledge, Dr. Yamada translates the fungus's life into scientific knowledge, something comprehensible in human language systems. Yet, his translation practices are implicated in multiple circles of world making. One of the circuits is the MAFF research led by the practices of capitalist economic value-making that is linked to rural agricultural development. Another is that of affectionate mushroom hunters guided by relations of trans-species attention and care.

This simultaneous belonging to multiple circuits suggests the quotidian nature of the politics of the world multiple. This is not a representational politics in which an actor is assigned to represent one position. Rather, each practice of an actor can be potentially connected to different translation circles, which could produce different material-semiotic effects. A simple action in everyday practice is always in negotiation and subject to contestation over which world-making assemblages are to be aligned. The same practice always faces a risk and a possibility of being incorporated into a different but simultaneously occurring translation circle. In this multidimensional politics, something that is not (yet) represented plays an important role for guiding the alignment.

The scientist's practices of "artificial cultivation" cannot be reduced to domestication or control of the fungus in terms of a human-centered manipulation of fungus vitality. They can be understood better as attempts to generate a hinge with which to connect the worlds lived by fungus, pine, and humans, and by extension, multiple beings that compose the world. The question is what kind of hinge and what kind of connection will be made. This question shapes the politics. The way different translation circuits have been coordinated in Dr. Yamada's practices suggests that his experiments with artificial cultivation were not geared to plantation-style cultivation, although this is temporal and always with the risk of being incorporated into more exploitative circuits. But at least at this moment, his research was aligned to the world-making translation circuit for cohabitation among fungi, plants, and humans. A mushroom boy is not represented in the artificial cultivation project, yet is folded into the research.

The charisma of the matsutake mushroom guides us to see how scientists' and meisters' translation practices have been shaped by the particular social and environmental predicaments that Japan has been facing as a consequence of the rapid and abrasive industrialization reflecting its position in the development of global capitalism in the twentieth century. At the same time, these practices also point us toward the possibility of unfolding the current coordination and the different ways that the world might be folded with care and attunement. Translation matters, as it is a practice of folding and unfolding relationships with other human and nonhuman actors in the world.

Acknowledgments

I thank Mr. Fujiwara Gihei and Dr. Yamada Akiyoshi for generously spending their time with me, and the officers in Nagano prefecture for facilitating my visit there. I am grateful to all the participants and attendants at a conference held in Osaka in 2016 for collective exploration of the world multiple, as well as to Brenton Buchanan, Elaine Gan, and Anna Tsing for reading an earlier version of this chapter and offering helpful comments. The research for this chapter was supported by the Social Sciences and Humanities Research Council of Canada.

Notes

1 According to MAFF (2017), the domestic harvest of matsutake mushrooms in 2016 was 69.4 tons. In 2016, about 981 tons of matsutake mushrooms were imported. The countries of origin, in order, are China, Canada, USA, Korea, Mexico, Turkey, and Bhutan.
2 The German word Umwelt literally means "surrounding world" (Uexküll 1982, 29). In Japanese, Umwelt is translated as the neologism kansekai, consisting of kan (um, or surrounding) and sekai (welt or world). Although Uexküll himself was only

concerned with the Umwelts of animals and he denied that of plants, I propose to extend this insight to plants and fungi.

3 While the plural form of Umwelt in German is *Umwelten*, I use Umwelts following the original English translation.

4 See Raffles (2010) for the similar yet more popular "symptoms" of *konchu shonen*, the boys who are fascinated by insects, mostly rhinoceros or stag beetles, in Japan, and the complex entanglements between the commercialization of insect trades and the awareness of the natural environment.

References

Callon, Michel. 1984. "Some Elements of a Sociology of Translation: Domestication of the Scallops and the Fishermen of St Brieuc Bay." *Sociological Review* 32 (S1): 196–233.

Fujiwara, Gihei. 2011. *Matsutakeyamazukuri no Subete: Seisangijutsu Zenkokai* (All about matsutake forest conditioning: Techniques open to the public). Tokyo: Zenkoku Ringyo Kairyo Fukyu Kyokai.

Gan, Elaine. 2017. An Unintended Race: Miracle Rice and the Green Revolution. *Environmental Philosophy* 14 (1): 61–81.

Haraway, Donna. 2016. *Staying with the Trouble: Making Kin in the Chthulucene*. Durham, NC: Duke University Press.

Latour, Bruno. 1988. *Science in Action*. Cambridge, MA: Harvard University Press.

—. 1993. *We Have Never Been Modern*. Cambridge, MA: Harvard University Press.

Law, John. 2015. "What's Wrong with a One-World World?" *Distinktion: Journal of Social Theory* 16 (1): 126–139.

MAFF. 2015. *Shinrin shigen o saitekiriyosuru tame no gijutsukaihatsu* (Technologies development aiming at the optimum use of forest resources). Tokyo: Ministry of Agriculture, Forestry and Fisheries. http://www.affrc.maff.go.jp/docs/project/2015/pdf/sub27_4.pdf accessed February 6, 2018.

—. 2017. *Tokuyo Rinsanbutsu Seisan Tokeichosa* (Statistical Data of Non-Timber Forest Products). Tokyo: Ministry of Agriculture, Forestry and Fisheries. http://www.e-stat.go.jp/SG1/estat/List.do?lid=000001191364 accessed February 6, 2018.

Raffles, Hugh. 2010. *Insectopedia*. New York: Vintage Books.

Stengers, Isabelle. 2011. *Cosmopolitics II*. Minneapolis, MN: University of Minnesota Press.

Tsai, Yen-Ling, Isabelle Carbonell, Joelle Chevrier, and Anna Lowenhaupt Tsing. 2016. "Golden Snail Opera: The More-than-Human Performance of Friendly Farming on Taiwan's Lanyang Plain." *Cultural Anthropology* 31 (4): 520–544.

Tsing, Anna Lowenhaupt. 2015. *The Mushroom at the End of the World: On the Possibility of Life in Capitalist Ruins*. Princeton, NJ: Princeton University Press.

Uexküll, Jakob von. 1982. "The Theory of Meaning." *Semiotica* 42 (1): 25–82.

Viveiros de Castro, Eduardo. 1998. "Cosmological Deixis and Amerindian Perspectivism." *Journal of the Royal Anthropological Institute* 4 (3): 469–488.

Chapter 15

A multispecies ontological turn?

Anna Tsing

Two prominent approaches of late have asked how anthropologists might explore *difference* in a world of unequal power relations: "the ontological turn" (Holbraad and Pedersen 2017; Kohn 2016), an approach that moves the analysis through alternative makings of reality; and "multispecies ethnography" (Kirksey and Helmreich 2010; Locke and Muenster 2015), an approach that opens anthropology to the more-than-human. Surveys of each of these developing fields tend to overlap quite a bit in the scholars they cite. Yet tensions have also emerged, suggesting problems in communicating across these two lines of thought—even as they constantly intertwine. This chapter situates itself in this gap, exploring how its tensions might also forge possibilities.

Following Strathern (1987), it would be possible to play up the "awkward relationship" between ontological and multispecies to show how the gap itself constitutes some of the more-than-academic challenges of our time. My stakes in this chapter, however, are humbler and more practical. I've seen scholars and students worrying through the divisions and lashing out at each other in anger and frustration. It is within the sometimes unintended insults of such confrontations that I want to show how it might be possible—even easy—to do both multispecies and ontological anthropology at the same time.

To make these approaches accessible as objects of reflection, I allow a certain amount of reification and simplification. Lots of related issues become caught up in the battles I've seen, from the question of how scholars should best advocate for indigenous interlocutors to the urgencies of environmental crisis. Every issue raised changes the debate. At the December 2016 "World Multiple" conference from which this volume draws its chapters, the quarrel was between ontological theorists and practitioners of a Japanese school of rich empiricism that reaches back to the legacy of Imanishi Kinji.[1] Multispecies anthropology was not the issue per se, and yet it has something in common with Japanese empiricism in that enthusiasm and curiosity about the world are expected to be co-eval with academic theory in producing the insights of research. Indeed, as often as possible, the former produces the latter. Japanese research traditions in anthropology are worth separate analysis. However, by working through the possibilities of multispecies-ontological dialogue, I hope to navigate not only the tensions that arise in my classes and supervisions, but also, perhaps, a group of related tensions including the one I witnessed in Osaka.

Imagining a gap between the ontological turn and multispecies ethnography is artificial, but good to think with, and thus a place to begin. Why is it difficult to work across these two literatures? They reflect differences in what catches practitioners' attention, exciting reflection. I'm oversimplifying, but bear with me. Ontological turn scholars are fascinated by radical difference. Multispecies anthropologists are amazed that touching occurs despite radical difference. This shapes, too, what ethnographic materials *do* for each group. Ontological turn scholars ask how practices reveal cosmologies, while multispecies scholars ask how practical encounters work within and beyond cosmologies.

The contrast stands out in the work of two respective pioneers. Eduardo Viveiros de Castro (2004) shows us the multinaturalism of Amerindian perspectivism through the figure of the jaguar: in Amerindian worlds, the jaguar is a *person* who drinks manioc beer where we see blood. Viveiros de Castro brilliantly teases out the implications of this way of doing world making. But he is not interested, as Eduardo Kohn (2013, 126) is, in women's fears in their gardens that jaguars might kill their dogs. Viveiros de Castro is excited by the encounter of humans and jaguars not because of its practical possibilities, but rather for the cosmological frames it reveals. In contrast, Donna Haraway introduces *Where Species Meet* (2008, 3) by asking, "Whom and what do I touch when I touch my dog?" The thrill, for Haraway, is her ability to engage in call and response with her dog despite their many differences. Where Carla Freccero (2011) traces Western ontological framings of the figure of the dog, as it emerges as a foil for the wolf, Haraway stands in awe of the contact zone in which a dog, multiply constituted, responds to her gesture.

This contrast, as I've said, oversimplifies to make sense of the conflict I've seen whirling around me in classrooms and conferences. In the paragraphs above, I identify scholarship in a nominalist way, referring to "ontological turn" and "multispecies ethnography" in relation to works held up as exemplifying each label. Yet this introduces problems. Eduardo Kohn, for example, has written a useful review of ontological anthropology (2016) while he is also embraced within the multispecies cannon. Kohn mentions Donna Haraway as a key ontological thinker even as she is perhaps the key pioneer for multispecies work. The dichotomy is always already wrong; everyone relevant is a member of both camps. Yet there is something to the difference that provokes passion, and this seems worth exploring.[2]

There is a difference in attention to humans and nonhumans that matters. Julie Archambault's (2016) rich and intriguing ethnography of young men's affective relations with plants in urban gardens in Mozambique speaks for many ontological-turn thinkers in stating outright that she is not interested in plants. "My inquiry into human–plant relations remains focused on human experience," she writes (ibid., 248). Her focus is the frame of human affect, and not its effect on plants. There are losses, even there: it might matter in regard to human affect's temporality, for example, that the gardeners she studies keep their plants' roots in plastic bags, which, if anaerobic, might encourage a short lifetime for the plants. But the plants do not catch her up *as plants*. In converse, Diogo de Carvalho Cabral's (2015) amazing account of the role of leaf-cutting ants in limiting colonial agriculture in Brazil ignores the agricultural ontologies of natives versus settlers. His article vividly brings to life the interactions of ants and crops in all their unexpected agency. Yet perhaps attention to indigenous relations to never fully domesticated crop diversity, of the sort Manuela Carneiro da Cunha (2017) offers, might amend our understandings of what happened.

I cite these essays because I admire them—and, while neither has the founding status of Haraway or Viveiros de Castro, they enact key pleasures and dangers of each approach, respectively. Both approaches include humans and nonhumans, but what excites researchers tends to be different. This is an element of the gap that encourages frustration and ire. Giving voice to nonhumans does not move ontological-turn scholars, who criticize their multispecies colleagues for using contaminated Western categories, and, worse yet, "bowing down to science." Meanwhile, multispecies scholars criticize ontological-turn practitioners for making dead puppets of nonhumans, refusing the liveliness of other beings. And yet the whole point of ontological materialism is to bring those nonhumans to life, but *through other means*. And one point of referring to science is to demonstrate the *importance of contaminated categories* in shaping interactions across multiple ontologies. Purification for its own sake is just as problematic as one-worldism. We will have to learn to read each other with more generosity.

This is where Annemarie Mol's *The Body Multiple* (2002), to which this volume is dedicated, can make an enormous difference. Mol takes both radical difference and touching seriously. She cares about both metaphysics and enactment, that is, the cosmologies arising from practices, on the one hand, and the conjunctural results of encounters across sets of practices, on the other. Mol starts with the assumption that there are always multiple ontologies in any situation. The job of the analyst is to separate and track the many strands of practice that gather in any social space. These lead to distinct ontologies. The analyst considers the framing assumptions of these strands of practice—the work of the ontological turn. But rather than stopping there, Mol continues by asking questions similar to those raised by multispecies anthropologists about touching across difference. The analyst considers how strands work together, not to form a singular whole, but rather to form a system of power asymmetries, interruptions, and hesitations within which social actors navigate and call out to each other despite their deeply rooted refusals of each other's projects. On one hand, then, Mol urges us to look at the ontological specificity of particular sets of practices. On the other, she encourages us to attend to what happens when these sets rub up against each other. This is a useful combination from which to work.

Yet Mol's study of doctors and patients in a Dutch hospital has two specifying characteristics worth discussing. First, it is inside "the West." It has been easier for scholars to evoke multiple ontologies involving social institutions in Europe and North America than in other places. Is an analysis of Molian multiplicity suited to places outside the West? Second, it concerns human-to-human interactions. Machines come into the story, but they are there as tools through which humans make worlds with each other; Mol does not focus on an assessment of nonhuman agencies. Would Mol's approach work if the goal was to understand nonhuman sociality? My answer to both questions is "yes," but I don't want to take for granted the ease of stretching Mol's approach to tackle new challenges. The purpose of the rest of this chapter is to work through what such stretching might entail. In the next section, I lay out some groundwork to give a sense of how I tackle the problem. Following that, I expand these points through a discussion of two in-progress projects. My tentative answers gain or lose traction by what they can do to make ethnographic situations come to life.

Mol and multispecies: Mixing and mulling

Multispecies anthropology concerns not just what humans make of nonhumans (and their projects for world making) but also what nonhumans make of humans (and our projects of world making). Nonhuman response does not have to involve human-like cognition or intention; indeed, despite the awkward label "multispecies," which perhaps might best be read as "concerning many kinds of beings," the nonhumans do not have to be living at all. The reciprocality of response has been a signature feature of the multispecies approach, differentiating it from "anthropology as usual." But how should one best study such responses? If nonhumans as well as humans make worlds, might their practices also be open to analysis as ontological frames? This seems to me the necessary next step in bringing "multispecies" and "ontological" into closer dialogue. However, this is not a simple combination. The questions I pose to Mol's framework about the West and the nonhuman suggest key challenges.

If ontological multiplicity of the sort Mol describes is found only inside the West, for example, this would foreclose the possibility of assessing as "ontological" that radical difference offered in nonhuman practices except in those very specified settings. To imagine that nonhumans have any autonomy in framing world making, indeed, would become a subset of Western ontologies, perhaps in the guise of science.[3] This is why the location of Mol's analysis matters—and opens questions. Yet perhaps the commonly practiced identification between ethnic groups and ontologies is a problematic habit rather than an analytic necessity. It is hard enough for an anthropologist to find one set of ontological frameworks during the course of fieldwork; how much harder to find more. Indeed, our willingness to stop there, with one ethnic group and one ontology, might be a holdover from anthropological expectations about culture. Despite the differences between ontological and cultural analysis, the former is influenced by the history of the latter. The anthropology of culture asked us to identify coherence amidst a set of disparate practices in a particular place; it is easy to transfer that convention to ontological discussions.

Mol, however, shows us quite reasonable techniques for overcoming these blocks. The hospital is a model: differentiating between the sets of practices of medical professionals, on the one hand, and patients, on the other, flows from the ethnographic material. There is no reason that such differentiations across sets of practices cannot be undertaken outside the West; the differentiation is not itself a feature of the ontology, in Mol's analysis. For earlier guides from the study of culture, I think of the French Marxists who asked whether hunting and agriculture in the same African society might be separate "modes of production" (Terray 1972). While this particular frame has disappeared from contemporary discussion, it suggests that there is precedent for identifying separate strands of practice in any social situation, Western or not.

Yet this changes the work that the analysis of non-Western ontologies can do. Multiple, non-Western ontologies cannot gain their interest *only* as foils for the West; they will also be foils for each other within a single setting. Furthermore, many of these frames will turn out to have connections with other places, even as they assume local forms. Without the expectation for a singular place-and-ethnicity-making ontology, analysis can note cosmopolitan connections, that is, ways that each ontological frame is emergent, shifting, and traveling within an indeterminate scale. To extend the multiplicity part of Mol's analysis outside the West requires opening our attention to alternative forms of cosmopolitanism. The ontologies we would learn to appreciate might involve appropriations and translations of projects that seem at first familiar from other places—but are perhaps quite different.

There is plenty of precedent among ontological-turn authors for just this move, although I have not seen an explicit discussion of contrasts among practitioners on this issue. Morten Axel Pedersen's *Not Quite Shamans* (2011), for example, offers an ontology of post-socialism in Mongolia in which ontology refers to a moving framework in which everything from national elections to unemployment takes on a coherence formed through cosmopolitan conjuncture. In his analysis, there is no "Mongolian" way of doing things. Instead, Mongolian ontologies are formed with the fragments of many cosmopolitan projects, from Buddhism to modernization. This kind of ontological analysis comes to life in motion. Rather than a commitment to a synchronic cosmopolitics, Pedersen's ontology is always already historical, that is, a practice of world making through time.

Shiho Satsuka's *Nature in Translation* (2015) also makes this point: Japanese translation of Canadian versions of the Rocky Mountains makes Japanese tourism possible, but it never re-creates "Japan." Japanese readings of the landscape partake of Canadian discourses even as they shift them into other registers. Their interplay does not offer that homogeneous "common world" mocked in stereotype by ontological critics of analyses of touching. Strands of practice remain separate, sometimes antagonistic, even as they create conjunctural effects in their cross-strand encounters. Those effects are historical trajectories with emergent ontological characteristics.

The identification of historically emergent, cosmopolitan ontologies is useful for imagining the conjunction of ontological and multispecies. It suggests a small addendum to Mol's scheme. Mol calls the touching of alternative ontological frames "coordination." I reserve that term for temporal synchronization (Gan and Tsing 2018, discussed below). But the word is not the issue; I stress the way that touching creates effects, even when there is no harmonization of frames or agreement in what counts as real. I call that kind of touching —the kind that has effects—"friction" (Tsing 2005). Friction sets off a historical trajectory, emergent from the encounter. Such trajectories are not calm currents; they are full of jolts, false starts, wild rides, and interruptions. New ontological frames may be formed, as well as what Viveiros de Castro calls equivocations. Pedersen's Mongolian ontology is of that sort: drunken aggression, post-socialist unemployment, and shreds of Buddhism and shamanism come together to make a "not quite"—a historical trajectory emerging in fits and starts from shifting practical exigencies. Satsuka's "translation" makes interruption the basis of the possibility for something new. By adding a historical dimension to Mol's analytical scheme, one can watch the effects of ontological difference as well as encounter as they realign each other—difference shaping encounter and encounter shaping new versions of difference.

Marisol de la Cadena offers another important way to track practice-based ontological frames: through watching how one frame can bury itself inside another. In Chapter 2 in this volume, for example, de la Cadena argues that the Quechua speakers she works with in Peru practice "religion—but not only" (see also de la Cadena 2015). Mountains as earth-beings have been transformed into mountains as the abode of the Virgin Mary. This is Christianity, but it exceeds Christianity; its religiosity is contradicted by non-Christian cosmologies. By adding the "not only" to the categories she uses for analysis, de la Cadena shows how scholars might have it both ways: cosmopolitan versions of Western ontologies are there, but, even within them, there is more. This modification of Mol's insights is an exciting entry into multiplicity.

But I have only made it through the first half of my stretching of Mol's framework. The second half concerns the practices of nonhumans, as they might have their own ontic characteristics.[4] Can we analyze a "world multiple" in which nonhumans as well as humans participate in world making?

The reason many anthropologists have hesitated to go there, I think, is a down-to-earth bewilderment about just how to study nonhuman ways of being. Luckily, many (although not all) nonhuman practices can be studied in much the same ways as anthropologists study humans, that is, by observation and attention to forms, gatherings, and transformations (Mathews 2017; Tsing 2013). Natural history practices have a close kinship to ethnography. If we can trust ourselves to learn something about unfamiliar humans, we might also learn to trust ourselves in working with nonhumans. It's a matter of having people show us—and also looking ourselves. This is the same set of knowledge-gathering practices we might employ to study doctors or patients at a hospital.

Still, one of the problems we face in following nonhuman practices is that nonhumans don't speak, at least not in human languages. If we want to appreciate nonhuman suites of practice, we have to move beyond language. As Kohn (2013) argues, we might want to do that anyway: language can be a limitation in how we imagine signification. Kohn's discussion of the philosophical issues involved is helpful. Here I merely offer a few practical suggestions. The following techniques have proved themselves useful to me in following nonhuman practices.

First, the researcher might learn from human informants the enthusiasm and curiosity necessary to get involved with nonhumans in a deep and serious way. In my work with mushrooms, I caught the "mushroom fever" that my human informants described, and it helped me care about the intimate details of fungal life—as many of them did also (Tsing 2015). Scientists were helpful in showing me fungal life, but so too were non-scientists, whose questions were often quite different questions from those of scientists. Only pickers, for example, cared about just when and where mushrooms might appear, and many had detailed observations and theories about this. The idea that learning about nonhumans reduces one's knowledge base to science is completely wrong. There are many kinds of human knowledge and practice concerning nonhumans—and each is a guide to the practices the researcher might use for his or her own observations and attunements. Indigenous scientists, indeed, have written passionately about overlaps as well as divergences in their tribal and professional training as each promotes attention to the forms of life around them (e.g., Kimmerer 2003). Conversely, while cosmological reflection is an important human practice for getting to know nonhumans, it is not the only one. To follow the reciprocal response of nonhumans to human projects, one might want to follow many kinds of vernacular human experiences of getting to know nonhumans through their practices and transformations.

Second, non-textual media can be useful in both learning about nonhuman practices and presenting them in ways that hold on to the fragile attunements of the research process. I've found myself wandering into projects involving sounds, diagrams, performances, drawings, film, and digital media, not only because of the charisma of such genres, but also because they show things that are hard to get at only using language. Presenting nonhuman practices through non-written media can sometimes better convey both the specificity and mystery of these arenas of practice.[5] Non-textual media are hardly a magic bullet, however. Consider the visual: plenty of nonhumans navigate with senses other than sight, and plenty of nonhuman practices do not lend themselves to viewing at all. Even when one presents the most visual of nonhuman practices through visual media alone, viewers often miss what you want them to see. Still, non-textual media can be an opening to what we might otherwise miss.

Third, attention to temporalities can guide us to nonhuman practices (Gan 2016). By watching temporal coordinations and disjunctures, it is possible to enter the worlds of nonhuman practice without communicating directly with each nonhuman. Human practices, too, are amenable to temporal analyses; taken together, a useful symmetry is possible.

Fourth, infrastructures can be an opening to understand the relation between materiality and ontology (Morita 2016). Infrastructures can lead us into world-making practices of humans—but also nonhumans. Sometimes nonhumans serve human infrastructural needs; sometimes they thwart human plans. Indeed, noting this makes it possible to consider nonhuman infrastructures, that is, landscape constructions that enable particular forms of nonhuman sociality and livelihood. Infrastructure, like temporality, can be a non-linguistic path to material-semiotic world-making projects.

In my own recent work, I've used some of these techniques to attend to the fractured becomings of landscapes that are simultaneously human and nonhuman. My "landscapes" are sites of struggle and negotiation among many ways of being, human and nonhuman. Beings need not agree on the worlds they make and inhabit. It's this feature of landscape, indeed, that makes the questions the ontological turn raises so important: landscapes are sites of radical difference both among varied humans and across species and assemblages, living and nonliving. Landscapes are also sites for touching; no single project of world making wipes out all the others. All this matters because in the course of encounters, some kinds of living beings will die, some will dwindle, and others will flourish. It is the *livability* of the landscape that most engages me, and no species, including humans, lives alone. Livability raises questions that, to me, need tools of both the ontological turn and multispecies anthropology. I can't say I've worked out all the answers. However, I've worried through a few options. In the next section of this chapter, I offer two collaborative projects to open out thoughts on how to care attentively about both humans and nonhumans. My goal here is to make palpable the challenges as well as the pleasures of a both–and approach.

Coordinating temporalities: "How things hold"

One way to track the world-making projects of nonhumans is to follow their temporal expressions, for example, their use of seasonal changes, their life histories, and their responses to historical changes involving other kinds of beings, human or nonhuman, and living or nonliving. Although we cannot question nonhumans directly, using language, we can follow their timelines and transformations. Elaine Gan and I do this in our paper "How Things Hold" (Gan and Tsing 2018). We are interested in both repeated temporal enactments and long-term, non-cyclical changes as each offers clues to the practice-based ontics of nonhuman beings. When temporalities of different living beings come together in a conjuncture, we watch how this has effects, which we call "coordination." Our project, then, explores both radical difference and touching as it involves humans and nonhumans.

At the center of our exploration stands the good-to-think-with and easy-to-love strangeness of Japan's *satoyama* forest, the village forest used for timber, firewood, and charcoal as well as all kinds of non-timber forest products. The term "satoyama" is quite new, introduced by conservation advocates, but it refers to a centuries' old practice in which farmers coppiced and pollarded trees, raked leaves for green manure, gathered mushrooms, vegetables, and wild fruit, and in the process encouraged certain kinds of ecological formations over others. Satoyama advocates argue that human disturbance is an essential part of the forest; without it, the satoyama formation degrades and its constituent biodiversity disappears. In contrast to Euro-American conservation truisms, more human disturbance is good for the more-than-human livability of satoyama. Without human practices, the assemblage falls apart.

From the first, questions of "Whose construction is this?" emerge in our exploration. I learned about satoyama from Japanese advocates who were already schooled in thinking across cosmopolitan difference. They showed me forests, talking me through their features. Sometimes, they gestured to international scientific perspectives, yet in the same explanations, they also offered distinctive frames. Advocacy was urgent, they showed, because humans only become fully human within a working relationship with the environment—just as satoyama forest only becomes fully forest through a working relation with humans. The emerging ontologies they showed me were simultaneously scientific, in an internationally legible way, and distinctively Japanese. This is the kind of cosmopolitanism we will have to consider to develop a multispecies ontological approach.

Gan and I explore the practices of particular kinds of beings, such as pine trees, oak trees, matsutake mushrooms, and farmers. Following satoyama advocates, we treat them as participants in making landscapes, each engaged in distinctive sets of practices. Humans are not exceptions. The distinctive role of language, planning, and cognition for humans, for example, never came up as a reason to remove humans from discussion of ecological transformation. Instead, advocates told me about *raking*, the farmers' practice of removing fallen leaves from the forest, which inadvertently produces the bare mineral soils preferred by pine and matsutake. In considering the sets of practices that formed both disparate ontological frameworks and the possibilities of touching, we were guided to treat humans and nonhumans with considerable symmetry.

The ontic enactments of my informants became the basis from which we trace temporalities and coordinations. Following the satoyama advocates I worked with, we do not opt for an exclusively Japanese vocabulary or sphere of reference: we open the project to the cosmopolitan science to which they guided me, but with its distinctive positionings of humans and nonhumans.

Figure 15.1 Pine trees, a mycorrhizalized seedling, and a rake stand in for the temporal coordinations of pine, fungal, and human practices in the satoyama forest

Source: Gan and Tsing (n.d.); illustration by Elaine Gan

Following the nonhumans, in turn, requires attention to temporalities. Rather than trying to explain these, we attempt an attunement involving diagrammatic exposition. Gan created a diagram of temporal coordinations.: Figure 15.1 is a sample page.

This particular part of the diagram shows the coordinations required to keep the satoyama assemblage in place. Our analysis, however, is equally concerned with ruptures and disjuctures, that is, forms of temporal coordination that make particular assemblages impossible. For example, the turn to synthetic fertilizers and fossil fuel among farmers has decreased farmers' cutting and raking, destroying the pine–oak–matsutake coordination. Coordination, our guide to both difference and touching, can be of different kinds; we turn, then, to questions of more-than-human livability to consider the political valence of varied forms of coordination. Because of coordinations between radiocesium and fungal metabolism, the destruction of the Fukushima reactors raised new problems for satoyama conservation, which had relied a good deal on mushroom incomes. Mushrooms are now radioactive, and radioactive coordination is hardly a recipe for livability. We end our chapter with a consideration of such temporal ruptures.

Caring for ghosts and other beings: *Golden Snail Opera*

As I was exploring questions of how to attune my analyses with nonhuman world making, I had the pleasure of meeting with Yen-ling Tsai, who told me of how "friendly farmers" in Taiwan—a group in which she includes herself—tackle the problem of the invasive spread of golden apple snails. The snails, introduced from Argentina in a failed plan for a food industry, devour the whole rice crop if farmers do nothing. Conventional farmers use poisons to kill the snails, but there are many reasons not to use these poisons, which spread through the water, killing many forms of life. Friendly farmers instead hand-pick snails in the middle of the night, when the snails are most active. It's a lot of work, but the snail picking has mobilized the friendly farming movement, giving it cohesion and national prominence. When we met, Tsai was finishing an article on the vitalization of the friendly farming movement through their focus on snails (Tsai 2016). But as she described the practice, it was clear that farmers get to know many other beings in and around the rice fields together with the snails; friendly farming is an effort at multispecies attunement. We agreed that thinking with snails might be a wonderful way to get to know the world-building projects of the varied beings who make their homes in Taiwanese rice fields. We enrolled the help of Isabelle Carbonell and Joelle Chevrier in a collaboration; together we made a film and a play that, in tandem, present the world-making projects of many beings—as these offer both the surprises of radical difference and the surprises of touching (Tsai et al. 2016).

Among the rice-field beings that stood out in our consideration were the ghosts of people who died in the World War II American bombing of Taiwan, then a colony of Japan. American development further altered the landscape after the war, unintentionally mixing the earth of newly flattened and modernized fields with the bones of the dead. As more recent farmers have turned the soil, the bones have erupted into their attention; the farmers made temples for them and asked for their help in their endeavors. At first, however, all this was lost on the young people who came to the area with the friendly farming movement. Only after the ghosts responded to being ignored by causing a shocking series of traffic accidents did the young people respond in turn by learning the rites to appease ghosts and to ask for their protection.

I can't remember how a ghost became a character in our play, but once it did, we had fun with it. In the process, we learned to think about kinds of beings ignored by observers who pride themselves on modern scientific views. Our ghosts have a double status: they are both objects within a human cosmology and world makers in their own right—as observed through the practices in which they participate. By sticking close to practices, from the traffic accidents they cause to the ceremonies that attract and appease them, we present ghosts as makers of farming landscapes along with snails and humans. If there is to be a multispecies ontological move, this double status, it seems to me, must be key to it. The objects that emerge from cosmologies must be considered through what they *do*, and not just in relation to how they cause us to reflect. Ghosts are best appreciated through their practices.

This same principle informs our attention to the living beings of the rice fields. There is one difference: since our play's ghost is a former human, we let it speak; in contrast, the other organisms we follow don't speak but perform their lifeways otherwise. This is where the film helps us attune to varied strands of practice. Our filming practices allow animals to help us navigate as they do: we have a dog carry a camera so that it can show us the landscape revealed as it runs back and forth across the rice field bunds; we even put a small camera on a snail (admittedly the much larger African land snail, another invasive species, the only one large enough to hold even the smallest camera). Our film does not just look *at* animals; it tries to look *with* them. We also explore temporalities through film: this is how we approach the life worlds of plants. Plants seem passive only to those who merely pass them by; farmers know them as dynamic beings—and we follow that lead. Time-lapse photography attunes our attention to the growth of the rice and the response of the landscape to darkness and light as well as to rain and sunshine. We bring into focus the flowering of the rice—in which flower parts shoot out suddenly from the developing heads. These organisms, as with ghosts, are both objects of farmers' cosmological reckonings *and* makers of worlds on their own. It is in that double status that we get to know them.

We designed our play-and-film as an amateur performance, in which users are asked to read parts aloud while the film is projected simultaneously. With this conceit, we refuse the seamless whole of a coherent and singular world. Each of the parts, oral and filmic, interrupt each other: they force moments of hesitation even as the rice field is composed in the friction of their rubbing together. We include scenes of complete refusal, such as a duck that refused to adjust to wearing a camera, instead spinning and shaking its head (Figure 15.2).

We call our project an "opera" in admiration of the hybrid Taiwanese *o-pei-la* that developed within the forced compliance and subtle refusals of Japanese colonialism, in which genres mix and match creating a story full of interruptions. Our creatures, human and nonhuman, interrupt each other, jolting into contested being a landscape of multiple agendas. And while one version exists as a paper in

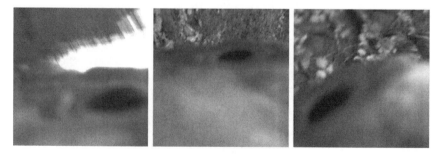

Figure 15.2 From *Golden Snail Opera*: a duck with a camera shakes its head
Source: Isabelle Carbonell and duck

the journal *Cultural Anthropology* (Tsai et al. 2016), it is central to our conceit that other versions are emerging. We have performed in a field site, a classroom, a conference, and a church. A Taiwanese version and an all-film version are being prepared, each shifting the storyline and the meaning of its interruptions.

Theoretical work in geographical motion

All this is situated. Writing this chapter in Denmark while reflecting on a conference in Japan offers a particular lens for considering ontological theories in anthropology. In contrast to Americans, both North and South, Danish ontological anthropologists have been playful and irreverent, caring more for the creativity of their interventions than for the political mobilization of advocacy (e.g., Pedersen 2011; Willerslev 2007). While this rests in part on the shameful Danish denial of the country's colonial legacy (Andersen 2014; Brichet 2012), it also offers advantages for decoupling theoretical approaches from particular political strategies, thus allowing the retooling and expansion of each. It is this feature of the Danish position that has opened the possibility of imagining a dialogue among multispecies and ontological approaches. Perhaps such openings can help keep theoretical tools flexible—and thus useful for varied political struggles. In the work described above, I have tried to forge description and advocacy tools for satoyama conservation ("How Things Hold") and alternative farming in Taiwan (*Golden Snail Opera*).

   In the conference in Osaka, which involved as many international participants as Japanese scholars, the deployment of international theories was colored by differences across national traditions and scholarly generations. Too often, it was hard to build bridges. While not all approaches can find an equitable space of negotiation, this chapter has argued that some can, including multispecies and ontological approaches.

Acknowledgments

I am grateful to the organizers of the Osaka University "World Multiple" conference, and to all the participants who took the time to try to explain the tensions of the conference to me. Pierre du Plessis, Zahirah Suhaimi, and Heather Swanson steered me away from my worst interpretations. The Danish National Research Fund, and the participants in Aarhus University Research on the Anthropocene, supported the infrastructure within which I could imagine and write this chapter.

Notes

1 The most accessible Imanishi in English, to my knowledge, is Pamela Asquith's translation of *The World of Living Things* (2002).
2 The question of what approaches count as "ontological" is complicated by divisions among practitioners. As Pierre du Plessis and Michael Vine pointed out in a recent

conversation, some practitioners pursue ontologies to clarify *concepts* (e.g., Holbraad and Pedersen 2017) while others are more intent on *practices* (e.g., Mol 2002). Those working through Latin American indigenous issues use ontologies to motivate *politics* (e.g., de la Cadena 2015). Each approach would require a different nuance in rapprochement with multispecies anthropologies.

3 Yates-Doer and Mol (2012) refuse this simplification, showing the heterogeneity of "the West." They do not address non-Western heterogeneity.

4 I use the term "ontic" following Helen Verran (2007). Nonhumans may not elaborate philosophies, but their practices enact ontics.

5 Moving beyond language using non-textual media can also be useful in learning with humans (Deger 2017; Forssman 2017).

References

Andersen, Astrid. 2014. "Islands of Regret: Restitution, Connected Memories and the Politics of History in Denmark and the US Virgin Islands." PhD dissertation, Aarhus University.

Archambault, Julie. 2016. "Taking Love Seriously in Human–Plant Relations in Mozambique: Toward an Anthropology of Affective Encounters." *Cultural Anthropology* 31 (2): 244–271.

Brichet, Nathalia. 2012. "Generating Common Heritage: The Reconstruction of a former Danish Plantation in Ghana." PhD dissertation, University of Copenhagen.

Carneiro da Cunha, Manuela. 2017. "Traditional People, Collectors of Diversity." In *The Anthropology of Sustainability*, edited by Marc Brightman and Jerome Lewis, 257–272. London: Palgrave Macmillan.

de Carvalho Cabral, Diogo. 2015. "Into the Bowels of Tropical Earth: Leaf-Cutting Ants and the Colonial Making of Agrarian Brazil." *Journal of Historical Geography* 50: 92–105.

de la Cadena, Marisol. 2015. *Earth Beings*. Durham, NC: Duke University Press

Deger, Jennifer. 2017. "Chased by Light: Digital Art, Luminous Ecologies, and Spectres of Rebuke." Paper delivered at "A Non-secular Anthropocene" conference, Copenhagen, June.

Forssman, Natalie. 2017. "Staging the Animal Oceanographer: An Ethnography of Seals and their Scientists." PhD dissertation, University of California, San Diego.

Freccero, Carla. 2011. "Carnivorous Virility, or Becoming Dog." *Social Text* 29 (1): 177–195.

Gan, Elaine. 2016. "Time Machines: Making And Unmaking Rice." PhD dissertation, University of California, Santa Cruz.

Gan, Elaine, and Anna Tsing. 2018. "How Things Hold: A Diagram of Coordinations in a Satoyama Forest." *Social Analysis* 62 (4).

Haraway, Donna. 2008. *When Species Meet*. Minneapolis, MN: University of Minnesota Press.

Holbraad, Martin and Morten Axel Pedersen. 2017. *The Ontological Turn: An Anthropological Exposition*. Cambridge: Cambridge University Press.

Imanishi Kinji. 2002. *A Japanese View of Nature: The World of Living Things*. Translated and with an introduction by Pamela Asquith. New York: Routledge.

Kimmerer, Robin Wall. 2003. *Gathering Moss: A Natural and Cultural History of Mosses*. Corvallis, OR: Oregon State University Press.

Kirksey, Eben and Stefan Helmreich. 2010. "The Emergence of Multispecies Ethnography." *Cultural Anthropology* 25 (4): 545–576.

Kohn, Eduardo. 2013. *How Forests Think: Toward an Anthropology Beyond the Human.* Berkeley, CA: University of California Press.

—. 2016. "Anthropology of Ontologies." *Annual Review of Anthropology* 44: 311–327.

Locke, Piers and Ursula Muenster. 2015. "Multispecies Ethnography." In *Oxford Bibliographies.* http://www.oxfordbibliographies.com/view/document/obo-9780199766567/obo-9780199766567-0130.xml

Mathews, Andrew S. 2017. "Ghostly Forms and Forest Histories." In *Arts of Living on a Damaged Planet*, edited by Anna Tsing, Heather Swanson, Elaine Gan, and Nils Bubandt, G145–1456. Minneapolis, MN: University of Minnesota Press.

Mol, Annemarie. 2002. *The Body Multiple: Ontology in Medical Practice.* Durham, NC: Duke University Press.

Morita, Atsuro. 2016. "Infrastructuring Amphibious Space: The Interplay of Aquatic and Terrestrial Infrastructures in the Chao Phraya Delta in Thailand." *Science as Culture* 25 (1): 117–140.

Pedersen, Morten Axel. 2011. *Not Quite Shamans: Spirit Worlds and Political Lives in Northern Mongolia.* Ithaca, NY: Cornell University Press.

Satsuka, Shiho. 2015. *Nature in Translation.* Durham, NC: Duke University Press.

Strathern, Marilyn. 1987. "An Awkward Relation: The Case of Feminism and Anthropology." *Signs* 12 (2): 276–292.

Terray, Emmanuel. 1972. *Marxism and Primitive Societies.* Translated by Mary Klopper. London: Monthly Review Press.

Tsai, Yen-ling (蔡晏霖). 2016. 農藝復興: 臺台灣農業新浪潮. *Router: A Journal of Cultural Studies* 22: 23–74.

Tsai, Yen-ling, Isabelle Carbonell, Joelle Chevrier, and Anna Tsing. 2016. "Golden Snail Opera: The More-than-Human Performance of Friendly Farming on Taiwan's Lanyang Plain." *Cultural Anthropology* 31 (4): 520–544. https://culanth.org/articles/851-golden-snail-opera-the-more-than-human accessed July 20, 2018.

Tsing, Anna Lowenhaupt. 2005. *Friction: An Ethnography of Global Connection.* Princeton, NJ: Princeton University Press.

—. 2013, "More-than-Human Sociality: A Call for Critical Description." In *Anthropology and Nature*, edited by Kirsten Hastrup, 27–42. New York: Routledge.

—. 2015. *The Mushroom at the End of the World: On the Possibility of Life in Capitalist Ruins.* Princeton, NJ: Princeton University Press.

Verran, Helen. 2007. "Metaphysics and Learning." *Learning Inquiry* 1 (1): 31–39.

Viveiros de Castro, Eduardo. 2004. "Perspectival Anthropology and the Method of Controlled Equivocation." *Tipití: Journal of the Society for the Anthropology of Lowland South America* 2 (1): 3–22.

Willerslev, Rane. 2007. *Soul Hunters: Hunting, Animism, and Personhood among the Siberian Yukaghirs.* Berkeley, CA: University of California Press.

Yates-Doer, Emily and Annemarie Mol. 2012. "Cuts of Meat: Disentangling Western Natures-Cultures." *Cambridge Anthropology* 30 (2): 48–64.

Afterword

Atsuro Morita

The contributors to this volume have explored the complex webs of relations that enact and compose the world multiple. As we note in the introduction (Chapter 1), the original conference call asked contributors to reflect on two key themes. One is the very notion of the world multiple; the other is quotidian practices as the loci of the world multiple's enactment. By closely engaging with these two themes, the authors collectively have revealed some central tensions in existing explorations of the world and practice. In this afterword, I will examine these tensions by noting shared and divergent themes in the authors' responses to the call. I will also contextualize the conversations in this volume in relation to the recent history of anthropology, and discuss how this volume reveals the challenges of exploring the complexity of the world, and indicates possible new directions.

Our initial provocation is well captured by the title *The World Multiple*. In analogy with the multiple enactments of atherosclerosis in Annemarie Mol's *The Body Multiple* (2002), it invited contributors to think about the multiplicity of reality. As Cristóbal Bonelli notes, both "body" and "world" "work as classes of things, generic abstractions that we can mobilize to think about situated socio-material realities" (Chapter 8 in this volume). He then goes on to ask: "What is at stake when we are invited to substitute the word 'body' with the generic word 'world'?" In different ways, these stakes became visible in the authors' diverse responses to this provocation. Here, I highlight some of these responses by paying attention to a certain tension that arises when one attempts to see the world as a sort of "thing."

It is, in fact, far from self-evident what it might mean to think of the world as a thing. Are we thinking of a planet? Or some kind of universe? Across the sciences and popular culture, there are innumerable reflections about what the world is and its shape. Their diversity ranges from the natural historian Alexander von Humboldt's (1849) depiction of the Earth as the *Cosmos*, to Buckminster Fuller's (1969) *Spaceship Earth*, to the magnificent notion of "Thousand-Cubed Great Thousands Worlds" from Buddhist cosmology (Morita 2017). However, the world is not only an object of reflection or depiction. It is also a certain kind of ground or horizon upon which we act. In my view, there is a certain tension between these two broad lines of conceptualization, and this tension is related to the changes in how anthropology has imagined and engaged with the elusive notion of "world."

What I have in mind can be made clearer through a somewhat unlikely comparison with an earlier edited volume, Marilyn Strathern's (1995) *Shifting Contexts*. This book was published about twenty-five years ago, following the Fourth Decennial Conference of the Association of Social Anthropologists of the Commonwealth. The theme of that conference had been "The Use of Knowledge: Global and Local Relations." At stake was a critical assessment of "the global." For anthropologists, the local has always been the focus of knowledge making. At the time, however, "the global," which seemed to both encompass and shape the local, was becoming a new matter of concern. *Shifting Contexts* offered a critical examination of this emergent imagination. Because of the simultaneous similarity and difference between "the global" and "the world," Strathern's way of addressing the former helps to clarify the stakes of the latter.

Questioning the image of the global as an abstract yet encompassing space, Strathern's critical engagement with the global appears quite close to *The World Multiple*. She wrote that

> Claims [. . .] to be able to encompass local facts by a global perspective take on a special meaning in the world-view of societies, such as those of the west, that imagine they are part of a life that is itself global in scale.
>
> (ibid., back cover)

This line of inquiry resembles the critique that science and technology studies scholar John Law (2015) has made of what he calls the "one-world world." To imagine the global in terms of encompassment, he observes, is to assume that everyone lives in a "container universe," "a large space–time box that goes on by itself" (ibid., 126–7).

In the afterword to *Shifting Contexts*, Strathern (1995, 179) refers to Donna Haraway's notion of "location" as "a point of relationality, a gathering together that makes visible relations between things," which rather closely resembles Marisol de la Cadena's notion of practices as "knots of connections" (Chapter 2 in this volume). Similarly to Mol's analysis of the body multiple, Strathern further considers both objects and persons in terms of location, since both are relationally composed. Accordingly, the local is simply a particular kind of location "where persons act, and act to make the world work"; it is "the point where they mobilize their resources, seek influence, labour, reproduce, spend energy, talk" (Strathern 1995, 179).

At this point, Strathern develops a view of the global that is of significant relevance to the present volume. Alluding to Bruno Latour's argument that macro-actors are an effect of assemblages of people, artifacts, and practices, Strathern argues that we never encounter the global per se. She goes on to draw attention to a particular kind of asymmetry between the local and the global. Since people never leave the local, the global cannot be another location, a relational site. Rather than relations, the global instead concerns people's capacity to imagine scales that make the world larger than the local, and that encompass the local:

> The continuities people see between their actions—their effect on others, the reactions of colleagues, antecedents and futures, setting things in motion, in short *the apprehension of a life that is larger than any of its moments*—would be equally part of making the world work.
>
> (ibid., 179, emphasis added)

Here, the local as a relational site is contrasted with imaginations about scale that enlarge the world beyond the immediate here and now. And this imagination in turn "produces a reflexive sense of context or locale" (ibid.). Imagining the world as larger than the local prompts people to compare and contextualize it in a way that produces an (ever) "expanding horizon" (ibid., 178; cf. Mohacsi and Morita 2013). At this moment, however, we can notice a stark contrast between Strathern's view of the global—and other scalar imaginations—as *horizons* and the present volume, which has invited contributors *to see the world as a relational object*. And I would suggest that this difference can be traced to the respective historical settings of the two volumes. Strathern's approach to the global is inseparable from a view of the world characteristic of the 1990s. Even as climate change had started to attract attention, anthropologists and social scientists mainly saw the world as a horizon, rather than a planet. Until recently, the image of planet Earth as a whole was often associated with science fiction and futuristic imaginations, like Buckminster Fuller's (1969) *Operating Manual for Spaceship Earth*. As the menace of climate change continues to grow, however, a view of Earth as a planetary system has become increasingly central, not only to environmental politics but also to public debate. At this moment, the many ways in which the Earth is disturbed by human activities have emerged as central matters of concern in very diverse fields, including environmental management, sustainable development, energy policy, and international security. The Anthropocene, the much-debated new geological era, epitomizes this shift, which has created a new ground for debates about the world. The starting provocation with which this volume began is by no means detached from *these* shifting contexts.

The implications of the Anthropocene for anthropology are arguably quite mixed. On one hand, many anthropologists are vocal critics of this discourse, drawing attention to colonialism and the unequal capitalist development that brought about planetary environmental change in the first place. They also point to the potential violence done by the Anthropocene in terms of flattening difference and creating a homogeneous "human" bearing equal responsibility.

On the other hand, the Anthropocene also makes it very difficult to imagine the world as an abstract "space–time box that goes on by itself" (Law 2015, 126–7)." When Westerners in the 1990s imagined themselves, as Strathern (1995, back cover) suggested, as "part of life that is itself global in scale," they were thinking of modern forms of life and institutions that had seemed to spread everywhere, but they were not conceiving of themselves as part of the biosphere. By locating everyone within a threatened biosphere, the Anthropocene has practically shattered the modernist delusion.

And this is indeed part of the trajectory that has led some scholars of science and technology studies to think of the world *not* as a self-evident horizon, but rather as a relational object that humans and nonhumans compose together. John Law's (2015) critique of the one-world world offers a clear illustration. So, too, does Latour's (2004) questioning of modern cosmopolitanism, which presupposed an already existing and shared natural world lying somewhere beneath conflicting cultures. As an extension of his general argument for the relational composition of things, Latour insisted that a common world does not exist as such, but must be composed.

When we drew on *The Body Multiple* in formulating our initial provocation, our inspirations from these approaches were clearly in evidence. By invoking a world multiple in analogy with a multiple body, we were encouraging contributors to engage with a world that was certainly relational and that did *not only* designate either nature or the planet.

However, the contributors' responses went beyond the world as a relational object. As if bringing back the question of scale that Strathern introduced twenty-five years ago, their contributions highlight the tension between the world as an object and as a horizon. For example, by focusing on the inscriptions of names—*Augusto Pinochet*, the ex-dictator of Chile and *Miguel Cuevas Pincheira*, one of the victims of his violent regime—Bonelli (Chapter 8 in this volume) elucidates a "politics of when," in which temporalities emerge through the perseverance of rocks. Similarly, by looking through particular entities, Mario Blaser, Keiichi Omura, Heather Swanson, Moe Nakazora, and Stacy Langwick (Chapters 4, 5, 7, 9, and 10) also show the practical enactment of objects as containing complex temporal and spatial dimensions.

Marisol de la Cadena (Chapter 2) illustrates one process out of which such complex spatio-temporal configurations emerge. Her starting point is that the practice of relating with mountains/earth-beings (*tirakuna*) in the Andes co-exists uneasily with what we call religion. By making explicit translations between tirakuna and religion, de la Cadena aims to makes it possible to glimpse "entities whose presence emerges in divergence from what is to 'us' (nature or religion, for example)—while also being with it." What emerges here is "the world being more than one and less than many" (Chapter 2).

Other contributors focus on aspects of world making that, while related to the concerns just mentioned, are also differently oriented. Thus, Shiho Satsuka and Anna Tsing (Chapters 14 and 15) elucidate the multiplicity of the world in the context of multispecies encounters. Since the *Umwelt* of fungi is very different from that of people, the latter have great difficulties figuring out how the former engage with other species, sense their surroundings, or get around. However, through gradual processes of attunement, some of these entanglements become visible to some humans, and this includes anthropologists keen on learning these arts. Making it possible to partially connect with the unknown world of fungi, our capacities for imagining and appreciating worlds beyond human ones are extended.

Dealing with diverse sorts of entanglements, contributors depict intricate and often perplexing configurations of relational things. Moreover, they show us that the time–space configurations of these worlds are not quite like horizons. And they make clear that these worlds are neither flat nor inert. Interestingly, the very strangeness of these worlds raises questions pertaining to the editors' original emphasis on quotidian practice.

By quotidian practice, we were referring to what people do in their daily lives. Because of its routine character, quotidian practice is obviously familiar to the actors. However, the anthropologist gradually becomes familiarized with quotidian practice through ethnographic immersion. This familiarity is then turned into writing and made available to readers. In this sense, quotidian practice is an artifact of ethnographic translation (Strathern 1987).

In fact, the effects of this translation can be observed in two orientations to ontology characteristic of science and technology studies and anthropology (Gad, Jensen, and Winthereik 2015). In *The Body Multiple*, Annemarie Mol traced connections between the daily routines of patients, including their discomforts and inconveniences, and an assortment of technologies, plans, and people. But she was particularly focused on the idiosyncratic details of individual entities and the contingency of their association. As noted by Christopher Gad et al. (2015) and Anna Tsing (Chapter 15 in this volume), however, this contrasts with the other orientation to ontology, as has been discussed in anthropology (Henare, Holbraad, and Wastell 2007; Viveiros de Castro 2004), which tends to emphasize what objects make thinkable.

These differences no doubt have to do with both ethnographic settings and writing strategies. Partly because she did fieldwork in a Dutch hospital, Mol could trace connections between entities and rely on the assumption that most Western readers *already knew*—at least in general outline—what kind of things happen in a hospital. These practices, in other words, are quotidian—mundane and familiar—to both Mol and many of her readers. In contrast, Eduardo Viveiros de Castro (2004), a central figure of the ontological turn, capitalizes on the distinctly *unfamiliar* nature of the Amazonian world in order to destabilize modern presuppositions. And thus he focuses on Amerindians' radically different assumptions about people and animals, which are furthermore not only unfamiliar, but also inherently elusive, due to unavoidable translational equivocations between the anthropologist and his interlocutors.

In different ways, both Gad and colleagues and Tsing advocate for something like symmetry between these two modes of studying ontology ethnographically. And, as if responding to this suggestion, many contributions to this volume indeed look at complex entanglements between apparently mundane practices through which relational things are composed, and their quite non-quotidian, strange backgrounds. Bonelli (Chapter 8), for example, focuses on the relation between the eminently material practice of inscribing names on rocks and the complex temporal horizons that it generates. Against this backdrop, in turn, the practice of inscription loses much of its familiarity. Similarly, we might say that glances at the surprising worlds of fungi (Chapters 14 and 15) make mountain walking and mushroom picking into something more and different than *just* everyday experience. And Marisol de la Cadena (Chapter 2) is explicit about the methodological import of grappling with such forms of excess, going so far as to contend that we might not know what the practice *is*. Thus, she pays critical attention to the varied forms of implicit translation that quietly turn her interlocutors' involvement with earth-beings into religion, something we might believe we already know.

In short, then, the contributions to this volume exhibit the recursive relationship between objects and their backgrounds. As Casper Bruun Jensen (Chapter 3) suggests, this unceasing motion can bring about a sense of vertigo. His suggestion that ethnography grapples with vertiginous worlds is meant as a challenge to how we conceive the time–space configurations emerging from practice.

It now appears to me that the term "horizons," which I borrowed from Strathern, cannot fully capture these strange backgrounds. For while a horizon suggests a certain commanding view, what characterizes the temporal and spatial dimensions depicted by our contributors is rather a sense of obscurity and the partial nature of both vision and connection.

Following Viveiros de Castro, Antonia Walford (Chapter 13) makes clear that her interlocutors in an Amazonian town are quite attuned to such obscurity. They are sensitive, she notes, to "the equivocations potentially occurring between themselves and their others". Such awareness of equivocation indexes a capacity for imagining that something quite impenetrable lurks behind seemingly shared communication. Rather than finding things in expanding horizons—or expanding horizons through things—equivocation in this sense seems akin to sounding unfathomable depths (Helmreich, Roosth, and Friedner 2016). But such depths are not like alterity, at least not in the conventional sense of a distant other—since equivocation happens recursively and, at any scale, obscurity is always in the vicinity, or even within.

If 1990s anthropologists realized that awareness of difference made people compare their location with others, thereby expanding their horizons, our contributions thus show that people's awareness of objects and relations that are more than one and less than many invite them (and their anthropologists) to sound the unseen depths. The difficulty of describing these time–space configurations—including in this afterword—also indicates that we are still searching for an adequate vocabulary. What seems clear from reading across the chapters, however, is that we are dealing with a vertiginous motion between relating things and persons and the emergence of depths behind these things and persons.

Perhaps, then, one way of describing the world multiple is in terms of a perpetual movement that gathers and disperses relations, while also generating new backgrounds. The latter would also be part and parcel of the practice of knots and connections, to which Haraway and Strathern (1995) so productively drew attention. But if this is the case, even as the modern imagination of the world as a container universe is challenged by the Anthropocene, the anthropological critique of its hegemony would also require transformation. Tracing the vertiginous motions of the world multiple can be seen as a response to this new challenge; one in which the Earth, the world, other species, and entities all reveal hitherto unseen aspects of one another. The present volume can hopefully be read as a stepping-stone to such forms of exploration.

Acknowledgments

I am grateful to Casper Bruun Jensen and Grant Jun Otsuki for helping me sort out the rather chaotic earlier draft of this afterword.

References

Buckminster Fuller, Richard. 1969. *Operating Manual for Spaceship Earth*. Carbondale, IL: Southern Illinois University Press.
Gad, Christopher, Casper B. Jensen, and Brit R. Winthereik. 2015. "Practical Ontology: Worlds in STS and Anthropology." *NatureCulture* 3: 67–86.
Helmreich, Stefan, Sophia Roosth, and Michele Ilana Friedner. 2016. *Sounding the Limits of Life: Essays in the Anthropology of Biology and Beyond*. Princeton, NJ: Princeton University Press.
Henare, Amiria J. M., Martin Holbraad, and Sari Wastell. 2007. *Thinking through Things: Theorising Artefacts Ethnographically*. London, New York: Routledge.
von Humboldt, Alexander. 1849. *Cosmos: A Sketch of a Physical Description of the Universe*. London: Bohn.
Latour, Bruno. 2004. "Whose Cosmos, Which Cosmopolitics?: Comments on the Peace Terms of Ulrich Beck." *Common Knowledge* 10 (3): 450–462.
Law, John. 2015. "What's Wrong with a One-World World?" *Distinktion: Journal of Social Theory* 16 (1): 126–139.
Mohacsi, Gergely and Atsuro Morita. 2013. "Traveling Comparisons: Ethnographic Reflection on Science and Technology." *East Asian Science, Technology and Society* 7 (2): 175–183.
Mol, Annemarie. 2002. *The Body Multiple: Ontology in Medical Practice, Science and Cultural Theory*. Durham, NC: Duke University Press.

Morita, Atsuro. 2017. "In between the Cosmos and 'Thousand-Cubed Great Thousands Worlds': Composition of Uncommon Worlds by Alexander von Humboldt and King Mongkut." *Anthropologica* 59 (2): 228–238.

Strathern, Marilyn. 1987. "Out of Context: The Persuasive Fictions of Anthropology." *Current Anthropology* 28 (3): 251–281.

—. ed. 1995. *Shifting Contexts: Transformations in Anthropological Knowledge*. London, New York: Routledge.

Viveiros de Castro, Eduardo. 2004. "Perspectival Anthropology and the Method of Controlled Equivocation." *Tipití: Journal of the Society for the Anthropology of Lowland South America* 2 (1): 3–22.

Index